D1420418

KING DAN

The Rise of Daniel O'Connell, 1775–1829

Patrick M. Geoghegan is a lecturer in the Department of History at Trinity College Dublin and is the author of *The Irish Act of Union* and *Robert Emmet*. He presents *Talking History*, a weekly radio show on Newstalk.

KING DAN

The Rise of Daniel O'Connell, 1775–1829

PATRICK M. GEOGHEGAN

Gill & Macmillan

Gill & Macmillan Ltd
Hume Avenue, Park West, Dublin 12
with associated companies throughout the world
www.gillmacmillan.ie

© Patrick M. Geoghegan 2008
978 07171 4393 1

Index compiled by Helen Litton
Typography design by Make Communication
Print origination by O'K Graphic Design, Dublin
Printed and bound in Great Britain by MPG Books Ltd,
Bodmin, Cornwall

This book is typeset in 12/14.5 pt Minion

The paper used in this book comes from the wood pulp
of managed forests. For every tree felled, at least one
tree is planted, thereby renewing natural resources.

A CIP catalogue record for this book is available from
the British Library.

5 4 3 2 1

CONTENTS

INTRODUCTION

'Ireland, it must be admitted, has been ungrateful to her great men'.
(SPEECH OF DANIEL O'CONNELL, 10 FEBRUARY 1827).[1]

D aniel O'Connell remains one of the most important and complex figures in Irish history. And yet, in recent years he has become unfashionable, sidelined by much lesser men and relegated to a position of relative obscurity. Perhaps this is because of O'Connell's rejection of violence, or perhaps because of the failure of his Repeal movement. When we think of O'Connell we think of him in his final years, 'the hugecloaked Liberator's form' of James Joyce's *Ulysses*, old and fat, engaged in constant compromises and, in the end, broken by the weight of expectations. The aim of this book is to show a different O'Connell, young, lazy, aggressive, reckless, uncertain and unsure, who became involved in the campaign for Catholic emancipation and who transformed the movement and himself. This is the story of how O'Connell became 'The Liberator'.

Determined to be the best at whatever he did, O'Connell trained to become one of the greatest orators of the age, with a magnificent voice that could move people to anger or to tears. One of the greatest lawyers in Irish history, O'Connell tormented judges, terrorised opposing barristers, and won fame for saving the lives of so many men who would otherwise have been hanged. He became 'The Counsellor', the fearless defender of the people. And he secured that reputation through his successful campaign for Catholic emancipation.

Recognising that a culture of defeat afflicted Irish Catholics, O'Connell set out from the beginning to confront authority, challenge the nature of British rule in Ireland, and make himself a symbol of defiance and resistance. Despite his hatred of the French Revolution, he became a radical in the 1790s and joined the United Irishmen, narrowly avoiding arrest during the 1798 Rebellion. In 1800 he took a defiant stand against the Act of Union, and it was his lifelong ambition to overturn that measure and restore the Irish parliament. First, he had to remove the remaining political and legal restrictions against the Catholics and secure the right to sit in Parliament. His campaign for Catholic emancipation was long and difficult, with an apathetic public and a divided Catholic leadership. His strategy was aggressive, ruthless and ultimately very effective. The climax came in 1828 when he stood for election in Co. Clare and defeated the Protestant Ascendancy after one of the most dramatic campaigns in Irish history.

But there was a darker side to O'Connell's character. In folklore he was a notorious womaniser, even after his marriage in 1802, although this has long been dismissed by historians unwilling to accept anything negative about their hero. The evidence presented here suggests that some of these stories were true. While he did not rape Ellen Courtenay in 1818, as she later accused him in print, he almost certainly had an affair with her and a number of other women. O'Connell was flawed. Incapable of managing his finances, he was constantly in debt, running the risk of bankruptcy and of leaving his family destitute. In 1815 he killed a man in a duel and nearly followed it by fighting another one. He was incredibly vain, and his vanity increased with the passing of time. Violent and aggressive in his speeches, he embarrassed friends and horrified his enemies by his refusal to follow a moderate line of conduct. Instead, as he later boasted, he became more violent, and he succeeded.

The list of things O'Connell has been blamed for is impressive. Seán O'Faoláin, who admired O'Connell, none the less traced the decline of Irish manners—the vulgarisation and cheapening of Irish society—to the aggression and vulgarity of O'Connell's speeches. And he added, 'How different it all is from, let us say, Robert Emmet with his plumed hat and his naked sword... Everybody who regards gracious living, nobility in thought and word and behaviour, must read this demagogue [O'Connell] with a curl of distaste'.[2] W.E.H. Lecky even concluded that it was debatable whether his life was a blessing or a curse for Ireland.[3] O'Connell was blamed for polarising Irish society along sectarian lines, for cheapening political discourse, for putting his own interests ahead of the Irish people. O'Connell would have expected these criticisms. He once complained that he would never receive the credit he deserved for winning Catholic emancipation, because people would never understand the extent of the problems he faced. But he did what was necessary in the context of the time, and he did it without resorting to physical force.

This book provides a radical new interpretation of O'Connell's early life, his career as a lawyer, and his titanic struggle to win Catholic emancipation over a quarter of a century. Recognising his flaws as well as his greatness, it shows the forces that drove him to create and lead an entirely new movement in Irish politics. The 1916 Rising is today hailed as the moment when the modern Irish state was born. But it was O'Connell who created the modern Irish nation, for better or for worse, in the nineteenth century. His constitutional approach, the way he channelled the power of moral force, did as much to create the modern Ireland and ensure that the institutions of the new state in the twentieth century were not still-born. This was the real legacy of 'King Dan', the man who persuaded the Irish Catholics that they were more than slaves, and who mobilised them to secure their freedom in 1828–29. In doing so, he helped create the modern Ireland.

ACKNOWLEDGMENTS

My thanks are due to the Irish Research Council for the Humanities and the Social Sciences (IRCHSS) for the research fellowship in 2006–2007 which made this book possible. I am also indebted to a number of individuals. Fergal Tobin of Gill & Macmillan helped shape the project in its early stages and his advice led to some crucial revisions at the end. As always it has been a pleasure to work with him. I am grateful to all the staff at Gill & Macmillan for their excellent work—Emily Miller who co-ordinated the design of the jacket, Deirdre Rennison Kunz for her editorial expertise, Helen Thompson, Claire Egan, Liz Raleigh and Esther Kallen. Professor Marianne Elliott and Dr Ian McBride were my IRCHSS referees and their encouragement and support was decisive. Professor Jane Ohlmeyer of the School of Histories and Humanities, Trinity College Dublin was an enormous help, especially with the initial IRCHSS application. My two colleagues —and friends—Dr Robert Armstrong and Professor Ciaran Brady were always available to debate ideas and problems. I would also like to thank Professor John Horne for his support and influence throughout my career. My friends in the School of History and Archives in University College Dublin were also an inspiration, in particular Mary Daly, Richard Aldous, John McCafferty, Michael Laffan and of course, James McGuire. Professor Tom Bartlett of the University of Aberdeen provided invaluable support, and I am also grateful to his colleague Dr Michael Brown who allowed me to present on aspects of this book at various (splendid) conferences and seminars. I am also grateful to Dr Seán Patrick Donlan for allowing me to discuss O'Connell at a legal history conference in Limerick. Dr Niamh Howlin provided important advice on the jury system in the nineteenth century and gave extensive feedback on the prologue; John Berry's legal expertise was also invaluable. Thanks to Professor Bill McCormack, I now have a complete set of the O'Connell Correspondence, and I am also grateful to Dr Brian Jackson, Ted Brady, Trevor White, Mary Connellan and Professor Paul Bew for their assistance. Honora Faul, of the National Library of Ireland's prints and drawings department, showed me numerous images and caricatures and her enthusiasm was much appreciated. Alastair McMenamin read a draft of the prologue and was a constant encouragement. Eoin Keehan advised on the introduction; Bridget Hourican helped with some literary points and translations; Rory Whelan, Jenny Scholtz, Paul and Lynne Geaney, Declan Lawlor, Dr J. Vivian Cooke, Nick Rowe, my brother, sister, sister-in-law, mother, and aunt were also a great support. Susan Cahill, my producer on *Talking History* on Newstalk, helped me think about history in an entirely different way, as indeed did my co-presenter, Dr Lindsey Earner-Byrne. I am also indebted to George Hook for his advice and encouragement. My god-son, Rowan Daniel Lawlor, shares a birthday with the subject of this book and I hope he and his brother, Declan, will some day enjoy it. My god-daughter Caitlin Ann and her brother, Jack, were also a welcome distraction. And, as always, I must thank the O'Connell family for all their support—Moira, Rory, Adrian and Benjamin.

I am particularly grateful to the staff at the various libraries and archives where I worked. Dr Gerard Lyne and the staff in the manuscripts room in the National Library of Ireland were an enormous help. So too were the archival staff at the University of Chicago Library, the Public Record Office of Northern Ireland, the Royal Irish Academy, the Dublin Diocesan Archives, and the School of History and Archives at University College Dublin.

Two people read the entire text in manuscript and deserve the greatest thanks. Cecelia Joyce was a shrewd commentator whose criticisms resulted in significant changes being made, both to the style and the interpretation. Mr Justice Adrian Hardiman also read a complete draft and spent many hours discussing O'Connell with me. The book is dedicated to him as it was his passion for the subject which inspired the writing of it.

PROLOGUE

The Doneraile Conspiracy, 1829

'Is he coming? Is he coming?' The only question which people wanted answered on the morning of Monday 26 October 1829 was whether Daniel O'Connell, MP for Co. Clare and the leading barrister in the country, had decided to take the case of twenty-two men on trial at the special commission in Cork for conspiracy to murder. As far as the people were concerned a conspiracy did exist, but an official conspiracy to persecute and judicially murder men innocent of the crime. Four men had been tried on the previous Friday, found guilty after five minutes' deliberation by the jury, and sentenced to death. Little hope was held out for the rest, who were due to go before the commission that week. But there was one chance. If only 'The Counsellor', the man who had defied the Protestant Ascendancy and had succeeded in winning Catholic emancipation, if only the man who was beginning to be acclaimed as 'The Liberator', could be persuaded to take the case. And so a messenger had been sent to O'Connell at his home in Derrynane, ninety miles away, on Saturday evening, pleading with him to defend the remaining men. But it was nine a.m. and the special commission was about to resume, with another four men to be put on trial, and he had still not arrived. The agent for one of the prisoners requested an adjournment, claiming that he had just received news that O'Connell was on the way. Baron Pennefather paused for a moment and looked to his fellow judge, Robert Torrens, before shaking his head. It was impossible to wait, he insisted, declaring that if the prisoners had wanted the professional services of O'Connell they should have asked for him in time, and he should already be in attendance. Another agent for the prisoners pleaded that the proceedings should be taken slowly, but he was told 'Certainly not.

Everything will proceed in the ordinary way'.[1] A jury was selected and was in the process of being sworn in when an incredible noise from outside the court brought everything to a halt. All that could be heard was loud cheering and shouting, which one newspaper reporter described as 'unequivocal demonstrations of applause by the populace'. Finally they could make out the chant: 'He's come! He's come!'[2] The door opened and 'a tall handsome man',[3] with a defiant military bearing, marched in. Daniel O'Connell had arrived.

The Doneraile conspiracy had been conjured into existence by a paranoid establishment anxious to believe the worst of the Irish peasants. However it did have its origins in a real plot. On 20 January 1829 the carriage of Dr John Norcott had been fired on by some members of the Whiteboys, an agrarian secret society, who had mistaken it for the carriage of Michael Creagh, an unpopular landlord and magistrate. Following this attempt plans were hatched to assassinate other local magistrates. But the problem was that spies and informers concocted a much larger conspiracy, inventing evidence and accusing innocent men of being involved.[4] On 29 April Patrick Daly, and his cousin, Owen Daly, both paid informers, went before the magistrates to claim that an extensive conspiracy had been formed to assassinate three prominent Protestants from the locality, George Bond Low, Michael Creagh, and Admiral Henry Evans. They claimed that in a drinking booth at the Rathclare fair, two days earlier, a number of men had sworn an oath to join together and commit the murders. They named a seventy-year-old man, (Daniel) John Leary, as the chief conspirator, and claimed he was in charge of a four-man committee to organise the assassinations. A large-scale investigation was conducted, and men came forward and did deals with the crown where, in return for immunity, they agreed to testify about the conspiracy. These were known as approvers, 'persons claiming to have been complicit in the alleged conspiracy who were giving evidence for the crown'.[5] And so Leary and twenty-one other men were brought before the special commission in Cork in October 1829 on trial for their lives. Some were guilty (of at least the initial outrage), most were innocent, and the problem was that the crown had no intention of discovering the real culprits and was determined to hang them all. John Leary, James Roche, James McGrath, and William Shine, were all tried on Friday 23 October, found guilty and sentenced to death. 'Oh, my lord,' said one of the men in a low tone after the sentence was announced, 'there is no justice for us! We know nothing but vengeance!'[6] Leary was completely innocent, though it appears the other three men were guilty of various agrarian crimes, and quite possibly the actual conspiracy (and certainly O'Connell thought so). But the conspiracy had taken on a life of its own and the ambitious solicitor general, John Doherty, saw this as an opportunity to win glory for himself at the expense of the Catholic peasantry.

O'Connell, the famed 'Counsellor', had been asked at the start of the summer to defend the men but had refused. He was worn out after a year in which he had finally won Catholic emancipation, following almost twenty-five years of continual agitation. His refusal had attracted much criticism and there were mutterings that he had abandoned his people. Stricken with terror following the first trial, the remaining prisoners decided to contact him again, as their last, desperate chance to escape being 'strung up like sheep'. William Burke, the brother of one of the prisoners, borrowed a horse and made the long ride to Derrynane. He arrived on Sunday morning just as O'Connell was sitting down to breakfast. O'Connell went to meet him in the library and was told that there was a hundred guineas for him if he took the case. The decision was presented in stark terms: 'If you come they'll be safe; if not, they'll all be hanged'.[7] O'Connell accepted the retainer. That day he set out for Cork, choosing to drive a gig, a light carriage with one horse. The road was bad and he was forced to stop for rest in Macroom for a few hours, before continuing his journey overnight. He arrived in Cork at ten o'clock in the morning. It was said that his horse fell dead from exhaustion almost as soon as he arrived, like in so many stories of the archetypal hero. Large crowds cheered O'Connell as he marched to the courthouse, shouting, 'Oh, he's come at last, thank God! Thank God!'[8] Thomas Sheahan, who was reporting on the trial, said that even though the court was packed with mainly crown supporters (who he called 'the well dressed savages'), the small number of people who supported the prisoners were energised by the appearance of 'the Great Dan': 'we felt as though we were a multitude, and with the strength of a multitude'.[9] When O'Connell walked into the courtroom the solicitor general, Doherty, went pale and appeared to take a step back.[10]

Throwing off his travelling coat, O'Connell bowed to the court and begged its forgiveness for his dishevelled appearance. Baron Pennefather, his old friend from the Leinster circuit, returned this courtesy, though Judge Torrens pretended not to have seen him.[11] O'Connell asked if he might have some breakfast in court, and Pennefather quickly agreed. A bowl of milk and some bread and meat was brought to his table. O'Connell's manners were messy at the best of times; here, they were appalling. Tired and hungry from having travelled all night, he regularly interrupted the prosecutors with his mouth full of milk and bread ('That's not law!'), unconcerned with what anyone thought. It was said to have made for a wonderful contrast, 'the big, massive Agitator slabbering his meal in a courthouse, and the graceful, aristocratic Mr Doherty talking in the most refined manner to the jury!'[12] The trial showed O'Connell at his very best: aggressive, sarcastic, vicious, unstoppable.

Doherty rose to state the prosecution's case and claimed that it would prove the existence of an elaborate and extensive conspiracy to murder. In his report, Sheahan described Doherty as 'a very theatrical sort of gentleman', pompous and self-important. O'Connell had come in the past few months to detest Doherty, and taunted him throughout the trial. Even Doherty's refined accent was abused. When Doherty told one witness that he could step down, he was interrupted by an exuberant O'Connell mimicking his voice who said 'Naw, daunt go daune, sir!' This was more entertaining than the theatre and the crowd loved it. Sheahan said that the entire courthouse began laughing, 'the well dressed savages' as loud as anyone.[13] At one point Doherty claimed that an allegation was based on 'false facts'. 'False facts, Mr Solicitor!' exclaimed O'Connell, 'How can facts be false?' Doherty stumbled along, replying, 'I have known false facts, and false men too,' while attempting a knowing look. The first witness was Daniel Sheehan, who was examined by Thomas Goold, another of the prosecution lawyers. Sheehan was an approver, having claimed to have been involved in the conspiracy, and receiving immunity in return for his testimony. Admitting that he was a Whiteboy, Sheehan insisted that he had witnessed a number of the accused men swearing an oath to murder Evans, Low, and Creagh, and that they had signed a paper to that effect.

Wiping some milk from his mouth, O'Connell rose to cross-examine. He immediately began poking holes in Sheehan's testimony, pulling at inconsistencies and unravelling the entire thing. Sheehan claimed not to understand O'Connell's questions and one of the judges intervened on his behalf and said, 'Mr O'Connell, I think the witness does not understand you.' 'My lord, I think differently,' replied O'Connell, turning around and shouting, 'Do you hear me, Sheehan?'[14] Over and over again, Sheehan insisted, 'I do not recollect', 'I cannot recollect'. 'You are a great fellow at recollection,' joked O'Connell. 'You are a perfect *non mi ricordo*'. This was a reference to the famous trial of Queen Caroline in 1820, when an Italian witness had given false testimony and then had answered any question 'Non mi ricordo', or 'I do not recollect.'[15] The court would have got the joke. It had become a popular saying and there was even a caricature from 1820 which showed a portly King George IV being asked his name and replying 'Non mi ricordo.'

O'Connell became convinced that Sheehan had received instructions from the police and had been told to say that very formulation of words whenever he was asked a difficult question. He directly accused Sheehan of having been drilled by a policeman called Vokes, but Sheehan denied that he had been told to say 'I don't recollect'. 'Then he forgot his usual practice,' replied O'Connell sarcastically.[16] The prosecution was furious with this allegation, and George Bennett rose to object that this 'observation is totally uncalled for'. He insisted that he could not allow O'Connell to accuse the police of suborning witnesses. But O'Connell feigned innocence and denied having suggested any such thing. Sheehan continued with his testimony, but was still hazy on details of his activities, claiming he couldn't remember: 'I don't recollect.' 'Just the answer I'd expect from an honest man like you,' laughed O'Connell. Turning to the crowd he asked, 'Well, what I am to do with this fellow?' Sheehan attempted to continue and listed all the people that he had seen joining the alleged conspiracy. He insisted that William Nowlan (another approver) was present, as well as his relative, Michael Nowlan. O'Connell sensed that something was not right and spent a considerable time questioning Sheehan about Michael Nowlan. It seemed an unusual line of attack, but O'Connell refused to give it up. Eventually Sheehan admitted that 'there was no such person' as Michael Nowlan. O'Connell was in the ascendancy and he proceeded to mock and humiliate the witness. Sheehan attempted to give a long explanation about what he had been doing, but O'Connell just joked that it was well for him that he had travelled ninety miles that day, 'I am not in sufficient wind for you'. When Sheehan again denied that the police had given him instructions, O'Connell just turned to the jury and exclaimed, 'This fellow is absolutely fatiguing me!' Goold attempted to redirect the questioning, but was prevented by O'Connell who insisted that this line of questioning did not follow from his own cross-examination. Sheehan stepped down, demolished and discredited.

The next witness was William Nowlan. He was first examined by Bennett, but O'Connell intervened successfully to prevent any reference being made to Friday's trial. O'Connell then rose to cross-examine, and Nowlan smiled nervously at him and said, 'It's little I thought, Mr O'Connell, that I'd be answering *you* this day!'[17] O'Connell despised Sheehan and Nowlan, men who claimed to have been involved in the conspiracy, but who had seen the error of their ways. Turning to the jury, he mocked them as 'the repentant sinners'.[18] In his cross-examination O'Connell discussed the nature of perjury and was interrupted by the court who asked him where he took his definition. 'My lord, I take it from the Catholic catechism,' he replied feigning innocence, to the delight of the Catholics in the crowd. Patrick Daly, another Whiteboy turned informer, was next to be deposed by the solicitor general. O'Connell repeatedly interrupted his examination, claiming that he was asking inadmissible or leading questions, and each time winning the point. When it was his turn to cross-examine, O'Connell attempted to unravel Daly's evidence. At one point Goold made an interjection, leading O'Connell to explode in rage, 'Good God! Am I to be interrupted?' Goold sat down, red-faced, and the examination continued. Daly stuck doggedly to his story, upon which O'Connell exclaimed in disgust, 'Such a drilling of witnesses I never saw'. Bennett was again furious and rose to ask O'Connell to repeat what he had said. O'Connell made his allegation a second time, at which Bennett announced that 'I can't sit down and hear such extraordinary language'. Doherty also rose to his feet and rather sententiously claimed that these observations, though intended to influence the jury, would make no impression. Bennett then demanded to know if O'Connell was accusing the prosecution of drilling the witnesses, but O'Connell interrupted to deny that he ever named the prosecution as the drill sergeants. Judge Torrens here intervened and called upon O'Connell to avoid making any further 'unpleasant remarks'. But O'Connell was never someone who was intimidated or impressed by the judiciary. With great vehemence he denied that he was making 'uncalled for observations'. 'Good God!' he exclaimed, 'four men upon trial for their lives, and with such evidence!'

Thomas Murphy was a witness who was examined through the Irish language. Murphy claimed to have been invited to a public house where the conspiracy was discussed, but insisted he had not been invited to join it. O'Connell was merciless in his cross-examination, asking Murphy why he had sworn that he couldn't speak any English, when in fact he could speak a little. Mocking the man's education, O'Connell wondered why the conspirators had not asked him to join their plot. 'Good God, witness!' he exclaimed, 'Did they, think you, invite you into the public house and there tell you their plans, for the mere purpose of having you as a witness here against them?' 'I don't know,' replied Murphy, completely bewildered. The prosecution rested its case. Beginning his defence, O'Connell produced two witnesses to show that Owen Daly, one of the prosecution's key witnesses, was a rogue and a scoundrel. It had been claimed by Doherty that Owen Daly was an innocent young boy, sixteen or seventeen years old, who had become unwittingly embroiled in the conspiracy. But O'Connell proved that he was, in fact, a twenty-four-year-old man who was employed as an informer under the game laws. After this, Pennefather made a concluding statement and the jury retired at ten forty p.m. to consider its verdict.

For forty minutes everyone waited tensely in the court. At eleven twenty p.m. Pennefather asked the bailiff to see if the jury was ready, and then fined the sub-sheriff £100 for taking his time in answering this request. A constable finally arrived at eleven forty p.m. and announced that the jury had 'all agreed, they say, but they want one *candidate*'. Pennefather 'appeared at a loss to comprehend what the constable was intending to convey'. Eventually he discovered that eleven members of the jury were in agreement, but with one dissenting voice. Pennefather adjourned the court for a further thirty minutes. The newspaper reporter was impressed that the court was as packed at midnight as it had been at noon, and that 'perhaps on no occasion, pending the verdict of a jury, was there more anxiety on the part of the public'. It was one twenty-five a.m. before the court resumed. The foreman of the jury, Horace Thompson, announced that there was agreement when it came to one of the accused, but there was no likelihood of a verdict for the other three men. Pennefather called on the jury to return the verdict for the prisoner they agreed upon, and the accused man, Thomas Barrett, was declared 'not guilty'. One of the jurors, Henry Hewitt O'Brien, then claimed that a verdict for the other three prisoners was unlikely as 'one gentleman says he does not believe a tittle of the evidence of those people'. And to much laughter, O'Brien added that the lone juror claimed there were 'eleven very obstinate men on the jury' and that 'he does not credit a word of the evidence'. This man was Edward Morrogh, the only Catholic on the jury. But Pennefather ordered the jury to retire and try and come to an agreement. This angered the jurors, who insisted they had done their 'utmost to convince the gentleman' and who claimed that the cold jury room would kill them if they were forced to remain there overnight. Pennefather was unmoved and ordered the jury to re-deliberate, giving them large coats and nightcaps, but no food or water, and insisting they were locked in the courthouse overnight.[19] Twelve angry men retired to consider their verdict. They debated the case until six a.m., before falling asleep with nothing resolved.

At ten fifteen a.m. the next day the court resumed. The jurors revealed that agreement was impossible on any case except that of Barrett. But Pennefather refused to discharge them and a stand-off ensured. One juror complained that 'we are starved alive!' But this was just greeted with laughter in the court. Another man claimed that he had been refused water the night before and, as he was just recovering from illness, he was incapable of continuing. There was little sympathy. The jury was obliged to retire again, but sent word through the sheriff that one man was 'extremely ill'. While this was going on, Goold and Bennett took the opportunity to praise the solicitor general for his handling of the trial, and defend him from the aspersions cast upon him by O'Connell. Accepting their praise, Doherty said he was proud of the way he had conducted the prosecution and prouder still of 'the disapprobation I have met from others'. O'Connell was unrepentant and said his observations had been 'founded on fact'. There remained confusion about how to proceed with the hung jury. O'Connell suggested that it should be discharged with a new trial held at the next assizes. The prosecution refused to offer any advice to the court, insisting it would not interfere in any way. O'Connell then began citing various precedents which showed a jury could be allowed to return home to their houses while making its decision, and could even be discharged if a juror became ill (as in the case of the *King v. Richards*). Bennett interjected to say that this was a *Nisi Prius* case and the precedent was therefore not applicable. O'Connell just turned to him and applauded him sarcastically, saying 'I am glad I got so much out of you'. Barrett was released, but the other prisoners were returned to jail, and the court was suspended. The jury remained sequestered to attempt to find a verdict, with a physician on hand if anyone became ill, but nothing further was agreed. It was an inconclusive ending, with victory for O'Connell in the case of Barrett, and stalemate in the other three cases. But O'Connell was not finished yet.

The next day, Wednesday 28 October, the special commission resumed its hearings at ten thirty a.m. Interest in the trials was growing all the time; one reporter said that excitement was 'hourly increasing'.[20] O'Connell spent much of this day discussing what should be done with the previous trial, and it was agreed eventually that it should be postponed until the next general gaol delivery, with the prisoners detained in custody in the meantime. The court adjourned for the day. The next trial began at one twenty p.m. on Thursday 29 October.[21] A new jury was selected from the large panel which had been called. One of the possible jurors was a man called Williamson, a man who O'Connell had problems with because he had heard that Williamson had either said or been told that to crush the conspiracy it would be necessary for the countryside to be decimated, with gibbets placed on all the crossroads. O'Connell wanted to discover who had said this, believing that it showed Williamson could not be an objective juror. Goold attempted to stop this line of questioning, but O'Connell's feelings about being interrupted had not changed since Monday: 'Am I to be thus interrupted? Have I not the legal right to examine?'[22] Both Doherty and Goold attempted to show that O'Connell's questioning was illegal, but O'Connell insisted that it was a fair question, as if the comment had been made by a relative, a father or a brother perhaps, then it would almost certainly influence him. Bennett rose to object, but O'Connell shouted that he would not be interrupted. 'Don't be vexed, O'Connell,' said Bennett. 'I'm never vexed with you', replied O'Connell, becoming calm again, before going on to explain that he was attempting to show that 'the expression of decimating or gibbeting on all crossroads' was 'a horrible, atrocious, and dreadful expression' and would affect a juror's objectivity. Doherty accused O'Connell of attacking Williamson unnecessarily, but Baron Pennefather intervened and said he was 'of the same opinion with Mr O'Connell'. O'Connell then called a witness, a Mr Hartnett, who had a different interpretation of the alleged comment. Hartnett said that after the first trial, when the four men were convicted, he heard Williamson say that 'if they go on this way, they will want gibbets on every crossroad'. O'Connell challenged Williamson peremptorily. In the event, fourteen men were challenged successfully by the prosecution, and forty rejected by O'Connell. The crown had learnt its lesson and ensured no Catholics were on the jury.

Following this, two more men were put on trial for being part of the conspiracy to murder. Pat Daly was called by the prosecution and made a detailed statement about what he had witnessed in the tent at the fair at Rathclare, on 27 April 1829, when he claimed the conspirators directed by Leary had signed a document to assassinate Low, Creagh and Evans. It is here that the case took a dramatic turn. Baron Pennefather stopped the examination and called O'Connell to the bar. They discussed the case for a few minutes as the entire courtroom looked on in confusion. Pennefather passed O'Connell a document. As O'Connell returned to his table to read it everyone waited in silence. It seems Pennefather had had enough of Daly's evidence as it was inconsistent with the evidence he had sworn two days after the fair when no mention had been made of a written assassination order. One of the finest judges of the period, and a model of integrity, Pennefather had realised that this evidence could not be withheld from the defence. It was clear that evidence was being manufactured and that the entire foundation of the prosecution's case was untenable. Pennefather had sent to Doneraile for the missing deposition, and when it had arrived discussed his concerns with O'Connell before presenting him with Daly's sworn testimony from 29 April, evidence that the prosecution should have supplied to him but which they had failed to do. It was the ammunition that O'Connell needed to open fire on the prosecution and kill their entire case. The real Doneraile conspiracy was exposed. There was suppressed evidence, lying witnesses, and a prosecution seemingly unconcerned with observing correct legal procedures. It is to Pennefather's credit that he was not prepared to remain silent, and acted courageously to assist the defence. With the suppressed evidence in O'Connell's hands it was easy to collapse the house of cards which the prosecution had constructed. Afterwards, O'Connell was full of indignant fury at how Doherty had conducted the prosecution. Reflecting on how key evidence had been withheld—'the awful warrant'—O'Connell questioned what this said about Doherty's 'parade of anxiety for public justice'.[23]

Discussing this case in a Supreme Court judgement on 30 March 2007, Judge Hardiman noted that O'Connell saved the defendants' lives 'by destroying the credibility of the principal approver in cross-examination. *He did this by cross-examining on the basis of a prior inconsistent statement.*'[24] Hardiman noted that 'it was clearly repugnant to the conscience of a judge… that a prior statement of a witness which made no mention of the principal point in his eventual oral accusation should be concealed from defending counsel.' O'Connell destroyed the credibility of the crown's witness 'using this knowledge of the difference between first evidence given in the privacy of a prosecutor's den and this oral evidence gently sieved by a crown prosecutor in court'.[25] O'Connell was able to show that Daly's testimony could not be trusted since he had not mentioned the assassination order in his original sworn deposition, and this was such a critical piece of information that he could scarcely have forgotten it. And, if this had been invented subsequently, then what else had also been invented? With the prosecution's case in shreds, the jury retired and quickly returned a unanimous verdict of 'not guilty'. Judge Torrens was overheard telling the prosecutor, Bennett, 'George, let me not see your face here again'.[26] The next day, Friday 30 October, the commission terminated itself. Pennefather was in no mood to continue and challenged Doherty, 'Well Mr Solicitor General, what do you intend to proceed with?' Doherty was forced to hold up his hands and admit that no further prisoners would be tried.[27] The remaining prisoners were released. It was too late for Leary and the three other men, but their sentence was changed from execution to transportation. The courtroom erupted into celebrations of 'general joy' and 'every tongue was loud in praise of Mr O'Connell, to whose exertions the result is universally attributed'.[28]

This was the last great occasion when O'Connell defended others in the courtroom. It was a triumphant performance in which he stood firm against the establishment, bullied and humiliated the crown prosecutors, and saved the lives of men who would otherwise have been doomed. In the words of Charles Phillips, a lawyer who knew him well, 'In 1829 he had reached the summit of his glory' and from there he could look down 'upon the millions he had liberated, he could hear their outburst of joy, and happiness, and homage'.[29] This was O'Connell at the height of his powers and the zenith of his career, the liberator of the Irish Catholics, feared and hated by the British government, and adored by his own people. It was perhaps no wonder that George iv had muttered darkly a few months earlier that O'Connell was now the 'King of Ireland'.[30]

Chapter 1

'THE FORTUNATE YOUTH', 1775–1793

'I was born with strong feelings'.[1] Daniel O'Connell was born on 6 August 1775, the eldest son of Morgan O'Connell, a farmer at Carhen, near Cahirciveen, Co. Kerry, and his wife, Catherine O'Connell (née O'Mullane). There are different accounts about where he was born, but he himself was certain he was born at the small farmhouse of his parents at Carhen.[2] His parents had married in 1771 at the church of the Holy Trinity in Cork, a Protestant church because of legal requirements for inheriting property, but with a Catholic priest officiating.[3] O'Connell took great pleasure in later years in pointing out that he was born at the start of what became the American War of Independence, and he liked to suggest that this coincidence 'shadowed forth his destiny as a champion of freedom'.[4] Even in his lifetime mythical stories were told of his birth. It was said that he was 'the gift of God', that his parents had been childless until his mother gave a generous gift to a priest, and in return was rewarded with the gift of a son.[5] The first-born of a large family, he had three younger brothers, Maurice, John, and James, and five sisters. Daniel liked to boast of his ancient and noble lineage, but the reality is that by the eighteenth century the family was fairly undistinguished. It was more accurate to say, as he also sometimes did, that he was 'the son of a country gentleman'.[6] The head of the family was Maurice O'Connell, the second but eldest surviving son of Donal Mór and Máire Ní Dhuibh, and the brother of Morgan. Maurice was known as 'Hunting Cap', after the velvet hat he took to wearing after a tax had been placed on beaver hats, his previous headgear of choice.[7] He lived in seclusion at Derrynane in Kerry, amassing a large fortune through various legal and illegal ways, including smuggling. A fourth son of Donal Mór and Máire Ní Dhuibh was called Daniel O'Connell, and he joined the French army at an early age, rising to the rank of general. Máire Ní Dhuibh was an extraordinary figure, revered and feared in equal measure for her wisdom and forthright views. Frequently consulted by the locals, she was unafraid to attack those who disagreed with her using vicious sarcasm and strong language, and it was later said that the future Liberator inherited from her 'his muscular mind and power of invective'.[8] She was also a poet of some renown and much of her work was political. In one poem in Irish she prophesised that 'A greater chief from me shall yet be born/ To triumph over ocean's haughty lord'.[9] As a baby, Daniel was sent to be nursed and fostered by the wife of his father's herdsman, who lived in a cabin on the Iveragh mountains, and he remained there until he was four.

   When O'Connell was three the American sailor Paul Jones hovered off the coast of Kerry. There was great excitement at the time, and O'Connell was brought to the shore in his nurse's arms. He later claimed to remember the whole thing 'perfectly', and it certainly appears to have been one of his earliest memories.[10] Two boats came ashore. On-board were men who had been sent by Paul Jones with 'towing ropes to get his vessel out of shallow water'. They were former prisoners of war, British and Irish, who had been imprisoned in Brest until given the opportunity to serve the other side at sea. However the men took the opportunity to escape, cutting the ropes and heading for the safety of the shore. Relieved to be free, the men left their fire-arms on the boats, and went to the nearest public house to get drunk. The locals, terrified of the men, drenched the weapons with water and then called the local magistrate, who arrested the sailors. O'Connell's memory, despite his young age, was probably accurate enough. He vividly remembered a tall man, mounted on a grey horse, who seemed to be 'the lawyer of the party' and who protested at the men being arrested.[11] This image of the man fighting against the authorities made a lasting impression. As no charges could be sustained, the sailors were released.

   'I was born within the sound of the everlasting waves'.[12] O'Connell loved the sea and as a child was spellbound by 'the varying sounds emitted by marine shells'.[13] He enjoyed greatly his visits to Derrynane, about nine miles away from Carhen, and in later years described poetically 'the mountain waves coming in from the illimitable ocean in majestic succession, expending their gigantic force, and throwing up stupendous masses of foam, against the more gigantic mountain cliffs that fence this my native spot'. Listening to the sea, O'Connell liked to imagine the adventures of long-dead Irish heroes. As he later recounted, 'Yes! My expanding spirit delighted in these day-dreams', and from them he developed an enthusiasm 'which no disappointment can embitter nor accumulating years diminish'. This enthusiasm was 'the high resolve to leave my native land better after my death than I found her at my birth and, if possible, to make her what she ought to be'.

At the age of four he returned to his parents' house. As a child he could be shy and silent and Hunting Cap despaired that anything would come of him; apparently he told O'Connell's mother that 'Daniel will be a blockhead'.[14] However at other times he could be unruly, especially when it came to his schooling when he was unwilling to take instruction. A travelling hedge-school master called David O'Mahony was hired to teach him but O'Connell was uncontrollable. Struggling to make any impression, O'Mahony gently combed his tangled hair one morning and this kindness apparently won him over.[15] O'Connell was now willing to learn and O'Mahony taught him the alphabet. O'Connell later boasted that he learned the alphabet in a single hour. From the beginning he was intensely competitive and this was a defining part of his character throughout his life. By his own admission, he 'desired to excel, and could not brook the idea of being inferior to others'.[16] His own family said of him that he had a burning desire to be the best at whatever he attempted, that if he 'was only a pothole digger he'd be the *first* of pothole diggers'.[17]

The first '*big* book' that he read was Captain James Cook's *A voyage towards the South Pole, and round the world*, published in two volumes, in 1784.[18] He took it everywhere with him until it was finished, reading it with 'intense avidity'. Even when the local children came and asked him to play with them he refused, running away and taking his book to the window in the housekeeper's room where he would sit, with his legs crossed, 'devouring the adventures of Cook'. For a brief time, O'Connell was obsessed with exploration and traced out the maps from the book. It made him, he said, 'a good geographer' and he could not recall 'a book that took a greater grasp' of him. And so he would ignore his friends, preferring to sit with his book, 'reading it, sometimes crying over it, while the other boys were playing'.

O'Connell was a lazy child. However 'the fear of disgrace' often motivated him to work hard at the last moment, and he boasted that he was 'remarkably quick and persevering'.[19] One day in school he was idling, and was caught by the teacher. Found 'imperfect in my lesson', he was about to receive a beating. But O'Connell, even then, was able to talk his way out of trouble. He 'shrank from the indignity, exclaiming, "Oh, don't beat me for one half hour! If I haven't my lesson by that time, beat me *then!*"' The teacher granted O'Connell his reprieve, and the lesson, though 'rather a difficult one, was thoroughly learned'.[20] O'Connell's lifelong love of the theatre began as a child and it was said that at the age of ten he composed a drama about the fortunes of the house of Stuart.[21]

Hunting Cap often bought the *Dublin Magazine*, which was sold at Carhen, and the young Daniel enjoyed looking at the portraits of important people and reading the biographical sketches which accompanied them. As O'Connell later admitted, 'I was always an ambitious fellow, and I often used to say to myself, "I wonder will *my* visage ever appear in the *Dublin Magazine?*" I knew at that time of no greater notoriety'.[22] In September 1810, when O'Connell was walking through the Dublin streets after a Catholic meeting he saw the *Dublin Magazine* in a window bearing a portrait of 'Counsellor O'Connell'. He remembered his childish ambition and 'said to myself with a smile, "Here are my boyish dreams of glory realised."'[23] It is an indication of O'Connell's vanity that he did remember and was still telling the story in his sixties. However he insisted that he 'had long outgrown *that* species of ambition' by 1810, although it had clearly been superseded, if not quite replaced, by greater ones.[24]

From the beginning O'Connell was precocious and had an extraordinary belief in his own destiny. Many children have fanciful ideas about their future, but O'Connell never forgot his dreams of making an impression on the world. Even at the end of his life he recollected that at the age of seven he had 'felt a presentiment that I should write my name on the page of history'.[25] This was the year 1782, when everyone was discussing the triumph of legislative independence and the victory of Henry Grattan and the Irish parliamentarians. O'Connell admired the Volunteers who had helped make legislative independence possible and, even as an adult, had a romantic attachment to them. When Lord Charlemont's son was considering reorganising them in the 1840s, O'Connell expressed an interest in becoming colonel of the first regiment of Dublin Volunteers.[26] When asked whether this contradicted his views on non-violence, he denied it saying would 'be a pacific band; its existence would quietly achieve our rights by showing the futility of resisting them'.

One evening at his parent's house in Carhen, sometime after the winning of legislative independence, the guests began discussing the political events of the day. Everyone had an opinion on who had made a greater contribution to Ireland, Henry Grattan or Henry Flood, and there followed a similar debate about the relative achievements of Henry Grattan and Lord Charlemont. During these debates O'Connell sat 'lolling back' in a large old chair, 'musing to himself and sometimes thinking aloud, apparently unconscious of anyone's presence'.[27] He had a serious look on his face and, whenever he was asked a question, answered only with a monosyllable, before returning to his reverie and staring out the window. Finally, a female relative asked him, 'Daniel, what are you doing? What are you thinking of?' His response was never forgotten by the woman: 'I am thinking that I'll make a stir in the world yet'.[28]

Henry Grattan was O'Connell's boyhood idol.[29] And the winning of legislative independence in 1782 was the event that O'Connell would return to throughout his career. But despite his admiration for Grattan, he supported his great rival, Henry Flood, over the question of renunciation in 1782–3, although it is not possible to date when he developed this belief, and it might well have been an adult opinion. Flood believed that legislative independence alone would never be enough and that the British government should be forced to renounce for ever any right to legislate for Ireland. In his later years O'Connell rambled, claiming that 'if Flood had succeeded, it is my firm conviction that the Union could never have passed'.[30] But here O'Connell was confused and in error: a Renunciation Act was passed in 1783, and it had no effect whatever on the Union seventeen years later.

O'Connell loved Kerry and, in particular, Glancara, near the lake of

Cahara, which had been in his family for generations. In old age he speculated that if he was ever to take a title it would be 'earl of Glancara'.[31] O'Connell had many happy memories of childhood adventures there. One story he was fond of telling involved an encounter with a bull in a field. The bull chased after him and O'Connell found his escape cut off by a ditch. So he turned round and coolly 'threw a stone at his forehead', stunning the bull. This gave O'Connell time to run for it and, as he made his escape, 'a number of boys came to my assistance and fairly stoned him [the bull] out of the field'.[32] He had another encounter with bulls when he was part of a six-man group, led by his cousin, the wild Marcus O'Sullivan, which was formed to put down a vicious herd on a nearby island. One of O'Connell's teachers, John Burke, assisted and was almost killed when he was charged by a bull and lost his nerve, running away rather than shooting.[33] O'Connell was not too concerned and confessed that, having been 'pestered' for too long by 'the bothering schoolmaster,' he was sorry he had not been killed.

In 1787 O'Connell was taken to the Tralee assizes, which were then 'a great mart for all sorts of amusements'.[34] O'Connell was more interested in the amusements than the legal cases on offer. As a boy he loved ballads and he went straight to the singers. He was particularly impressed with two singers, a man and a woman, who took turns singing the verses. The man sang the first two lines, the woman the third line, and they both sang the fourth. Fifty years later he was still able to sing a verse from memory, 'I leaned my back against an oak/ I thought it was a trusty tree/ But first it bent; and then it broke/ 'Twas thus my love deserted me.'[35]

One of O'Connell's best friends in this period was Darby Mahony and they spent much of their time hunting together. At the end of 1796 O'Connell reflected that 'the happiest days of my life' were a couple of Sundays when Mahony was allowed to join him at Carhen.[36] The boys went to the same school and delighted in persecuting the teacher, a man called Linahan. However in 1790, over Easter, they had an 'unfortunate quarrel' which interrupted their friendship for some months until both boys went to Harrington's boarding school in the summer.

Beginning to show some talent and potential, O'Connell was watched closely by Hunting Cap, who took a keen interest in his development. It was said that Daniel was 'the fortunate youth', his uncle's favourite nephew and possibly his heir.[37] Certainly his uncle enjoyed giving him responsibility and, around this time, entrusted him with £300 in gold which he asked him to get changed into notes at Cotter and Kellet's Bank.[38] The clerk made a mistake and handed him £400, £300 in small notes and a single £100 note. O'Connell pointed out the error, but the clerk refused to check, insisting that he never made a mistake. 'I persisted', O'Connell later said, even though the clerk was 'sulky and obstinate'.[39] Finally one of the owners came over and counted the money. O'Connell was right and the banker took away the £100 note. But O'Connell was still not happy and he pleaded to be allowed keep the large note, in exchange for the same amount in smaller notes, because his uncle wanted the largest notes available.

Great things were planned for O'Connell and his brother Maurice. Hunting Cap decided to send the two boys to the continent to be educated and he sought advice from his brother in France in 1789, shortly before the outbreak of the revolution. While these plans were being made, the boys were sent to board at Dr Harrington's school at Reddington, in Long Island, near Cork, in 1790. O'Connell later boasted that he was 'the only boy who wasn't beaten at Harrington's school', and credited this to his diligence and concentration.[40] However, he was unable to escape beatings from the other students. Shy and aloof at school, O'Connell was not a popular student. His preference for 'study, or secluded reflection', instead of play, made him appear unsociable and the other students delighted in tormenting him.[41]

Despite the warnings of General O'Connell, who was disturbed by events in France, Hunting Cap was still determined to send his nephews to the continent. They set out from Cove in late 1790 in a brig heading for England, and disembarked on a small boat at Dover. This small boat capsized near the shore, and the boys were soaked as they swam to safety.[42] The rest of the journey was uneventful and they made their way to Ostend and then Liège. The first college they went to was in Liège, but there Daniel discovered that he was too old to be admitted. So the boys rested at Louvain for six weeks while they waited for instructions from home. During this period they attended the university schools, and made good use of the library of the Franciscans, and Daniel impressed by rising to a high place in a class of 120 students. Eventually the new instructions arrived and they were told to go to St

Omer, one of the most distinguished colleges for Irish and English
Catholics, and they travelled from Louvain to Ostend and from there to
Jurens and then Dunkirk. They finally arrived at St Omer in January
1791.

In his lifetime it was a popular belief, endorsed by some reporters
and historians, that O'Connell had been intended for the priesthood
when he went to France.[43] He himself repeatedly denied the story, but
certainly that perception was prevalent in his locality. For some years
after his return to Ireland he was known as 'Father Dan' by the peasants
in Iveragh.[44] It is unlikely that Hunting Cap would have wanted him to
become a priest for, as O'Connell told him in late 1793, 'I will (please
God) employ in preparing for that [the law] or any other profession
you choose'.[45] Had Hunting Cap wanted O'Connell to be a priest it
would have been difficult to avoid that course. However it is also
possible that, as new career paths opened for Irish Catholics after the
1793 Relief Act, O'Connell's direction was changed.

Hunting Cap took a great interest in O'Connell's studies, and so did
Hunting Cap's brother, Daniel, whom O'Connell called 'the general'.
The general gave the boys advice on what they should study at St Omer
and recommended them they should take 'mathematics, logic and
rhetoric'.[46] Daniel immediately went to the president, Dr Gregory
Stapleton, and made this request, but was told that 'the price of
learning mathematics here is a guinea a month'. The answer did not go
down well, and Daniel wrote to the general suggesting that 'if he wished
we should follow that system of education, it would be better to send
us elsewhere'. That issue aside, Daniel had no complaints at St Omer
and enjoyed studying Latin and Greek authors, French, English, and
geography. The classes in rhetoric had already begun by the time he
arrived, so he and Maurice struggled to catch up.[47] He kept busy and
during his recreation hours took lessons in music, dancing, fencing,
and drawing. Frederick Hill, who was at school with the O'Connells,
later remembered that 'one was very studious, and the other something
like myself, very wild'.[48]

The studious one was Daniel. He later boasted, 'I was first in the first
class and got premiums in everything'.[49] This was not quite true. On 3
February 1792 he reported to Hunting Cap that he had come 'second in
Latin, Greek and English, and eleventh in French'.[50] But O'Connell took
these things very seriously as an adult. At St Omer he was able to

indulge his love of theatre, and was looking forward to a whole play being acted by the school in August. He also purchased a violin, and began taking music lessons. The Latin authors studied were 'Mignot's harangues, Cicero and Caesar' while the Greek authors were 'Demosthenes, Homer and Xenophon's *Anabasis*'.[51] Years later a school friend recounted how at St Omer O'Connell was 'a gay and thoughtless youth of more abilities than application'.[52] But O'Connell took offence to this suggestion, and insisted that in this period he was not idle, rather, 'I shook my constitution by intense application'.[53]

Anxious to discover how the boys were doing, and if his investment was worthwhile, Hunting Cap wrote to the president of the college, Dr Stapleton, for a confidential assessment. Stapleton wrote that one of the worst things a teacher could ever do was to 'gratify the parents of those under their care, by ascribing to them talents and qualities which they do not really possess'.[54] Having sounded this warning he reported that Maurice's

> manner and demeanour are quite satisfactory. He is gentlemanly in his conduct and much beloved by his fellow students. He is not deficient in abilities, but he is idle and fond of amusement. I do not think he will answer for any laborious profession; but I answer for it he will never be guilty of anything discreditable.[55]

Stapleton's report on Daniel was short but spectacular. He wrote that 'with respect to the elder, Daniel, I have but one sentence to write about him; and that is that I never was so much mistaken in my life unless he be destined to make a remarkable figure in society.' But despite this glowing testimony, Hunting Cap was not satisfied with the education the boys were receiving at St Omer and made enquires about moving them to the English college at Douai.

Early on 18 August 1792 O'Connell and his brother left St Omer, arriving late that same evening at Douai. Money was a worry, as here the boys were expected to furnish their own rooms and pay for their washing.[56] They were forced to borrow money from John Duggan, a young man from Newmarket, in Co. Cork, and had a further sum advanced by the procurator at the school. Eating at the school was also expensive. The portions at dinner were small, but most of the boys paid for seconds, which cost an extra three or four pounds a year. But Daniel was already becoming a master at how to request money from Hunting Cap without causing offence and he made a successful application for an increased allowance. Despite the additional charges, O'Connell admitted that 'this college is much better in every respect than the other'.

The Roman Catholic Church had become one of the targets of the French revolutionaries and by remaining at the college the boys made themselves targets as well. The revolution soon began to encroach on their day-to-day life, and one afternoon the boys fled in panic when they were abused on the streets by a soldier.[57] By 17 January 1793 O'Connell had come to realise that 'the present state of affairs in this country is truly alarming'.[58] King Louis XVI was on the verge of being executed, and war with Britain appeared inevitable. O'Connell knew that war would make staying at the school impossible and he wrote to Hunting Cap for instructions. Four days later, without waiting for a reply, O'Connell made the decision to withdraw from school and return home. He left his furniture and his violin behind to be sold, but the goods were confiscated as 'national property'.[59]

Fleeing from Douai, Daniel and Maurice headed to Calais. Their carriage was attacked along the way, and they were abused by supporters of the revolution as 'little aristocrats' and 'young priests'.[60] In some towns soldiers struck their muskets on the roof of the carriage, and the terror of the journey was never forgotten. For safety, Daniel wore a tricolour cockade on his hat, which he ripped off and threw into the sea in disgust as soon as he arrived at Calais. Some fishermen rescued the cockade from the water and spat curses at him.[61]

Calais was alive with the news that the king had been executed on 21 January. Glad to be escaping France, Daniel and Maurice boarded a ship which was travelling to England. There were a number of Englishmen on board and O'Connell admitted that they, like himself, 'seemed to have been made confirmed aristocrats by the sanguinary horrors of the revolution'.[62] Their views were not shared by two young Irishmen who boarded at Calais, John and Henry Sheares. They entered the cabin one evening when the execution was being discussed and boasted that they had been present to watch it, having bribed two national guardsmen into letting them borrow their uniforms. One Englishman was horrified and exclaimed, 'But, in God's name, how could you endure to witness such a hideous spectacle?' The reply of

John Sheares made O'Connell shudder and he never forgot 'his manner of pronouncing the words: "*From love of the cause!*"'.[63] Later on the journey John Sheares made a throw-away comment about how this was the only time he had ever been at sea when he hadn't been worried about being shipwrecked, a strange aside that also stayed with O'Connell. When the ship landed in England, O'Connell prepared to return to Ireland, relieved to have escaped the uncontrolled violence in France. He later told his daughter, Ellen Fitzsimon, that at this period he was warmly attached to the French monarchy and 'thoroughly detested the revolutionists and the democratic principle'.[64]

In the years ahead much would be made of O'Connell's limited experience of the French Revolution and how it had given him a horror of violence and bloodshed. O'Connell himself encouraged such a belief in the 1840s. But his views in the 1790s were far more complex. He had certainly been horrified by what he had witnessed and had little time for the abstract idealism of the revolutionists. He believed the obsession with abstract rights had resulted in France being 'deluged in blood; liberty was sacrificed'.[65] But it was also true that in the 1790s he sympathised with radical attempts to overthrow the existing system in Britain and Ireland. During this period he came to realise that violence was not the way to secure lasting liberty for a people: 'The altar of liberty totters when it is cemented only with blood, when it is supported only with carcases'.[66] Instead he vowed to devote his life to the pursuit of a genuine liberty 'that would increase the happiness of mankind'.

Chapter 2

YOUNG DAN: LIFE IN LONDON, 1793–1796

Arriving in London, O'Connell was reunited with his old childhood friend, Darby Mahony, now a soldier, who had returned from a military campaign.[1] They spent their days strolling around the city, sometimes amusing themselves by looking at the caricatures on sale at the Haymarket. O'Connell's wild cousin, Marcus O'Sullivan, was also in London and it had been arranged that he, Daniel, and Maurice would return to Ireland together. But these plans changed when General O'Connell, who had also fled France, intervened to persuade Hunting Cap to allow the boys to remain in London and be educated there. O'Connell thus spent a number of weeks studying at home, using his Douai books for guidance until a teacher was found. Hunting Cap still kept a close eye on any unusual expenditure and threatened harsh punishments if he was not obeyed. Daniel was often obliged to write home apologising for wasting money. In October he was forced to act quickly when Hunting Cap demanded an explanation over nine guineas which he and Maurice had spent foolishly.[2] He was getting used to assuaging Hunting Cap's anger, and was learning how to plead his case before a critical judge. Addressing the 'continued chain of offences' which had alienated Hunting Cap, he explained that there was 'no excuse' for 'such folly'. But he admitted 'the fault' and assured him 'of our sincere sorrow for it'.[3] The proof of this sorrow, he insisted, would be 'shown by our future conduct'. Skilfully addressing the frequency of these offences, and the apologies which followed them, he admitted that 'it is true we have often before assured you of our resolution of never again offending you, and as often broken our promise'. But this was explained away as 'the age we are' which 'adds considerably to our fault'.

A friend of the family, Christopher Fagan, formerly a captain in the French army but now an émigré, was hired by General O'Connell to teach Daniel and Maurice and they visited him once a fortnight. There were a number of boys in the class, and Fagan devised daily exercises for them, but the teaching came to an abrupt end in October when he announced that he could no longer continue.[4] Fagan was the father of O'Connell's future biographer, and later claimed that O'Connell was just an ordinary scholar, displaying no great ability. Despite the loss of his teacher, O'Connell was not too worried; he informed his uncle that his difficulties with logic were almost at an end, and that he was almost ready for more advanced training. This was confirmed by General O'Connell later in the year, when he reported that 'Dan is indeed promising in everything that is good and estimable'.[5]

In his dealings with Hunting Cap O'Connell had to learn quickly how to handle people, and especially how to bargain from a position of weakness. Hunting Cap meant well, he wanted his nephews to get an education and have successful careers, but he was also a bully, and kept such a tight rein on money and such a close control over the two boys that at times his good intentions were oppressive. He was also too old (he was in his sixties) to remember the indiscretions of youth. In the autumn of 1793 Hunting Cap reacted furiously to some offence of Maurice's, threatening to disown him and force him to find employment. Daniel intervened and, in a very skilful negotiation, persuaded his uncle to back down. He admitted that 'thoughtlessness is my brother's failing', but none the less 'he is my brother and I am bound to serve him in as much as lies in my power'.[6] The argument deployed to calm Hunting Cap was a clever one: Daniel claimed that if Maurice was required to earn his own living as a lawyer or merchant, having not grown up to expect such a career, he might very easily be reduced 'to despair' and 'plunge headlong into the greatest vices'. Daniel's final point was the decisive one. Such a young man could very easily 'become a dishonour to his family'.[7] The argument was settled, the offence forgiven.

Not all of his manoeuvres were successful though. Home-sick over Christmas 1793, he resolved to return to Ireland to study law in Dublin. To do this he had to convince his uncle, and here he failed to twist him to his will. The arguments, none the less, were ingenious. He claimed that the living expenses would be far greater in London, as he would be required to maintain the lifestyle of a gentleman in London: 'I could never go to the [Middle] Temple unless in full dress, with silk stockings etc. I could scarce appear in the streets after twelve o'clock otherwise'.[8] Also, in Dublin he could visit Derrynane easily and for far less expense than if travelling from London. The final argument was intended to clinch it: in London he might fall in with a bad crowd, students who would 'spend their time in riot and idleness'. With his 'youth and inexperience' he could easily fall victim to dishonest men, however in Dublin he could rely on Hunting Cap's 'credit and character' and so meet 'the most eminent lawyers in the kingdom'.[9] Hunting Cap was not fooled and so O'Connell took terms at Lincoln's Inn on 30 January 1794 to train as a barrister.[10] Middle Temple had been the preferred option, but there was still in place a bond requiring members to receive the sacraments according to the rites of the Church of England.[11]

In March 1794 Maurice returned to Ireland having rejected any attempts to make him a lawyer.[12] He stayed at Carhen while he made plans to become a soldier. It took him two years to secure a place in a regiment, almost certainly because of Hunting Cap's reluctance, and he was sent to the West Indies in November 1796, bidding his brother 'adieu, perhaps for ever'.[13] O'Connell, meanwhile, was determined to be an orator, and in his spare time studied 'history and the *Belles Lettres*, objects absolutely necessary for every person who has occasion to speak in public, as they enlarge the ideas, and afford that strength and solidity of speech which are requisite for every public speaker'.[14] He was still anxious about money and sent Hunting Cap a list of books, suggesting that as books were cheaper in Ireland they might be purchased there and sent over. O'Connell was determined to show his uncle that he was no longer careless with money. He claimed not to have gone 'to one single place of public entertainment since I came to London' and wrote of how he shunned 'idle amusement'.[15] There was nothing 'more ridiculous', he insisted, than 'putting money into the pockets of London tradesmen or shopkeepers'. This was a lie, for O'Connell was profligate in London and had become addicted to boating on the Thames. As he later remembered, he enjoyed it so much that it was only a short time before 'the waterman's fare made inconvenient inroads' on his purse.[16] During this period O'Connell lived in a *cul-de-sac* on the north side of Coventry Street, in what he later recalled was an 'excellent accommodation'.[17] A fishmonger's shop was on the same street, and when he passed by fifty years later he was amazed at how little had changed. He noted it was 'the same sized window, the same frontage; I believe, the same fish!'[18]

At Lincoln's Inn O'Connell found it necessary to complete a certain number of dinners, or, to use his own phrase, eat a certain number of legs of mutton.[19] When speaking he still had traces of a French accent, which drew comment, and even in his later years it was said upon that he had 'a peculiar pronunciation of some words'.[20] He remained careful in how he presented his requests for money to his uncle. One letter ended with the postscript: 'I am perhaps the only law student in London without a watch. But this is a thing that may be done without'. O'Connell knew how to play his uncle and the money for the watch was duly sent.[21] During this period O'Connell received much advice on his studies from Counsellor Stephen Henry Rice, and together they devised a plan for the study of law, which involved, for a large part, gaining mastery over Sir William Blackstone's *Commentaries on the laws of England*.[22] Blackstone's *Commentaries* has been described as a 'do-it-yourself guide to becoming a lawyer', and it was required reading for law students in Britain, Ireland, and the United States.[23] The *Commentaries* did not just provide legal information, it also encouraged mental discipline, and through it O'Connell learned a great deal about logic and order.[24]

O'Connell had returned from France, in his own words, 'half a Tory'.[25] But the political repression he witnessed in London shifted his beliefs again. In the autumn of 1794 he attended the trial of Thomas Hardy, the secretary of the London Corresponding Society, who was accused of high treason. He was shocked by what he saw as a blatant attempt by the government to oppress the people, and it helped make him a radical democrat.[26] He also seems to have followed the trial of John Horne Tooke, the man who had helped draft the constitution of the London Corresponding Society and who was arrested in May 1794 on suspicion of planning an insurrection. Like Hardy, Horne Tooke was acquitted when the evidence was shown to be almost non-existent. When Horne Tooke ran for election to the House of Commons in 1796 for the Westminster constituency O'Connell followed his campaign closely. It seems likely that he was present at the famous speech in June when Horne Tooke denounced the home secretary, Henry Dundas, for being a scoundrel, but then withdrew the accusation claiming that he was wrong, but only because Dundas deserved to have a stronger word used about him.[27] In 1827 when O'Connell was criticised for calling a man a scoundrel, he paraphrased Horne Tooke and said 'I believe I was wrong, I am sure I was if there be a harsher word in the English language.'[28]

In August 1794 O'Connell became ill, suffering from a nervous condition, or, as he described it, 'a weakness of nerves'.[29] He fell prey to a 'slow nervous fever' and for three weeks had 'a most unaccountable weakness', fainting whenever he attempted to rise.[30] After lengthy treatment by an Irish doctor, Prendergast, he recovered, though it took him some time to regain his strength.

A visit to the House of Commons had a long-lasting impact on O'Connell's development. He attended a major debate on 24 March 1795 on the state of the nation.[31] It was an opportunity to hear the prime minister, William Pitt, who had been in power since 1783 (and who was still only thirty-five) and his chief antagonist, the celebrated Whig MP, Charles James Fox. Although O'Connell's political sympathies were with Fox, he learnt more about oratory from Pitt. Years later he recalled how, 'he struck me as having the most majestic flow of language and the finest voice imaginable. He managed his voice admirably'. There was a lesson here for O'Connell as he studied to be a great orator:

> It was from him I learned to throw out the lower tones at the close of my sentences. Most men either let their voice fall at the end of their sentence, or else force it into a shout or a screech. This is because they end with the upper instead of the lower notes. Pitt knew better. He threw his voice so completely round the House, that every syllable he uttered was distinctly heard by every man in the House.[32]

When training his own voice O'Connell took this point very seriously, until he had honed his voice so that it could be projected across Merrion Square in Dublin with perfect clarity.[33] Fox also spoke in the Commons that day, for three hours, and O'Connell admired his contribution: 'He spoke delightfully; his speech was better than Pitt's'.[34] But it was to Pitt's speech that he returned to again and again, praising his 'majestic declamation' and his 'inimitable felicity of phrase'. He was astonished at how whatever word Pitt used 'was always the very best word that could be got to express his idea'. Throughout his career, O'Connell would reflect on Pitt's 'majestic march of language' and his 'full melodious voice'.[35]

A young man about town, O'Connell got into scrapes, some of them serious. In the spring of 1795 he met and befriended an Irish law student, who would be called to the Irish bar the following year, Richard Newton Bennett. Bennett was six years older than O'Connell, but they shared the same outlook about the world, and became lifelong friends. On Sunday 26 April O'Connell invited Bennett and another friend, De Vigonier, an émigré, 'to take a bottle' with him at the Old Packhorse Inn at Turnham Green. They were joined by another young man, Douglas Thompson, a local who was the son of a Chiswick porter brewer, and they stayed drinking until ten o'clock p.m.[36] Thompson left, and the three friends entertained each other as they staggered home. De Vigonier was 'heated with wine' and had to be dragged away by O'Connell and Bennett after harassing a woman. Then De Vigonier amused himself by knocking randomly on doors as he walked by. They stopped at the home of a Portuguese man, a Mr de Faria, and De Vigonier 'rapped repeatedly (twice) and loudly'. A servant, George Middleton, eventually came out and shouted abuse at the men, challenging any, 'or, I believe, all', to fight. O'Connell stepped forward and accepted the challenge. As he later wrote in his journal, 'We made some blows at each other without effect, when De. V. rushed at my antagonist and gave him a kick in the belly'.[37] Bennett joined in and was struck in the face. Furious, he grabbed the servant and began to beat him with his cane. However the disturbance had woken the household and most of the neighbours, and Faria and his daughters rushed out; one daughter began hitting Bennett. The three men made a run for it, but were apprehended by a watchman. And so they all set off for the watch-house, followed by 'half of the inhabitants of the village'. Along the way O'Connell 'abused Faria grossly'. Only Bennett was charged, for injuring the servant, and O'Connell and De Vigonier were told they could leave. But O'Connell would not abandon his friend and remained. De Vigonier did not understand what was being said and also remained; somewhat maliciously, O'Connell refused to translate for him. The incident proved expensive for O'Connell as legal actions were taken by Faria and he later regretted 'its consequent expenses, troubles and inconveniences'.[38]

In the summer, O'Connell returned home to Ireland on a short visit. He went first to Iveragh where he met Darby Mahony and they quickly returned to old habits, going to a 'hunting match at Therboy', and shooting hares.[39] It was the last time he saw Mahony. That autumn he left with his regiment to go to the West Indies, where he was killed. O'Connell also visited Hunting Cap at Derrynane and, at an unpleasant meeting, had all his bad habits pointed out to him.[40] However on his return to London, to placate his uncle, he promised to try and correct these defects. There was also time to take to the stage. As O'Connell loved the theatre it was easy to persuade him to take part in a private performance in Tralee. He had no problem learning his lines, and later boasted he 'got sixty lines by heart, with ease, in an hour'.[41] His friend in later years, William J. O'Neill Daunt, had no such ability and confessed that it took him 'three days to get ten lines by heart, to repeat in a private play'. O'Connell was unsympathetic: 'Yes,' he replied, 'some persons are curiously stupid in such matters'. For the Tralee performance his friend Ralph Hickson had a single line. All he had to say was 'Put the horses to the coach,' but he made a mess of it. Instead, he said, 'Put the horses *into* the coach.'

O'Connell returned to London in October and kept a close eye on events in France: 'Unfortunate distracted people! Their misfortunes will never have an end'.[42] His hatred of slavery was also evident at this early stage. His émigré friend, De Vigonier, claimed that the emancipated former French slaves at St Domingo were 'tired of liberty' and that they wanted a return to slavery.[43] O'Connell's dismissive comment was 'I have enough of nonsense of my own'.

Ambitious and determined to succeed, O'Connell was insistent that he would never 'be satisfied with a subordinate situation in my profession'.[44] And he had no doubt that he would 'appear with greater *éclat* on the grand theatre of the world'. To track his development, he started keeping a journal, which was both self-absorbed and revelatory. He was now at a new residence, staying at Mrs Rigby's in Chiswick, which was then outside the city of London. By an extraordinary coincidence, Rigby's landlord was de Faria, who O'Connell had abused the previous April. But even though O'Connell was 'anxious to become a great lawyer', he was also keen to study more than just the law.[45] He also read 'history, rhetoric, philosophy, and sometimes poetry', determined to master the English language and 'unite purity of diction to the harmony and arrangement of phraseology'.[46] To perfect his speaking style he attended meetings of 'The Honourable Society of Cogers', a liberal debating society of some repute which met at the White Bear Tavern on Bride Lane. As the 1793 minute book of the society explained, its objects were 'the promotion of the liberty of the subject and the freedom of the press; the maintenance of loyalty to the laws, the rights and claims of humanity and the praise of public and private virtue.'[47] John Wilkes and John Philpot Curran had been members and it was seen as training ground for some of the finest orators of the age.[48] Meetings were held on the ground floor of the White Bear and the entrance had a sign over a lamp which said 'Coger's Hall'. When members entered or left they were required to remove their hat and salute the chairman, who was also required to acknowledge them.[49] Refining his speaking style at the meetings (usually held on Wednesdays and Saturdays), O'Connell acquired 'a great fluency of speech'.[50] But in December he decided to stop going, despite what he had learned, because of the money it was costing and the amount of time he was spending on the pursuit. As he wrote in his journal, 'I have entirely lost this day owing to my being in town'.

On 29 October 1795 the king, George III, was almost assassinated in London. O'Connell witnessed the incident, having gone through St James's Park with his friend, Richard Newton Bennett, to see the king return from the House of Lords. They took a position by a tree near Whitehall. There a crowd had gathered and a man threw a coin at the king's carriage, shattering the glass. The dragoon escort immediately went into action, drawing their sabres and clearing a way in front of the carriage. The mob was in a foul mood, 'groaning' and jeering the king as he moved on. As the procession drew near to where O'Connell was waiting, he leaned forward to get a good look at the king. A twitchy dragoon made 'a furious cut' at him with his sabre, missed, and made a deep notch on the tree about an inch or two over his head.[51] Soon the king arrived safely at St James's Palace, where he changed his clothes quickly, and then exited by the opposite side, near Cleveland Row, getting into a new coach drawn by two large black Hanoverian horses. O'Connell seems to have moved to Green Park, for he saw the mob rush around the carriage and grab hold of the wheels, preventing any movement. Two men approached the door of the carriage, as if to open it, and O'Connell later speculated that 'had they dragged the king out, he would, doubtless, have been murdered'.[52] But he was saved by an armed man in the crowd who threatened to fire on the mob and they shrank away. Taking advantage of the wheels being released, the driver sped away, 'at a gallop to Buckingham Palace'. O'Connell believed that 'the French revolutionary mania had tainted' the minds of the crowd, who were 'full of Jacobinism'. O'Connell later recollected that the man who saved the life of the king was given a clerkship in the naval department at Somerset House. Some of the mob were tried for treason, including a man who was indicted 'for *grinning* at the king'. O'Connell was amused by the man's defence: he got some friends to prove that 'he was always *grinning*'.

'I remain in general too long in bed'.[53] At the age of twenty O'Connell still struggled with his idleness. In many ways he was living a typical student lifestyle, going to bed late, and then staying in bed for anything up to eleven hours. But it was something he regretted deeply, and in his journal he lamented that his laziness was 'equally detrimental to the constitution and to the mind'. This may very well have been one of the 'bad habits' criticised by his uncle. He was also beginning to struggle with his financial affairs. His brother, James, later claimed that Daniel had been in financial difficulty from the age of fourteen.[54] There is no evidence for that, but certainly by this point he was struggling to pay his bills and berating himself for his negligence. Every day he read through law reports, studying carefully Espinasse's *Nisi Prius* collection of legal decisions, as well as Blackstone's *Commentaries*, and Lord Coke's edition of *Littleton on land tenures*.[55] In politics, William Godwin's *Inquiry concerning political justice* became an influential text.[56] He was also struggling with his writing style, making a real effort to improve his presentation of ideas.

O'Connell's best friend, Bennett, got married on Monday 14 December 1795. This prompted him to reflect on the married state and his belief that it was either 'the source of pure happiness or unmixed sorrow'.[57] He was philosophical about the nature of happiness. His understanding of the nature of want and desire was sound: he realised that men always looked to some future event as the thing that would make them happy but, once it was achieved, they inevitably switched their attention to a different 'unattained desire'.[58] On Monday 14 December he attended the theatre, watching a double bill at Drury Lane Theatre, a tragedy, *Alexander the great*, and a farce, *The devil to pay.* O'Connell loved analysing and critiquing acting styles and here he found much to criticise. But O'Connell judged the delivery of the lines, rather than the acting, in other words he was evaluating the actors as public speakers, and his criticism of 'modern actors' was that they mangled the delivery of their lines.[59] He believed that the celebrated John Philip Kemble, who played Alexander, delivered his lines badly, without the 'smoothness' which made them 'remarkable'.[60] Instead, 'he pronounces them as if they consisted of a number of disjointed half-sentences'. When Kemble swelled his cheeks to emphasise his feelings, O'Connell merely found the scene 'truly pantomimic and highly ridiculous'.[61] He found more to admire in the performance of Mrs Siddons who played Roxana. Others had been critical of Siddons but he defended her style, praising the 'strength and modulation of her voice' which enabled her to be 'clearly understood in every part'.

By his own admission O'Connell was a womaniser in this period. In 1800 he told his future wife that he would not pretend that this was the first time he had spoken to a woman about love.[62] And in 1816 she teased him, not so gently, about 'your female *acquaintances before I knew* you'.[63] These entanglements also brought with them financial obligations. He had a sexual relationship with a woman we only know as 'Mrs Y' and felt obliged to contribute to her support when it ended. The nature of this obligation is not clear.[64] It does not necessarily mean a child; in this period men sometimes paid women to compensate for what was called 'ruined prospects'. At a party on 17 December 1795 O'Connell came close to striking a rival for a young woman's affection. The incident took place at a large party in Hammersmith, at the home of General Morrison. O'Connell had gone to the party with two women, a Mrs Atkinson and a Miss King. At eleven thirty p.m. Mrs Atkinson asked O'Connell to call Miss King. Douglas Thompson, the brewer's son from Chiswick, was sitting with the girl, and reacted jealously when O'Connell moved to take her away. He seized her free hand and led her from the room. When Thompson returned to the room O'Connell went up to him and said, 'in an undertone, "You have behaved in a rascally manner to me and you shall hear about it"'.[65] Thompson replied angrily, 'I tell you what, sir: if we were not at General Morrison's I would see which of us should quit the room first'. The next morning, while at breakfast, O'Connell received a letter from Thompson requesting an explanation, the first step on the path to a duel.[66]

The conflict escalated. O'Connell needed someone to act on his behalf (and potentially act as his 'second' if it came to a duel) but Bennett was still on his honeymoon. So instead O'Connell decided to act on his own behalf and he set out for Thompson's home. He met Thompson at the door of the house and their conversation quickly became heated. Thompson rushed inside and grabbed a cane before striking O'Connell three times. Even though O'Connell carried a cane he did not return the blow. That Saturday O'Connell sent a message to Bennett asking him to act as his second and arrange the duel. Bennett met with Thompson, but while Thompson pretended to arrange the details his father called for a constable who arrested Bennett. O'Connell was forced to visit the magistrate to release his friend and was obliged 'to give security that I would keep the peace'.[67] There were further repercussions. General O'Connell was forced to come down to the station the next day and become O'Connell's bondsman and Bennett was also forced to become one of his securities. Thompson's father began legal proceedings against O'Connell, although it is not clear what his grounds were, and the incident was a source of some anxiety for O'Connell over the following months.

So why didn't O'Connell strike back? This was something that haunted him over the weeks and months ahead. Even General O'Connell, who opposed duelling, 'railed at me for not having returned the blow'.[68] O'Connell reflected ruefully that had he struck the blow his uncle would almost certainly 'have blamed me as much, if not more'. O'Connell tried to convince himself there were better ways of 'revenging an injury than that of fighting with cudgels like common porters'. In his private journal O'Connell made a list of reasons for why he had not responded. O'Connell was close to six feet, which would have been considered very tall for the period.[69] Thompson was his 'inferior in stature and in strength' and O'Connell claimed that had he struck him he might have killed him: 'My apprehension was founded on the consciousness of my superior strength and of the weight of my cane'. He also thought back to the incident with de Faria's servant and, 'having no witnesses, I was afraid of the law'. But there was probably more to it than this. O'Connell was afraid. Unsure of his own courage, he also feared the effects of violence. Indeed he made a resolution at this very time 'not to fight a duel from the time that I become *independent* of the world'.[70] That said, he did not accept that this showed a want of courage, in fact he reflected 'with pleasure on the courage which I *felt* on this occasion'. But he worried about 'plunging' himself into future quarrels. He believed that 'duelling was a vice' though he understood its 'certain charm'—'the independence which it bestows on a man'—which 'endears it even to many thinking minds'.[71]

In this period O'Connell was a radical and willing to express and argue his beliefs in public. From William Godwin he had come to the belief that 'government is best which laid fewest restrictions on private judgement'.[72] After the Thompson incident, General O'Connell lectured his nephew about his behaviour and took the opportunity to speak 'of my folly in being a democrat' and 'my absurdity in displaying my political opinions'.[73] O'Connell was also a sceptic when it came to religion. Miss Hunter, a blind young woman who was boarding with her mother at Mrs Rigby's, was so astonished at O'Connell's capacity to doubt that she observed that in fifty years he would be unsure about whether he was 'a man or a cabbage-stump, so much was [he] inclined to scepticism'.[74]

At this time O'Connell became a firm opponent of the death penalty. On Friday 15 January 1796 he attended the trial of two highwaymen at the Old Bailey. This was the trial of Philip Parry, aged twenty-eight, and Thomas Thompson, aged twenty-six, who had robbed a carriage on 16 December but had been captured afterwards.[75] The men were found guilty and sentenced to death. This prompted O'Connell to reflect on 'the inefficacy of punishment'.[76] He did not approve of the way society became a force of destruction when executing a death sentence: 'And this is what we are thought to call justice. O, justice, what horrors are committed in thy name!'[77] As a lawyer, O'Connell continued to detest the death penalty. After a trial at the Limerick assizes, on 13 March 1807, three of his clients were sentenced to death. He accepted that they were guilty, 'and certainly deserve[d] their fate', but he could not help 'feeling out of spirits', even though he had done everything possible to save them.[78]

During this period O'Connell read voraciously. He enjoyed Thomas Paine's *The age of reason*, and said that it gave him 'a great deal of pleasure'.[79] Continuing his study of Godwin, he believed that 'his work cannot be too highly praised... The cause of despotism never met a more formidable adversary'.[80] He also read Godwin's socio-political novel, *Caleb Williams*. After finishing Mary Wollstonecraft's *A*

vindication of the rights of women, he reflected on the status of women
in society. He had 'long entertained' the opinion that 'women are
unjustly enslaved' and that education should be equal for men and
women ('mind has no sex').[81] But he disapproved of Wollstonecraft's
style: 'She is too fond of metaphor. Images crowd too fast on the reader.
And in the decoration we lose sight of the substance'.[82] This is an
interesting insight into O'Connell's views on style versus substance. As
an orator O'Connell hated decoration and believed the most important
thing was to make yourself understood. Therefore he always chose
simple language, often repeating the same words and phrases over and
over to emphasise his points. O'Connell's style was in how he delivered
his speeches, not in what he said, and it clearly reflected a decision he
made early in his career.

Novels were read and then discarded. O'Connell read a three-volume
novel called *The ring*, which he dismissed as 'the most stupid, insipid
work I ever met with', but which he still made sure he completed.[83] He
took greater enjoyment from Henry Mackenzie's sentimental novel *The
man of feeling*, which had first been published anonymously in 1771. He
found a 'melancholy in it that pleases and sympathises with my soul'.[84]
O'Connell read much Shakespeare in this period, but was not
enamoured of his style. When reading 'a patched-up piece' attributed to
Shakespeare the following year, he dismissed it as 'very bad', but then
joked that this 'was no argument' that it was not by Shakespeare.[85] This,
of course, was the typical bluster of youth. In later years O'Connell
recognised the genius of Shakespeare and he became one of his
favourite authors when he was looking for a stirring quote.

To take his mind off the Thompson incident, O'Connell wrote a
sketch of the character of his landlady and his fellow-lodgers. Mrs
Rigby was about forty-five years old and O'Connell was merciless in his
description of her looks.[86] She was an alcoholic and O'Connell believed
she would get drunk more often except she was afraid of losing her
lodgers. He also mocked her 'foolish and absurd' attachment to cats.[87]
But he approved of her beliefs: she was 'a most violent and inveterate
democrat, as well as a Deist'.[88] Occasionally she made sexual advances
on O'Connell. He noted that at all times she was 'familiar', and when
'heated with drinking' she became 'rude in her familiarities'. It is not
clear whether O'Connell took advantage of the offers. It seems unlikely
as he concluded his sketch of her by saying that she lacked 'common

decorum and cleanliness', although young men have not let worse things stop them.[89] When it came to matters of business she was hopeless: her servants neglected their work and stole from her. De Faria, the landlord, served her an eviction notice in early 1797 and O'Connell predicted 'her ruin'.

Female psychology fascinated O'Connell. Following the trial of the highwaymen in London he dined at the home of a married friend and spent the night there. He was intrigued by his friend's wife, 'a fine young woman' who gave every appearance of being partial to him.[90] O'Connell was a little shocked—'she is a most debauched woman'— but, all the same, 'endeavoured to improve this partiality'. Nothing happened. Reflecting on the incident a few days later, O'Connell was unsure about whether she 'had really taken a great liking to me' or if she was merely 'an artful woman who meant to take me in'. And he regretted that, even if she had really liked him, he would have been unable to 'profit of her good graces... for want of an opportunity'. The feelings of her husband—his friend—were not mentioned.

O'Connell was friends with his fellow-lodger, Mrs Hunter, an American who had come to Britain to try and find a cure for her eldest daughter's blindness. He enjoyed reading novels to this daughter[91] and greatly enjoyed meeting her two sisters, both unfortunately married. O'Connell believed that the youngest one 'was truly beautiful' and admitted that he 'never was so struck by female beauty as by hers'.[92] Mrs Hunter knew Arthur Murphy, the Co. Roscommon-born playwright and lawyer who had written a highly praised life of Samuel Johnson, and O'Connell enjoyed discussing politics with him.[93] Murphy would attempt 'to argue me out of my democratic opinions', but in such a bad way that it only gave O'Connell further evidence for his side. Murphy was also a friend of the Thompson family and on 6 January 1796 O'Connell decided to visit him to discuss the affair. Someone had called for O'Connell that morning and he had hesitated about meeting the man in case it was a bailiff waiting to arrest him.[94] Worried about this failing of nerve, he decided it was time to settle the quarrel. Murphy admitted that the Thompsons had 'acted in a blackguard manner' and appointed himself and General Morrison as arbiters. But O'Connell was reluctant to shake hands with Thompson, given that he had been struck and had received no reparation. The reconciliation did not get far. At first Thompson's father was willing to drop the prosecution, but he reacted angrily when Murphy pointed out that O'Connell also had grounds for a legal action. Murphy was furious and advised O'Connell 'to revenge' himself 'by violence'.[95]

In February 1796, O'Connell decided to amuse himself by writing a novel. He never fixed completely on a story, but he had a definite hero, a man who was the illegitimate son of King George III and his Quaker mistress, Hannah Lightfoot. The hero had been taken from his mother as a child, educated at Douai, and from there various adventures had taken him to the West Indies. 'He was to be a soldier of fortune, to take part in the American war, and to come back finally to England, imbued with republican principles.'[96] The novel did not get very far. O'Connell was still unhappy about his inability to cure his laziness, and he continued to stay in bed late.[97] As he admitted in his journal, 'I have likewise begun a novel which I shall probably never finish'.[98]

As O'Connell prepared to return to Ireland he was criticised by Hunting Cap for his expenditure during his two years' training to be a lawyer.[99] One of the more legitimate charges was for £11, which was the cost of transferring from Lincoln's Inn to Gray's Inn. This was to facilitate his return to Ireland and enable him to keep Trinity Term in Dublin. Having kept seven terms in Lincoln's Inn, he made a petition to be removed on 26 April 1796 so that he could attend Gray's Inn, and it was approved.[100] He was admitted to Gray's Inn the same day.[101] He gave a detailed defence of what he had spent, but Hunting Cap was not convinced and continued to berate him.[102] Arriving in Dublin on 12 May 1796 O'Connell knew that he had to complete nine terms at the King's Inns to be called to the bar, but that there was nothing else he needed to do.[103] Even though he had been living in London, he had still been able to register at King's Inns on 4 March 1795, his memorial signed by the respected barrister Jerry Keller.[104] Back in Ireland, he assured Hunting Cap that he had 'arrived at a new stage of my life' and regretted the times in the past when he 'had been displeased with my conduct'.[105]

Defiant and occasionally deliberately provocative, O'Connell was still able to assert his independence. On a visit to Derrynane, some time in this period, he borrowed his uncle's favourite horse, without asking, and left for a fortnight. Hunting Cap was furious and wrote angrily to O'Connell's mother about this affront. O'Connell had decided to go hunting, and had visited 'the seats of Hares at Kularig, the earths of foxes at Tarmon, the caves of otters at Direen', before going on to Direen to take part in Miss Burke's wedding celebrations.[106] 'Useful avocations, laudable pursuits, for a nominal student of the law!' snorted Hunting Cap. He threatened that O'Connell's numerous failings (in addition to taking his horse) would not be forgotten: 'The many indications he has given of a liberal mind in the expenditure of money has left a vacuum in my purse, as well as an impression on my mind not easily eradicated'. The offence, when added to his careless spending habits, ensured that O'Connell ended the year much fallen in his uncle's estimation.[107] In private O'Connell admitted that he had not known how to be economical in London, 'I spent foolishly what I bitterly regretted since'. It was a weakness he was never quite able to shake.

Chapter 3 ~

'IN THE SERVICE OF LIBERTY: O'CONNELL IN DUBLIN, 1797–1799

'The man who conceives strongly is the man of genius.
He is the friend and the patriot'.[1]
(DANIEL O'CONNELL'S DIARY ENTRY, 29 DECEMBER 1796).

A s a young man, O'Connell believed in ghosts. Even though he knew all the evidence was against their existence, he still had 'a strong superstitious dread of them'.[2] But he convinced himself 'There are none. Philosophy teaches me there can be none'. When planning a visit home he decided to spend the night in Derrynane Abbey, to give 'a practical proof of my disbelief in ghosts'. He admitted that he 'would be ashamed that anyone thought I believed in them'. In deciding to confront his fears in this way he was following in the footsteps of his great hero, Henry Grattan. Grattan had been so determined to rid himself of his fear of ghosts, he visited a local churchyard every night until he had conquered his terror.[3]

Living in Dublin, O'Connell continued to read voraciously. In December 1796 he began Adam Smith's increasingly influential *The wealth of nations*, and every day he read a number of pages of Edward Gibbon's enormous *Decline and fall of the Roman empire*.[4] The six volumes were finished in January 1798 and O'Connell praised Gibbon for mending his style, improving his thoughts and enriching his memory.[5] On 6 December 1796 O'Connell joined the Dublin Library Society at Eustace Street, even though the cost of two guineas was 'a great sum of money for me'.[6] But he was determined to spend four days a week in it, and so get 'very ample value of it'. O'Connell would stay reading books until closing time at ten p.m. and even then only leave with great reluctance. One night he was frustrated because he had to leave two pages short of finishing the eighteenth chapter of the second volume of Gibbon.[7] Gladiators fascinated him and he researched their history in the *Encyclopaedia Britannica* and the *Encyclopédie* on his very first day as a member. He returned to the subject on a later day, even though he found 'the passion for this *amusement*' to be a 'strong proof of the malevolence of the human disposition'.[8] 'In the perusal of a favourite author', he threw away hours, and he admitted he would have stayed reading until one a.m. if allowed.[9]

Despite some initial reservations, O'Connell enjoyed reading Boswell's life of Samuel Johnson. He was intrigued by the character of Johnson, someone he loved one moment and almost hated the next.[10] Reflecting on Johnson's aphorisms, he approved thoroughly of his belief that he could not love anyone who was jealous for nothing. O'Connell shared this belief and wrote excitedly in his journal that 'the man whose mind is not forcibly excited by some object is not capable of receiving any strong impression'. This made O'Connell idealise the man of 'ardent enthusiasm', the man who was only apprehensive from 'excess of desire and anxiety for success'. Such a man, for O'Connell, was 'the man of genius. He is the friend and the patriot'.

The celebrity patriot of the day was the dashing Lord Edward FitzGerald. Like many young men at the time, O'Connell admired him greatly. FitzGerald was a leading figure in the United Irishmen and it was believed that his name alone would be enough to raise an entire army. One day when O'Connell was walking by the entrance of Trinity College Dublin he spotted FitzGerald and, anxious to get a good look, he 'ran on before him, and turned about to enjoy a good stare at him'.[11] O'Connell remembered this incident years later, and described FitzGerald as 'a nice, dapper-looking fellow, with keen dark eyes'. Around this time O'Connell renewed his friendship with Richard Newton Bennett, who had been called to the Irish bar.[12] Bennett had joined the United Irishmen and the friends often discussed the crisis in Irish politics. After one long walk together, O'Connell went home and made a journal entry praising democracy: 'Hail liberty! How cheering is thy name!'[13]

O'Connell still attended mass on occasion, though he no longer really considered himself a Catholic, and thought that mankind had suffered too much because of organised religion.[14] He could best be described as a Deist, a sort of late-eighteenth-century existentialist, believing in some 'eternal being', remote and unmoved, and having made a deliberate decision to substitute philosophy for religion.[15] On 9 December 1796 he dined with some friends of General O'Connell, four men who had served in the Irish brigade in France. There was not much drink on offer and he was not 'much amused' by their company.[16] But he believed that two of them men, Marshall and Bland, were useful contacts and he speculated that they would make 'a valuable triumvirate'.[17] A few days later he had need of Marshall's pistols. He discovered that a relative, John Segerson, had abused him in a letter and resolved to settle the matter with a duel. He asked Marshall for the use of his pistols, but was told that he did not lend them to anyone. In the meantime a reconciliation was arranged and the duel did not take place.

O'Connell was still interested in developing his speaking style and began attending debates of the Historical Society. In the 1790s this prestigious society had split, with one group continuing to meet in Trinity College Dublin, and a more radical group meeting outside the grounds of the university. O'Connell attended this second group on Wednesday 14 December prepared to speak on the motion that elections for parliament every two years were better than elections every seven years. However upon his arrival he discovered that it had, for that night, changed into a law society and the debate had been cancelled.[18] He returned to the Historical Society on Wednesday 28 December and spoke twice against the partition of ancient Greece. He always analysed his performances afterwards and here admitted that he 'spoke pretty well, better, indeed, than I expected'.[19] At these meetings it was normal to have an examination before the debates on some assigned text. That night, members were examined on a section of Blackstone's *Commentaries* and O'Connell was proud that he answered 'better than any individual'.

During the winter of 1796, Theobald Wolfe Tone attempted to land with a French fleet at Bantry Bay in Cork. The incredible gamble caught British intelligence and the British navy by surprise, but bad weather prevented a landing and the mission was aborted. Hunting Cap was hostile to the French and sent news of the fleet to Lord Kenmare's agent.[20] O'Connell received word on 29 December, while the ships were still attempting to land, and reflected on whether the French might succeed if the soldiers came ashore. On the whole he was sceptical; he believed that they would 'meet with a greater resistance than they have been in all probability led to believe'.[21] O'Connell always insisted that he loved, from his heart, liberty. But he was not convinced that a French landing was the best way of achieving this liberty for Ireland: 'The Irish people are not yet sufficiently enlightened to be able to bear the sun of freedom'. He feared that freedom would descend into licentiousness and men would take advantage of the confusion to rob and murder. It was a significant observation by a young radical and suggestive of the future line of conduct he would adopt. O'Connell decided he wanted a different liberty, one which would 'increase the happiness of mankind'. It was 'in the service of this liberty' that he pledged his life and his talents. The year ended with O'Connell receiving news that his childhood friend, Darby Mahony, had been killed in the West Indies. 'Oh, my friend,' he lamented in his journal. It made him reflect on the shortness of life and he believed people should use their time to 'acquire what knowledge we can'. 'For my part,' he wrote, 'I will endeavour to be as happy as I can. I will make my heart a heart of love; that, and [that] alone, is the way to be happy'.[22]

Enjoying a busy social life, O'Connell dined out regularly. On 4 January he dined with the Rice family on Eustace Street, and was impressed by how much the father, Stephen, knew. O'Connell admitted that he seemed 'to possess more information than any man in whose company I have ever been'.[23] Because of all the reading he had been doing, and all the information he had accrued, O'Connell had allowed himself to become cocky about his own cleverness. But Rice's superior knowledge embarrassed him: 'He made me creep into my ignorance'. O'Connell was also beginning to feel guilty about the number of lies he told. At a dinner on Thursday 5 January he told a point-blank lie: he claimed to have been at the same theatre as King George III on the night of the attempt on his life. Ashamed of the lie, he made the wonderful resolution not to depart 'from the truth in any one instance tomorrow'.[24]

On Monday 2 January 1797 O'Connell joined the lawyers' artillery, the yeomanry corps for lawyers established to assist in the defence of the country.[25] In part he joined because it was necessary as an aspiring barrister, in part because he was caught up in the excitement which accompanied the abortive French landing: 'surrounded as I am with young men whom the moment has inspired with enthusiasm; with the blood of youth boiling in my veins'.[26] There was a final reason. Quite simply he was attracted to the romance of the volunteer corps. As he recorded in his journal, even though it interfered with his reading and writing, 'Yet the recollection of having been in one will hereafter be pleasant. It will still be more pleasant to be always able to say, "I was a volunteer."'[27] The next day O'Connell wrote to Hunting Cap, ostensibly to ask his permission, but really to get the £20 he needed for his uniform and equipment before he could appear in public. In this letter he tried to give the impression that his uncle would have the final say: 'I need not add that your decision will be religiously obeyed'.[28] The problem was that trouble was inevitable if his uncle refused.

The same month O'Connell fell madly in love with a woman called Eliza. Between the military drills at the King's Inns, and his pursuit of 'Sweet Eliza!', he found little time for his reading or studies, and even neglected his journal.[29] Consumed by his love for Eliza, O'Connell could not think clearly. Depressed and demoralised, he wrote of how he wanted his love for her 'to mingle in the cup of my sorrows'. And in one of the most over-the-top journal entries, he expressed a wish that he might go mad: 'Then, Eliza, I would rave of thee; then should I forget my uncle's tyranny, the coldness and unfeelingness of his heart, my own aberrations'. His mind gradually cleared, and he resumed his history readings, a good sign that equilibrium had been restored.[30] However at the end of January his thoughts were still with his 'Sweet Eliza' and he remembered her with 'satisfaction and delight'.[31] But, as quickly as he had fallen in love, O'Connell fell out of love. In February 'Sweet Eliza' was banished from his thoughts. She was, understandably, upset and wrote reproaching him 'with having *deserted* her'.[32] O'Connell was 'astonished' by this reaction: 'How blind are unfortunate mortals to their defects'. He was amused that she had 'imagined that she had made an impression on me!'

This was an emotional time for O'Connell and his journal shows much evidence of him being in the grip of deep and uncontrollable passions. Everything became an intense melodrama. On Monday 16 January he learned that his brother, John, was due to fight a duel at home and he was deeply upset at the thought that he might have been killed while the letter was in the mail: 'John, if you have perished, if you have deserted me so early in life, if you should render my path clouded and cheerless, why should I remain here, the sport of contingencies and the victim of regulated events?'[33] He was also distressed by the news that arrived from Derrynane, news which he had been dreading. Hunting Cap sent a stern letter forbidding him from entering the yeomanry corps. Devastated, O'Connell grandiloquently imagined that he would prefer to be 'quietly in my grave!'[34] He wrote a number of letters to Hunting Cap, using every argument he could think of, pleading with him to change his mind. The most persuasive point was that Lord Clare, the lord chancellor, might block him being called to the bar if it appeared he deliberately avoided service in the corps. In one letter he even threatened to quit Dublin. Finally Hunting Cap relented, though he refused to give O'Connell the money he needed for his uniform. Instead O'Connell was forced to ask his father.[35]

It was only on Sunday 5 February 1797 that O'Connell finally appeared in the uniform of the lawyers' artillery. He had been drilling regularly, but this was the first time that he appeared in public in the attractive blue jacket.[36] He served as a private and quickly became adept at the rapid loading and firing of cannon.[37] His sergeant was William Waggett, who went on to have a brilliant, if desultory career as a barrister and Recorder of Cork.

This was a time for much introspection. Thinking about the nature of glory, he admitted that 'praise is useless to the dead'. But he was also adamant that he would not like to die unknown.[38] At times he feared that he would never achieve anything, but at other times he was confident that he would 'cut a great figure on the theatre of the world'. O'Connell was well aware that he was sometimes carried away by his own 'vanity and ambition'.[39] Engaging in much self-reflection, he attempted to make a proper estimate of his talents. In the end, he decided that 'nothing could shake the steadiness' with which he planned to pursue the good of his country.

As far as O'Connell was concerned the best way of pursuing the good of his country was through political activity. He was determined to become a member of the Irish House of Commons, even though Catholics were prevented from sitting in it. This restriction did not seem to bother him too much and for some reason he seemed to believe his ambition would soon be achieved. On Saturday 28 January he spent much time thinking about how he would act 'when I come into parliament'.[40] He recognised that the easiest way to distinguish himself immediately was 'by becoming a violent oppositionist'. But he preferred 'to serve my country' and therefore thought that 'moderation' was the best policy. 'Moderation is the character of genuine patriotism', he insisted, 'and through it came 'the happiness of mankind'. But he also recognised the passion of 'hating oppression'.

Curious to see the standard of debate in parliament, on Monday 20 February 1797 he attended a debate at the Irish House of Commons. The chief secretary, Thomas Pelham, was too tired to attend, so there was no business before the house. Sir Lawrence Parsons spoke for nearly half an hour on the defence of the country and O'Connell was harsh in his assessment of his speaking abilities: 'His oratorical abilities do not rise to mediocrity'.[41] Leaving the gallery, O'Connell made a vow to work for 'the real interests of Ireland' and avoid 'the profligacy of corruption and the violence of unreasonable *patriotism*'.[42] Seeing the poor quality of speakers in the Commons, he was even more determined to enter parliament: 'I too will be a member'.

Such confidence was hard to sustain. Other days, O'Connell despaired because of his inability to make an impression on the world. He spoke of suicide: 'At this moment I know not why I should not shoot myself. I have the means at hand'.[43] But he hesitated: 'life—damn life!' He wished, as he often did, that he was a philosopher and 'superior to all circumstances'. 'But no,' he wrote with sadness, 'I am more weak than a woman'.[44] Too much should not be read into these outpourings. They were the tentative thoughts of a young man, unformed and vulnerable, trying to find his way in the world. In part he was upset because he was suffering from a terrible cold, in part he was beginning to despair about what would happen in Ireland in the event of a rebellion. And worse, this was a rebellion which he believed was being forced on the country by the wilfully destructive actions of the government. He did not believe that violence would solve Ireland's problems: 'a revolution would not produce the happiness of the Irish nation'. The stresses of the period were taking their toll: 'I am really tired with living'.

There was a 'celebrated tavern' on Eustace Street, and it was here that many reformers met to discuss their ideas. In 1797 O'Connell attended one of these meetings, organised by the city's lawyers, and also present was his old travelling companion from France and now a leading United Irishman, John Sheares.[45] As he had not been called to the bar, O'Connell was unable (or, more likely, was unwilling) to participate in the proceedings, but he said afterwards that he 'learned much by being a *looker on* about that time'. He was glad in later years that he had remained silent as he was too full of anger and passion and he believed that a young Catholic student taking a stand would in all probability have been hanged. Ireland was in crisis, and few had any idea how disaster could be averted. This period in Irish history made a deep impression on O'Connell and he always spoke of it being 'a terrible time'.[46] In years later he told stories of the loyalist atrocities, for example the story of a man called Sneyd who casually shot dead a messenger boy outside Mrs L'Estrange's public-house in Fleet Street, after he had delivered him a note.[47]

Richard Newton Bennett had risen to become an adjunct to the Directory of the United Irishmen and through him O'Connell got a further glimpse into the revolutionary undercurrent in Irish life. It also convinced him to take a part and, despite his fears of revolution, he seems to have joined the United Irishmen. 'I was myself a United Irishman,' he admitted privately in the early 1840s, and he confirmed this to a group of visitors on 2 October 1844.[48] What he observed in the 1790s convinced him that no one could be trusted and that therefore secrecy was vital when it came to action. Even men 'on whose fidelity you would have staked your existence' would betray you when faced with a massive bribe on one side and threat of hanging on the other.[49] Ironically his flirtation with the physical force movement only reinforced his belief in constitutionalism, but for pragmatic rather than (or perhaps as well as) emotional reasons. He became convinced that 'in order to succeed for Ireland, it was strictly necessary to work within the limits of the law and constitution'.[50] Secret fraternities would never be safe. In later years he confirmed that 'the United Irishmen taught me that all work for Ireland must be done openly and above board'.[51] What becomes clear is that O'Connell rejected the 1798 (and later the 1803) attempts at securing Irish independence, not because they were violent and unconstitutional, but because they failed and were doomed to fail. Noble aspirations unleashed evil forces, and the flaws contained within any revolutionary movement made success unlikely. Containing both a capacity for uncontrollable violence and a self-destruct button, all revolutions were doomed to explode (1798) or implode (1803) with disastrous consequences for the people they were trying to help. O'Connell himself admitted in 1826 that he refused to contemplate whether a future Irish insurrection might be justified if it had any chance of succeeding.[52] The implication is that, in that case, he might very well be tempted to support it.

In later years O'Connell spoke harshly about the 1798 Rebellion. Once in the 1840s he was criticised for this by some American visitors, but was uncompromising in his response. He dismissed the rebellion as 'an ill-digested, foolish scheme, entered upon without the means or the organisation necessary to ensure success'.[53] Nor did he have much sympathy for the leaders. While he accepted that some were 'pure, well-intentioned men', he believed the majority were 'trafficking speculators, who cared not whom they victimised in the prosecution of their schemes for self-aggrandisement'.[54] O'Connell had much greater respect for the people who had risen up, and he accepted that many had been provoked by 'the cruelty of the administrators, great and small, of English power in Ireland!'[55] He insisted that the examples of 1798 and 1803 had convinced him that 'physical force could never be made an available weapon to regenerate' Ireland: instead, 'the best, the only effective combination must be that of moral force'.[56] When R.R. Madden, the great chronicler of the United Irishmen, presented O'Connell with one of his volumes he returned it, saying that he had a horror of their proceedings.[57] And yet, while O'Connell repudiated the motives and methods of the United Irishmen, he never shook off their interpretation of Irish history. For the rest of his life he continued to peddle United Irishman propaganda from the late 1790s, for example that members of Orange lodges swore oaths to exterminate all Catholics and wade in their blood.

O'Connell certainly knew Thomas Addis Emmet in this period. In a speech on 4 June 1812 he talked of how they 'had once the pleasure to be personally acquainted' and that 'a more worthy gentleman, in private life, never lived'.[58] He also drew on his personal knowledge in a speech on 31 December 1813 when he said the leaders of the United Irishmen had been motivated by a 'pure, though erroneous love for Ireland'.[59] However post-rebellion Thomas Addis Emmet despised O'Connell. When O'Connell contacted him in late 1818 about some favour for his son, Maurice, he did not receive a friendly response.[60]

Around this time O'Connell became a Freemason and by doing so he came into contact with many of the United Irishmen leaders. In 1797 he joined the Old Lodge, 189, which was also apparently the lodge of Lord Edward FitzGerald, Hamilton Rowan, Robert Holmes, and Thomas Addis and Robert Emmet; John Philpot Curran was also a member.[61] O'Connell rose to become master of the lodge in 1800 and was later a member of Lodge 13 in Limerick as well as a charter member of the lodge in Tralee.[62] For about fifteen years he was an active and prominent member. In 1800 he was selected to complain to the grand master about the unpopular district deputy master and he successfully secured his removal. It seems he also acted as standing counsel for the grand lodge in Ireland during a major legal dispute between 1808 and 1814. While O'Connell was described as 'a most enthusiastic mason' in this period,[63] he later rejected their secrecy and was expelled quite publicly in 1837, having ceased to attend or consider himself a member for some years. It seems he had become uneasy about the number of oaths which were administered and taken by the Freemasons. While in the popular imagination the Freemasons conjure an image of shadows and conspiracies, the reality is that, certainly in Ireland in this period, they were just another kind of social club, where men holding diverse views could meet, exchange ideas, and relax. Petra Mirali has shown that the Freemason lodges in Ireland in the 1790s represented all shades of political opinion, liberal, radical, conservative, loyalist, and O'Connell himself defended freemasonry in 1814 as a 'philanthropy unconfined by sect, nation, colour or religion'.[64] In 1837 O'Connell explained that he had renounced freemasonry unequivocally after becoming aware of the Catholic Church's censure of it, and had told Archbishop Troy that he was willing to make this public, 'but he deemed it unnecessary'.[65] There was a renewed papal attack on freemasonry in 1814, which prompted the Irish Catholic hierarchy to join in condemning it, thus ending what Mirali has called its 'de facto toleration of freemasonry'.[66] Troy died in 1823, and O'Connell's rejection of the Freemasons probably occurred in 1816 given that this was when he returned (completely and decisively) to the Catholic faith.

'I love liberty,' wrote O'Connell on Friday 24 March 1797 as he reflected on what was needed for Ireland.[67] He was certain that liberty was 'conducive to increase the portion of human happiness'. Conversely, misery could usually be blamed on the form of government the person lived under. His thoughts were clearly on whether a revolution in Ireland should be supported or rejected. But he could not decide. The very next day he was preoccupied by the concept of virtue and wondered whether it might help him see what was best for the country. He admitted that he trembled as he asked himself, 'how much of myself entered into my desire or dread of a revolution'.[68] The fear of dying was also something that bothered him and he resolved to accustom himself 'to consider death without shrinking'.[69] O'Connell was still radical in his political beliefs and was not slow to express these beliefs in public. He was well aware that he was too reckless and 'must avoid disclosing my political sentiments so frequently as I do at present'. Given the state of repression, he knew there was a real chance of being arrested: 'It would be a devilish unpleasant thing to get *caged*!' But then he thought better of this: 'Nonsense! *Liberality* can never become dangerous'.[70]

Bennett's wife was ill in April and, as Bennett was away on circuit, O'Connell stayed almost four weeks at his house to care for her. For a time it seemed that she would die, but by the end of the month she was recovering slowly.[71] By 30 April Bennett had returned and he and O'Connell attended the funeral of a millwright named Ryan, which became something of a political demonstration.[72] It was later alleged that on the way to the funeral Bennett proposed to O'Connell 'that they should deliver up' to the United Irishman the cannon of the Lawyers' Artillery.[73] It was also alleged that both men stopped several people and asked them to join in this adventure. The declaration of martial law convinced O'Connell that 'a great change in administration' was upon the country. He later tore out pages from his journal from this time, afraid that if it was discovered he would be prosecuted. As the country became more radical so too did O'Connell.[74]

On 23 June 1797 he returned home to Derrynane, staying there until November. At the end of the year he regretted that he had 'misspent' much of his time in this period.[75] He left his lodging at Mrs Jones's on Saturday 13 January 1798, for reasons that he never explained. All he said was that 'some other time I will descant of my reasons. My heart is now sick'.[76] Possibly it was because he was spending too much; certainly at this time his uncle was urging him to live in cheaper accommodation.[77] Hunting Cap may have been strict with O'Connell about money, but he had detected a weakness that would afflict his nephew for most of his life. O'Connell was careless with money, indeed reckless, and he never followed his uncle's maxim that it was better to start out in life prudently 'than to set out ostentatiously and soon be obliged to recede and retrench'.[78]

O'Connell moved to 14 Trinity Place, a house owned by Matthew Regan, a fruit-seller who traded at 1 Kevin Street.[79] The country was on the brink of open rebellion and O'Connell was uncomfortable with the 'inveterate' odium against the Catholics. He blamed the distracted state of the country on the 'ferment which reigns all over Europe' and also the weakness and cruelty of the government's own measures.[80] Sometime in March 1798 O'Connell dined at the home of Bernard Murray, a respectable cheesemonger, at 3 South Great George's Street. The state of the country was discussed during the meal and O'Connell did not hold back and he attacked the government in strong language. Murray's son, Peter, remembered the dinner well and narrated an account for W.J. Fitzpatrick some years later. He claimed that O'Connell was 'so carried away by the political excitement of the day and by the ardour of his innate patriotism' that he called for a prayer-book so that he could 'swear-in some zealous young men as United Irishmen'.[81] Administering this oath was a capital offence so if the story was true then O'Connell was certainly putting his life in danger. Indeed Peter Murray believed that 'there can be no doubt that private information of O'Connell's tendencies and haunts had been communicated to the government' and that this prompted him to leave the city.

On the way home from this dinner, O'Connell came across a man being beaten up by a gang of thugs. His blood up, he rushed to the defence of the man, knocking down three of the attackers. But, outnumbered, he was grabbed from behind and 'beaten savagely in the face'.[82] The attackers then ran off. Because of his injuries, he was forced to his bed for a number of days, and his landlord took the opportunity to lecture him against committing himself politically.

The same month O'Connell was included in a report given to Dublin Castle on radicals in the city. The source was Francis Higgins, a key informer, and he reported on a meeting which took place in a private room in the Eustace Street library which was sometimes used by the United Irishmen. Higgins was unsure about who O'Connell was, and confused him with his uncle and namesake. He said that 'Mr Connell' held 'a commission from France (a colonel's)' and was waiting for a letter from James Tandy, son of Napper Tandy. According to Higgins, O'Connell spoke at the meeting and 'he is one of the most abominable and bloodthirsty republicans I ever heard. He is open and avowed in the most daring language'.[83] Some of the details were correct: 'He wants to be called to the bar here, merely to please a very rich old uncle'. The report is probably accurate enough. It certainly fits with other evidence, including the fact O'Connell felt compromised enough by pages from his journal to have removed and destroyed them.

As martial law had been declared, O'Connell spent many nights on patrol with his Lawyers' Artillery Corps. He told two stories afterwards to show his disgust for the harsh treatment of civilians which was normal at this time. On one occasion he was posted as a sentry on a canal bridge and was ordered to fire on some people who were out after curfew. He refused.[84] Another time he intervened when a man and his wife were being dragged out of their bed in James' Street after a random house search. A yeoman lashed out at the man with his sword and O'Connell blocked the blow with his musket. It was said that the deep indentation the sword-cut made on the barrel of his musket 'proved how fatal the blow would have been'.[85] Sergeant Waggett intervened and prevented further violence. In later years O'Connell spoke with horror about the loyalist atrocities of this period, the desperate attempt to terrorise the population into submission. He talked of 'three permanent triangles, constantly supplied with the victims of a promiscuous choice made by the army, the yeomanry, the police constables and the Orange lodges' and how 'the shrieks of the tortured must have literally resounded in the state apartments of the Castle'.[86] He recalled a man strung up outside the Castle, 'naked, tarred, feathered, with one ear cut off, and the blood streaming from his lacerated back'.

Like many of the radicals of this period, O'Connell came to detest Lord Castlereagh, the chief secretary who crushed the 1798 Rebellion and then co-ordinated the passing of the Act of Union. In March 1797, though, he admired him as 'a very valuable man'.[87] Few Irish politicians were more abused by O'Connell in the years ahead, although in private he was sometimes generous. He would tell the story of Cornelius McLoughlin, a man who was passing by Kilmainham Gaol when he was thrown a manuscript from one of the windows with a message to get it published. McLoughlin arranged for publication and, as a result, was brought before the select committee of the House of Commons. When asked why he had arranged to have the pamphlet printed he answered, 'Because I approved of the principles contained in it'.[88] Impressed, Castlereagh exclaimed, 'That's a brave fellow! We won't inflict any punishment upon him'. Listeners were often surprised by this story in favour of Castlereagh, but O'Connell would reply, 'Oh, he had a great deal of *pluck*, and liked spirit in others'.

Tragedy struck at this time. Maurice O'Connell, his younger brother, died of disease while serving in St Domingo in December 1797. News of the death, however, only reached Ireland in April 1798. O'Connell was devastated. At the end of the year he wrote the following lament, 'Oh, Maurice, oh my brother, how early in life hast thou forsaken me. Oh, accursed be the authors of the war, and accursed be the breeze whose pestiferous breath brought death to my brother.'[89]

O'Connell became a lawyer just as the 1798 Rebellion finally erupted into open violence. His memorial for call to the bar had been presented on 19 April 1798, signed by Dom Rice, and he had gone into the court of common pleas a week later, on 26 April, where he took the oath of allegiance.[90] On 19 May, the day Lord Edward FitzGerald was seized by the government and fatally wounded in the process, O'Connell was formally called to the bar. He received his first fee on 24 May 1798, just as the rebellion was starting, one guinea for drawing a declaration on a promissory note in a case in the court of exchequer (*Duckett v. Sullivan*). He received two briefs that month, each for a guinea. The outbreak of the 1798 Rebellion closed the courts and the summer circuit was late starting (O'Connell had decided to 'go' the Munster Circuit). With the outbreak of the rebellion making it dangerous for him to remain in Dublin, he decided to return home to Kerry in early June.

Communications had been cut off with the countryside, so he decided to travel by sea rather than land. With seventeen others he secured passage on a potato boat and sailed for Cork, paying the pilot half a guinea to be put ashore at Cove. The entire journey lasted thirty-six hours.[91] From there he made his way to the Iveragh peninsula, and then to Carhen, where he stayed with his parents for the rest of the year. What he learned about the rebellion horrified him. He heard stories of the rebellion in Wexford, where he believed that the people had been 'driven into insurrection by the insane cruelty of Lord Kingston'.[92]

Safe at Carhen, O'Connell tried to distract himself by hunting, one of his favourite pursuits.[93] One night he got soaked after a heavy rainfall and spent the night in a peasant's hut. But, instead of changing his clothes, he left them on and drank three glasses of whiskey as he went to sleep by the fire. The next day was sunny and he resumed his hunt, but he had no energy and soon fell asleep in a ditch. He was feverish and when he went home 'he became much worse'. As he later remembered, 'I spent a fortnight in great discomfort, wandering about and unable to eat.'[94] Finally, unable to take any more, he took to his bed. The elderly local doctor, Moriarty, visited and diagnosed the fever. O'Connell recollected that he was in such pain that he wished he was dead and, in his 'ravings', 'fancied that I was in the middle of a wood, and that the branches were on fire around me'.[95] For a time, O'Connell was convinced that he was terminally ill, he felt his backbone 'stiffening for death', and he later believed that the only thing that saved him was his effort to get up and show his father that he recognised him. During the illness, O'Connell reflected on his life and regretted that he would never get the opportunity 'to write his name on the page of history' as he had so long wanted.[96] His self-belief—what later became his overwhelming vanity—can be seen in the choice of poetry he quoted during his illness. It was four lines from the tragedy of *Douglas*:

> Unknown I die, no tongue shall speak of me;
> Some noble spirits, judging by themselves,
> May yet conjecture what I might have proved;
> And think life only wanting to my fame.

Drifting in and out of his fever, he heard Dr Moriarty say that Napoleon Bonaparte, in his mission to Egypt, had led his army all the way to Alexandria. 'That is impossible,' said O'Connell, lifting his head. 'He cannot have done so; they would have starved.'[97] 'Oh no,' replied Moriarty, 'they had a quantity of portable soup with them, sufficient to feed the whole army for four days.' 'Ay,' said O'Connell, 'but had they portable water? For their portable soup would have been but of little use if they had not the water to dissolve it in.' O'Connell's father stirred upon hearing this and, for the first time, began to feel hopeful. Moriarty turned to O'Connell's mother, 'His intellect, at any rate, is untouched.'[98] O'Connell also remembered hearing about the battle of Ballinamuck at this time although the result was not then known.

Returning to Dublin at the end of the year, he also resumed his journal after 'a year of silence'. He believed his year had been 'wretchedly misspent' and he made a vow to improve. Again his thoughts were on the idea of virtue and living the virtuous life. This was his key resolution as he was certain that 'to be virtuous, is to be happy'.[99] O'Connell was writing all this in the middle of a terrible hang-over, following 'last night's debauch'. His head ached, his stomach was nauseous, and his thoughts were embittered as a result. He reflected that drinking was 'a vicious pleasure' which always led to punishment: 'stupidity, sickness and contempt'. And so, like many men in the grip of a hang-over, he resolved to drink less.[100] His thoughts were with his dead brother, Maurice, and his spirits were low: 'Would I had never been born!' His new, pessimistic philosophy was that 'life is short and full of sorrow. Man is born to trouble as the sparks fly upwards.'[101]

On 2 January 1799 he had dinner with his good friend, Richard Newton Bennett. Talk, inevitably, turned to the recent rebellion, which O'Connell called 'the late unhappy rebellion'.[102] O'Connell regretted that 'a great deal of innocent blood had been shed'. His sympathies were clearly with the rebels, who he believed were 'ignorant and oppressed' and provoked into rising. But he still feared mob violence and believed this 'ignorance' had turned the rebels into 'brutes'. As a lesson, he believed that every 'virtuous revolutionist' should remember 'the horrors of Wexford'. This was a reference to atrocities like Scullabogue, when Protestant prisoners were burnt to death in a barn following a rebel defeat. His private comment on the rebellion reflected his deepest thoughts: 'Oh, Liberty, what horrors are perpetrated in thy name!'

Chapter 4

THE COUNSELLOR: DANIEL O'CONNELL AND THE LAW, 1799–1830

The Irish assizes were described in the nineteenth century as a theatre, where 'tragedies and comedies, melodramas and burlesques, succeed each other with marvellous rapidity'. But with one crucial difference: 'in the theatre the characters are fictitious, in the court-house they are real'.[1] O'Connell chose to 'go' the Munster circuit, the circuit of John Philpot Curran, which was 'ranked the first in Ireland'.[2] It was here that he studied human nature, and perfected his talents for performing legal as well as political theatre. O'Connell was not necessarily the best at any one thing as a lawyer, but in the range of talents he had no equal. Of these talents he had 'some in perfection, all in sufficiency'.[3] It was said that William Waggett was as eloquent, that Charles Burton and Richard Pennefather knew more law, that Harry Deane Grady was as skilful at cross-examination, and that Thomas Goold 'could brow-beat and bluster with as much vehemence and stimulated fury'.[4] But it was in the 'variety of his resources' that O'Connell excelled: 'he was like a bundle of lawyers and advocates rolled into one'.[5] At *Nisi Prius*—in other words courts of original jurisdiction before a judge and jury—he was unequalled, turning his 'mingled talent for abuse and drollery to great effect. He covered a witness with ridicule, or made a cause so ludicrous, that the real grounds of complaint became invested with absurdity'.[6] Being a great barrister, though, required more than showmanship. Dramatic outbursts and fancy tricks were well and good if they helped the case; if misjudged, they could be fatal. O'Connell's greatest characteristic was his caution. Although he could appear reckless in his manner, the reality is that every gesture, every outburst was finely calculated.[7] He 'affected to be careless, but a more wary advocate never stood in a court of justice. Perhaps no great advocate ever had the same relish for the legal profession'. For him, it was a game that was there to be won. He never made the mistake of confusing a jury with too much evidence.[8] Instead he would put illegal questions to a witness and, when they were overruled, make asides to the jury which enabled him to carry his point. In so many ways he was the consummate performer:

> He acted the part of an indignant lawyer to perfection; caught up his brief-bag in a seeming fury, and dashed it against the witness table—frowned—muttered fearfully to himself—sat down in a rage, with a horrid scowl on his face; bounced up again, in a fit of boiling passion... threw his brief away—swaggered out of the court house—then swaggered back again, and wound up by brow-beating and abusing half-a-dozen more witnesses, and without any real grounds whatever.[9]

And in doing so, O'Connell became not 'merely the advocate but the partisan of his client'.[10]

After recovering from fever in 1798, O'Connell was determined to resume his legal career. One early morning he set out at four o'clock from Carhen and travelled all the way to Tarbert, about sixty old Irish miles away, arriving at five p.m. His brother, John, went some of the way with him before turning off at the mountains so he could go hunting, 'and oh, how I did envy him... while *I* had to enter on the drudgery of my profession'. O'Connell was later met along the way by Robert Hickson, twice high sheriff of Kerry, who wanted to know where he was going, and why he had started out so late. He was astonished when O'Connell revealed that he had been travelling all day, 'You'll do,' he said, impressed. 'You'll do'.[11] There were no free rooms at the inn at Tarbert, and O'Connell began to regret 'the prospect of a long, stupid evening'. But he was relieved when a friend, Ralph Marshall, appeared, inviting him to a ball in the town that night. At first O'Connell declined the invitation, exhausted from the long ride, but given the scarcity of lodgings he was persuaded to go, and he stayed up until two in the morning, dancing, before spending the night there. He rose the next morning at eight thirty a.m. and made his way to the Limerick assizes. At Tralee he was given a brief by James Connor, and assisted as a junior alongside Jerry Keller, the respected lawyer who had signed his memorial to enter the King's Inns, and other experienced barristers.[12] It was standard to take turns with the examination of witnesses and, as it happened, the examination of a crucial witness fell to O'Connell, a man called Darby, who was described as 'half foolish with roguery'.[13] Most junior barristers declined these cross-examinations, given how much was at stake, and left them for more experienced counsel. But O'Connell was determined to make an impression and, without consulting anyone, decided to lead himself. Cross-examining Darby, O'Connell asked if he was telling the truth. 'Yes, your honour', he replied. 'Well, you are a good-humoured, honest fellow', O'Connell said. 'Now tell me Darby, did you take a drop of anything that day?' 'Why, your honour, I took my share of a pint of spirits.'[14] But ordering him to tell the truth under oath, O'Connell forced Darby to admit that 'his share' had been the entire contents, or 'all but the pewter'. Upon hearing this, 'the court was convulsed' with laughter and 'it soon came out that the man was drunk, and was not, therefore, a competent witness'. O'Connell later said that 'the oddity of my mode of putting the question was very successful and created a general and hearty laugh'.[15] Jerry Keller turned to O'Connell and repeated the words which Hickson had said to him the day before, 'You'll do, young gentleman! You'll do!'

After completing this, his very first circuit, O'Connell rested at the inn of Fermoy while on his way back to Dublin. He was sharing the journey with Grady and they had decided to take shelter because it was 'a dreadfully wet evening'.[16] However they discovered that the inn was so crowded with judges and their yeomanry escort that they were forced to eat their dinner in a corner of the room.[17] O'Connell's cousin, Captain Henessey, commanded the yeomanry escort and was 'thoroughly drenched'. Given his own recent illness, O'Connell pleaded with him to change his clothes, but Henessey refused. He fell victim to a fever and died a few days later. 'How people will fling their lives away,' regretted O'Connell afterwards.[18]

Both O'Connell and Grady were worried because they would have to pass through the Kilworth mountains on their journey, home to all kinds of brigands and robbers. They were discussing ways of getting a supply of ammunition for their pistols, when a corporal and four privates from a cavalry corps 'clattered into the hall of the inn'.[19] Grady decided to chance his luck and asked the corporal, 'Soldier, will you sell me some powder and ball?' But he refused. Grady then asked him if he would help purchase some for him, but was told bluntly, 'I am no man's messenger but the king's.' 'Grady,' said O'Connell in a low tone,

> 'I wonder that you, who have so much mother wit, should have been guilty of the blunder of calling the corporal 'Soldier'. Did you not see the mark of his rank upon his sleeve? You have grievously wounded his pride, and turned him against us, by thus undervaluing him in the eyes of his own soldiers, whom, doubtless, he keeps at a distance, and amongst whom he plays the officer.'[20]

O'Connell waited for a moment and then addressed the offended corporal: '*Sergeant,* I am very glad that you and your brave fellows here had not the trouble of escorting the judges this wet day. It was excellent business for those yeomanry chaps.' The corporal was delighted to have been mistaken for a sergeant and replied 'Aye, indeed, sir, it was well for those that were not under these torrents of rain.' The weather discussed, only then did O'Connell enquire about the ammunition:

> 'Perhaps sergeant you would have the kindness to procure me some powder and ball in town. We are to pass the Kilworth mountains and shall want ammunition. *You* can of course have no difficulty in purchasing, but it is not to everyone they'll sell these matters.'[21]

The flattery worked and the corporal willingly handed over some ammunition saying it would fit his pistols, and advised him not to spare the powder 'for there are some of those out-lying rebelly rascals on the mountains'. Grady was astonished at O'Connell's triumph: 'Ah Dan,' he said, 'you'll go through the world fair and easy, I foresee!'

Becoming a great lawyer was of course not all 'fair and easy'. O'Connell was still raw when it came to the detailed workings of the law. Recognising this, he devised a programme of study to master common and statute law, and eventually equity, and in January 1799 admitted that it would take him a year before he was 'a tolerably good lawyer'.[22] Laziness was still a major failing and he continued to criticise himself for sleeping late. He was also tough on himself when he made a mistake and this self-criticism kept him sharp. On 2 June 1802 he acted in the case of *Gallway v. Rice* but was poorly prepared. In the event, he argued the case well, but he was dissatisfied afterwards and admitted that 'in point of preparation I am but too negligent'.[23] In his final two journal entries, on 3 and 4 June 1802, he was rising early, getting up at 7 a.m. and 7.30 a.m. and spending most of the days reading law.[24] He was angry because of a case he had lost, *Gorham v. Corneberry*, where he had been badly prepared. It was an action of ejectment and O'Connell admitted that 'had I gone down to the assizes as well prepared as I am at present, we should not have been defeated'.[25] O'Connell hated being beaten and the determination to address his weaknesses played as much a part in his success as a lawyer as any of his talents.

From his fee-books we can see the range of cases O'Connell was involved with in his early years. His very first entry was for a declaration on a promissory note at the court of exchequer on 24 May 1798, for which he received a fee of one pound, two shillings, and nine pence (or one guinea).[26] This was his regular fee (or for larger cases two pounds, five shillings, and six pence) until 1802, when he began to earn considerably larger fees. One brief at this time earned him eleven pounds, seven shillings, and six pence, while the majority were for five pounds, thirteen shillings, and nine pence. On 24 August 1803 at Cork he prosecuted a man called McDougall for a murder which had taken place on board a privateer in Bantry Bay. Later in the year at Tralee, on 16 October 1803, he prosecuted a mother for assaulting her son in the case of *Hennessey v. Hennessey*. Many of his briefs involved the recovery of debts; there were also cases which involved cow stealing, various arbitrations, and forgery. On 2 February 1804 he took part in a suit which involved a woman suing a man for breaking his promise of marriage.[27] In his early years at the bar he received a high fee from Jerry Connor, an attorney who was representing a farmer called Lalor who was fighting to keep his farm at Lisnababie, Co. Kerry. Lalor was angry that O'Connell should have been paid so much when he was so inexperienced. But O'Connell performed brilliantly in the courtroom and the judge made a point of praising him afterwards. As a result,

Lalor wrote to Connor acknowledging that he had been worth the money. Years later when O'Connell passed the farm he pointed it out and said, 'with honest pride, that I was a good help to keep that farm in the hands of its rightful owner, Lalor of Killarney'.[28] O'Connell later boasted that 'no man ever got into business at the bar more rapidly than I did' and that the only one who had come close was William McMahon, who was called to the bar in 1799 and who became Master of the Rolls in 1814.[29] As a barrister, O'Connell was 'in full business' by 1806, and by 1810 he was called '"the eagle of the bar", soaring above all competitors'.[30]

At the Cork assizes in April 1806, O'Connell represented a relative, Charles Connell, who was bringing an action against his guardians for giving out leases to some of his property against his wishes. Harry Deane Grady represented the guardians, and in the course of his defence made some harsh comments about the plaintiff. Charles Connell was furious and threatened to horse-whip Grady. The judge was determined to punish him, but Daniel O'Connell intervened and spoke for 'about an hour before the most thronged audience you ever saw or that even I ever witnessed'.[31] Instead of a fine of £500 and a three month term in prison, Connell escaped with 'a fine of thirteen shillings and four pence'. Daniel was proud of his performance and told of how he 'spoke vehemently and with perhaps some feeling'.

It was usual for barristers to tense up as they waited for their case to begin in court. Some would deliberately attempt to create the impression that they were lost in concentration. But O'Connell had little time for these games, and rarely if ever showed signs of nerves. Rather, as he waited his turn to 'blaze away', he gave every indication that his fun was about to start.[32] In a sketch of his court-room behaviour in 1823 he was described as routinely disrupting 'the gravity of the proceedings by a series of disorderly jokes, for which he is duly rebuked by his antagonists, with a solemnity of indignation that provokes a repetition of the offence'.[33] The sheer force of O'Connell's personality tended to win through and it was said that 'even the judges, when compelled to interfere and pronounce him out of order, are generally shaking their sides as heartily as the most enraptured of his admirers in the galleries'. O'Connell, by his own admission, loved 'the bustle of the courts'.[34] He also had enormous stamina for the business at hand and on a busy day in court could go until ten p.m. without eating and without it affecting his health or spirits.

O'Connell detested the abuse of power and had little time for judges who acted tyrannically. It soon became known that 'any attempt to put him down was sure to meet with immediate retaliation'.[35] In the court of exchequer a young Kerry attorney was being examined by opposing counsel about a piece of evidence. O'Connell did not hold a brief for the case, but had been promised one if a new trial took place. He therefore advised the attorney not to concede the point. The judge on the bench, Baron McClelland, was not impressed by his intervention and turned on him, 'Mr O'Connell, have you a brief in this case?' 'No, my lord,' he replied, 'I have not; but I will have one when the case goes down to the assizes.' 'When I was at the bar,' McClelland retorted dismissively, 'it was not *my* habit to anticipate briefs.'[36] O'Connell's response was devastating. 'When *you* were at the bar I never chose you as my model, and now that you are on the bench I shall not submit to your dictation.'

The strategy was to match the judges point by point. It was said that 'if they were haughty, he was proud. If they were malevolent, he was cuttingly sarcastic... he badgered pompous, despotic and hostile judges until they ultimately yielded. He could not be awed'.[37] This refusal to be intimidated by authority can also be seen in a major chancery case in which O'Connell acted with another lawyer, John Richards. The lord chancellor, Manners, refused to let Richards speak towards the end of the case because, he said, he had 'made up his mind, and would hear no more arguments'. Richards feared that the case was lost if he didn't discredit some previous testimony so again pressed to be allowed to speak, but once more the lord chancellor replied that he 'would not hear him'. In 'his deepest and most emphatic tones' O'Connell rose to speak. He did not wait for permission, nor was he concerned with what the lord chancellor might think. 'Well then, my lord, since your lordship refuses to hear my learned friend, you will be pleased to hear me,' he said, as he launched immediately into a detailed analysis of the case. In an instant he had the attention of the lord chancellor. 'Every five minutes, as he opened up fresh ground, he prefaced it with— "Now, my lord, my learned young friend beside me would have informed your lordship, in a more impressive and lucid manner than I can hope to do"' and so on.[38] The next day the lord chancellor decided in favour of their client. Richards never forgot this favour and was quoted, on a number of occasions, praising O'Connell's 'ability, firmness and perseverance'.[39] O'Connell enjoyed setting 'those fellows' —the judges—'at utter defiance'.[40] He knew it went against the practice of most other barristers, 'many of whom are guilty of vile untruths to ingratiate themselves with the judges', but he declared that he would rather get no work than submit to any of them.

Judges who were weak could be intimidated and brow-beaten. O'Connell had great personal regard for Judge Day, but had little respect for his legal abilities. 'Ah, poor Day,' O'Connell once said, 'most innocent of law was my poor friend Day'.[41] This view was prevalent: Curran had said that Day's attempts to understand a point of law 'reminded him of nothing so much as the attempt to open an oyster with a rolling pin'.[42] On one occasion O'Connell was before Day defending a man who had stolen some goats. The case seemed clear-cut, but O'Connell produced an old act of parliament which stated that the owners of corn-fields, gardens, or plantations could kill and destroy all goats that trespassed. O'Connell contended that 'this legal power of destruction clearly demonstrated that *goats were not property*'.[43] Therefore the stealer of goats was not technically a thief, nor punishable as such. Day instructed the jury accordingly and the prisoner was acquitted. Another time O'Connell was refused permission to make a speech at the end of a case, because Day admitted that he was 'always of opinion with the last speaker, and therefore I will not let you say one word'.[44] This phenomenon persists today in some quarters and is known to lawyers as the 'last man standing' rule. In this case O'Connell was determined to be the last man standing and insisted on the right to speak. As he said afterwards, 'I *had* the last word, and Day charged in favour of my client'.[45] At the Ennis assizes, which O'Connell hated, he had 'a singular *row*' with Baron Smith (formerly William Cusack Smith) in March 1803.[46] O'Connell believed he had been treated badly and stayed behind to remonstrate with Smith in private. At first Smith threatened to report O'Connell to the other judges, but by the end of the conversation he was 'paying me all kinds of compliments and offering me any retribution in his power'. O'Connell was privately dismissive of Smith's character: 'He is a singularly capricious animal'. However he was proud of the command he had over his own temper which 'fits me for scenes of this kind'.[47]

In his fee-book, O'Connell kept a record of the judges who were on the bench. He was never complimentary. He noted how John Toler, the attorney general during the passing of the Union, succeeded Lord Carleton as chief justice of the common pleas in 1800, with the title of Lord Norbury. He had thought Toler 'a *pretty gentleman* at the bar', but as a judge he found him 'ridiculous'.[48] It is a sign of how much he despised Toler that he referred to him as 'the thing'. He wrote that 'the thing is fond of blood and has often reminded me that "Nero fiddled while Rome was burning"'. Another man who benefited from the Union was Luke Fox, who was raised to the bench as a result of changing his vote. O'Connell dismissed Fox as 'morose, sour and impetuous'. Nor did he have much time for Arthur Wolfe, who was raised to the bench as Lord Kilwarden, and who had won a great reputation as a liberal barrister in the 1790s. O'Connell wrote that 'much was expected from Wolfe... but his pompous inanity is insufferable'. When George Ponsonby retired as chancellor in 1807 he had some kinder words, though they were still barbed: 'Ponsonby was, to say the utmost for him, but a *decent* judge.' O'Connell reflected on what was required to be a good judge and decided that it was necessary to be 'a good *practical* lawyer'.

O'Connell was withering in his assessment of the judges on the bench. Sir Michael Smith was made Master of the Rolls in 1801. O'Connell admitted that he was 'a gentleman and a scholar, polite, patient, and attentive'. But as a judge he found him 'indifferent' and 'tedious to a fault' and, as 'the business multiplies, very little is done'. St George Daly succeeded Smith as a baron of the exchequer and O'Connell was not impressed:

> Daly is extremely ignorant, knows nothing of the law, and has not the art to conceal any part of his want of knowledge. These qualities, added to a difficulty of enunciation, have brought him into contempt with the bar and country.[49]

That said, he still thought Daly had more merit than a judge of the common pleas, Robert Johnson. Johnson, he believed, shared Daly's 'want of knowledge and discretion' but combined it with 'a peevishness of temper which is as ungentlemanly in its expressions as it is undignified in his situation'. The final, damning indictment was that he had 'no confidence in the man's honesty'. His assessment seemed vindicated in 1805 when Johnson was extradited to England and convicted of criminal libel.

Once, at the Cork assizes, a judge made a decision against O'Connell, refusing him permission to call a certain witness and submit evidence. However by the next morning the judge had changed his mind having consulted a legal text during the night. He called upon O'Connell to reproduce the evidence and call the witness. Most lawyers would have been grateful or would, at least, have remained silent. O'Connell was merciless: 'Good God, my lord. If your lordship had known as much law yesterday morning as you do this, what an idle sacrifice of time and trouble you would not have saved me, and an injury and injustice to my client.'[50] 'Crier,' he added, 'call up the witness.' The judge was humiliated, but 'remained absolutely silent'.[51]

In one of his early cases, O'Connell's aggression almost resulted in a duel. He had a brief on a prosecution of John Segerson for assault. O'Connell had a long running feud with Segerson and, in the course of his speech, criticised him using very harsh language.[52] Segerson jumped up and called O'Connell 'a purse-proud blockhead'.[53] O'Connell reacted first cleverly, and then intemperately. He told the man that 'in the first place, I have no purse to be proud of; and secondly, if I be a blockhead, it is the better for you, as I'm counsel against you.' But he then took the exchange too far and added, 'However, just to save you the trouble of saying so again, I'll administer a slight rebuke,' and whacked him on the back with the president of the commission's cane. The next day Segerson sent a challenge, but the proposed duel did not get very far. Segerson discovered that O'Connell had a lease on some of his land, and so was unwilling to fight him. He told O'Connell, 'Under these circumstances, I cannot afford to shoot you, unless, as a precautionary measure, you first insure your life for my benefit. If you do, then heigh for powder and ball! I'm your man.'[54] O'Connell rightly found this 'so ludicrously absurd' as to be 'almost incredible'. He later believed that Segerson, despite his bravado, was a timid man, and had fought all of his duels 'out of pure fear'.

So how good was O'Connell as a lawyer? 'He was a man of business, and his business was to win.'[55] He had little time for barristers who were more concerned with their own performance rather than the result. Thomas O'Hagan, the future Roman Catholic lord chancellor for Ireland, who knew him well, said that he 'regarded his facility of speech as an instrument and not as an end. He had little pride in it, save as the means it gave him of working out his purpose'.[56] As O'Connell, himself, often stated, 'Ah, a good speech is a good thing, but the verdict is *the* thing after all!'[57] He cited the example of a time when he appeared at the Galway assizes and was required to reply to a speech of three hours, which itself had followed three days of evidence against his client. O'Connell always believed that in law and in politics one should 'endeavour to condense'.[58] He responded in a speech of two-and-a-half hours and got the verdict.

O'Connell learned much of his skill in discrediting witnesses from Harry Deane Grady, who impressed him as a 'dexterous cross-examiner'.[59] Grady once defended some illegal still-owners at the Tralee assizes who had been arrested after a scuffle with five soldiers. Grady cross-examined the first soldier and cajoled him into admitting that he had arrested the still-owners single-handedly as his comrades had been too frightened. He proceeded to extract similar accounts from the other four soldiers, and as a result their evidence was completely discredited.[60] At the Tralee assizes O'Connell defended a smuggler called Connor, who had been captured with a valuable cargo of tobacco by a magistrate called Flood, himself a former smuggler. Connor's friends decided to assist O'Connell in his endeavours, and plied Flood with 'all sorts of liquors—whiskey, brandy, gin and rum' on the day of the trial.[61] Though drunk, Flood was still capable of telling his story coherently and he described clearly how he captured Connor and the contraband goods. After giving his evidence, Flood got up to leave the witness-chair when O'Connell called to him, 'Come back, Alonzo'.[62] Flood loved the theatre, regularly attending Crow Street Theatre in Dublin, and organised his own theatricals in Dingle. He caught instantly O'Connell's reference to a play in which he had appeared in Dingle, and sat down with a smile, quoting 'Alonzo the brave and the fair Imogene'. 'And who was your Imogene in Dingle?' asked O'Connell gently, prompting Flood to give a full account of his production of the play, the cast details, and the roles he played himself. There was a reason behind O'Connell's line of questioning. Flood had organised lavish suppers after each performance in Dingle and had encouraged his friends to steal fowl from neighbouring areas to feed everyone. This is what O'Connell was getting at and he continued to probe Flood about the Dingle theatricals, the suppers which followed, and the geese, turkeys, chickens and hens which had been robbed for them. 'Between the drink and bewilderment in which he found himself, Flood became involved in a web of contradiction, so that it was impossible to credit what he had said.'[63] Finally he lost the run of himself and quoted the line, 'My love, my life, my Belvidere,' attempted to embrace O'Connell, and then fell off the stand. There was much amusement, and after five minutes' discussion the jury acquitted Connor. When O'Connell was reminded of this case in later years he claimed to have completely forgotten it. But the next day he said that 'Alonzo' and 'Belvidere' had been haunting his memory ever since and he boasted that this was his greatest success in a courtroom, even including Doneraile.[64]

In February 1810 O'Connell destroyed an opposing witness who was testifying in a case, a former magistrate known as Lame Galen because he had only one leg. In a vicious attack of his character, O'Connell declared that Galen 'had been a vendor of quack medicines', an informer, 'an outcast of his profession, a very excrescence of the community'.[65] Galen attempted to argue back and present a nobler version of his career as a magistrate. But O'Connell would not let him get far. He interrupted to describe how, on the night of Emmet's rebellion in 1803, 'this hobbling anatomist' led his soldiers into Cork Street, but, once he heard the rebels were advancing, he ran into a laneway and 'fell prostrate on his face'. He was discovered by some rebels, but because he had soiled himself they assumed it was a dead body and moved on.

O'Connell was particularly skilled when it came to discrediting witnesses. At the Clare assizes in Ennis he defended two brothers named Hourigan who were charged with setting fire to a police-barrack, the property of Darby O'Grady. The prosecution said that a half-consumed jar of pitch had been found near the barrack, and stated that this had been used to start the fire. Before the trial O'Connell surreptitiously placed a skillet containing pitch near the witness chair, and covered it with his broad-brimmed hat so that it couldn't be seen. The principal witness was examined by the prosecution and swore that 'he discovered the barracks on fire and knew it was set on fire by pitch, for he got the smell of it.'[66] O'Connell was quick to cross-examine. 'You know the smell of pitch, then?' he asked. The witness replied that he did. O'Connell learned forward:

'You seem a man able to smell pitch anywhere?'
'Anywhere I found it.'

'Even here in this court-house, if it were here?'
'No doubt I would.'
'And do you swear you don't get the smell of pitch here?
'I do solemnly. If it was here I'd smell it.'

At this, O'Connell removed his hat from the skillet of pitch, revealing it to the court-room. Turning on the witness he dismissed him saying 'Now you may go down, you perjured rascal. Go down.' The accused man was acquitted.

From many of the stories it becomes clear that O'Connell saved men who were almost certainly guilty. But he believed in the legal principle that everyone deserved a fair trial, and felt no uneasiness about doing his duty as a lawyer. In 1821 O'Connell defended successfully a man called Lucy who had been involved in various agrarian outrages. When he entered the record court later, he sat next to Joseph Devonshire Jackson who lamented the fact that he had not been able to assist him earlier in the day. 'I could not get away from the crown court,' replied O'Connell, 'I was engaged defending Lucy.' Jackson wanted to know the result and was horrified to learn that Lucy had been acquitted. 'Then,' he said, you obtained the acquittal of a wretch who is unfit to live'. The reply of O'Connell captures the man and his beliefs: 'Well my friend, you will, I am sure, admit that if his crimes render him unfit to live, he is still more unfit to die.'[67] There were also times when O'Connell failed to save men who he believed were innocent. He long remembered the case of three brothers called Cremin who were found guilty of murder. O'Connell always believed 'the evidence was most unsatisfactory', but that the men were doomed because 'the judge had a leaning in favour of the crown'.[68] The brothers were sentenced to death and led by armed guard back to the prison and O'Connell remembered their mother breaking through to hold them:

> I saw her clasp her eldest son, who was but twenty-two years of age; I saw her hang on the second, who was not twenty; I saw her faint when she clung to the neck of the youngest boy, who was but eighteen—and I ask, what recompense could be made for such agony? They were executed, and—they were innocent![69]

However, with particularly brutal crimes and when convinced the accused was guilty, he was less upset at losing a case. He defended John Scanlan in March 1820 for the murder of Ellen Hanley, a fifteen-year-old girl who Scanlan had eloped with, robbed, and then murdered. O'Connell was disgusted by this 'horrid villain' and admitted that, unusually for him, he was quite 'satisfied' that he was being hanged.[70] The murder formed the basis of Gerald Griffin's novel *The Collegians* (1829), which in turn was used by Dion Boucicault for *The Colleen Bawn* (1860).

The murder had taken place on 13 July 1819. Scanlan and another man, Michael Sullivan, had gone on a boat journey with Ellen where they murdered her and disposed of the body. Back home, Scanlan kept changing his story, saying first that his wife had been left at Kilrush, then that she was visiting her sister at Kilkee, and finally that she had run off with the captain of a ship. When Ellen's body was discovered everything pointed to Scanlan. O'Connell and George Bennett represented Scanlan and it was said that they 'did all they could in cross-examining the witnesses to elicit discrepancies and contradictions in their statements... but it was impossible to beat down the facts'.[71] Scanlan was found guilty and hanged. Michael Sullivan was captured soon afterwards and admitted both men's guilt before his execution. In later years O'Connell enjoyed reading *The Collegians*. He told his friend, O'Neill Daunt, that he read it

> with a melancholy interest. Scanlan was the real name of the man who is called Hardress Cregan in the novel. I was Scanlan's counsel at the trial and I knocked up the principal witness against him. But all would not do—there were proofs enough besides, that were quite sufficient to convict him.[72]

There were so many different levels to O'Connell as a lawyer. During an important case on the Connaught circuit, such was O'Connell's skill that one of his fellow counsel, T.B.C. Smith, admitted afterwards that 'we were all like babies in comparison'.[73] He had a great eye for detail, and was just as good dealing with figures as he was with concepts. In his early days at the bar, O'Connell had a brief for a client who was trying to get a debt of £1,100 set aside. The senior barristers who had been retained spent their time 'abusing the adverse witnesses, detecting flaws in their evidence, and making sparkling points'. As O'Connell recounted years later, 'In short, they made very flourishing and eloquent, but rather ineffective speeches'.[74] O'Connell ignored what was going on, and instead began working on the client's books, taking a seat immediately under the judge's bench. He wrote down numbers for each voucher and compiled a simple double entry system. The result was that instead of his client owing £1,100, 'there was actually a balance of £700 in his favour'.[75] O'Connell explained this to the judge and jury when his turn came to speak and the jury was so impressed a member asked if it could give a verdict of £700 in favour of the client. This was a story O'Connell told in his later years, 'to show that I kept an eye on that important branch of my profession'.

Sometimes when O'Connell was called upon for legal advice he came across some extraordinary stories. He was amused by the story of an attorney's clerk, out to make a quick fortune, who forged a document purporting to be the will of a certain Duke O'Neill, who had recently died, childless, in Spain, leaving a fortune of over a million pounds. This fortune was to be left to any Irish person bearing the name of O'Neill, and the attorney sold copies of the forged will to the gullible for half a crown. Several victims of the scam went to O'Connell for advice about how to get their share of the inheritance. 'Nothing', said O'Connell, 'could exceed their astonishment when I assured them the whole thing was a delusion.'[76] The victims went away 'indignant at the fraud, and lamenting they could ever put faith in the tale of the "ould duke"'.

One of O'Connell's favourite legal anecdotes concerned a criminal called Checkley, known widely as 'Checkley-be-damned'.[77] Checkley had been arrested for burglary and criminal assault at Bantry and was tried at the Cork assizes, where he was defended by Jerry Keller. Checkley had arranged his own character witness, and when this witness took the stand he shocked Keller by testifying that there was 'devil a worse' character than Checkley. Keller flung down his brief and looked furiously at Checkley, but Checkley asked him to continue with his examination as the witness could provide an alibi. And so it transpired. On the night of the crime the witness said that he had observed Checkley stealing a brand new spade, as well as carrots and parsnips, from the estate of Lord Shannon, sixty miles from Bantry. The judge was satisfied that Checkley was innocent and released him, on the understanding that he would be arrested for the other crime. It was only afterwards when both Checkley and the witness disappeared that everyone realised they had been conned. O'Connell later told this story to a group of English barristers with whom he was dining and they applauded 'Checkley's unprincipled ingenuity'.[78] One lawyer claimed that he had such a high 'admiration of this clever rogue that he would readily walk fifty miles to see Checkley'.[79]

When all else failed with the jury, O'Connell would tell a good story. Once, when defending a man in Cork, he entertained a jury with the (apocryphal) tale of a man on trial at the Clonmel assizes for murdering his neighbour. The evidence was circumstantial, but seemed enough to convict the prisoner, who had a terrible reputation in the county. But the prisoner surprised everyone by calling the dead man as a witness. It turned out that a different man had been killed, and had been falsely identified as the accused man's neighbour because of the similarity of their clothing. The jury still retired to consider its verdict and shocked the judge by returning a verdict of 'guilty'. 'Good God,' exclaimed the judge, 'of what is he guilty? Not of murder, surely?'[80] The foreman nodded in agreement, 'No, my lord, but if he did not murder that man, sure he stole my grey mare three years ago!' The Cork jury laughed when O'Connell told the story and he took the opportunity to explain to them that his client was being punished for things he did in the past, not the crime which he was presently accused. The client was acquitted.[81]

O'Connell's talent for abuse was another useful weapon to neutralise an enemy or win a jury's sympathy. When O'Connell once introduced a motion to change the venue of a case from Dublin to Tralee, he was opposed 'by a very ugly barrister, Mr Scriven'. O'Connell first tried flattery, stating that he trusted that his 'learned friend opposite will not resist my application to have this case tried in Kerry. We shall do our best to give my learned friend a kind welcome, and I'll undertake to show him the lakes of Killarney'.[82] But Scriven was not won over and growled, 'I dare say you'd show me the bottom of them.' 'Oh no,' replied O'Connell, 'I would not frighten the fish'. On another occasion, when defending a client against a barrister who kept interrupting him, O'Connell finally lost his patience and roared at him to 'Sit down! You audacious, snarling, pugnacious ram-cat.'[83] Those gathered in the court-room roared with laughter, although his opponent shook with silent rage; he was known as 'ram-cat' for the rest of his career. But the genius of O'Connell as a barrister lay not in his ability to abuse—although few could match him when he was in the mood—or in his ability to intimidate a judge or persuade a jury—and again few could match him when he was at his best. Rather it was his ability to know, almost instinctively, what was the correct tactic to use and when. He had so many weapons to deploy, and his genius lay in knowing when to attack or fall back, when to use humour or when to abuse, when to rely on the law to win, or when to resort to tricks and stratagems.

Even in the early days of his career O'Connell was considered 'matchless as a scold'. His talent for vituperative language soon became infamous, although there was one person who came close—Biddy Moriarty, a woman who sold goods at a stall on the quays near the Four Courts. Her 'powers of abuse' were notorious and it was said that 'the dictionary of Dublin slang had been considerably enlarged by her'.[84] Soon barristers began to speculate about who would win in a contest between the two, and soon O'Connell was challenged by his friends to engage her in a contest. 'Bets were offered and taken'—O'Connell bet on himself—and a large group gathered at Moriarty's stall to see what would happen. But O'Connell had prepared the ground carefully and beat her with a mixture of Euclidian geometry and 'a scoffing, impudent demeanour'.[85] After a long and heated debate over the price of her goods, he left her so confused that she was no longer able to speak. She began gasping for breath, struggling to find more insults to throw at O'Connell, before grabbing a saucepan and moving to attack him. O'Connell wisely retired from the fray. The wager was won and he was handed his winnings.

O'Connell detested the bullying of younger or weaker barristers which was a feature at the bar. For years he took the side of one of his contemporaries, William McMahon (later Master of the Rolls), who, because his father had been a state-trumpeter, was looked down upon by some members of the Munster circuit. This only encouraged O'Connell to be nicer to McMahon. However circumstances changed. McMahon's brother began to receive royal favour in the 1810s from the prince regent.[86] The effect on McMahon's fortunes was immediate. Those who had abused him now toadied up to him. But just as O'Connell had treated him as an equal when he was despised, he was now just as determined to give him no special treatment. One day in

Limerick, when it had been raining, McMahon changed from his boots into a pair of slippers before entering the bar-room. A young junior, anxious to make an impression, immediately brought the boots inside and placed them by the fireplace. When O'Connell arrived and saw the muddy boots he demanded to know who they belonged to and, when told they were McMahon's, he kicked them with force towards the door. He roared that they should be outside as 'placing them in the fire-place under our noses is a great outrage'. Rather than being offended, McMahon was amused: 'O'Connell, you are quite right.'[87]

John Martley was another young barrister who had reason to be grateful to O'Connell. At his first appearance addressing a court, he was prevented from stating his motion by two of the judges, Johnson and Norbury, who took turns mocking him. None of the seniors were willing to help, so O'Connell, who was waiting in the court for a later case, intervened. "'My lords," he said, "I respectfully ask your lordships to hear this young gentleman. Mr Martley is not personally known to me, but I submit he has a right to be heard." "Oh, Mr O'Connell, we have heard Mr Martley," said Lord Norbury, "and we cannot allow the time of the court to be further wasted." "Pardon me, my lord, but you have not heard him," replied O'Connell, "He has not been allowed to state his motion; I am sure he is quite capable of doing so now if your lordships permit him." "Mr O'Connell," asked Judge Johnson, with an air of defiance, "are you engaged in this motion that you presume to interfere?" "My lord, I am not," replied O'Connell, "but I rise to defend the privileges of the bar, and I will never permit them to be violated, either in my own or the person of any member of the profession." "Well, well," interposed Lord Norbury, "we'll hear Mr Martley; sit down Mr O'Connell."'[88]

O'Connell enjoyed being unconventional. Dining at the bar-mess in Ennis during a summer assizes he was helping himself to an Irish dish called *sleabhcán*, a kind of edible seaweed, dipping his table-spoon into it with great rapidity. A fashionable young barrister then entered the mess, a man who dressed like a dandy and delighted in 'squiring young ladies round the squares in Dublin'.[89] He took a seat near the bottom of the table and ordered in a loud voice some *sleabhcán*. O'Connell watched as the plate went by, and then 'very coolly took his own table-spoon, which had paid such frequent visits to his own mouth, [and] darted it into the dish before him'.[90] The dandy was furious but, afraid of provoking O'Connell's wrath, instead took out his anger on the waiter. The rest of the diners 'were half-suffocated with ill-suppressed laughter', but O'Connell continued with his meal as if nothing had happened.

The more difficult problems sometimes demanded ingenious solutions. Once, at the Cork assizes, O'Connell was engaged in a case which hinged on the successful examination of a key witness. Unfortunately for O'Connell a king's counsel had also been retained, and according to rules of precedence, was required to depose the very next witness, in this case the key one. The senior barrister was 'in agony', dreading the prospect of the case failing because he was not as quick-witted as O'Connell. But his face brightened when O'Connell whispered something in his ear. Emboldened, he called 'Timothy Hegarty' as his next witness. Hegarty had nothing to contribute to the case, being merely 'a gaping clown' that O'Connell had spied in the crowd, but that was not the point.[91] He was questioned briefly by the senior, which meant that it was O'Connell's turn for the following witness—the material witness on which the case depended. The case was won.[92] It has been speculated that O'Connell's frustration at having to defer to inferior lawyers, because they were king's counsels and he, as a Catholic, was not, induced him to perfect an unrivalled ability at cross-examining.[93] One of the most famous examples of O'Connell's brilliance at cross-examination occurred when he was representing clients who were challenging the validity of a will. The plaintiffs— O'Connell's clients—insisted the will had been forged. But despite all of O'Connell's best efforts he was unable to shake the story of a witness who swore on oath that the deceased man had signed the will 'while life was in him'. However O'Connell became curious because no matter how he asked the question, the witness kept using the same phrase, that 'life was in him' when the will had been signed. And, as if by magic, O'Connell read the truth into what was being said. He asked the witness to swear solemnly—'and answer me at your peril—was it not a live fly that was in the man's mouth when his hand was placed on the will?' The witness fell to his knees, terrified, and confessed everything: the defendants had placed a fly in the mouth of the dead man so that they could swear on oath 'that life was in him' when they had scrawled his signature on the forged will. When the deception was exposed the witness countered, 'Ah, Mr O'Connell, you know all the roguery of it, but you know none of the honesty of it.' Those present in the court-room were amazed at O'Connell's 'intuitive quickness' and his reputation grew as the story spread.

'Nothing advances an Irish barrister more than the talent of ridicule.'[94] Humour was another weapon to be deployed to get a judge or jury on-side. At the Limerick assizes in March 1808 he secured the acquittal of all his prisoners and kept the county court-house 'in a roar of laughter' for nearly an hour.[95] Once, when O'Connell was leading in an action for the conversion of a water-course, he took the opportunity to poke fun at his own attorney, a stout man named Fogarty who had a reputation for being abstemious. O'Connell was representing a man who had suffered by the diversion of a river stream, which meant that his fields were no longer irrigated. To illustrate his point, O'Connell turned to 'the jolly-faced attorney by his side' and told the jury that 'instead of the flowing stream that used to meander through the plaintiff's ground, there is not now, gentlemen, as much water remaining as would make grog for Fogarty!'[96] As O'Connell would boast in his later years: 'I kept the court alternately in tears and in roars of laughter.'[97] Once, when defending a man who was accused of stealing a dead cow, O'Connell succeeded in changing the indictment to stealing beef.[98] Later, the defendant gave O'Connell advice on how to choose the best cow to steal in the dark. It would be the one farthest from the ditch, as the thin ones always went to the ditch for shelter.[99] O'Connell would also play on the emotions of a jury. On 3 April 1813 at the Cork assizes he made what he called 'a *famous speech*', which reduced the jury to tears and prompted them to acquit his client 'for the sake of *his wife* and children'.[100]

A fishery case tested O'Connell. He was representing the members of a company which had established at salmon fishery near Youghal. However the previous proprietors were Danish merchants who had called the fishery 'The Lax Weir' and who challenged the right of the company to set up nets to fish for salmon. However O'Connell found a translation for '*lax*' or '*lachs*' as meaning 'salmon' in German, and thus proved that the weir was therefore in fact a salmon fishery.[101] On another occasion, at Limerick, he defended two men indicted for robbery. A young priest had been called as a character witness, but he infuriated Judge Torrens by 'parading his learning by the use of big words'. For example, he praised the men saying 'their reputation for rectification of habitual propriety was exemplary and commendable'.[102] Torrens grew increasingly impatient and asked the priest directly: 'are they honest?' The priest replied, 'As far as my experiences of their deportment, I am under that impression.' Torrens snorted, 'You think they are! That comprehends a great deal,' before dismissing the priest from the witness chair. O'Connell now rose and assumed 'an air of great indignation'. Turning to the prisoners, he said 'My poor fellows, bigotry is on the bench, and when your excellent young priest has been so ignominiously turned out of court, I am in despair of being able to serve you. Here's your brief and fee.'[103] He then flung down his brief and his notes and began putting on his cloak, muttering 'My innocent clients, I despair altogether now of your acquittal; you'll be hanged, and never were men hanged more unjustly. The only hope I can look to is, that, if your sentence is not carried into execution before the twelve judges meet, I'll bring this outrageous case before them.' Torrens grew pale and, terrified that it would be reported that he had acted in a bigoted manner against the priest, pleaded with O'Connell to resume his defence. O'Connell hesitated, but allowed himself to be persuaded to continue. The trial restarted and the judge went out of his way to praise the honesty of the prisoners, and a not guilty verdict was secured.

The celebrated American actor, John Howard Payne, visited Ireland in 1814. Towards the end of his production of *Hamlet* in Cork on 20 August 1814, the editor of the *Cork Freeholder*, John Boyle, interrupted proceedings by taking to the stage to address the audience and complain about the performances. Boyle denounced the company as being worthless, and when the sheriff attempted to remove him he lashed out and struck him. The case attracted much interest, and O'Connell agreed to represent Boyle. During the course of the trial in January 1815 he demonstrated that 'the house, scenery and performers, with one or two exceptions, were wretched beyond all endurance'.[104] He took care to praise the performance of the Ophelia in the production —a young Irish actress called Miss O'Neill—saying that her 'talents are an ornament to her country, and her virtues are an honour to her sex'.[105] And he also made clear that Payne had not been attacked because he was an American, given that Britain and the United States were at war: 'monstrous and unfounded charge! Had this been the case I would not have opened my lips in his defence'. Boyle, however, was found guilty, fined fifty pounds and sentenced to six months' imprisonment.[106] As is clear from this, O'Connell did not win all his cases. The many published collections of O'Connell legal anecdotes create an impression that he was invincible which is as unrealistic as it is misleading. The lawyer who wins all his cases is a lawyer with an incredibly small practice.

The reputation O'Connell developed as 'The Counsellor' came from the times he achieved the impossible, when he seemed to be able to conjure a victory out of nothing. When defending a man named James at the Cork assizes charged with murder, O'Connell realised that his entire defence depended on discrediting the principal witness. A hat had been found near the scene of the crime and the witness refused to change his testimony that it belonged to the accused:

> 'Now', said O'Connell to the witness on cross-examination, 'you are quite sure about this hat?' 'I am', replied the witness. 'Let me look at it again', said O'Connell, taking it from the witness and examining it carefully. He then looked inside and spelled J-A-M-E-S. 'Now do you mean to tell the court and jury this name was in the hat when you found it?' 'I do, on my oath', replied the witness. 'Did you see the name then?' 'I did—surely'. 'This is the same hat, no mistake about it?' 'Och, no mistake—tis his hat'. 'Now you may go down' said O'Connell triumphantly. 'My lord, there is an end of the case—there is no name whatever in the hat.'[107]

The prisoner was acquitted.

On another occasion in 1822, also in Cork, O'Connell found himself out of ideas when representing a man accused of murder. The case looked hopeless as there was overwhelming evidence against his client. One of the judges had fallen ill and the inexperienced Serjeant Thomas Lefroy presided in his place. O'Connell could read men and decided to gamble everything on the character of Lefroy. Knowing that a genuine defence was doomed, he immediately began putting some irregular questions to the first witness. Thomas Goold, the crown prosecutor, objected, and Lefroy concurred. This was what O'Connell had been hoping for and 'after a little expostulation', said, 'Well then, my lord, as you refuse permitting me to defend my client, I leave his fate in your hands'.[108] And with that he grabbed his brief and stormed out of the court, turning once to admonish Lefroy, 'The blood of that man, my lord, will be on your head, if he is condemned.' For half an hour O'Connell paced up and down outside, waiting for the verdict. Finally the attorney for the defence rushed out to him and announced that their client had been acquitted. 'O'Connell is said to have smiled meaningfully on the occasion, as if he had anticipated the effect of the *ruse*, for it was a *ruse* he had recourse to, in order to save the unfortunate culprit's life.' By 'flinging the onus on a young and a raw judge' O'Connell had given his client a chance. Lefroy, fearing that the man would not get a fair trial, had taken it upon himself to cross-examine the witnesses and developed a bias in favour of the accused. He charged the jury to return a not guilty verdict and the result was 'the unexpected acquittal of the prisoner'. 'I *knew*', said O'Connell afterwards, 'the only chance was to throw the responsibility on the judge.'[109] O'Connell despised Lefroy, mocking him for 'preaching bad sermons and displaying as little law as possible', and believed he was 'the most complete *failure* which any times' had produced.[110]

On the Munster circuit in the summer of 1822 O'Connell was in much demand. He was given a retainer by a solicitor to defend a man who had been caught red-handed robbing a plantation belonging to a wealthy landowner. The evidence against the man was overwhelming and included the testimony of no less than three eyewitnesses, servants of the landowner—the gamekeeper, the butler and a labourer—who had all helped apprehend him. The case seemed hopeless and, believing that nothing could be done, O'Connell sent the fee back to the solicitor. The next morning the solicitor accosted him in court, furious that the fee had been returned. Demanding an explanation, the solicitor was not mollified by O'Connell's reasoning that the money would be wasted. Indignant, the solicitor insisted that O'Connell had no right to refuse the case, and demanded that he accept both the fee and the case. 'Oh,' said O'Connell, 'there is not the slightest necessity for you putting yourself into a passion about the matter. If you will insist on my receiving these fees, notwithstanding that I tell you I cannot give you value for them, have it your own way. I am quite satisfied since you are, and I *will* take the matter up.'[111] When the case got to court the prosecution confidently announced that it had three eyewitnesses who would all testify. The solicitor whispered to O'Connell, 'Get two of them out of court, while one is under examination'. It seemed obvious that the only chance of getting an acquittal was in securing three different testimonies from the men. But O'Connell refused. 'No, no,' he replied, 'they shall all remain in. It is our only chance, as you will see'. This was O'Connell at his best, reading the terrain and deciding in an instant where to attack. The butler was the first witness. He told the story clearly, though giving himself the greatest share of the glory for the capture. O'Connell had the measure of the man, and encouraged his pomposity and self-regard during the cross-examination. Then, with a series of trick questions, he led him into a web of 'inconsistencies and contradictions, as utterly to invalidate his testimony'.[112] The labourer was the second witness. Even though he was annoyed that the butler had attempted to seize most of the credit, he was more concerned with getting a conviction. And thinking that a conviction rested on telling the same story, as the prosecutor had warned him beforehand, he attempted to repeat the butler's narrative, all the time trying to explain away or reconcile the inconsistencies. This only made the story more confused, and by the end of his account he was 'in a state of greater *botheration* than even the butler'. The gamekeeper was the final witness. Brimming with confidence, despite what had happened to the other two witnesses, he happily set about attempting to tell the same story, convinced he was clever enough to explain away all the inconsistencies and contradictions. But O'Connell was merciless during cross-examination and tormented him to such a state that when told he had only to answer one further question, he replied, 'Oh, if it's only one question more and you'll let me go, then I'll answer it any way you like!' O'Connell seized upon this and reminded the gamekeeper that he had made this promise under oath. Then he asked him, 'by virtue of your oath, isn't the client innocent?' The gamekeeper was trapped and confused. Bewildered, he replied 'By virtue of my oath, he is!' The man was acquitted and O'Connell left the court amused that the he had won the case despite all his misgivings.

The same summer, O'Connell defended a man accused of a particularly brutal agrarian murder. The case hinged on the testimony of a young boy who had witnessed the murder and who swore that he could identify the accused by a mark on his cheek. O'Connell blocked the boy's line of sight to his client and then began questioning him about the murder, drawing him out about what he had seen.

Distracting the boy by asking some questions on unimportant matters, he eventually seized upon two separate claims that the mark was on the right cheek. When it was revealed that the mark was actually on the left cheek the accused man was acquitted. A short time later another man was arrested who had a mark on his right cheek and it was discovered that he was the real culprit.[113]

It would be easy to get the impression from stories like these that O'Connell triumphed by relying on his quick wit and intelligence rather than his superior knowledge of the law. The problem is that the stories which have survived are the ones which make for a good anecdote, whereas the ones that relied on a detailed knowledge of the law were much less entertaining and so have not been passed on. This gives a misleading impression, for at the heart of all of O'Connell's legal triumphs was his mastery of the law.[114] At the Cork assizes, O'Connell was once engaged in two cases running in parallel, one in the crown court and one in the record court. His attentions were fixed on the case in the crown court, which involved the defence of a man charged with murder. Meanwhile the case at the record court was falling apart, and the other barristers who had been retained alongside O'Connell feared that it was about to be dismissed as a non-suit. Out of ideas, they sent for O'Connell. O'Connell was just concluding a brilliant cross-examination and was 'quite radiant with triumph'. When he heard how things were going at the record court he set off at once, 'with that lively, rollicking manner that made him so popular, jesting with all he knew as he strode along'.[115] He glanced through his brief while he received an update on what had taken place, all the time reading his extensive notes on the margins. Sweeping into the court, O'Connell immediately addressed the judge on the critical point, demonstrating that the argument of the opposing counsel was not applicable in this case and that there were no grounds for a non-suit. The judge ruled in his favour and announced that the case must go to the jury. It was said afterwards that he had 'found the able men with whom he acted sprawling like a parcel of children, and it was he only who set them on their feet'.[116] The point won, O'Connell replaced his brief in his bag and returned to the crown court, where he completed the successful defence of his client charged with murder.

A story from 1825 demonstrates O'Connell's mastery of the law. He was called into court by the agent of his clients very suddenly, without much time to prepare his thoughts. Without opening his brief-bag, O'Connell made a quick estimation of the particulars of the case and then argued strongly for a non-suit. He won the case and was applauded by the solicitor for an 'unexpected success'.[117] But O'Connell was not happy. He rebuked the solicitor for not having paid him his fee. The solicitor was astonished and assured him that it had been left with the brief at his lodgings. O'Connell was about to challenge the man's honesty but a friend whispered in his ear that he was incapable of speaking a lie. So instead he wrote out a short receipt for the fee on the brief and gave both to the solicitor. The solicitor opened the brief and there, attached to the first sheet, was a five pound note. O'Connell realised he had been found out—he had never read the brief. The story became a popular one, as it demonstrated O'Connell's success even without preparation.

After emancipation O'Connell rarely returned to the courtroom but on one occasion when he did he was similarly unprepared. In the 1830s he represented a group of merchants suing the government for compensation for the loss of goods following the great Custom House fire of August 1833. Charles Haliday, a member of Dublin corporation, was enlisted to advise O'Connell, but O'Connell was distracted and had not paid attention to the particulars of the case. During his speech he delivered an argument in direct opposition to the side he was meant to be on. Haliday listened in bewilderment, but was unable to interrupt. Fortunately there was a break for a few minutes and Haliday quickly whispered to O'Connell that he was arguing the wrong side. O'Connell seemed unconcerned. When the case resumed he showed 'the utmost coolness' and told the court, 'When we left off, I was engaged in showing what might be said by my adversaries' before delivering a brilliant argument rebutting all the points he had just made.[118] Haliday would later tell the story 'with much zest as an instance of O'Connell's dexterity'.

Numerous stories of O'Connell's legal triumphs entered folklore. Many of these stories are amusing, few are plausible. In one story O'Connell was defending a man accused of a crime and decided to provide a testimonial about his character. Before the trial O'Connell put the man into a child's cradle and rocked it for a little while. Then, when before the judge and jury, O'Connell swore that he had never known the man to do anything wrong for 'as long as I know him'. 'Is that long?' the judge asked. 'Since I used to rock him in the cradle,' answered O'Connell with a straight face.[119] In another, he dealt with a judge who had been bribed with ninety gallons of wine. O'Connell pretended to fall asleep in the court and, when woken by the judge, he pretended to be startled and claimed that he had dreamt of a horse drowned by a large quantity of wine. The judge realised O'Connell knew about the bribe and made sure the prisoner was acquitted. The stories were important for creating the image of O'Connell as a folk hero, relying on his instincts, his superior intellect, and almost supernatural powers to defeat his enemies.

When at the Cork assizes O'Connell stayed at a lodging in Patrick Street, and as his fame grew crowds would gather at his door to catch a glimpse of 'The Counsellor'. Once O'Connell was visited by an old friend, just as he was finishing giving a legal opinion to a 'shrewd-looking farmer'. O'Connell rushed to greet his friend and the farmer, sensing an opportunity to avoid paying for the consultation, took the opportunity to make for the stairs. Seeing what was happening, O'Connell raced after him and, realising that he couldn't catch him, leant over the banister, and made a grasp at the farmer's hair.[120] Unfortunately for O'Connell the man was wearing a wig, which came away in his hand. The farmer escaped. But O'Connell was jubilant, and returned to his room with the wig held aloft in triumph. He passed the wig around for inspection saying, 'Ah boys! Here's the wig of a rascal that has just bilked me of a fee.' The crowd which had gathered laughed and shouted, 'Three cheers for the Counsellor!'

As well as possessing a detailed knowledge of the law, O'Connell also had a prodigious memory when it came to remembering people. At Derrynane he often settled grievances, indeed he insisted his own tenants went to him rather than the law, and on one occasion was asked to adjudicate in a dispute between a wealthy farmer and a neighbour. The wealthy farmer boasted that, unlike his rival, he had never been before a judge or sent to jail. But O'Connell stopped him and reminded him that 'it is now just twenty-five years ago, last August, that I myself saved you from transportation, and had you discharged from the dock'.[121] The man was thunderstruck, having assumed that O'Connell would never have remembered him, and then 'shrunk away, murmuring that he should get justice elsewhere'.

One of O'Connell's rare cases after the winning of emancipation was in 1831 in Kilkenny. Twenty-five men were charged with the murder of eighteen policemen during a riot at Carrickshock. O'Connell had been retained by the prisoners but many doubted if he would arrive in time. On the day of the trial the same question was asked, 'Is the Counsellor come?' When finally it was revealed that he had arrived the night before there was relief, 'Glory be to God! The poor boys are all safe!'[122] The first prisoner tried was a farm labourer, Michael Kennedy. A constable who had survived the riot was the prosecution's key witness and he stuck resolutely to his story despite O'Connell's best efforts. A conviction appeared inevitable, but just as O'Connell was about to bring the cross-examination to an end he was passed a note: the constable's father had been a sheep-stealer. O'Connell returned to the cross-examination, making no reference to the note. Drawing it to an end, he asked the constable with a smile 'one more question. Are you fond of mutton?' 'I like a good piece well enough,' came the reply.[123] O'Connell continued, 'Did you ever know any expert sheep-stealers?' The constable blushed, but thinking his father's past was long forgotten he said simply, 'I have met some in the discharge of my duty as a policeman'. But O'Connell pressed him about whether he had known any before he became a policeman. 'Never,' was the emphatic response. Again O'Connell pressed the question and again it was denied. At this point O'Connell, 'with that power and vehemence which none could assume more impressively, dragged from the witness the fact that his father was a notorious thief, and before long forced the bewildered green-coated, black-belted peeler to admit himself a perjurer.' But this was only the first part of the defence. The principal witness discredited, O'Connell then produced an alibi for Kennedy. He called upon Kennedy's employer, who swore that during the time of the riot Kennedy had been engaged in bringing a ladder from a neighbour's farm. Kennedy was acquitted and no convictions were made at the special commission.

By 1828 O'Connell was earning over £8,000 *per annum* in legal fees. This, he boasted, was 'an amount never before realised in Ireland in the same space of time by an outer barrister'.[124] What he meant was that, prevented by religion from obtaining a silk gown and becoming a king's counsel, he was limited in the type of work he could do and the amount of money he could make. He later speculated that had he been a king's counsel he would have increased his income, 'by probably one half'.[125]

As O'Connell's fame grew he was retained even by men who detested his politics. A leading Orangeman, Hedges Eyre, was always prepared to hire O'Connell. Once during a trial, he was censured for this by a friend and asked why he gave his money 'to that Papist rascal'.[126] Eyre said nothing, but continued to watch the trial. The opposing counsel were pressing for a non-suit and the judge was prepared to go along with them. O'Connell protested but the judge was unimpressed. Still O'Connell persisted, 'Well, hear me, at all events!' The judge again refused, saying, 'I've already heard the leading counsel.' This only angered O'Connell more and he insisted even more firmly: 'But I am conducting counsel, my lord, and [am] more intimately aware of the details of the case than my brethren. I entreat, therefore, you will hear me.' Finally the judge relented, and within five minutes O'Connell had argued him out of the non-suit. Hedges Eyre turned to his friend in triumph: 'Now! Now do you see why I gave my money to that Papist rascal?' Likewise Lord Chief Justice Bushe admitted that O'Connell was 'at the head of the bar, and deservedly so, and that if he had a suit at law, he would certainly employ him'.[127]

Perhaps the greatest tribute to O'Connell's legal abilities came from one of his greatest enemies, Robert Peel. One evening in the 1830s the great orators of the day were being discussed at Lady Beauchamp's. O'Connell was mentioned and one man dismissed him as 'a broguing Irish fellow', asking, 'Who would listen to him? I always walk out of the House when he opens his lips.' Lord Westmorland asked Peel for his opinion. Peel did not hesitate: 'If I wanted an efficient and eloquent advocate, I would readily give up all the other orators of whom we have been talking, provided I had with me this same "broguing Irish fellow".'[128] Long before Daniel O'Connell became 'The Liberator' he was revered as 'The Counsellor'. And as the Counsellor his reputation was assured.

Chapter 5

'THE TEXT-BOOK OF MY POLITICAL CAREER': OPPOSING THE ACT OF UNION, 1800

'It was the Union that first stirred me up to come forward in politics.'[1] Daniel O'Connell liked to remind people of his public stand against the Act of Union and his opposition became an integral part of his political biography. It was a defining event for him and he often referred to it afterwards. In 1812 he spoke of how it was, 'and I thank God for it, the first act of my political life'.[2] Some historians have speculated that for O'Connell repeal of the Union (especially in the 1830s) was only a trump card to be played or discarded depending on political expediencies. But this is to misread profoundly his political priorities. O'Connell always insisted that repeal was his defining ambition; everything else, including the quest for Catholic emancipation, was secondary. The restoration of an Irish parliament (and one where he was a member) became a lifelong ambition and his opposition to the Union in 1800 was an expression of his deepest held political principles. He delivered his speech at the Royal Exchange on 13 January 1800 despite much opposition. Hunting Cap certainly did not approve and, while O'Connell later pretended that his uncle had opposed the Union, the truth is that he was viewed by the government as a friend. His uncle's position made any opposition difficult. But O'Connell did not consult with him beforehand and did not tell him about it afterwards. Nevertheless, Hunting Cap could read and he was furious when he discovered from the newspapers what had happened. He reacted immediately, telling O'Connell that had he known about it in advance, 'or suspected it', he would 'by no means have consented'.[3] 'Popular applause is always short-lived', he told him firmly, but 'the inconveniences may be serious and lasting'. However in this, as in everything else, O'Connell was determined to be independent.

The meeting at the Royal Exchange had been organised to demonstrate that Catholic Ireland was not supporting the Union. By January 1800 the anti-Union forces were in disarray. They had failed to agree on a coherent strategy and had failed to build on their success the previous year when they had blocked an initial attempt to introduce the measure. They were also divided on the Catholic question, with some MPs opposing the Union precisely because they wanted to maintain the Protestant Ascendancy. Catholic Ireland remained inactive. While their support could not pass the Union, it was believed that a popular, concerted opposition could block it for ever. After the rejection of the Union in 1799, the government had made concerted efforts to secure the support of the Irish Catholics. The chief secretary, Castlereagh, had even secured a pledge from the British cabinet that emancipation would follow the measure and, although this promise was not made public, the Irish bishops were left in little doubt that a Union would soon bring full rights. Anticipating emancipation, the bishops were prepared to concede to the government a veto on the appointment of future Catholic bishops. Their support for the Union helped create an impression that Catholic Ireland was also in favour.[4] It was this impression that O'Connell and other anti-Unionists were determined to dispel.

Private meetings were held at the home of Sir James Strong to discuss how the Union should be opposed by the Catholics. The aim was to generate heat against the measure, demonstrate that not all Irish Catholics supported the measure, and prove that Catholics were also concerned with defending the Irish constitution. It was agreed to hold a public meeting at the Royal Exchange, under the shadow of Dublin Castle, in which the Catholics as a body would denounce the measure. But, although Strong was active at first, he began to lose his nerve as the day came closer and refused to chair the meeting. Ambrose Moore was persuaded to replace him. Resolutions were drawn up by John Philpot Curran which were 'very fiery and spirited', however these were toned down by 'the timidity of some of our friends'.[5] It was a time 'of terror and brute force' and O'Connell readily understood how the resolutions could be modified into 'comparative tameness'.

And so O'Connell got ready for his first political speech and his first major speech of any significance. He decided not to write the entire speech out in advance, instead he made a list of headings and spoke from them. This became his future practice and he almost 'never wrote a speech beforehand'.[6] But for this maiden speech he clearly worked out what he wanted to say, and remembered it so well that he was able to give a full version to the *Dublin Evening Post* afterwards. O'Connell later said that it was 'a curious thing enough, that all the principles of my subsequent political life are contained in my very first speech'.[7] O'Connell always liked to think out loud, and he would have rehearsed his ideas many times. For years O'Connell had studied the English language and the nature of oratory, preparing for precisely this moment when he could make his entrance on 'the great stage of the world with brilliancy and solidity'.[8] However just as he was about to speak there was a loud noise from outside and 'the measured tramp of soldiery became audible'.[9]

The meeting was being raided by Major Sirr and a group of armed yeomanry, 'who grounded their arms with a heavy clash on the stone pavement' outside.[10] In 1834, when O'Connell was sitting for the artist, Benjamin Robert Haydon, he was asked about his early life. He immediately jumped into this story of the soldiers interrupting the meeting. Haydon wrote in his autobiography that 'the poetical way in which he described the crashing of the muskets on the stones at "Order arms" was characteristic'.[11] There was panic at the meeting, but O'Connell and a few others advanced to meet the redcoats. Sirr demanded to see the resolutions, but when he had read them 'he threw them back on the table, saying, "There is no harm in them"'. The meeting was allowed to continue and a nervous and blushing O'Connell was called to speak.

He began the speech hesitantly. 'My face glowed', he remembered, 'and my ears tingled at the sound of my own voice, but I got more courage as I went on.' His voice remained steady, giving him confidence, and his fear passed. O'Connell would later contrast 'his embarrassment making his first speech with the ease and self-possession acquired by subsequent practice'.[12] From the outset he was clear that the Union was a momentous issue on which everyone must take a stand: 'Sunk, indeed, in more than criminal apathy, must that Irishman be, who could feel indifference on the subject.'[13] He also addressed the prevailing belief that the Irish Catholics were supportive of the Union. This, he insisted, was a false assertion. The Catholics had resisted the measure individually and now they would 'oppose it collectively'.[14]

Few men had studied oratory as carefully as O'Connell, few obsessed over every detail, few analysed their speeches as closely afterwards. This was O'Connell's consuming passion, even more than his career at the bar, and in part it was driven by frustration from being prevented from entering, first, the Irish House of Commons, and then, after 1801, the united House of Commons at Westminster. O'Connell's voice was trained to perfection, like that of a great stage actor. If his oratory soon became legendary, to a large extent it was due to this training which gave a unique power, range and beauty to his voice. It was an incredible instrument, half wand, half weapon. There are numerous witnesses who heard O'Connell speak from the balcony of his house at Merrion Square and who testified that you could hear, 'with ease', every word he spoke from the opposite side of the square.[15] William Fagan attended some of O'Connell's 'monster' meetings in the 1840s and was astonished that where other speakers strained their lungs in the hope of being heard by the crowds which had gathered, 'O'Connell was able, without any exertion whatever, to send his voice to the most distant outlayers in the vast crowd around him.'[16]

Many orators succumb to shouting, but O'Connell had learned much from watching Pitt in the House of Commons and knew how to project across great spaces while making it appear effortless. He also had the advantage of being able to speak extempore and this always made a greater impression on his listeners than, say, the scripted brilliance of Richard Lalor Sheil. Whenever he wrote a speech in advance it was somewhat flat, but speaking from the briefest of notes he wielded, as Pitt once said of Fox, 'the wand of the magician'.[17] William Henry Curran later analysed O'Connell's oratory and described his style as 'vigorous and copious, but incorrect'.[18] What he meant was that his delivery was often better than his content. He had 'phrase in abundance' and an ear for melody, but few of his speeches deserved to 'survive the occasion'. Curran believed that 'in a popular assembly he is supreme', with a style that, 'though far from graceful', had 'a steady and natural warmth' and a voice that was 'powerful', with 'intonations full and graduated'. William Tait also analysed O'Connell's oratory and drew similar conclusions: his 'eloquence is more to be felt than admired'.[19] He believed that what distinguished O'Connell from other speakers was that he cared more about convincing his listeners, in sweeping them away with the force of his beliefs, than in creating phrases that would read well in newspapers after. In other words he was aiming at a popular, rather than a critical response. By 'a glance, a curl of the lip, or a change of the voice' he could produce 'an electric effect on the listener'. It was not just what he said but how he said it; a line like 'But they shall never succeed', would be delivered with a 'triumphant glance of the eye, and the bold menacing attitude of defiance suddenly assumed by so powerful a looking man' ensured that there was 'a startling and rousing effect'.

This speech, though short, was one of O'Connell's most effective. Robert Moore, the son of the earl of Drogheda, was present at the Royal Exchange and the speech made a huge impression. Thirteen years later he discussed it with O'Connell, calling it 'one of the best and most patriotic speeches that was ever uttered in any assembly'.[20] O'Connell ended the speech with a famous and often-quoted declaration:

> Let every man who feels with me proclaim that if the alternative were offered him of Union, or the re-enactment of the penal code in all its pristine horrors, that he would prefer without hesitation the latter, as the lesser and more sufferable evil; that he would rather confide in the justice of his brethren, the Protestants of Ireland, who have already liberated him, than lay his country at the feet of foreigners.

This produced much cheering. The resolutions were then read and passed unanimously.

Despite O'Connell's attempts to rally the Catholics the Union passed inexorably through the Irish parliament in 1800 with very little public opposition. The majority of people seem to have been unenthusiastic about it but were unwilling to take a major stand. During this time O'Connell was friends with John Collis, the writer of an anti-Union pamphlet.[21] They were on the Munster circuit together and O'Connell told a story of how they once amused themselves on the Tullamore boat by firing pistols at the elms along the canal. A group of soldiers were also on board and ordered them to stop shooting. 'Ah, corporal, don't be so cruel,' said Collis, who continued firing. Spotting an opportunity to score a hit, O'Connell asked the man if he was a corporal, and received a sullen affirmative. 'Then, friend,' replied O'Connell, 'you must have got yourself reduced to the ranks by misconduct, for I don't see the V's upon your sleeve.'[22] Everyone laughed and the soldier 'slunk off to the stern quite chopfallen'.

In later years O'Connell met a man who boasted that he had been a repealer from the age of ten. 'Thank God,' replied O'Connell, 'I opposed the Union *ab inito*, and the grounds on which I did so are singularly coincident with my whole public life.'[23] There is no evidence that O'Connell attended any of the great set-piece Union debates. He certainly never heard any of Grattan's famous speeches, although he did hear him speak in public in later years.[24] As O'Connell became consumed by the struggle for emancipation in the first part of the nineteenth century it is easy to see this as his great defining issue. But O'Connell was always clear about his priorities in the 1800s and 1810s. More than anything, he wanted a repeal of the Union and a return to a parliament in Dublin. This was his driving ambition. Emancipation was a necessary first step before that could be achieved, but his mind was always looking ahead. When Benjamin Robert Haydon told O'Connell in 1834 that it was somewhat ungrateful to demand repeal so soon after winning emancipation, O'Connell was unrepentant. 'Not in *me*,' he insisted. 'I always said repeal would be a consequence of emancipation, and I always avowed such to be my object.'[25]

A newspaper reporter in the 1840s, who followed the meetings of the Repeal Association, once admitted that 'Mr O'Connell always *wears out* one speech before he gives another.'[26] This was a fair comment. When O'Connell found a formulation of words that worked, or an idea that captured the imagination, he recycled it until near exhaustion. A speech O'Connell delivered on the Union, at an aggregate meeting at the Royal Exchange on 18 September 1810, contained elements that had been adapted from his 1800 speech, most notably of all the famous peroration. The speech is worth analysing for O'Connell's thinking on the Union a decade after it had passed. He had also grown in confidence. This was the speech of a consummate performer. In his opening O'Connell discussed the 'ten years of silence and torpor' which had ended as 'Irishmen began again to recollect their enslaved country'.[27] He declared that it had been 'a melancholy period', a period in which Ireland saw 'her tradesmen begging, her merchants become bankrupts, her gentry banished, her nobility degraded'. It was also a time when Ireland had fallen victim to 'domestic turbulence... open violence and murder... and had been degraded by one rebellion [1803]'.[28] O'Connell denied that the old Irish parliament had a right to 'commit political suicide'. The MPs had been elected as the delegates of the country, and by voting away its independence for bribes and patronage, 'they added to the baseness of assassination all the guilt of high treason'.[29] He name-checked all the men who had claimed the Union was a crime in 1799 and 1800, and who now supported the government. But, he asked, surely if it was a crime then it must be a crime now, 'unless it shall be ludicrously pretended that crime, like wine, improves by old age?'[30] His audience laughed, but O'Connell reminded them, 'in sober sadness,' that they must recognise that the continuance of the Union made 'crime hereditary'.

Using far more aggressive language than in 1800, O'Connell declared that the Union was 'a consummation of evil'. He also denounced the bribery and corruption, or 'official *management*', which had accompanied it. It was one of his cherished beliefs that the 1798 Rebellion had been encouraged by the government to enable a Union and he developed this theme here. And he deliberately, provocatively, echoed the key principle of the United Irishmen later in the speech, when he spoke of uniting Protestant, Catholic and Presbyterian into the name of Irishman so that the Union could be repealed.[31] His argument was that the passing of the Union had been illegal and unjust, and that the reality of the Union had been disastrous for Ireland. The British MPs knew nothing about Ireland, so that when they spoke of Irish affairs they were 'vile and profligate'. Nor did he have much respect for many of the 100 Irish MPs, some of whom were not even Irish-born. Carrying out some research on the men who represented Irish constituencies he was disgusted to find that one-fifth were cyphers, who knew nothing and had done nothing. His use of humour to mock them was typically crushing:

What, for example, do we know about Andrew Strahan, printer

to the king? What can Henry Martin, barrister-at-law, care for the rights or liberties of Irishmen? Some of us may, perhaps for our misfortunes, have been compelled to read a verbose pamphlet of James Stevens; but who knows anything of one Crile, one Hughan, one Cackin, or of a dozen more whose names I could mention, only because I have discovered them for the purpose of speaking to you about them... What are they to Ireland or Ireland to them? No, Mr Sheriff, we are not represented.[32]

The speech ended, as the one ten years earlier had, with a dramatic declaration on the future of the Catholics. The language was even more explicit than before, even more aggressive. He announced defiantly that he would 'trample under foot the Catholic claims if they can interfere with the repeal; I abandon all wish for emancipation if it delays that repeal'.[33] The next part of his speech was almost identical to 1800: 'Nay, were Mr Perceval, tomorrow, to offer me the repeal of the Union upon the terms of re-enacting the entire penal code, I declare it from my heart, and in the presence of God, that I would most cheerfully embrace the offer.'

This was a revised, updated edition of his political text-book. The O'Connell of January 1800 was a callow twenty-four-year-old boy orator, just starting off at the bar, lazy, uncertain, and a political unknown. The speech reflected his timidity and uncertainty; his caution understandable just two years after the 1798 Rebellion. The O'Connell of September 1810 was a thirty-five-year-old man, a celebrated barrister, energetic and industrious, and on his way to becoming a leader of the Catholics. Self-confidence encouraged his aggression, his instinct for abuse, and his use of dramatic exaggeration to make his point. The false dichotomy of Union and the penal laws was classic O'Connell. So too was his idealisation of the period of legislative independence, and his assertion that the Irish Catholics must take responsibility for securing their rights, rather than remaining passive onlookers always waiting for someone else to set them free.

After the Union passed in summer of 1800, O'Connell travelled through Kerry, his heart 'heavy at the loss that Ireland had sustained'.[34] It was 'a wild and gloomy' day. As he travelled the 'bleak solitudes' he had many 'wild and *Ossianic* inspirations', and, away from any people, he gave in to his feelings of 'solemnity and sadness'. As he later admitted, he was always 'of a desponding disposition when anything' went against him. He could not help it. He was, he claimed, 'the spoiled child of fortune and fell naturally into despair when he met an unexpected reverse'.[35]

The Act of Union came into effect on 1 January 1801, and with it came the creation of the United Kingdom of Great Britain and Ireland. O'Connell was in Dublin that day and was surprised to find 'less excitement than you would imagine'. Instead, he believed, 'the hatred which all classes (except the small government clique) bore to the measure, had settled down into sulky despondency'.[36] Bells rang out across the city to celebrate the passing, and O'Connell was furious: he felt it was 'a joyful peal for Ireland's degradation'. His 'blood boiled' and he made a vow, 'on that morning, that the foul dishonour should not last, if *I* could ever put an end to it'.[37] He would spend the rest of his life trying to honour that vow.

Chapter 6 ∾

CONFRONTING A CULTURE OF DEFEAT, 1801–1810

O'Connell was still a man of high spirits and reckless adventures. In the winter of 1801 he got uproariously drunk after celebrating with a party at the Freemasons' Hotel, on the corner of Golden Lane. He had drunk 'a good stoup of claret' and was making his way home, when a fire broke out at a nearby timber-yard and began to spread rapidly. A man attempted to get water from the water-pipes, underneath the street, and began hitting the ground with a pickaxe. But O'Connell, drunk, took offence at how the man was doing the job and 'shouldered him away, seized the pickaxe, and soon got at the plug'.[1] However he was not content with this and continued working away, destroying much of the street in the process. As he later recalled, he 'would soon have disturbed the paving stones all over the street, if I had not been prevented'. An old auctioneer, Sheriff Macready, arrived with a troop from the Buckinghamshire militia, but still O'Connell refused to stop: 'I was rather an unruly customer,' he admitted sheepishly afterwards, 'being a little under the influence of a good batch of claret, and on my refusing to desist from picking up the street, one of the soldiers ran a bayonet at me'.[2] The only thing that saved O'Connell was the cover of his hunting-watch, which deflected the bayonet. As he later said, 'If I had not had the watch—there was the end of the Agitator!'[3]

O'Connell in love
On 7 November 1800 O'Connell fell in love.[4] And, for the first time in his life, he was prepared to commit. The object of his affection was Mary O'Connell, his penniless twenty-two-year-old cousin,[5] and he

decided after a few weeks to marry her. His impulsive, impetuous marriage proposal was typical of him once he had made up his mind:

> I said to her, 'Are you engaged, Miss O'Connell?' She answered, 'I am not'. 'Then', said I, 'will you engage yourself to me?' 'I will', was her reply. And I said I would devote my life to make her happy.[6]

Few men try such a direct approach and even fewer have such success. A couple of years later O'Connell told her that he had been first attracted to her by her 'greater capability of everything that is great and really virtuous', which was more 'than any other young woman I met with'.[7] And as he approached their twenty-fifth wedding anniversary he reminisced about how he had loved her ever since she was 'the prettiest little girl that ever picked a clean spot for a sweet little foot to tread on amidst the mud of a dirty pavement'.[8] The relationship risked everything. Hunting Cap had his own plans for O'Connell and wanted him to marry a wealthy heiress, a Miss Mary Ann Healy of Cork. But she was, to put it politely, unattractive (or to put it less politely 'so grotesque that the younger members of the family always felt ashamed of her') and O'Connell was not interested.[9] But despite the risk of disinheritance, O'Connell did not waver: 'I did not care for that. I was richly rewarded by subsequent happiness.'[10] The relationship with Mary was kept secret for as long as possible. As O'Connell warned her, 'you know as well as I do how much *we* have at stake'.[11]

At the time Mary lived in Tralee with her grandmother. Once, when visiting, O'Connell amused himself by complaining to the grandmother about an imaginary problem:

> 'Madam', said I, 'Mary would do very well, only she is so cross'. 'Cross, sir? My Mary cross? Sir, you must have provoked her very much! Sir, you must yourself be quite in fault! Sir, my little girl was always the gentlest, sweetest creature born.'[12]

O'Connell was happy to agree. In his widowed final years he remembered her as having 'the sweetest, the most heavenly temper, and the sweetest breath'.[13] O'Connell admitted his womanising past to Mary, but promised her repeatedly that 'you are my first and only love' and that he had 'never before seriously thought of marriage'.[14] 'Mine is not the idle love of a romantic boy', he insisted, rather it was 'the affection of a man who loves you almost as much for his own sake as for you'. For Christmas 1800 he sent her some expensive ear-rings, and promised to bring her a picture of himself along with a lock of his hair. He also advised her against following 'the present fashion of female dress' which was to 'wear half as many clothes' as before.[15] This, he claimed, was responsible for more female deaths that winter than in 'any other within the memory of man'. He loved complimenting her and told her how her 'image is like a fairy vision [which] visits my dreams and makes my sleep blessed'.[16]

In April 1801 O'Connell told Mary's mother about the attachment. This made her 'the happiest of women' as O'Connell was 'one of her great favourites'.[17] But Mary rebuked O'Connell the next month when it appeared he spent a large amount of money on a veil for her.[18] He denied that it was too expensive and she was satisfied: 'I do consider you as my husband'.[19] Various ruses were adopted to keep the relationship a secret; once, O'Connell wrote to her ostensibly about a lottery ticket so that the letter wouldn't attract any suspicion.[20] Another time he started a rumour that she was involved with someone else. In February 1802 he told her to think of how much she loved him 'and then add ten hundred thousand times as much and you will still have a feeble idea of the measure of my affection'.[21] They married, in secret, at the home of Mary's brother-in-law, James Connor, at Dame Street, Dublin, on 24 July 1802.[22] O'Connell now called her 'the partner of my soul'.[23] By November Mary was one month pregnant and O'Connell wrote of his hopes that it was a daughter, 'and as like you as possible'.[24] He looked forward to when he could 'cherish the little stranger coming'. The love letter has echoes of a previous tribute to 'Sweet Eliza': 'Sweet Mary, I rave of you! I think only of you! I sigh for you, I weep for you! I almost pray to you!'[25]

There were complications with the pregnancy and O'Connell blamed himself. In his desperation to keep anyone from realising they were married he had told Mary to avoid certain things—including going outside for regular exercise—and this, he felt, had damaged her health. Mary was living with a Mrs Pembroke in Tralee, while he was working in Dublin. He began to despair and his wife's 'cold perspirations' and 'shiverings' filled his heart 'with apprehension and horror'.[26] He began reading books on pregnancy and even became an amateur expert 'on every species of illness which accompanies pregnancy... I filled my head with them and trembled for every one of them'.[27] Escaping from the courts, O'Connell rushed home to be with Mary, and she made a slow recovery, but still he worried. Mary was deeply religious and O'Connell's lack of faith had always been a difficulty. Now he admitted to her that if he was 'a religionist' he would spend every moment praying for her, and he lamented that 'this miserable philosophy which I have taken up and been proud of—in the room of religion—affords me now no consolation in my misery'.[28]

The death of his grandmother, Honora O'Mullane, over Christmas 1802, brought O'Connell home to Carhen. He visited Derrynane for nine days and tried to find a way to tell his uncle about his marriage. He knew that it would be 'devilish[ly] awkward', especially as his uncle did not want him to marry a woman without a fortune.[29] Losing his nerve, he avoided telling him face-to-face, and instead sent him a letter after he left.[30] O'Connell was in 'a state of suspense' while he waited for a response.[31] The response was quick coming and justified all of his fears. Hunting Cap was enraged and had burst into 'a most violent flood of tears' upon reading the letter.[32] O'Connell's father also disapproved of the match, but only so far as it would damage Daniel with his uncle. And the damage was immense. Hunting Cap decided to punish this perceived betrayal with disinheritance. O'Connell was furious but his brother, John, wrote to him urging restraint. He advised Daniel that this was 'the most critical period of your life' and he cautioned against giving way 'to those acute feelings which I know you possess'.[33] General O'Connell wrote to Hunting Cap at this time, and suggested that his nephew's

> fate must be truly deplorable if you have irrevocably cast him off. The bare prerequisites of his profession are probably very inadequate to the support of a wife and family... Much will depend of his professional abilities, but, great as they might be, I conceive it will require time and labour to bring them under notice.[34]

But General O'Connell seemed to share Hunting Cap's disappointment and was not willing to intervene any further on his behalf.

O'Connell was optimistic, at least when writing to his wife, that his uncle's anger was 'a storm that will soon blow over'.[35] He was hopeful that, because he had 'gratified every other wish of his', he would be allowed this one act of defiance.[36] Daniel and Mary's child was born on 27 June 1803, a boy, who they named Maurice.[37] 'Poor thing I cannot tell you how much I doat of him,' wrote O'Connell to his wife during one absence.[38] Mary was too weak to breast-feed and so Maurice was given to a wet-nurse.[39] Despite the loss of his uncle's favour, O'Connell was able to make enough money for his family on the Munster circuit, although he did badly in Limerick, which he dismissed as 'this damned town'. He looked forward to when he could 'have my poor little squalling brat to pull by the nose—a pleasure that I assure you I long very much to enjoy'.[40] His family would grow steadily in the years ahead. Mary O'Connell was pregnant for much of the next thirteen years: she had twelve children between 1803 and 1817, seven of whom survived infancy. O'Connell delighted in his new role as father. Once, his friend Peter Hussey rebuked him for allowing his children to join the adults after dinner, for it was 'a heavy tax upon the admiration of the company'. 'Never mind, Peter,' replied O'Connell, 'I admire them so much myself, that I don't require any one to help me.'[41]

Questions about O'Connell's fidelity surfaced occasionally, as did evidence of his past adventures. In 1812, for example, Mary O'Connell received a number of anonymous letters, all mailed from Bristol, and all sent when Daniel was away.[42] The letters were full of poison about O'Connell and Mary initially suspected that they had been sent by one of her husband's former lovers. It seems the letters suggested that O'Connell had cheated on Mary and that the woman was pregnant. The writer was apparently looking for O'Connell's help in securing some appointment. Mary appears to have been worried about the financial implications rather than anything else as she did not think that O'Connell could 'in justice to your family contribute to *her* support'. Then the letters stopped. This was not the first time O'Connell had been harassed by letters. For a number of years, a man he barely knew, Tom Codd, sent him letters asking for money, claiming that he had brought O'Connell forward in the world. Once, when Hunting Cap visited Cork, he was stopped by Codd, who complained bitterly about O'Connell's ingratitude. The man was, as O'Connell realised, 'quite mad'.[43]

'As wild as anything in romance': Daniel O'Connell and Robert Emmet's rebellion

When Emmet's rebellion broke out on the night of 23 July 1803, O'Connell was in Dublin. As a member of the Lawyers' Artillery Corps, he was called up and spent one night searching every single room of the Grand Canal Hotel for rebels.[44] After three nights on call he was approached by a friend, Nicholas Purcell O'Gorman, who was recovering from illness and hesitant about being exposed to the night air. He told O'Connell his dilemma: 'If I refuse, they'll accuse me of cowardice or croppyism; if I mount guard it will be the death of me!'[45] And so O'Connell took his place, standing guard and sometimes patrolling, for a further three nights. One of these nights they captured a young boy on Dame Street, after midnight, who claimed he was delivering a message for his master, a public notary, who was complaining about a bill he had received. The yeomanry searched the boy for treasonable documents and discovered in his waistcoat pocket a sheet of paper, 'on which were rudely scrawled several drawings of pikes'.[46] The boy 'turned pale with fright, and trembled all over' but stuck to his story. Some of the men went off to check his story and found the boy's master, who confirmed everything, but as a precaution they searched the house for pikes. Finding nothing, they released the boy and O'Connell and the men returned to the guard-house at three in the morning.

O'Connell was contemptuous of the 1803 rebellion. His famous put-down was often repeated, though not attributed, in later years: 'Poor Emmet's scheme was as wild as anything in romance!'[47] At the time he was also critical and believed that the organiser of 'so much bloodshed, so many murders—and such horrors of every kind has ceased to be an object of compassion'.[48] He was insistent that Emmet 'merits and will suffer the severest punishment. For my part I think pity would be almost thrown away'. In the 1840s O'Connell reflected afresh on Robert Emmet's rebellion: 'Poor man, he meant well.'[49] However he was pragmatic in his analysis: 'But I ask whether a madder scheme was ever devised by a Bedlamite?'[50] O'Connell was very familiar with Emmet's famous speech from the dock, and in one letter years later even paraphrased the ending, 'Let me, then, implore "the charity of silence" until my experiment is worked out and that I take the lead in the field again.'[51] At O'Connell's house in Merrion Square in 1842 the subject of

Emmet's rebellion was raised. O'Connell was brutal in his assessment of the planning and the result:

> There never was a more rash or foolish enthusiast. At the head of eighty men, armed only with pikes, he waged war on the most powerful government in the world, and the end of the mad fiasco was the murder of the best of the Irish judges, Lord Kilwarden, a really good and excellent man. His nephew, Wolfe, who happened to be in the carriage with him, was also murdered; for this murder, even if it stood alone, Emmet deserved to be hanged.[52]

This was somewhat different from O'Connell's assessment of Kilwarden before his death: 'his pompous inanity is insufferable'. O'Connell believed that Emmet was remembered for the wrong reasons: 'But for the romance which his attachment to Miss Curran threw around the case he would have long since been forgotten.'

O'Connell enjoyed greatly his role in the yeomanry corps. Even the extensive drilling, which he took seriously, did not diminish his sense of fun. One day in November 1803 he was 'tired as a dog' after seven hours of drills in the Phoenix Park, 'firing, marching, running and counter-marching'.[53] But it was still 'a lovely day—clear, cool and frosty'. He decided to join Sir Edward Denny's corps back home, which meant that he would be stationed in Kerry in the event of an invasion.[54] His career was starting to take off and he was rising at the bar. On Wednesday 16 November he was one of four barristers who presented an important case before the court of exchequer. O'Connell's argument lasted an hour and, even though the court was divided in its judgement, all the judges praised his display. 'The thing has made some noise here,' he boasted.[55] And the following week he insisted that he would not swap his position for that of any other rising barrister.[56]

O'Connell's brother, John, got engaged at the end of 1803. Hunting Cap approved of the match and agreed to 'settle the entire of his landed property on John'.[57] But he hesitated about settling more than £10,000 on him and Mary believed that this was a good sign that 'the *old sinner*' had not entirely abandoned Daniel. This hope was misplaced. Hunting Cap revenged himself on O'Connell by attacking, and possibly cutting off an annual allowance of £100 that his father gave him.[58] O'Connell was disgusted by this 'mean and shabby conduct' and believed it

afforded 'a vindication of my *quarrel* with him'. By now h
respect for his uncle and admitted that he was only surprised
so long a favourite of his and indeed I am almost ashamed o
recognised that 'in every action my mind scorned the narrow bo
of his'. A new will was made by Hunting Cap (or 'the king'
O'Connell's uncle, John O'Mullane, called him) in December 1803 in
favour of John. The reason given was that Daniel had 'run counter to
his wishes'.[59] Mary was glad, however, that that was the extent of the
damage he could do. She assured her husband that 'the old sinner will
never have such a representative as the one he has so shamefully given
up'.

Confronting the culture of defeat

Having made his mark with his anti-Union speech, O'Connell was
determined to renew the fight. What he was learning as a lawyer proved
to be of great help as he embarked on a career in national politics. Most
importantly, he was learning about the Irish people. As Carl Sandburg
said of Abraham Lincoln's legal career, he 'came to know in whispered
consultation and public cross-examination the minds and hearts of a
quarrelling, chaffering, suspicious, murdering, loving, lavish,
paradoxical humanity'.[60] From the beginning, O'Connell had little time
for John Keogh, the merchant who had been a leading figure in the
Catholic agitation since the early 1790s. One day, 'soon after he entered
the political arena', Keogh said to him, ''Twas I made men of the
Catholics.'[61] 'If you did,' replied O'Connell with barely concealed scorn,
'they are such men as realise Shakespeare's idea "of nature's
journeymen having made them, and made them badly"'.[62] O'Connell
was quoting, inaccurately, lines from *Hamlet*, but his meaning was
unmistakable.

Casting an eye over Irish society, O'Connell believed that you could
tell a Catholic by 'his subdued and slavish look and gait'.[63] This is one
of the reasons O'Connell was so imperious and volcanic in his public
displays. He was determined to make men of the Catholics by making
himself a symbol of defiance and resistance. It was also why he
marched rather than walked to the Four Courts every day, shouldering
his umbrella as if it was a pike.[64] A magazine profile in 1823 described
him as flinging 'one factious foot before the other, as if he had already
burst his bonds, and was kicking the Protestant ascendancy before

...t to shuffle off "the oppression of seven
...ll was aided by his size: 'His frame is tall,
...recisely as befits a man of the people—for
...ok with double confidence and affection
...nts in his own person the qualities upon
...ust recent defeats such as 1798 and the Act
...ed the spirit of the Catholics. O'Connell
...lures had steadily eroded Irish confidence
...they automatically felt inferior when facing the British. It was
this culture of defeat which O'Connell was determined to confront.
The challenge for O'Connell was to find a way of attacking the state of
slavery without confirming the Catholics in that state. His solution was
to deny that Ireland had ever been conquered—'this unconquered, this
unconquerable island'[65]—and instead claim that Ireland had lost her
freedom through 'fraud and treachery', never through defeat in battle.
Britain was often conquered, he claimed—by the Romans, the Saxons,
and the Normans—but Ireland was 'never subdued; we never lost our
liberties in battle, nor did we ever submit to armed conquerors'. It was
an argument designed to raise Irish confidence and shake off the
trauma of defeat. In private, O'Connell was more scornful. In later
years he insisted that he would never get proper credit for winning
emancipation, because people would never understood 'the species of
animals with which I had to carry on my warfare with the common
enemy'.[66] They were nothing more, he claimed, than 'crawling slaves'.

The return of Pitt as prime minister in 1804 briefly raised hopes that
Catholic emancipation might be forthcoming. But Pitt had pledged to
never again raise that question before the king, and the hopes were
quickly dashed. In late 1804 O'Connell regularly attended the Catholic
meetings at Marlborough Street at the home of James Ryan, who acted
as secretary to the Catholic body, held privately in case they were
suppressed.[67] As one important meeting on 17 November approached,
he 'resolved to take a part'.[68] Unfortunately 'we had not much *speeching*',
though he still 'was *on my legs*'.[69] The aristocratic leadership under Lord
Fingall attempted to block the forwarding of a new Catholic petition to
parliament. O'Connell opposed them, vigorously, and won the point.[70]
He was one of twenty-five members appointed to draw up a new
petition and report on 15 December. This would give him additional
trouble, he admitted, 'but *that* is immaterial'.[71] Energised by his task, he

was one of five men who were part of a subcommittee that actually wrote the petition, and he was proud that 'the fate of millions perhaps depends on my poor pen'.[72] The meetings of the subcommittee were held at his lodgings, 7 Upper Ormond Quay, and although O'Connell was kept busy between politics and law, 'my heart was light and my health excellent'.[73] On Saturday 15 December the petition was discussed favourably, although a final decision on it was postponed until 2 February 1805. John Segerson, O'Connell's old nemesis, went to the meeting on 15 December fully prepared to speak. He was so convinced it would be worth recording that he had even brought his own note-taker. But he was 'completely put down' by O'Connell and only managed to say three sentences.[74] O'Connell was proud of his work. He believed it was 'a most *beautiful* petition' and looked forward to it being formally presented.[75] He was also thinking about the composition of the delegation to London, and he volunteered for this job, then withdrew his name for consideration in case this was seen as presumptuous. However he was careful to leave the matter open.[76] It was a reflection of his junior status that he wasn't selected.

The petition, signed by one hundred leading Catholics, including O'Connell, was sent to London in March with the delegation. Pitt met with them reluctantly on 12 March 1805, but refused to act on their behalf. The petition was then championed by Fox in the Commons, and Lord Grenville in the Lords, but both motions were defeated.[77] Pitt died on 23 January 1806 and a new ministry of all the talents was formed, with Grenville at the head, and Fox in a key ministry. But Fox urged the Irish Catholics—in a letter to James Ryan—to hold off on agitating until the appropriate time.[78] Most were willing to do this, to avoid embarrassing the new government, but not O'Connell. He was one of only a handful of members who argued for petitions every parliamentary session no matter who was in power. Fox's abandonment of the Catholics, now that he was in office, was never forgiven.

Nor did O'Connell have much faith in his associates. On more than one occasion he was to dismiss their efforts. Years later he reflected that when he 'took the helm, I found all the Catholics full of mutual jealousies—one man trying to outrival another—one meeting rivalling another—the leaders watching to sell themselves at the highest penny!'[79] Ryan was one of the men who was thought to have sold out, and he was heavily criticised at this time for applying to the government for a post for himself.

From this time on, until emancipation was won, O'Connell threw himself whole-heartedly and energetically into the Catholic question. Years later, when he was attacked in the 1830s about receiving contributions from the Irish people, O'Connell launched a vigorous defence of the payments. He believed they were compensation for having sacrificed his 'buoyant youth and cheerful manhood' to the Catholic cause.[80] He recounted how 'the burden of the cause was thrown' upon him:

> I had to prepare the meetings, to prepare the resolutions, to furnish replies to the correspondence, to examine the case of each person complaining of practical grievances, to rouse the torpid, to animate the lukewarm, to control the violent and the inflammatory, to avoid the shoals and breakers of the law, to guard against multiplied treachery, and at all times to oppose, at every peril, the powerful and multitudinous enemies of the cause.[81]

Further details were given. He explained how, at a time when

> my meals were shortened to the narrowest space, and my sleep restricted to the earliest hours before dawn; at that period, and for more than twenty years, there was no day that I did not devote from one or two hours, often much more, to the working out of the Catholic cause.

This was a time when O'Connell's only external income was from the bar, his existence dependent on his 'physical and waking powers'. So O'Connell believed these payments were justified, because of what he had sacrificed in this period, and who would compensate him for 'the lost opportunities of acquiring professional celebrity, or for the wealth which such distinctions would ensure?'

An olive branch was offered to Hunting Cap. A consignment of brandy had ended up with Hunting Cap, after the ship carrying it sank off the Kerry coast. It was an enormous amount, roughly 2,400 gallons.[82] O'Connell discovered that his uncle was still liable to pay duty, risked having the brandy confiscated, and, worse, risked being prosecuted. He investigated the case as well he could, and was leaked a confidential document on the subject, prompting him to send Hunting Cap a detailed warning.[83] He refrained from adding any personal information, acknowledging 'how disagreeable that subject is to you'. By this time Hunting Cap seems to have lost interest in John and changed his will again so that the last surviving brother, James, inherited everything.[84] This caused much tension between the brothers and was probably the origin of some later conflict. But the peace offering from O'Connell had been much appreciated and that August the two men were reconciled. Following the Tralee assizes, he told his wife that 'the old gentleman and I are upon the best possible terms. He met me with as much cordiality and talked to me with as much familiarity as ever he did'.[85] By March 1806 O'Connell had been restored to close to his previous place in his uncle's affection. Hunting Cap told Robin Hickson that he had forgiven O'Connell and O'Connell said he 'felt it completely'.[86] Within weeks O'Connell had returned to calling him 'the best of parents and my first my *only* friend'.[87] Mary was relieved by the rapprochement, especially, as she noted archly, because it would be 'a great disappointment' to others.[88] But there was still a price to be paid for his act of rebellion. O'Connell went from being Hunting Cap's only heir to sharing this honour with his two brothers. By marrying for love his inheritance had been reduced substantially, although he would still inherit Derrynane and the land around it. Soon Hunting Cap was taking immense pride in O'Connell's achievements as he continued his advance at the bar. Mary learned that whenever he heard of O'Connell making a great speech 'he sheds tears of joy'.[89] Such displays even made her like him a little.

O'Connell's family was expanding rapidly and he delighted in receiving reports on their progress from his wife when he was on circuit. The eldest, Maurice, kissed O'Connell's picture every morning and called it 'Dan'.[90] He talked 'a great deal, but all in Irish'. With his mother he was more difficult: 'He sometimes calls me a bitch and desires me to go to Tralee to Dada Dan.'[91] O'Connell realised he would have to buy a house for them in Dublin and in January 1806 he purchased his first house at 1 Westland Row. As a young man O'Connell had read the works of William Godwin and his future wife, Mary Wollstonecraft. Therefore when he discovered that two sisters of Mary

Wollstonecraft had established a preparatory school at 17 Hume Street, Dublin, it was a simple decision to send Maurice there.[92]

In 1807 the Catholics regrouped and resolved to start petitioning again. There was also a new willingness to meet without fear of arrest, and so a new Catholic Committee was formed. The meetings were still held at private venues, just in case, and were centred around the figure of Lord Fingall.[93] O'Connell was appointed a member of the committee and on 24 February delivered an important speech on Catholic affairs at a meeting at the Rotunda Rooms.[94] The government was trying to reward the Catholics for their loyalty by extending the 1793 relief act so that Catholics could hold commissions in the army in England, as well as in the army in Ireland. This concession was mocked by O'Connell as 'the privilege of shedding our blood and sacrificing our life in their defence'.[95] Lord Fingall was in the chair, and he supported the attempts to postpone the new Catholic petition until the sentiments of the country districts were known. This was attacked by O'Connell, and his eloquence was credited with defeating the motion.[96] It had been claimed that forwarding the petition would damage the empire and O'Connell was scornful, asking how the service and loyalty of five million Irish Catholics could ever be 'an injury to the empire'. He ended his speech with a vehement attack on the Union:

> The Union interfered, it swept away with rude violence, amidst the wreck of the country, every opportunity of kindness and liberality on the one hand, every occasion for gratitude and affection on the other... It was a small but wretched consolation that no Catholic sat in the parliament that voted away the country.[97]

Fingall was disturbed by this direction, and begged O'Connell to avoid discussing the Union as it was not relevant to any subject before the meeting. O'Connell apologised and explained that he had been borne away by his emotions: 'It was impossible for him to stand over the grave of his country without shedding on it a tear.' But he then insisted that it was relevant—for emancipation had been promised with the Union. O'Connell knew that the king was again a massive obstacle, but he believed the campaign could not wait. In a daring and dramatic conclusion he insisted that 'the prisoner counts by hours; he who would hug his chains even for a day, may well seem not to merit freedom.'[98] He noted that the existing government had abolished the slave trade, but added that the king should have added a clause to that bill raising the Catholics from slaves to freemen. 'That is all I require,' he concluded. 'It cannot be attained too soon'. The speech produced 'a very considerable sensation at the meeting'.[99] O'Connell had made his mark.

At a later meeting, after 'a warm and angry debate', it was decided to send a petition to Grattan to present in parliament, rather than giving it to delegates as in 1805.[100] Again O'Connell spoke and in a memorable discussion of Grattan's merits said that he had 'sat by the cradle of Irish independence' and had afterwards been 'doomed to follow its hearse'. And he predicted that Grattan would someday blow 'the trumpet of its resurrection'.[101] O'Connell's oratory in this period was not as developed as it later became. It lacked the intensity of later efforts and those who followed his oratory said that at this time 'there was not that bold and dashing manner about him, which added so much to his delivery'.[102] There was much truth to this, for O'Connell was still finding his range as a speaker but, even in 1807, he knew how to deploy humour to great effect. On a visit to Kerry at this time, O'Connell joined with the knight of Kerry at a public meeting to support anti-tithe resolutions. Here he demonstrated his powers of rebuttal by ridiculing the previous speakers, who supported the tithe system, and he was said to have 'produced a decisive impression'.[103] The resolutions were carried.

In later years, O'Connell reflected on the nature of leadership. He believed it was a mistake to always talk about leadership and put oneself forward at every opportunity. Instead he had 'always professed myself quite ready to follow the lead of anybody who should work harder or better than I did; and my command is only the more readily obeyed on that account'.[104] In the 1800s, his rise, and the rise of a more middle-class leadership, was challenged by the Catholic aristocracy, the men who considered themselves the 'natural leaders' of the Catholics and who despised 'the vulgar violence' of the lawyers and merchants.[105] O'Connell had little time for the old leaders, men he believed were 'incapable of managing'. He remembered one 'aristocratic banker' visiting the Catholic Committee in 1807 and delivering advice which 'savoured suspiciously of Castle influence'. The man accused the

Catholic barristers of fighting for emancipation purely out of self-interest, so that they could be promoted. O'Connell opposed him in strong terms and was assisted by Peter Hussey who attacked his advice as 'dishonest'. In 1806 and 1807 Robert Marshall, inspector-general of exports and imports , a minor Dublin Castle official, compiled notes on the leading Irish Catholics and described O'Connell as 'impatient for emancipation—ambitions very warm—uncle rich—probably a J[acobi]n—fled about the time of the rebellion'.[106]

O'Connell's position within the Catholic Committee was still a junior one. He was mocked by one faction as 'the door-keeper', a man who abused his job of allowing and refusing entry to the meetings so as to control who attended.[107] In January 1808 the Catholic Committee met again in Dublin, with Lord Fingall in the chair. It was agreed to submit another petition but there was some division in the group, with one member wanting greater consultation with the greater Catholic body before proceeding. O'Connell was always keen to prevent divisions, and here he intervened to persuade the member to withdraw his motion so that there could be unanimity. In May 1808 the veto question first appeared on the agenda and it would go on to exert a long influence. In 1799 the Catholic hierarchy had been willing to concede a veto on the appointment of Irish bishops to the British government in return for emancipation under the Union.[108] But emancipation had not been granted and by 1808 the veto was a much more contentious issue. From the British government's point of view securities like the veto were essential before emancipation could even be considered. The fear was always that Catholics owed their allegiance to a foreign power and could never be trusted. Some control over the appointment of bishops was therefore seen as a necessary safeguard. The so-called aristocracy of Fingall and his friends supported the veto, as did Grattan. But O'Connell, from the beginning, was hostile and his inveterate opposition would help shape the debates of the Catholic Committee for the next decade. Over the next two years O'Connell had but one doctrine, 'agitate, agitate, agitate', and but one strategy, 'petition, petition, petition'.[109] In 1809 the Catholic Committee was reformed on formal lines and during the year O'Connell drew up a report on the penal laws, which ran to 300 folios for discussion.[110]

This was a period of sustained success. At the Cork assizes in April he secured the release of a young officer in the Westmeath militia who had stolen money from the post office. Although the man had been guilty, O'Connell had won the case 'on a point of law', and was relieved, 'Poor fellow, I felt much for him.'[111] O'Connell had conquered his old problem of laziness and he rose early and worked late without difficulty. For example, on 6 April he worked on arbitrations from six a.m. to ten p.m.[112] He had also success closer to home. For years he had been working to try and get a post office built at Cahirciveen, but with no luck. However in 1809 he acted successfully in a legal case for Edward Lees, the secretary to the post office, and as a result had a favour he could call in. The post office was built soon after.[113]

Despite the money he was making at the bar, O'Connell's reckless expenditure was beginning to become a problem. In March 1809 his wife pleaded with him, 'I *want money, love.*'[114] O'Connell was always profligate and his brother, James, said in 1823 that he believed he had failed to meet all his debts every year since 1808.[115] In the autumn O'Connell moved again, purchasing an expensive house on 30 Merrion Square.[116] His wife was anxious because of the expense and pleaded with him to sell it immediately, but he refused.[117] Debt was becoming a major worry and Mary was beginning to fear, correctly, major problems in the future. But O'Connell was always good at hiding things from her and concealed the extent of his problems.

For reasons that are not clear, but which probably had a lot to do with his wife's ungentle encouragement, he had a short-lived return to the Catholic faith at this time. His wife was delighted and told him how she couldn't tell him 'what real happiness it gives me to have you this sometime back say[ing] your prayers and attend[ing] mass so regularly, not to say anything of your observance of the days of abstinence'.[118] Joking, O'Connell thanked her for her 'sermon' and noted how difficult it was to abstain from meat (it was Lent).[119] However he did not follow devotional practices too strictly, or else he relapsed, for it was only in 1816 that he returned fully to the Catholic faith.

O'Connell dated his 'first great *lift* in popularity' to 1810.[120] It marked the time when he went up against the aging Catholic leader John Keogh and emerged from the contest with his standing enhanced. For years Keogh had resisted attempts to renew petitioning parliament for emancipation, always urging caution and moderation. At these meetings Keogh saw that O'Connell had the makings of a future leader and met with him privately to win him over to his way of thinking. As

O'Connell remembered dismissively, 'He urged that the Catholics should abstain altogether from agitation, and he laboured hard to bring me to adopt his views. But I saw that agitation was our only available weapon.'[121] O'Connell was determined to agitate, viewing it as a 'legitimate weapon' of the Catholics, which could not be allowed 'to rust'. A Catholic meeting was arranged for Friday 13 June 1810 and leading figures pressed Keogh to attend. O'Connell was sent with a deputation to collect Keogh, and discovered that he was willing 'to talk away on all sorts of subjects, *except* the business which had brought his visitors'. After some lengthy digressions, the men again invited Keogh to come with them to the meeting. But he was becoming irascible and spent a quarter of an hour haranguing them about 'the impolicy of public assembling at all'.[122] This done, he then attended the meeting after all, much to O'Connell's astonishment. At the meeting, Keogh supported a resolution denouncing 'the continued agitation of the Catholic question at that time'. 'Proceeding as it did from a tried, and tired old leader', it was clear that it would be carried.[123] Beginning to show some real political cunning and insight, O'Connell chose not to oppose the resolution. Instead he rose to suggest an amendment. This amendment pledged 'us to incessant, unrelaxing agitation'. When O'Connell would tell this story in later years he would claim that his amendment (he remembered it as a motion) was passed 'in the midst of enthusiastic acclamations', without anyone realising that it ran directly counter to what Keogh wanted. The reality is that O'Connell's amendment was defeated by 150 votes to 112, a majority of 38 against him.[124] But O'Connell was not finished. He immediately rose to propose an adjournment until 1 November, when the same committee should prepare a petition to parliament, an address to the king, and an appeal to the people. In other words, to reject Keogh's advice and continue as before. 'A very irregular and violent discussion took place', but this time O'Connell was victorious. The anti-petitioners were defeated. O'Connell later declared that this was his first serious victory: 'Thenceforward, I may say, I was the leader.'[125]

A few days later Keogh called to O'Connell's house. It was a last, desperate attempt to persuade him to alter course. During the meeting Keogh paid him 'many compliments, and repeated his importunities that I might alter my policy'.[126] But O'Connell was, in his own words, 'inexorable'. He had committed himself and would not be shaken: 'I refused to yield.' Keogh left 'in bad humour'. It was last time the two men would ever meet in private. In later years O'Connell would speak dismissively of Keogh, and in terms that were then being used about himself: 'Keogh was undoubtedly useful in his day. But he was one who would rather that the cause should fail, than that anybody but himself should have the honour of carrying it.'[127]

O'Connell was becoming a national figure. A government spy reported around this time that O'Connell was someone who 'ought to be watched'.[128] On 7 August 1810 he was mocked in a satirical poem in the *Freeman's Journal* for being a briefless barrister, though the reality was that his practice was thriving.[129] The poem or, more accurately, 'new song' was called 'The popish orators' and attacked the 'arrogant prate' which was spoken at Catholic meetings. O'Connell was described as 'A sweet smiling lawyer, who talked very big...About children of his that were slaves, sir'.[130] Rather than being offended, O'Connell claimed to love the publicity. His portrait and a speech of his also appeared in the *Dublin Magazine* in September (a childhood ambition fulfilled). Delighted, he asked his wife to 'inquire the first day you go to town about it'.[131] Mary purchased a copy and teased him that he looked 'the image of Prince *Le Boo*'.[132]

As the year came to a close O'Connell was in an aggressive mood. He was determined to continue agitating and at a meeting of the Catholic Committee on 15 December he suggested laying before the House of Commons his statement on the penal laws.[133] Beginning to make a name for himself, O'Connell was invited to dinner by an uncle of the O'Conor Don. The guest of honour was Henry Grattan. O'Connell was not disappointed by his childhood hero and was entertained greatly by his 'anecdotes of the men with whom he politically acted'.[134] The dead-pan style of delivery was also of interest. Grattan 'never relaxed a muscle' when he told his stories, even as 'his hearers were convulsed with laughter'. A story which stayed with O'Connell concerned Lord Kingsborough, a man who dressed like a Cromwellian roundhead, and who was a mass of contradictions. He was defiantly independent, yet was servile before ministers; he read a portion of the Bible every day, but marked his place with an obscene ballad. O'Connell believed that Grattan had been behind his invitation to the dinner. As he later noted, 'I was then beginning to be talked of, and people like to see a young person who acquires notoriety.'[135]

Most people outgrow, but rarely abandon, their childhood heroes. O'Connell never lessened in his admiration for Grattan. But as the 1810s were to prove, he was also determined to follow his own path, even if that meant going against Grattan or anyone else who opposed him. In that decade, when the debate over the veto was at its height, O'Connell turned on Grattan with a viciousness that was astonishing. He knew Grattan's place on the page of history but he also knew his own. Towards the end of his life O'Connell was questioned about who was the greatest Irishman. He replied, without hesitation, 'Harry Grattan.' The key to understanding O'Connell's character is in remembering how he prefaced the answer: '*next to myself*'.[136]

Chapter 7 ~

'HATED BY SOME, DISLIKED BY MANY': THE AGITATOR, 1811–1814

'I am an agitator with ulterior views! I wish for liberty — real liberty'.

(SPEECH OF DANIEL O'CONNELL, 24 DECEMBER 1813).[1]

In October 1810 the major obstacle blocking Catholic emancipation was hurled from the throne. King George III relapsed into the madness that had afflicted him many times before and the prince of Wales was appointed prince regent formally on 6 February 1811.[2] This created a new mood of optimism amongst the Irish Catholics who believed that change would follow. George III had been instrumental in preventing emancipation in 1801 and now he had been replaced. But no change came. The prince regent persisted with the existing administration and showed little interest in changing course. The Catholic Committee was forced to continue its work. During this period O'Connell faced enormous pressure from his relatives, Hunting Cap especially, to abandon his agitation and concentrate on his legal career. There was little support for his activities and there was even a sense of embarrassment about some of his more aggressive speeches. He was given advice regularly—sometimes directly, more often indirectly. On 17 January 1811 his brother, James, was the bearer of the following message from Hunting Cap: 'Tell him I fear his political avocations occupy too much of his time and thoughts, and may possibly have the effect of taking him off from his professional pursuits.'[3] Moves were underway to send a new Catholic petition to the British parliament and Hunting Cap urged his nephew, in unequivocal language, not be part of the delegation. O'Connell relented, and refused the invitation to travel to London with the new petition on 20 April 1811, citing his professional commitments.[4]

Hunting Cap was also concerned about O'Connell's 'softness and facility of disposition' when it came to financial matters.[5] Here he was justified in intervening, for O'Connell was notoriously feckless when it came to his own money. He was also far too trusting of friends and his extended (and, as he became more famous, ever-increasing) network of relations. Far too often O'Connell acted as security for various debts and loans, and all too often he was forced to pay the price. In part O'Connell was playing the part of the traditional Irish chieftain, but his generosity was proving expensive and would cripple him in the years ahead. In May 1811 Hunting Cap was deeply concerned that O'Connell would act as a security for John Primrose. Hunting Cap feared that any help might well ruin O'Connell 'beyond redemption'. Knowing his nephew's weakness when it came to money, he forbade any support absolutely and threatened that any disobedience would 'create a breach between us never to be healed'; indeed he would never speak to him again for the rest of his life. Hunting Cap was, by now, well used to O'Connell's artfulness when it came to persuasion and warned him that he would not tolerate any 'feeble or temporizing excuses'.

In the meantime O'Connell was renovating his house on Merrion Square. The work was not without its difficulties and he soon learned to have little faith in builders, 'who are of all others the greatest rogues in the community'.[6] His widowed mother (his father had died in 1809) was in regular contact asking for money, though O'Connell had little sympathy as she had an annual allowance of two hundred guineas: 'It would be just the same if she had £2,000 a year.'[7] However he remained close to his mother and before she died in February 1817 she 'very, very often' gave her blessing to O'Connell and his family.[8]

Sustained attempts were made to suppress the Catholic Committee in 1811.[9] In February the government considered arresting the leading troublemakers, having collected a mass of evidence from spies. One of its targets was O'Connell, who was aware of what was being planned and was determined to remain in custody if arrested. He believed it was better to avoid bail so as to 'keep the business alive' and 'punish their oppressors'.[10] It was reported in July that O'Connell had spoken of how the rights of Catholics could only be achieved by force of arms and the government looked for proof so that it could make him the subject of 'a most necessary and useful prosecution'.[11] Using the Convention Act of 1793, which enabled the government to declare certain assemblies illegal, a proclamation was finally issued against the Committee on 1 August.[12] To discuss this, a major Catholic meeting was held in Cork on 2 September 1811, with James Roche in the chair. O'Connell spoke for two hours and then stayed up all night preparing a version of the speech for the press. Even though O'Connell had not written his speech in advance (he never did), he was able to remember it afterwards almost perfectly, and was also able to include incidental matters which had also been discussed.[13]

Recognising that O'Connell was one of its most troublesome opponents, the government made an attempt to purchase his silence. This marked a new strategy, for in July the Castle had called for 'decisive measures' to be taken against him, insisting that 'no compromise could be thought of'.[14] But a compromise was indeed considered, and an offer was made. O'Connell was told that if he was 'not so violent and intemperate as previously' he would be given an annual pension of £1,200.[15] This was a considerable sum, especially given his financial problems, and the offer was made by someone 'so high in rank' that there were '*few* higher in rank or influence in the country'. 'With quiet and unaffected contempt', O'Connell rejected the offer. As he reflected in 1825 (when he made the attempted bribe public), 'I did prefer my violence and intemperance'.

A new Catholic Committee, composed of delegates from around the country, met on 19 October, and O'Connell attended having been appointed a delegate by Townsend Street parish, but it too was suppressed.[16] Magistrates raided the meeting and took Lord Fingall into custody when he refused to vacate the chair. O'Connell was full of rage. When told by the leading magistrate that this was an illegal meeting, O'Connell responded furiously that 'your belief is of no consequence to us. We are not bound by your opinions.'[17] Leonard McNally, the key government informer who pretended to help the Catholic Committee, recommended challenging the arrest, declaring that the lord lieutenant had authorised an illegal action. But O'Connell, wisely, urged caution and persuaded the Committee away from taking a stand that would have made further prosecutions inevitable.[18] Instead the secretary of the Catholic Committee, Edward Hay, published a letter calling on every county in Ireland to elect delegates to prepare petitions for parliament and meet in Dublin to form a 'General Committee of the Catholics of Ireland' on 23 December.[19] But this meeting was also declared illegal and a magistrate dispersed the gathering. Unbowed, the delegates withdrew to the Crown and Anchor Tavern and resolved to hold a new aggregate meeting of the Catholics of Ireland on 26 December. As this meeting drew near, Lord Fingall prepared resolutions with O'Connell assisting.[20] At the new meeting it was decided to dissolve the Catholic Committee and replace it with a new board, of named individuals thus bypassing the Convention Act. The new body was an assembly, but did not claim to be a representative body, and by disclaiming representation it was safe from the Convention Act.[21] This board would then prepare an address to the prince regent. It was at this aggregate meeting that the Catholic Board was established.[22]

The government kept a close eye on the meetings of the new body. Frederick W. Conway, a journalist who occasionally acted as secretary and chairman, was a secret informer and sent regular reports to Dublin Castle.[23] In one report forwarded by the lord lieutenant to the home secretary it was said that 'Messrs O'Connell, Dromgoole and Scully' usually took 'the least temperate line' at the meetings and regularly dissented from the leadership of Fingall. The address to the prince regent was passed at the aggregate Catholic meeting of 28 February 1812 and a deputation from the Catholic Board was sent to London. The delegation presented the address at a levee on 16 April, but its request for a private interview was rejected.[24] In a haughty dismissal, the prince's secretary also revealed that any address to the prince should be submitted the usual way; there would be no special treatment for the Catholics.

The British prime minister, Spencer Perceval, was assassinated in the lobby of the House of Commons on 11 May 1812 by a deranged insurance broker. Afterwards, many ministers broke down in tears in the chamber when they paid tribute to him, and a new ministry was formed under the anti-Catholic Lord Liverpool. O'Connell was following a murder of his own. On 17 February 1812, William Hall was sentenced to death for the murder of a seventeen-year-old Catholic boy called Byrne. But Hall, an Orangeman, was pardoned by the lord lieutenant on the grounds of insanity.[25] O'Connell was visited by Byrne's mother, a widow, and upon hearing her story was enraged. It was only a matter of time before he responded publicly. His opportunity came on Thursday 18 June 1812 when there was a major meeting of the Catholics at Fishamble Street Theatre, with Lord Fingall in the chair. There was much anger when the indifference of the prince regent was reported along with the rejection of the request to secure a personal interview.

Addressing the large gathering, O'Connell threw away the scabbard and with it any pretence of trying to conciliate. The sword had been drawn and he was determined to draw blood. His attack on the prince regent was uncompromising, and he publicly accused him of four distinct breaches of faith, over a long period, to the Irish Catholics. He then addressed the assassination of Perceval. This was a subject that called for tact and sympathy: O'Connell showed none. His violent language was a good indication of just why he offended so many British listeners (and readers) and some Irish ones too. O'Connell expressed 'unaffected horror' for Perceval's fate, but refused to allow this to obliterate his crimes: 'he was a narrow-minded bigot, a paltry statesman, and a bad minister', an advocate of public corruption and an enemy of reform.[26]

'But are all our feelings to be exhausted by the great?' O'Connell reminded his audience of the murder of Byrne, in a masterful attempt to redirect their sympathies. He was making the point that all the papers were full of the murder of Perceval, but no one was paying any attention to 'the wretched Irish widow' who had lost 'her boy—her hope, her support'. The murderer had been convicted by a jury of his peers, and O'Connell was horrified that the lord lieutenant had decided to pardon him, even speculating mischievously that 'perhaps he [Hall] has been rewarded'. But how, he asked, 'can this be done with impunity? Is there no vengeance for the blood of the mother's son?' O'Connell was impudent, bordering on the presumptuous. He even suggested that Perceval deserved his fate. In a highly controversial section he speculated whether the head of a government which 'had allowed the blood of Byrne to flow unrequited' might have been the victim of 'a providential visitation for the unpunished crime'.[27]

Towards the end of the speech O'Connell quoted some lines from Byron's latest work, *Childe Harold's Pilgrimage*, which were to become his rallying call in the years ahead: 'Hereditary bondsmen! Know ye not/ Who would be free, themselves must strike the blow.' It was his way of asserting that the Irish Catholics could not wait passively for Britain to emancipate them; if serious about freedom they must act themselves. If they acted as slaves they deserved to remain as slaves. Warning that Napoleon could very well conquer Russia and then Europe, he suggested that emancipating the Catholics could ensure that every village produced a regiment. The speech ended abruptly and dramatically: 'My feelings overpower me—I must be silent'.[28] It was this meeting which passed O'Connell's infamous 'witchery resolution', accusing the prince regent of being bewitched by his mistress, Lady Hertford—it lamented 'the fatal witchery of an unworthy secret influence'—into abandoning the Catholics.[29] It was an insult that was never forgiven by the future king.

About the violence of O'Connell's language: his aggressive style was often criticised by figures in public and friends in private. Following the winning of Catholic emancipation, O'Connell remembered that for years he had been told: 'O'Connell, you will never get anything as long as you are so violent!' But he laughed when he remembered this: for 'what did I do? Why, I became *more* violent—and I succeeded!'[30] This was always his opinion. In 1813 he noted how the modest campaign for relief between 1805 and 1807 had produced nothing: an attempt by the sympathetic Lord Grenville government to allow Catholic officers was defeated. But a more violent agitation six years later had persuaded a government hostile to the Catholics to propose a relief bill that offered everything except seats in parliament. This convinced him that agitation, and aggressive agitation at that, was the only strategy.[31]

By October 1812 the Catholic Board had amassed debts of £3,000 threatening its continued existence. O'Connell was put in charge of the finances and immediately set about fundraising. Like Pitt, O'Connell was terrible with his own finances but ingenious when it came to public monies. This is where he first had the idea of a national subscription, what later became the Catholic rent, taking the idea from a recommendation by Lord Kenmare in the 1780s.[32] He introduced a temporary subscription to pay the debt, and O'Connell later claimed that he would have continued with it only for the split over the veto.

Within seven months he had cleared the debt, and even managed to leave the account in credit.[33] In 1824 O'Connell boasted, with typical hyperbole, that he had cleared £2,500 of the debt 'in the space of one fortnight'.[34]

On 5 November 1812 O'Connell spoke at an aggregate meeting of the Dublin Catholics, held in Kilmainham, and reviewed the results of the recent general election, constituency by constituency. It convinced him that if there was a Protestant parliament in Ireland it would vote for emancipation.[35] Upon hearing this report, there was a loud and prolonged cheering from the crowd, described by one reporter as 'enthusiastic almost beyond any former experience'.[36] The applause was 'taken up again and again' and it was some minutes before O'Connell was allowed to continue. In this speech he was also cheered loudly for declaring that 'sorry, sunk and degraded as my country is, I still glory in the title of Irishman.'[37] Developing a clever argument about inconsistencies in the British government's position, he mocked its insistence that Catholics were too slavish when it came to the doctrines of the Catholic church, while also claiming that Catholics were too fond of freedom. Again there was much laughter and loud cries of 'Hear, hear!'[38]

Division was seen by O'Connell as the enemy of the Catholic Board and on numerous occasions he struggled to maintain a united front. On 14 November 1812 he had a run-in with the noted firebrand, and rival agitator, Jack Lawless, at a meeting of the Board. Lawless enjoyed censuring members and wanted to punish some men who had not supported the celebrated John Philpot Curran during his recent election campaign at Newry. But O'Connell opposed him strongly, all the time anxious to prevent divisions which could fester or be exploited by their enemies. O'Connell attempted to delay the discussion for a fortnight, and succeeded in adjourning the debate. On 28 November huge crowds gathered to hear the debate, and again O'Connell moved for a postponement, but this time he was defeated. There followed a series of heated speeches, and O'Connell spoke of his hatred of individual votes of censure, which transformed the Catholic Board from 'an assembly instituted for the advancement of constitutional freedom', with the full confidence of the Irish people, into 'a terrible inquisition'.[39] He suggested that regular censures would ensure that no one would feel safe and, if someone could muster twenty or twenty-five votes, then how soon might someone come forward and say 'Daniel O'Connell does not deserve the confidence of the Catholic people'? But he was unable to carry the point. Despite his growing influence, he was defeated and the censure passed. It was clear that O'Connell was not in charge, he did not carry every issue, and he had his rivals, such as Jack Lawless.

In later years O'Connell was asked his opinion of Lawless's speaking style. O'Connell always analysed oratory and found it easy to give an answer. Lawless, he said, 'began admirably and proceeded wretchedly. His first four or five sentences were exceedingly good; the language excellent, the sentiments impressive, the delivery admirable'.[40] But then, he said, he fell apart, 'and continued to the end in a strain of incoherence'. If he was interrupted he performed well, as he would repeat his opening points 'with excellent effect', but if allowed to continue unchallenged he was lost. O'Connell found Lawless a difficult person to deal with. Once at a committee meeting, before a large Catholic gathering, he told O'Connell that he planned to bring forward a matter which O'Connell preferred to avoid. After much persuasion, Lawless finally agreed to drop the matter. O'Connell thanked him and then, to make doubly sure, checked again as they were entering the room: 'Now, Jack, you'll be sure to hold your tongue about that affair?' Lawless was offended and replied angrily, 'Do you mean to doubt my word? Have I not promised to be silent? I consider my honour as pledged.' Inside, O'Connell sat down to read a letter and immediately Lawless jumped up and began speaking on the very topic that he had promised to avoid. 'Of course I had to draw the sword upon him in reply,' laughed O'Connell when telling the story.[41]

In 1813 the lord mayor of Dublin, Abraham Bradley King, gathered together a Protestant 'no popery' petition, signed by 2,800 people. The petition was aimed at countering the almost annual Catholic petitions and show that there was genuine opposition to relief in Dublin. In May King went to London and presented this petition to the House of Commons along with a petition complaining of the commercial monopoly of the East India Company. George Canning, the protégé of Pitt, joked at this inconsistency in supporting a religious monopoly and opposing a commercial one.[42] On 8 May O'Connell addressed the Catholic Board and lashed out at the petition. Many of the signatures, he believed, were forged or fabricated, and there was much evidence for his belief.[43] O'Connell had brought a copy of the petition with him and he had great fun in examining it before the audience. This was O'Connell in theatrical lawyer mode, sifting through the evidence, poking and pulling at the inconsistencies and flaws, and finally taking the whole thing apart.

First, O'Connell examined the genuine signatures. He regretted that there were three or four barristers on the list, a profession which was normally 'the friends of every freedom', and he said that he regretted, 'from my soul, the discovery'.[44] He was pleased that there were few clergymen on the list, but saddened to find about ten attorneys, a large number of placemen, holders of government pensions, and people who wanted an office. But that still left almost two thousand signatures unaccounted for. Some, he showed, were forgeries, like the case of Mr Stephens who discovered that his name was on the petition even though he had not signed it and who had made a formal complaint. But when forgery was exhausted, 'mere fiction was resorted to'.[45] Here O'Connell was devastatingly funny as he went through the names which had been invented for the purpose, from the improbable to the downright impossible: 'They produced names which no man ever bore or will bear.' To increasing laughter and cheers he spoke of how

> The fabricators of this petition set disavowal at defiance... they invented John Hedpath... they united the noble families of the Feddlies to the illustrious race of Fiddlies; they created the Jonneybones, and added the M'Coobens to the Muldongs; to the uncleanly Rottens is annexed the musical name of Navasora—the Sours and the Soars—the Dandys and the Feakens—the Gilbasleys and the Werrillas—five Ladds and five Palks—the Leups and the Zealthams—the Huzies and the Hozies—the Sparlings and the Sporlings—the Fitzgetts and the Fibgetts—the Hoffins and the Phantons, and the Giritrows, and the Hockleys and Breakleys, the Russinghams, and the Favuses, and the Sellhews, and the Mogratts and Calyells all, poor innocents, are made to combine against us, and to chime with the Pithams and Paddams—the Chimnicks, and Rimnicks, and Clumnicks, and the Rowings and Riotters; they threw in the vulgar Bawns, and after a multitude of fantastic denominations, they concluded with Zachariah Diamond. (Great laughter.)

According to O'Connell one thousand of the names could be accounted for this way, 'one thousand children of the brain of those worthy managers of intolerance'. There had never existed 'a more tasteless group of imaginary beings... conjured up by the delusions of magic'. He poured scorn on the twenty-five Armstrongs on the list, and the eighteen Taylors. This, he said, should really have been 'four-and-twenty Taylors all in a row' as then there would have been 'some pleasantry in it'. As far as O'Connell was concerned a deliberate fraud had been brought before the House of Commons. Laying down a challenge to the petitioners, he asked them to produce the men in question:

> Mr. Riotter may head their party. I should be glad to see the gentleman. If he does not live in the city, this Riotter, I presume he is to be found in the Liberties. After him our enemies can show off Mr. Wevilla, hand in hand with Mr. Navasora, and Johnny Bones, Esq., may appear with Fibgetts, gent., and even Mr. Knowing can be summoned to come forward in company with Mr. Dandy. (Cheers and laughter.)[46]

In the speech O'Connell also defended the honour of the princess of Wales, the estranged wife of the prince regent. Adapting Edmund Burke, O'Connell suggested that thousands of Irish swords should have leaped from their scabbards to defend her from the charges that had been laid against her.[47] She had married the prince of Wales in 1796, but there was little affection in the relationship. The princess could not shake the suspicion that her husband was still in love with his mistress, which was probably true enough, and they separated soon after the birth of a daughter. From then on, the princess's every move was watched and she was accused of having a number of high-profile affairs. In the 1810s siding with the princess became the easiest way of killing your political career. But O'Connell had little time for the prince regent and was determined to cause him embarrassment.

The veto was also becoming a divisive issue. The veto, or the question of 'religious securities' as it was properly called at the time, was whether the British government would be allowed have a say on the appointment of Irish bishops in the event of emancipation. Looking back on it, it is difficult to see why the veto was so controversial. After all, it was a power already given to most European monarchs who ruled over large Catholic populations. As S.J. Connolly has noted, 'the different schemes for a veto were perfectly compatible with the doctrines of the Catholic church' and if 'later historical writing' has taken it for granted that it should have been opposed that only reflects 'the extent to which it was the anti-vetoists who won the contemporary debate'.[48] A case can easily be made for those who were prepared to compromise and who were baffled by the intransigence of O'Connell and the others. So why was O'Connell so prepared to wreck Catholic unity in opposing the veto? It seems he genuinely believed that the veto was fatal for long-term Irish interests. He equated acceptance of the veto with a fatal servility and saw it as a compromise that destroyed the integrity of the case they were making. There may also have been a cynical aspect to his opposition, using the issue to establish his own leadership and destroy the credibility of his opponents. In the years ahead O'Connell showed a remarkable willingness to accept various securities when it looked like a deal could be done and it was him making the deal.

The Catholic hierarchy backed O'Connell in his opposition to the veto and their support proved decisive. And so, when the 1813 relief bill was defeated, he was not too disappointed. It had been tainted by the question of securities. Attacking the bill publicly, he said it was based on things that if meant to be facts were 'unsupported' and if meant to be fiction 'made very bad poetry'.[49] At the Catholic Board on 29 May 1813 O'Connell read the unanimous repudiation of the Catholic prelates of Ireland for the religious securities in the relief bill. He then delivered a powerful attack on the measure, which he dismissed as the work of the lord lieutenant, the duke of Richmond, and his chief secretary, Robert Peel. The master of invective, O'Connell lost no time in abusing Peel. He was 'Orange Peel', 'a raw youth, squeezed out of the workings of I know not what factory in England', an expert in justifying absurd policies, and appointed to Ireland precisely because he was 'a lad ready to vindicate anything—everything!'[50] The speech ended with much cheering and O'Connell moved a motion thanking the Catholic prelates for their letter 'and for their ever vigilant and zealous attention to the interests of the Catholic church in Ireland'.

But this second part of the motion caused controversy. Anthony

Strong Hussey wanted to delete it, and was supported by Sir Edward Bellew, who delivered an extraordinary and what he claimed was an extempore speech. O'Connell rose to defend the bishops. Teasing Bellew, he questioned whether it was really an extempore speech, or whether it would appear in that exact form in the newspapers the next day, as he doubted whether Bellew could produce such an 'artful' though 'mischievous' speech without preparation.[51] Full of scorn, O'Connell delivered a hard rebuttal of what had been said, mocking Bellew for claiming a special right to be heard because he spoke so rarely. O'Connell said this reminded him of the soldier who prayed before a battle, for the first time in forty years, and demanded that his prayer was answered because it was his first. O'Connell took great care to unravel Bellew's 'spider-web of sophistry'. He insisted that no securities were necessary, denying Britain's right to ask for them as well as its need for them. As far as he was concerned it was Britain which had regularly broken its word to Ireland. He denied that the English disliked the Irish because they were Catholics, 'they simply hate us because we are Irish'.[52]

On 29 May, at another meeting of the Board, O'Connell went on the attack. He pressed the earl of Fingall to reveal the pledge the prince of Wales had given him, years earlier, about the Catholic question. The motion was passed by thirty-six votes to six. He also attacked Henry Grattan for supporting the recent relief bill, a bill so limited that the government had been obliged to send William Plunket over to Ireland to reconcile Catholics to it. 'Strange mission!' exclaimed O'Connell, mocking the idea of having to reconcile Catholics to a bill for their own relief. O'Connell also found the opportunity to attack the English Catholics, whose willingness to always compromise he believed amounted to selling out the cause.[53]

Fishamble Street in Dublin was the location of an aggregate meeting on 15 June and O'Connell again took the opportunity to attack 'this modern cant of securities'.[54] Grattan was also attacked for not understanding the significance of the securities and why they were such an insult: in doing so he had given up 'our honour and our religion'.[55] Castlereagh, the foreign secretary, was also attacked, as the man who had disgraced himself in 1798 and again during the passing of the Union. Later in the meeting O'Connell presented a motion for an address in favour of the princess of Wales. Addressing the allegations that had been levelled against her, he quoted one of the judges who had shown that the charges against her were 'false as hell'; this became one of his favourite phrases for a short time afterwards.[56]

O'Connell was becoming a contentious figure in Ireland and he was accused of wanting a complete separation between Britain and Ireland. Speaking to the Catholic Board on 29 June, he declared that such a charge was 'false as hell'.[57] This was a controversial speech as O'Connell was unambiguous in claiming that repeal of the Union was his most important consideration. It was 'my great, my ultimate object'.[58] Indeed he went so far as to suggest that had emancipation been granted with the Union then the country might have 'relapsed into apathy'.[59] But the refusal of the British government, which had become outright resistance, had 'roused the sleeping lion of Ireland to awaking activity'. Therefore the long wait for emancipation was something to be applauded, he claimed for rhetorical effect, because it created the momentum for repeal. In this speech O'Connell admitted that he had long made it 'a scrupulous duty' not to wear anything that wasn't made in Ireland, and he called on his listeners to boycott the 'produce of England'.[60] He was also determined to make this official policy and in July 1813 he successfully brought forward a motion insisting that no one could speak or vote at the Catholic Board unless they were wearing Irish-made clothes.[61]

On 27 July 1813 O'Connell delivered one of the most famous speeches of his career. His defence of John Magee would be hailed by contemporaries and historians as one of his finest, but there are problems with this interpretation. It should be remembered that Magee was found guilty and O'Connell's behaviour only made such a verdict inevitable. True, he gave a great speech, but it was a political speech, rather than a legal one. In doing so, he abandoned his client for the sake of making some, albeit powerful, political points. O'Connell justified this on the grounds that he knew his client was doomed, and therefore it was worth seizing the opportunity to strike out against the British government. But his client did not see it quite so clearly. This was O'Connell at his most cynical and opportunistic. He knew the case would be reported extensively in Britain and Ireland and thus give him his biggest ever audience. The Magee trials were probably the only time that O'Connell acted as a politician in the courtroom rather than as a lawyer.

Magee was the proprietor of the *Dublin Evening Post* and was being prosecuted for an alleged libel on the duke of Richmond, the departing lord lieutenant for Ireland. The actual libel was relatively mild, but the government was determined to make an example of the press. The prince regent was also unhappy with the newspaper for reporting O'Connell's speeches against him and wanted a case to be taken. In addition, the new chief secretary, Robert Peel, saw the *Dublin Evening Post* as the most subversive of all the Irish newspapers and the cause of much of the trouble in Ireland. The trial began on 31 May, though it was postponed as key witnesses were not present. The prosecution team consisted of William Saurin, the attorney general; Charles Kendel Bushe, the solicitor general; Thomas Kemmis; and three serjeants. Defending Magee were O'Connell, who was leading counsel, John Finlay, Charles Phillips, and two junior barristers. As soon as the case was called on, Finlay rose and asked for an adjournment so that four key witnesses could be called, including William Wellesley Pole, the former chief secretary, and Peel, the current one. Saurin opposed any adjournment, and was attacked in turn by O'Connell for giving the court 'assertion instead of argument, abuse instead of logic'.[62] O'Connell then questioned the validity of an affidavit the prosecution had secured from a 'James Murphy, of the city of Dublin'. Wondering why there were no specific details about the person's profession or address, he compared it to the recent anti-Catholic petition and suggested that the prosecution had imitated that example 'of imposition, of perjury, and of forgery'.[63] After discrediting the prosecution's precedent for refusing a postponement, O'Connell presented a number of precedents of his own. The solicitor general wisely intervened and agreed to a postponement.

When the case was called again on Monday 26 July O'Connell once more pressed for an adjournment, because of the continued absence of two key witnesses, but this time he was unsuccessful. A jury was called (though there was no balloting of names, a point that O'Connell raised an objection to and later appealed), and Kemmis and then Saurin delivered the case for the prosecution. Saurin's blood was up and he delivered a stinging indictment of Magee's character, calling him 'abominable', a 'ruffian', 'seditious', 'revolutionary', 'a brothel-keeper', and 'a kind of bawd in breeches'.[64] The trial broke for the evening, and the next day, Tuesday 27 July, O'Connell had an opportunity to respond. Abandoning the caution which characterised much of his legal career, he delivered one of his most vehement attacks on British misrule in Ireland. For all its faults as a legal speech, it was still spectacular. One observer, who was not known to O'Connell, called it 'dazzling and overpowering'.[65] O'Connell began as he meant to continue. He praised the previous day's break because it had allowed him to calm down. While he said he was still angry, he claimed this anger arose from his feelings of pity; what 'roused my indignation, now only moves to contempt'.[66] He was scathing when he came to Saurin's treatment of Magee, dismissing his comments as 'a confused and disjointed tissue of bigotry, amalgamated with congenial vulgarity'. Saurin's speech was 'violent and virulent' and contained 'very little logic, and no poetry at all'. O'Connell admitted that he was departing from his normal 'rigid rule' of not mixing politics with his 'forensic duties', but claimed that he was justified in doing so on this occasion because of the example of the attorney general.[67] He attacked Saurin for accusing the Catholics of being seditious and treasonable, an allegation that he said he noted seventeen times. Even though Saurin had ended his speech disclaiming any real significance to these words, O'Connell was not appeased. He declared that if any man dared charge the Catholic body or the Catholic Board with treason or sedition he would stand in the court, in the city, or in the field, and 'brand him as an infamous and profligate *liar*'.[68] This was a clear digression from the case being tried and the chief justice interrupted to question its relevance. O'Connell was unbending. He insisted that since Saurin had been allowed to 'traduce and calumniate us', and had been heard with 'patience and with temper', then he should be allowed to deliver a vindication. Saurin had boasted that he would one day suppress the Catholic Board and O'Connell dared him to do so. He said he would 'hurl *defiance* at the attorney general', challenging him to find any law, statute or proclamation that had been violated by the Catholic Board. And he taunted him by saying that emancipation would be achieved, and achieved soon: 'we will—we must soon be emancipated'.

Only then did O'Connell address the alleged libel on the duke of Richmond. One of the disputed paragraphs had accused Richmond's administration of errors and O'Connell wondered aloud how this could be seen as libel. He also reminded the jury that Saurin had claimed that a good press protected the people against the government and he asked how this was possible 'if it is a crime to say of that government that it has committed errors, displays little talent, and has no striking features?'[69] Magee had not just attacked Richmond, he had also catalogued the errors of previous administrations, and these were examined by O'Connell and supported. Lord Westmorland had been called 'profligate and unprincipled', and this was defended by O'Connell as fair comment. O'Connell was also prepared to go further. He suggested that the women of Ireland were less chaste after Westmorland's administration (1790–1794) because of the 'depraved example of a depraved court'.[70]

Camden, the viceroy from 1795 until the outbreak of the 1798 Rebellion, had been called 'cold-hearted and cruel'. O'Connell cited the court records of the period, when hangings were almost official policy, to prove this point, and also enlisted the support of Ralph Abercromby and John Moore, two distinguished generals who had been critical of the British army abuses in Ireland. Magee had called Cornwallis, the viceroy who put down the 1798 Rebellion and supervised the passing of the Union, 'artful and treacherous'. Here O'Connell decided to attack the 'artifice and treachery' which had been used to pass the Union, and he blamed the government for manipulating the 1798 Rebellion to secure the measure. His blood boiled, he said, whenever he thought of that period and how the Union had been achieved. It would have been impossible a year later, and would have provoked a revolution a year earlier. But the government had 'artfully and treacherously seized on' the perfect moment, 'and our country, that *was* a nation for countless ages, has dwindled into a province, and her name and her glory are extinct for ever'.[71]

The betrayal of the Catholics after the Union was also addressed. O'Connell said that he was glad the Catholics had been deceived and that emancipation had not accompanied the Union, because the man who 'trafficked for his own advantage upon his country's miseries deserved to be deceived'.[72] O'Connell mentioned his own small role in opposition in 1800 and said he still rejoiced that 'my first introduction to the stage of public life was in the opposition to that measure'. 'In humble and obscure distance' he had followed the debates over the Union and he noted that some of the men who now prosecuted Magee had made radical statements in 1800. He teased the solicitor general, Bushe, for his anti-Union stand, and quoted the title of his pamphlet against him: 'Cease your funning.' Saurin's speech against the Union on 22 March 1800 was also used in Magee's defence. Saurin had claimed then that 'debates sometimes produce agitations, but that was the price necessarily paid for liberty'. O'Connell joked that the price had been paid, but the goods had not been given. Paragraphs from a speech of Saurin's on 13 March 1800 were also quoted, which suggested that if the Union passed it would be a 'nullity' and that 'resistance to it would be a struggle against usurpation and not a resistance against law'. O'Connell affected astonishment that Magee could be prosecuted for calling Cornwallis's administration artful and treacherous when Saurin, in an earlier incarnation, had said so much worse. He joked that he and his friends were 'poor and timid agitators' in 1813 when compared to the violent agitator' of 1800, who had 'sounded the tocsin of resistance and summoned the people of the land to battle against it'. Put alongside Saurin in 1800, O'Connell suggested that Magee in 1813 should be praised for his moderation. O'Connell also mocked Saurin for his French descent. He attacked the French Revolution and then the French people, adding, 'Yes, my lords, they *are* insolent, even when transplanted and to the third and fourth generation.'[73]

Nor was O'Connell concerned with befriending the jury. He was blunt in his assertion that he would have deselected 'at least ten of you' if he had been allowed. Instead he asked them to act for a moment as if they were 'a dispassionate and an enlightened jury', an insult which was surely counter-productive. Later he was even prepared to exclaim, 'Would to God I had to address another jury!'[74] The jury was entirely Protestant and O'Connell claimed that it had been fixed that way because of a belief that no Catholic could be trusted, and that this was surely a libel the government should wish to challenge.[75] After a brief defence of Denys Scully's *A statement of the penal laws*, O'Connell returned to the alleged libel. It had been written that Richmond had come over to Ireland 'ignorant, he soon became prejudiced, and then he became intemperate'.[76] O'Connell defended each part of this statement, insisting that there was no shame in a military man coming to Ireland without any previous knowledge and nothing wrong with developing beliefs which might be called prejudices. As for the charge of being intemperate, O'Connell denied that this conjured up images of 'midnight orgies' or 'morning revels' as Saurin had alleged. Instead, he insisted that what was being discussed was political intemperance, and that was merely the justified violence with which a man defends his political opinions. O'Connell was attempting to show that while there may be a harshness in the sound of the words, there was none when they were examined and defined. It was clever sophistry, but its effectiveness was diluted by the aggression of the rest of the performance.

Phillips, acting as junior counsel, was shocked by some of O'Connell's language. At one point O'Connell accused Saurin of some mistake, but Bushe interrupted to accept responsibility, saying 'If there is blame in it, I alone must bear it' and quoting from Virgil, '*Me, me, adsum qui feci, in me convertite ferrum*' ('Me, me, I'm here, I did it, turn your swords on me'). But O'Connell snarled 'Finish the sentence, Mr Solicitor' and demanded that he complete the quote: '*Mea fraus omnis.*' ('Mine was all the fraud').[77] A hurricane had been unleashed upon the government, and O'Connell's abuse was ferocious and unrelenting. Robert Peel was so shocked that he wrote a report afterwards declaring that O'Connell 'had avowed himself a traitor, if not to Ireland, to the British empire'.[78] And he claimed the speech was 'more scurrilous and more vulgar than was ever permitted within the walls of a court of justice'.

Comparing Magee to the proprietor of the *Hibernian Journal*, O'Connell wondered why the *Hibernian Journal* was supported by the government with pensions and advertising, even though it libelled the Catholics of Ireland in its pages. O'Connell wanted to know why one proprietor was prosecuted and the other rewarded. Knowing that Peel, the chief secretary, was in the courtroom, O'Connell turned round theatrically to where he was seated and asked 'Would I could see the man who plays this proclamation money and these pensions at the Castle'.[79] O'Connell ended his speech by calling upon the jury to show that they were sincere men of genuine religious zeal and real piety, rather than 'slaves and hypocrites', by acquitting his client. Unsurprisingly, Magee was convicted. From prison, Magee published on 7 August 1813, in the *Dublin Evening Post*, an account of a series of resolutions passed by the Catholics in Co. Kilkenny three days earlier. Again the government decided to prosecute him, claiming that this was another libel on the duke of Richmond's administration.[80] Despite the conviction of Magee, O'Connell's reputation was undamaged and his attack on the British government reverberated.

Soon after the Magee trial, O'Connell took to the field to fight a duel. The affair of honour had resulted from a courtroom clash between O'Connell and his opposing counsel, Maurice Magrath, on 12 August 1813. Angry at some comments that had been made on a legal point, Magrath surreptitiously kicked O'Connell under the box. O'Connell immediately raised his brief and struck Magrath across the face with it.[81] Afterwards, O'Connell was still furious and went to find his friend, Nicholas Purcell O'Gorman, for advice on how to proceed. O'Gorman believed that O'Connell had had the better of it: he had struck Magrath publicly, while Magrath's kick had not been seen by anyone. But O'Connell was not satisfied and asked O'Gorman to carry a challenge to Magrath and act as his second. The next morning at six a.m. the two men, and their entourages, met to settle the matter with pistols. While O'Gorman was measuring the ground one of Magrath's party, Nicholas Philpot Leader, who was also friendly with O'Connell, attempted to effect a reconciliation. O'Connell took the opportunity to say that he had no unkind feeling towards Magrath and did not wish to fire on him. Leader negotiated a compromise: if O'Connell would repeat these sentiments to the crowd, Magrath would apologise. O'Gorman, however, was furious. As the second he felt, rightly, that he should have been consulted, and was angry with O'Connell for talking to one of Magrath's friends in his absence. O'Connell insisted that the conversation had happened innocently and that he would abide by O'Gorman's decision. Hearing this, O'Gorman asked him to take his ground and put a case of pistols into his hands.[82]

By now word of the putative compromise had spread throughout the crowd and there was much anger that a deal had not been reached. A group gathered around O'Gorman and insisted he back down, but he refused and declared that it was too late for such a course. Upon hearing this, the crowd told him that if anyone was killed he should be hanged for it. O'Gorman was visibly upset and went over to O'Connell to resign as his second. The compromise which had been suggested by Leader was then agreed, apologies were made, and no shots were fired. The parties shook hands and returned to Limerick. For two years the affair cast a shadow over O'Connell. It was rumoured that he had not the stomach for a fight and would back down rather than risk death. This made him a target. His behaviour was certainly suspect by the standards of the day. O'Connell himself, when commenting on another duel in November 1804, had praised one of the participants for conducting himself with honour and for leaving 'the ground without making the slightest concession'.[83] However O'Gorman later admitted that Leader's proposition had been 'most unprecedented and embarrassing' and there was no alternative but to agree to it.[84]

The veto continued to occupy O'Connell's thoughts. A series of meetings were held in the south of Ireland to rally opposition to it, and a large aggregate meeting took place in Cork on 30 August 1813. It was believed that leading figures of the Catholic Board in Cork supported conceding securities to the government and O'Connell was determined to crush their momentum. The aggregate meeting took place at the Lancastrian School, but as the room had not been prepared for the meeting, there was no podium and very few seats. The meeting began with a dispute over who should chair it, with various suggestions opposed and rejected and, offended by the disorganised proceedings, the dissenting Board members withdrew. O'Connell arrived late at the meeting to great cheering and gave a short speech about the need for unanimity. Then he departed to attempt a compromise with the Board members who had left, and in his absence there were further disagreements. O'Connell returned to calm the meeting before gathering ten men to return to the dissenting Board members and discuss the veto issue. The meeting took place in a bed-chamber and lasted two hours, but O'Connell returned triumphant. He had persuaded the Board members to agree to 'simple repeal', in other words 'the unconditional abrogation of the penal code', and to return to the aggregate meeting.[85]

Unanimity still proved difficult. Seventeen resolutions were proposed, most of which were uncontroversial, but three towards the end were opposed. These were votes of thanks to the Catholic prelate Dr Milner, John Magee, and Daniel O'Connell. The vote for Milner, who had acted for many years as the agent of the Irish bishops, was opposed because he had initially supported the veto. The vote for Magee was opposed because he was 'a convicted libeller'.[86] The vote for O'Connell was opposed, in a direct attack on his character, because of his questionable 'public conduct'. This was a clear challenge and O'Connell rose to respond. He joked that he supported two of the votes of thanks, but joined in opposing one, his own. However he was uncompromising that the other two should be supported. Addressing the case of Milner, he said that a man had a right to change his mind and should not be punished for a previously held belief. Defending Magee, he insisted that the judgement of the Castle should not be allowed to discredit a man who should be praised for trying to publish the truth. O'Connell pleaded for unanimity. He said it was division which damaged Ireland, while unanimity could make Ireland 'the paradise of the world'. The speech ended strongly. O'Connell claimed that language had failed him and he stopped abruptly with the line, 'I will stand by you while I live; I will never forsake poor Ireland.'[87] The three contentious votes of thanks were passed by the meeting. However some members of the Board were still unhappy and decided to secede from the body afterwards, despite all of O'Connell's efforts. This problem of the seceders would afflict the Catholic cause for the next eighteen months. At a meeting of the Cork Catholic Board on 3 September O'Connell again called for unanimity and spoke of his regret at the secession, which he recognised as having its roots in the veto controversy. To encourage these 'security-men', as he called them, to return, on 20 October he moved a general resolution that no future Catholic relief measure would be approved unless supported in advance by the Catholic bishops. But this was in turn rejected as offering an indirect kind of security, and O'Connell withdrew it.

Sometime before the decisive battle of Leipzig in October 1813, 'when the fate of Europe was in suspense', O'Connell made an extraordinary offer to Peel.[88] Through an agent, he sent a message, signed in his own name and Denys Scully's, offering to raise one hundred thousand Irish Catholics to fight in the British army against Napoleon if emancipation was granted immediately. O'Connell promised that the men would all be 'serviceable' and that if they were not raised within three months then the emancipation bill need not pass. There were no other conditions, except a pardon for a printer who had been jailed for something Scully had written, and O'Connell gave his word that they would not insist on the nomination of officers or interfere in any way. The offer, however, was rejected and another opportunity for conciliation was lost.

On 19 November Magee was again in court for publishing the Kilkenny resolutions. He was indicted on eleven counts and O'Connell moved for a postponement, but this was opposed by Saurin. After long arguments about the rights of the subject to traverse *in prox,* in which

O'Connell quoted from Blackstone's *Commentaries* and cited many historical precedents, it was agreed to hold the trial in the early new year. However before that, O'Connell was forced to defend Magee in court on a separate but related charge. On Saturday 27 November Saurin moved to increase Magee's sentence because the *Dublin Evening Post* had published O'Connell's original speech in Magee's defence, which, he insisted, contained a libel against himself. Saurin spent much of his time suggesting that the case involved 'a senseless and shameless question', and unsurprisingly O'Connell heard in this a personal attack. He also interpreted some of Saurin's comments as accusing him of complicity in the crime of his client and of having a 'low and vulgar mind'.[89]

When it was his turn to speak, O'Connell responded in force. He began by asserting that he was the equal of Saurin in birth, fortune, education, and talent (though he admitted there was little vanity in claiming equality on that final point). This equality asserted, he admitted that he was willing to accept Saurin's personal abuse because of his respect for 'this temple of the law' because if the attack had been made elsewhere it 'would have merited *chastisement*'.[90] This created a sensation. Chastisement was code for horse-whipping, and O'Connell's language was readily understood in the court. Judge Day was startled from his slumber and asked, 'Eh! What is it that you say?' Judge Osborne had been more attentive. Visibly upset, he declared that he would not listen to such an outburst, warning O'Connell, 'Take care of what you say, sir.' But O'Connell was relentless. Aware that he was leaving himself open to prosecution, he restated the comments, suggesting that the attorney general had been prudent in making 'that foul assault upon me here' because if it had been made elsewhere it 'would lead me to do what I should regret—to break the peace in chastising him'. Day was astonished: '*Chastising!* The attorney general! If a criminal information were applied for on that word, we should be bound to grant it.' Again O'Connell was unrepentant. Deliberately provocative, he was daring the judges to punish him. He insisted that he was willing to pardon Saurin the offence, and was merely saying that had he been assailed elsewhere, he would have been 'carried away by my feelings to do that which I should regret—to go beyond the law—to inflict corporal punishment'. The challenge had been offered three times. Judge Osborne did not appreciate O'Connell's proffered distinction and immediately consulted with the other judges to see if O'Connell should be arrested on the spot. The chief justice warned O'Connell about his language and Day berated him for claiming to be suppressing his feelings, when in fact he was indulging them. Saurin also intervened, insisting that his comments had not been directed against O'Connell personally. The judges joined in this attempt to mollify O'Connell, assuring him that he had not been attacked. O'Connell was willing to accept this interpretation, but he put his own spin on it and claimed it showed that Saurin's words had been disavowed publicly. Continuing to provoke, O'Connell declared that he would never compromise the principles of the Irish bar, and he suggested that Saurin had taken this prosecution because it was personal; he wanted 'to check the popish advocate'.[91] O'Connell was astonished that a man could be prosecuted for reporting the account of a trial, if that report was a fair and accurate one. O'Connell had plenty of legal precedents on his side, especially from British courts, which established that 'nothing is a libel, or can become the subject matter of a criminal prosecution as such, which occurs in the course of proceeding in a court of justice.' As far as O'Connell was concerned this was not a case where Magee was threatened double punishment for one offence. Rather it was the 'greater atrocity' of being threatened punishment for no offence. He also asked why Magee should be punished for what he, O'Connell, had said. The judges had not interrupted him at the time, and O'Connell asked if this meant that Magee should have become a censor of the judges and taken it upon himself to interrupt. O'Connell ended his speech by pleading with the judges not to set a dangerous precedent which could be abused by judges in the future. Not that he expected the present bench to do so— 'I admit the perfection of the bench,' he insisted in a moment of playful irony.[92] But moving away from 'the utopian perfection' of the present period, O'Connell speculated about what might happen at some future point. In this discussion of a hypothetical future, he cleverly lined up another hit on Saurin. He claimed that in some future period an attorney general might be found, 'some creature, narrow-minded, mean, calumnious, of inveterate bigotry, and dastard disposition'. Such a man would store up his resentment for four months (the length of time since the first Magee trial), before his virulence would 'explode by the force of the fermentation of its own putrefaction, and throw forth its filthy and disgusting stores to blacken those whom he would not venture directly to attack'.[93] O'Connell was still convinced that a deliberate attack had been made upon him and he refused to back down. He ended his speech with another defiant statement of intent, confirming his belief that he had been right to attack the attorney general:

> As to him I have no apology to make. With respect to him I should repeat my former assertions. With respect to him I retract nothing. I repeat nothing. I never will make him any concessions. I do now, as I did then, repel every imputation. I do now, as I did then, despise and treat with perfect contempt every false calumny that malignity could invent, or dastard atrocity utter whilst it considered itself in safety.[94]

Magee listened in horrified silence to this speech. He was already breaking under the strain of prison and this performance convinced him that further punishment was inevitable. He instructed Thomas Wallace, his other counsel, to intervene and Wallace requested permission to speak before the solicitor general responded to O'Connell. Wallace distanced his client from the speech and suggested that O'Connell and not Magee should be held responsible for anything that had been said and for any impropriety which had occurred. O'Connell was furious and denied that he had been guilty of any impropriety, but Wallace went on to discuss 'the sins and crimes of counsel' and suggested that O'Connell was the person who should be punished.[95] Chief Justice Downes added his voice to the attack, grandly stating that he regretted not having stopped O'Connell years earlier at the start of his career. Despite Wallace's best efforts, Magee was found guilty, given a £500 fine and a further two years in prison from the date of sentence. In 1824 O'Connell insisted publicly that he had made an offer to Magee to take responsibility for the speech and that he made the same offer to Saurin. However neither offer appeared in the Dublin newspapers, prompting O'Connell to take this as evidence that they were 'a base press'.[96]

Many shared Magee's unease at O'Connell's behaviour. It was speculated that O'Connell had damaged his client by attacking Saurin so strongly, and that a more moderate line might have secured a lighter sentence.[97] Reports of the trial reached Kerry and Hunting Cap was horrified by what he read. He was shocked at the violence of the language used, the open attacks on the government, and the aggressive way his nephew had behaved in the court-room. In a strongly worded letter he requested, indeed 'insisted', that in future O'Connell would act with 'calmness, temperance and moderation', and would not be 'hurried by hate or violence of passions to use any language unbecoming to the calm and intelligent barrister or the judicious and well-bred gentleman'.[98] Hunting Cap was aware that there was going to be another Magee trial over publication of the Kilkenny resolutions and here he ordered O'Connell not to behave in a similar manner, but to act with 'calmness, discretion and decency'. This was the dark side of Hunting Cap's patronage. He was desperate to share in the reflected glory of his protégé, and was distraught that he seemed to be throwing everything away.

O'Connell was unapologetic. In an uncompromising defence of his actions he insisted that he had been placed 'in the novel situation of a barrister put upon his trial'.[99] He was convinced that Saurin had arranged beforehand with the judges to ambush him and had packed the court with as many friends as possible to heckle and jeer him. The newspaper, he insisted, only gave 'an insignificant idea of the tenor of his language' and 'of his insulting manner it can give you no idea whatsoever'. Challenging him to a duel was out of the question as he might very well have been arrested. And so, 'there was but one course to be pursued... the fixing *on him* a decided insult at all risks'. This, he believed, fully 'vindicated my violence'.[100] As for the upcoming trial, he would not make any promises, though he said he would follow 'a line of moderation in tone, manner and language unless I am first attacked'. But in that event, he would not allow 'any man to tarnish my character or honour with impunity'. In a later letter he again repeated that, if attacked, he would 'repel the assault with interest'.[101]

For a time, O'Connell's position was precarious. An attempt was made to arrange a meeting of the benchers to censure him, and possibly try and strip him of his gown, but this did not get far.[102] None the less it is an indication of just how vulnerable he was perceived to be that two very public tributes were paid to him at this time. In other words, the tributes were a public demonstration that he still had the backing of the Irish people. First, the Catholic Board decided to give him 'some solid and lasting memorial' to show its support.[103] Thus he was voted a silver plate, worth one thousand guineas, for his services, on 11 December 1813.[104] John Finlay made a speech on this occasion where he paid tribute to O'Connell's legal and political work, describing how he rose at five in the morning and was still working 'in the public service' at five in the evening. O'Connell's style was also praised: he was 'proud with the haughty' and with 'his frown rebukes arrogance to inferiority'.[105] But it was also recognised that he was divisive: he was 'hated by some, disliked by many'. According to Finlay, O'Connell's greatest strength was that he could speak well every day. Many men could give a good 'holiday speech', but O'Connell could speak often without sacrificing anything. 'This power of continual exertion' made him 'an opposition in himself'.[106] Accepting the tribute a week later, O'Connell said that he was now the bribed servant of Ireland, 'and no other master can possibly tempt me to neglect, forsake, or betray her interests'.[107] The manufacturers in the Liberties also decided to reward O'Connell, and he was presented with a silver cup at his house in Merrion Square on 14 January 1814. Accepting the tribute, O'Connell insisted he would only ever allow one toast from the cup, that of 'Repeal of the Union'.[108]

Securities was still the dominant question. At a meeting of the Catholic Board on Wednesday 8 December 1813 O'Connell saw for the first time the extraordinary oratorical talents of the twenty-year-old Richard Sheil (later Richard Lalor Sheil) who opposed the uncompromising position of the Board. A recent graduate from Trinity College Dublin, where he had been a leading debater at the College Historical Society, Sheil was a small man, and wore what was described as 'negligent attire'.[109] Earlier in the meeting O'Connell had passed a motion urging the northern Catholics to avoid joining the ribbon societies and thus giving the government evidence of illegality. This had been followed by a long-postponed motion from Dromgoole declaring permanent and unqualified opposition to any securities. Sheil delivered a stirring oration against the motion, which was described by the *Dublin Evening Post* as 'one of the most brilliant harangues ever delivered in a public assembly'.[110] Some people had claimed that the hard-line position on securities had retarded the cause of emancipation by fifty years, and Sheil wondered if the next generation would be slaves for the sake of a principle. He questioned whether the Catholic Board was following the right strategy. The English ministers mistrusted the Irish Catholics; therefore, securities should be given to reassure them. Sheil was a very different kind of speaker to O'Connell. He prepared his speeches carefully in advance, then memorised them, and sometimes even gave the text to journalists before it was delivered. His weakness was his voice, sometimes 'a shriek', and often compared to 'the noise of a rusty saw'.[111] But despite 'the shrill intonation' and 'awkward delivery' his 'magical vehemence' never failed to entrance his listeners.[112]

O'Connell immediately rose to applaud the speech, praising its 'brilliant and glowing language' and quoting Thomas Gray by acknowledging 'the thoughts that breathe and words that burn'.[113] But he would not accept the validity of the arguments. He insisted that emancipation in the circumstances outlined by Sheil was worthless, it was 'a participation in the servitude of slaves'. Nor did he accept the argument about the next generation being slaves for the sake of the country: 'It is indeed to confer the blessings of liberty on the nestlings of my heart (my children) that I struggle against obloquy, conspiracy and calumny.'[114] He ended the speech by calling on Sheil to join him in opposing securities, predicting that soon he would be a leader. And he called on him to 'reject party and adopt Ireland, who in her widowhood wants him'.[115] The gathering took their lead from O'Connell and Dromgoole's motion was passed.

Henry Grattan and Lord Donoughmore were the appointed spokesmen of the Catholic Board; the former to act in the Commons, the latter in the Lords. In the autumn of 1813 the Catholic Board had agreed to send the men a series of twelve 'suggestions' related to the approaching Catholic relief bill. But Grattan refused to read the suggestions, or allow his conduct to be influenced by them in any way, and Donoughmore replied that he would 'not condescend to receive instruction'.[116] The imperious manner of the men, and the way they were supported by the Catholic aristocracy, infuriated O'Connell. He knew their power would have to be broken before real progress could be made. In a speech six months later O'Connell discussed the 'style of superiority' which Grattan and Donoughmore had adopted at this time, a style, 'better suited, perhaps, to periods when the Catholics were more depressed, the Protestants more elevated'.[117] In Clare, O'Connell intervened to prevent a vote of thanks to Donoughmore for his general support to the cause.[118] Still angry about the securities issue, he attacked Grattan at a meeting of the Catholic Board on Saturday 8 January 1814, held in the Shakespeare Gallery on Exchequer Street in Dublin. 'Would to God that I could revive in the mind of Mr Grattan his former feelings for the Catholics of Ireland,' he declared.[119] Comparing Grattan's activities in the 1790s with those in the 1810s, he wondered why Grattan had not bothered about securities then, or had not been alarmed about the danger of emancipation. O'Connell called on 'the ghosts of the illustrious dead' to remind Grattan 'of what he was, and what he ought to be, unsophisticated by the delusions of English politics'. At the end of this speech there was a disturbance when a man was discovered taking notes of the meeting in a area separate from the reporters. The man was grabbed by the crowd and he revealed, under pressure, that he was employed by the police. But O'Connell intervened and said 'that all was perfectly fair'.[120] He said that he would arrange for there to be a desk or a table at the next meeting to allow for two or three police reporters to take notes comfortably. Again O'Connell was determined to give no excuse to the Castle to suppress the Board. By now O'Connell was much discussed in the media. For example, the *Irish Magazine, and Monthly Asylum for Neglected Biography* in January 1814, in an otherwise critical article, declared that he was 'the best man in the Catholic Board and inferior to no man in the purity of his heart and the splendour of his talents'.[121]

Magee's new trial for publishing the Kilkenny resolutions took place on 3 February and he was again found guilty and given an additional six months in prison and a fine of £1,000.[122] George Bryan, the chairman of the meeting which had passed the Kilkenny resolutions, was heavily criticised at this time by some members of the Catholic Board and in the pages of the *Dublin Evening Post*. It was felt that he should have taken responsibility for the libel, which he had refused to do. O'Connell supported Bryan at a meeting on 5 February 1814, but there was much opposition and he had his share of 'hissers'.[123] At the meeting of 12 February Jack Lawless moved a resolution censuring Bryan and on 26 February a modified version was passed, despite O'Connell's best efforts.[124] This was a difficult time for O'Connell and he also had to deal with personal tragedy: his youngest son, Daniel Stephen O'Connell, died aged two.

The securities issue was splitting the Catholic Board and a minority, who became known as 'the seceders', decided to withdraw from the meetings. They were horrified by the new uncompromising spirit, and especially the attacks on Donoughmore and Grattan. Lord Fingall, the nominal leader of the Catholic Board, was the most significant seceder, and he was joined by his right-hand man, Sir Edward Bellew. O'Connell continued to have great respect for Fingall—despite his harsh attacks on him he thought he was 'personally as pure as gold'— but suspected he was 'subject to some influence from less clean quarters'.[125] In late March 1814 O'Connell took part in a debate on the securities issue in Clare. The future chief baron, Stephen Woulfe, a seceder, had made a powerful speech urging moderation, criticising the attacks on Donoughmore and Grattan, and calling for an end to the hard-line opposition to securities. The speech made an impression and O'Connell felt obliged to answer. Deciding to use humour and ridicule to win the crowd over, rather than reasoned argument, he told the fable of the sheep who abandoned their guard dogs and were left to the mercy of the wolf. As he said the word 'wolf' he pointed to Woulfe and the crowd erupted into laughter.[126] Woulfe was furious and complained later about how all his arguments had been undermined by a simple pun. O'Connell showed little regret for the loss of the high profile seceders and insisted that 'Lord Fingall is not the Catholic cause, nor is Sir Edward Bellew the Catholic strength.'[127] His position was challenged in April when Monsignor Quarantotti, writing from the Vatican, came out in favour of allowing the British government a veto on the appointment of bishops. But O'Connell stood firm and declared defiantly in public that he 'would as soon take my politics from Constantinople as from Rome'.[128] Refusing to be bowed, he carried the debate.

Following months of rumours, the Catholic Board was suspended by proclamation on 3 June 1814. General O'Connell, in Paris following the abdication of Napoleon, was relieved by the news. He advised his nephew that this could allow him to withdraw from all political activity without losing face. It was clear that he shared Hunting Cap's views and preferred if O'Connell devoted his time to his legal career. General O'Connell believed that 'a prudent, peaceable and loyal deportment' was the only way to gain full rights for the Catholics, and that 'tumultuous assembles, intemperate speeches and hasty resolutions' would only damage their cause. He urged O'Connell to obey the proclamation and was clear that if he disobeyed he left himself open to 'a rigorous' and, 'I must say, a merited prosecution'.[129] But O'Connell ignored the advice. He refused to submit to the government and arranged a meeting at his house on 8 June to discuss resistance.[130] Already the idea of a new body was being discussed, with O'Connell as secretary. O'Connell also ensured the passing of a long series of resolutions deploring the proclamation at an aggregate meeting. Some more radical members even suggested renewing the meetings to see if a Dublin jury would convict.[131] But O'Connell opposed any illegal action and counselled for a moderate line. At this point Hunting Cap intervened. He was terrified that O'Connell would be prosecuted and he believed the government would rather target him 'than any other man in the kingdom'.[132] But again O'Connell refused to alter course.

Grattan and Donoughmore now abandoned the Catholic cause. Both men refused to submit a new Catholic petition to parliament in September 1814. Nevertheless, the Cork Catholics voted to present a petition to both men to do with it what they saw fit. A few days before the decision was taken, O'Connell had spoken at a meeting in Cork, chaired by his brother, John. He was the only speaker, and by his own admission 'spoke very badly'.[133] When he discovered the new vote, he was disgusted, attacking the 'submission of the people of Cork'. He believed it showed that they were only 'fit to be slaves'.[134]

The splits which O'Connell had been attempting to avoid now rose to the surface. O'Connell decided to arrange a new meeting of the Catholics, in their private capacity, at 4 Capel Street on 26 November 1814, and he sent the notices signed by himself, Dromgoole, and Scully.[135] This meeting was boycotted by Fingall and Sir Edward Bellew, who both wanted to postpone all agitation until the result of the negotiations with Rome on the subject of the veto was known.[136] The break with so many friends and colleagues was traumatic, but O'Connell believed it was necessary. This was how he operated throughout his political career. O'Connell was incapable of doing things on anyone's terms except his own. As his friend and junior colleague Charles Phillips noted with regret, 'Implicit obedience was the homage he demanded.'[137] Phillips observed O'Connell closely in this period, and noted that when provoked, O'Connell could produce 'an instant hurricane of rage', ready to sweep away friend or foe who challenged him.[138] Phillips believed that this was O'Connell's great weakness, that he was incapable of accepting any opposition. 'Oppose him in his wildest whims, or contradict him on the veriest trifle' and he would become 'the slave of some ungovernable impulse'. While O'Connell, himself, was always prepared to change strategy, and compromise, he was instantly offended if others did not follow him without hesitation. Once, Phillips disagreed with O'Connell on a political issue and 'Daniel fell into one of his paroxysms... For six months and upwards, when we met, his look was a wild glare.'[139] Finally he relented and walked up to him, saying, 'Charles, shake hands—I'm tired not speaking to you. I forgive you!' Phillips respected and admired O'Connell, but he was not blind to his defects: 'Contradiction incensed him, equality affronted him; and while invoking "liberty", he waved an iron sceptre.'

During the secession crisis a series of small meetings were held at Lord Fingall's house. The purpose was to discuss a petition for the removal of civil restrictions, and it was agreed that divisive religious matters would not be discussed. The press was not allowed to attend and admission was so limited the group was given the nickname of the 'Catholic divan'.[140] Cake and wine were always provided for the members of the board, but the meetings were unpopular and Fingall had by now lost much of his status.[141] O'Connell gained permission to attend, and became a key figure at debates even though he was criticised for attending by some of his supporters. Fingall was anxious that Counsellor Bellew, the brother of Sir Edward Bellew, should draw up the new petition for parliament. But this was opposed, and instead Richard Sheil, a key supporter of securities, was invited to present a draft. This draft contained various concessions, but these were opposed by O'Connell and a number of 'animated and somewhat sharp' discussions followed.[142] At a meeting on 10 January 1815 O'Connell attacked the opening paragraph which praised the 'generosity and liberality' of the British parliament, declaring that he would oppose the petition on this ground alone. Other sections were also opposed for creating a loophole on the securities issue; when pressed Shiel conceded the ground. At a meeting a week later, 17 January, O'Connell again went on the offensive. He decided to draw out the seceders and force a confrontation. It was an aggressive strategy but was aimed at bringing the matter to a head. At the start of the meeting he introduced a resolution which reopened the securities debate. Ostensibly it was uncontroversial, for it had been approved four times before by the Catholics, in 1809, 1810, 1811, and 1812. But it was controversial in 1815 because it called for 'the unqualified repeal of the penal statutes', and since the summer of 1813 this had been the dividing line between those who accepted securities and those who did not.[143] O'Connell must have known that he was on a collision course with Lord Fingall, he must have realised that a permanent breach was inevitable, and he must have deliberately encouraged it. Pointedly, he noted in his speech that his very resolution had been unanimously adopted, with the earl of Fingall in the chair, on 9 July 1811. Fingall was upset that the securities issue was being raised again, especially as the meetings were meant to avoid the controversy. But O'Connell persisted. Sheil delivered a lengthy speech against the introduction of the words 'unqualified emancipation'. Attempting to put O'Connell on the defensive, he asked if he would drop the word 'unqualified' if it meant restoring unanimity in the Catholic body. But O'Connell refused: he would not abandon 'a word which has been used at every Catholic meeting in Ireland'.[144] There was a vote on the issue, with eight siding with O'Connell and two with Sheil. A new subcommittee was formed and the meeting adjourned. Another meeting took place on 21 January at Fitzpatrick's in Capel Street and O'Connell reported on the resolution that had been passed the previous week. There followed an open discussion on the new petition and how it should be transmitted to parliament. There was still considerable support for giving the petition to Donoughmore and Grattan and, despite O'Connell's opposition, this was agreed.

Fingall's involvement with the Catholic question was drawing to an end. His name was used on the notices for a new aggregate meeting of all the Catholics on Tuesday 24 January in Clarendon Street Chapel, even though he opposed its calling.[145] The meeting began shortly after one p.m. with Owen O'Conor, the O'Conor Don, who claimed to be the lineal descendent of the last king of Ireland, temporarily in the chair. Fingall attended the meeting and was offered the chair, but he refused, insisting that he opposed O'Connell's resolution, opposed discussing any matter until a decision from Rome was known, and opposed his name being used to call the meeting. Still he was pressed to take the chair, but still he refused, insisting his mind was fixed. O'Connell rose to speak. Defending his resolution, he reminded everyone that it had been approved many times before and had even been approved by Fingall. In a defiant statement O'Connell insisted that though he wanted unanimity, and had long worked to obtain it, he would 'now disclaim it for ever' if it must be accompanied with this concession.[146] His declaration was unambiguous: 'I will for ever divide with the men who, directly or indirectly, consent to vetoism of any description.' After making this declaration, and knowing there was no way back, O'Connell invited Fingall to take the chair. But he warned Fingall that he was only the head of the Catholics while he remained 'at his natural post'. If he refused, if he chose 'to give our enemies this triumph', then although 'we know his value, and shall regret his refusal, the Irish Catholic people are too great to feel the loss'. Insulted and cornered, Fingall was deeply distressed and again refused to take the chair. He left the assembly, with some friends, seceding again, this time for ever.

In this, the moment of his long-desired victory over the old Catholic aristocracy, O'Connell was not prepared to sit back. After a number of men spoke, he decided to press the point and he delivered a speech full of contempt for Fingall, who he called 'a Catholic nobleman coldly departed from the cause of his children and his country'.[147] Comparing the present secession with the secession in 1792, he joked that sixty-eight men had departed then, whereas now Fingall had taken with him 'just the number of Falstaff's recruits—only three-and-a-half'.[148] There was much laughter. His victory was complete. 'It was at this meeting' that O'Connell established his leadership of the Catholic committee, 'and rendered the question of unqualified emancipation triumphant'.[149] According to one account, Fingall accepted he had been wrong on his death-bed. He admitted that he had been mistaken about O'Connell and now accepted that his 'rough work had mainly assisted in winning for them religious freedom'.[150] But this qualified tribute was more a recognition that O'Connell's methods had succeeded rather than a realisation that they were right.

O'Connell preached unanimity, but he practiced division. At every turn he widened the breach with the seceders, making reconciliation impossible. O'Connell was not just determined to win, he wanted a victory on his own terms. The anti-securities group, which became the core component of the Catholic movement, was forged by the fires of O'Connell's rage and defiance. At a meeting on 23 February 1815 he announced that 'we are for independence, the seceders are for its dependence.'[151] A sense of being abandoned by friends and besieged by enemies was created deliberately and O'Connell did everything he could to encourage the new mentality. Reviewing how the Irish Catholics were treated by 'our friends, and our enemies, and our seceders', he declared that 'the first abandon, the second oppress, the third betray us'.[152] Having eviscerated the old Catholic body, it remained to be seen what O'Connell would achieve with the new one.

Chapter 8

'A BAD BUSINESS': AFFAIRS OF HONOUR, 1815

The affair of the abortive duel with Maurice Magrath continued to exert an influence. It was said that O'Connell had stopped the fight by exclaiming 'with that dramatic pathos in which he had no superior either on the stage or off it "Now I am going to fire at my dearest and best friend".[1] This was a much-modified and embellished version of the story, but if reflected the widespread confusion about what had transpired. Even O'Connell's relatives were uneasy at the manner in which the duel had been resolved. His brother-in-law, Rickard O'Connell, admitted that for two years an 'unfavourable impression' had 'remained fixed on my mind and which I could not divest myself of, relative to the manner in which your affair with Mr Magrath was patched up by that miserable meddler in Catholic affairs'.[2] This gave him 'the most serious uneasiness', presumably about O'Connell's courage. Doubts about O'Connell's courage under fire were also entertained by his enemies. It was believed that he would always back away rather than risk his life. In January 1815 these doubts were tested deliberately and O'Connell was forced to take the field once again to fight a duel. This time there could be no compromise.

Given the aggressive nature of some of O'Connell's speeches, what is surprising here is that the crisis was provoked by something relatively innocuous. Certainly no personal offence had been intended when O'Connell had denounced Dublin corporation, during a speech on the new Catholic petition on Saturday 21 January, as 'a beggarly corporation'. But offence was taken by one member of the corporation, John Norcot D'Esterre. D'Esterre was described as 'a brave, wiry man... skilled in dealing death with cutlass or musket'.[3] He was a former royal marine, and it was said that he had stood firm against the mutineers at Nore in 1797, even when tied up at the yardarm with a halter around his neck. His defiant response was 'Haul away, ye lubbers! Haul away and be damned. God save the king!'[4] The mutineers were said to have been so impressed with his courage that they cut him down and he later escaped. D'Esterre went on to become a merchant and contractor but he was not a good businessman and by 1815 was heavily in debt. Given his precarious finances it is possible that D'Esterre took the reference to 'beggarly' as a personal insult. But it is more likely that he was goaded into a challenge by men who were determined to break the power of O'Connell. D'Esterre was ambitious and saw attacking O'Connell as a good way of escaping his debts and securing advancement, and even achieve his ambition of becoming high sheriff.[5] As the *Irish Magazine* put it, 'D'Esterre imagined he saw fortune beckoning to him through the perforated corpse of O'Connell.'[6] The attacks on Saurin during the Magee trials were a factor too and Saurin's son was one of D'Esterre's supporters. He was also encouraged by Sir Richard Musgrave, the noted Orangeman and historian of the 1798 Rebellion, and Sir Abraham Bradley King, an alderman and former lord mayor. It seemed a guaranteed win. If O'Connell refused to fight he would be branded a coward and lose his standing with the people. If he agreed to fight it played into their hands, for D'Esterre was a noted marksman. It was said that he could 'snuff a candle at twelve paces' and that a gambler would have given odds of 'five to one in his favour'.[7]

D'Esterre wrote to O'Connell on 26 January demanding to know whether he had used the words recounted in *Carrick's Post* three days earlier, language which was 'not warranted or provoked'.[8] Though he had waited three days to write he was now impatient, and he insisted upon a response that evening. Replying the next day, O'Connell neither admitted nor disclaimed the contentious phrase, but explained that because of the 'calumnious manner in which the religion and character of the Catholics of Ireland are treated by that body' he could not hide the 'contemptuous feelings I entertain for that body in its corporate capacity'.[9] O'Connell was not naive and understood what D'Esterre was attempting to arrange. After recognising that the corporation contained 'many valuable persons', he ended the letter sharply, 'this letter must close our correspondence on this subject'. But D'Esterre responded that evening, using a different address from the previous

The home of Daniel O'Connell's parents at Carhen, Co. Kerry, where he was born in 1775. (*Mary Evans Picture Library*)

Hunting Cap (Maurice O'Connell), Daniel's uncle and patron. (*Department of the Environment*)

Drawing of Derrynane, which O'Connell inherited in 1825. (*Mary Evans Picture Library*)

Painting of Derrynane House from the 1830s. (*National Library of Ireland*)

Counseller D. O'Connell

Portrait of O'Connell in the *Dublin Magazine* in September 1810. His wife, Mary, teased him by saying he was 'the image of Prince Le Boo'. (*National Library of Ireland*)

O'Connell's wife, Mary, with their youngest son, Daniel. (*Department of the Environment*)

Portrait of Counsellor O'Connell in the *Dublin Magazine* in March 1813. (*National Library of Ireland*)

This Profile was
taken many years
ago, when o'Connell
was in his prime —
given to me by
Mr Michael Sprull

T. M. Ray
1846

Silhouette profile of O'Connell in his prime as a lawyer, marching to work with an umbrella.
(*National Library of Ireland*)

Representation, of a late unfortunate Duel.

A contemporary engraving of the duel between O'Connell and D'Esterre in February 1815. (*National Library of Ireland*)

SHOOTING OF D'ESTERRE,

O'Connell was upset by this engraving of the duel with D'Esterre which appeared in the *Irish Magazine* in March 1815.

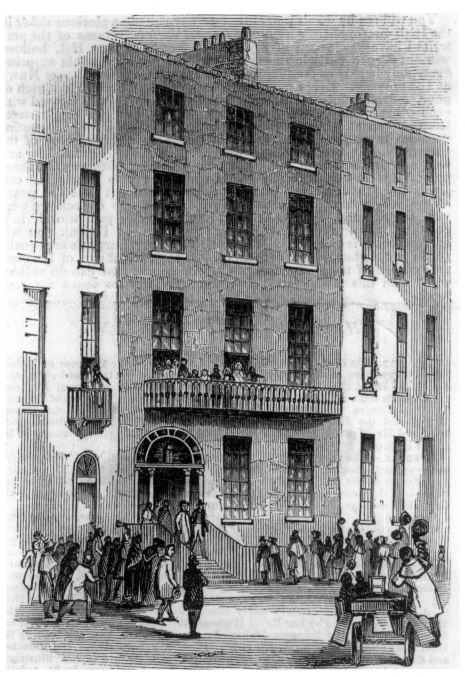

O'Connell's home at 30 (now 58) Merrion Square, Dublin. *(Mary Evans Picture Library)*

Sketch of the Catholic Association, showing Richard Barrett, John Lawless, Richard Sheil (speaking) and Thomas Wyse. (*National Library of Ireland*)

A caricature showing Richard Sheil and O'Connell and commenting on the 'wings', O'Connell's ambitions, and the question of securities. (*The Board of Trinity College Dublin*)

'The Mighty Agitators': a caricature dated August 1828, following O'Connell's victory in the Clare by-election. (*The Board of Trinity College Dublin*)

Caricature dated 17 March 1829, showing O'Connell celebrating with his supporters in London. (*Getty Images*)

Painting by Charles Russell of the centenary celebration of O'Connell's birth, on Sackville (later O'C

Dublin on 6 August 1875. (*Photograph courtesy of the National Gallery of Ireland*)

Statue of Daniel O'Connell on O'Connell Street, Dublin. The statue was designed by John Henry Foley, the leading sculptor of the day, and was unveiled in 1882. (*The Heritage Office, Dublin City Council*)

O'Connell's tomb at Glasnevin Cemetery in Dublin. (*Alamy*)

day's correspondence. This letter was returned opened by O'Connell's brother, James, who said that he had been asked to open his brother's letters in his absence. However 'upon perceiving the name subscribed I have declined to read it and by his directions I return it to you enclosed and *unread*'.[10] O'Connell had deliberately absented himself from his house, following the advice of his friend George Lidwell, a Protestant barrister.[11] He knew that a challenge seemed inevitable. The next day, Saturday 28 January, he called round to his friend Nicholas Purcell O'Gorman, his second for the Magrath affair, to seek his help. O'Gorman was out and O'Connell left a short note. His tone was light: 'My dear Purcell—*This* is perhaps the only moment when you could be of singular use to me.'[12] But was clear that the matter was urgent (the note was endorsed 'haste'), and it ended with O'Connell imploring his friend to let him know when he was back. O'Connell had probably decided in advance, given what had happened with Magrath, to have a different second, though with O'Gorman assisting on the field. He appears to have settled on George Lidwell, but Lidwell was called away to Roscrea on the Monday.[13] It seems a chance meeting with Major William Nugent McNamara, a Protestant friend who was a noted duellist (indeed his nickname was 'Fire-ball'), led O'Connell to ask him to act as his second. It proved an excellent choice as McNamara had plenty of experience of this kind of business and it was said that no-one was 'better versed in the strategics of Irish honour'.[14] He could choose the ground with 'an O'Trigger eye' and had a 'peculiarly scientific genius' when it came to measuring the distance between protagonists, essential when it came to knowing how much grain to load in the pistol. All of this was to prove decisive. O'Connell wrote to his old friend, Richard Newton Bennett, and asked him to join McNamara and O'Gorman on the field if it came to a duel. Bennett rushed to help, lending O'Connell his late uncle's duelling pistols.

But still no challenge came. D'Esterre told his friends that he did not send one because he was afraid that O'Connell would bring legal proceedings against him, but Lidwell sent back a message that O'Connell was 'ready to meet him without a moment's delay'.[15] On Sunday 29 January D'Esterre sent a nasty letter to James O'Connell, who swore he would fight D'Esterre himself after the matter with his brother was resolved. O'Connell himself was astonished that he had not heard in 'the proper way' from D'Esterre.[16] By Monday 30 January nothing further had happened, and Lidwell became convinced that the affair, which had originated 'in folly, and perhaps urged on by party', had been abandoned. In public, however, D'Esterre still boasted about what he would do to O'Connell. In the grand jury room, in front of many members of the corporation, he declared that he would either flog O'Connell on the streets or shoot him.[17]

On Tuesday 31 January D'Esterre set out with a whip to confront O'Connell. He marched to the hall of the Four Courts and made a great noise about being there to horse-whip and humiliate O'Connell. However by the time O'Connell went out to meet him he was gone again. D'Esterre was more interested in creating a public spectacle than confronting O'Connell and went walking along the quays. At three p.m. Richard O'Gorman (Nicholas Purcell O'Gorman's brother) went to meet D'Esterre and carried this message from O'Connell: that he would fight him 'in three minutes whenever he chose'.[18] D'Esterre refused, saying the challenge should come from O'Connell himself. O'Gorman laughed. Upset, D'Esterre insisted that in that case he would horse-whip O'Connell and O'Gorman told him, 'He is a large man, you are a small one, and he may destroy you. Call him out.' But D'Esterre replied, 'The man is a poltroon [a spiritless coward] and will never fight.' O'Gorman got angry: 'I'll undertake to have O'Connell on the ground and, if he fails to fight, I'll take his place.'[19] D'Esterre then marched to College Green, where he was flanked by Saurin's son, Musgrave, and King. The use of the horse-whip was obviously influenced by O'Connell's threat to chastise Saurin and it was clear to the public that larger issues were at stake. Excited crowds gathered to see what would happen next. O'Connell met with Major McNamara and together they went to confront D'Esterre. But when they arrived at College Green at around four p.m. they found that 'the delinquent had fled'.[20] The crowd was so large that O'Connell was unable to make his way home and instead was obliged to take refuge in a house on Exchequer Street. There he was intercepted by Judge Day, who had been sent to arrest him. O'Connell was adamant, 'It is not my duty as a duellist to be the aggressor. I therefore pledge my honour that I shall not be the aggressor.' Day seemed satisfied and bound him to keep the peace on his honour. 'Was there ever such a scene?' wondered O'Connell afterwards. Denys Scully was convinced that 'publicity was the original end and purpose of this aggression' and urged O'Connell to make sure the correct narrative was published in the newspapers.[21]

The affair became pure street theatre. Later, when O'Connell made his way from his house in Merrion Square to the Four Courts, he was pursued at a distance by D'Esterre brandishing his horse-whip. Expectant crowds gathered to see the inevitable collision, but somehow it never came. A journalist writing about the affair a few years later was more cynical: 'The town was dominated by two factions, who traversed the streets in opposite directions, ostensibly in search of one another, but never once contriving to come face to face.'[22] The chamberlain of Dublin Castle, Sir Charles Vernon, was said to have taken a position overlooking the city so that he could follow the show. The two men were described as Homeric heroes, traversing the field for an entire day without collision.[23] This could not continue indefinitely and so at nine a.m. on Wednesday 1 February Sir Edward Stanley, D'Esterre's second, called on O'Connell at his home. Stanley demanded an explanation for O'Connell's conduct during the affair, but O'Connell refused to talk with him, insisting that he visit Major McNamara. This was unexpected and Stanley was unsure how to proceed. He attempted to discuss the matter with O'Connell a second time but left defeated when this failed. For almost three hours Stanley, D'Esterre, and their friends discussed their next move. At noon Stanley finally visited McNamara and demanded an apology on behalf of D'Esterre. But McNamara was insistent that this was 'a waste of words', no apology would be forthcoming.[24] Upon hearing this a formal challenge, at last, was issued. 'Very well,' said McNamara, 'it is my right to appoint a time and place and I fix on this day at three o'clock for the meeting, and Bishop's Court in the county of Kildare as the place.' Expecting to find prevarication, Stanley was astonished at the speed at which things were being arranged. He attempted to postpone the duel until one o'clock the next day, or at least until the next morning, but McNamara refused. Recognising that McNamara was within his rights, Stanley then pressed for a later time that day, after four o'clock, but McNamara would only agree to a postponement until three thirty p.m. They discussed briefly how the duel should be arranged. McNamara told him that since the duellists had no personal quarrel, or any private animosity, it might be sufficient if they each just fired one pistol. Stanley scorned that offer and insisted that even if they exchanged twenty-five shots D'Esterre would never leave the ground until O'Connell had made an apology.

'Well then,' shouted McNamara with a curse, 'if blood be your object, blood you shall have!'[25]

The site of the duel was about twelve miles from the city, at Bishop's Court, near Naas, Co. Kildare. O'Connell's wife was in Dublin at the time, apparently 'in delicate health'.[26] O'Connell kept the entire affair secret from her—'my wife never heard a word of it until I returned from the ground'[27]—and set out with McNamara, Bennett, O'Gorman, Surgeon Macklin, and his brother, James. He was in high spirits, as men sometimes are when they know they might not survive the day. Duels were forbidden by the Catholic church. However, Fr O'Mullane, a rebel priest who was at war with his bishop, went to Bishop's Court and prayed in a nearby cabin, ready to give absolution to O'Connell if he was fatally wounded.[28] O'Connell's carriage arrived at three p.m. A large crowd had gathered at the ground, which was near the foot of a hill, and more were on the hill so they could get a close view. O'Connell recognised a distant relative, Jerry McCarthy, in the crowd and shouted to him, 'Ah, Jerry, I never missed you yet from an aggregate meeting!'[29] D'Esterre was late, his carriage only arriving at four p.m. He also had his supporters in the crowd, though not as many. The son of Alderman Smyth, who was present, was told growing up that close to the entire Dublin corporation attended.[30] Surgeon Peile, the deputy inspector general of the forces, was also there in case D'Esterre required medical treatment. It seems D'Esterre's supporters expected a pitched battle, for many were armed and O'Gorman counted thirty-six pistols. Stanley approached McNamara and discussed postponing the duel. He believed that given the large crowd which had gathered it might not be safe for D'Esterre to fight. But Connell O'Connell, another of Daniel's relatives, was in the crowd and he informed Stanley that, since D'Esterre was the aggressor, if he left the ground without fighting he would expose himself as a coward and a ruffian. This settled the matter. The seconds then discussed the details of the duel, the positioning, mode of firing, and so on. This took forty minutes and D'Esterre took the opportunity to make a speech to the crowd, saying that his quarrel with O'Connell was not of a religious nature and that he had no animosity towards the Catholics.[31] Charles Phillips, the young lawyer who sometimes acted alongside O'Connell, was present. O'Connell took him to one side and told him that this was a political, not a personal affair, and that his enemies had adopted a false pretence to cut him off.[32] But O'Connell revealed that he was 'one of the best shots in Ireland at a mark, having, as a public man, considered it a duty to prepare, for my own protection, against such unprovoked aggression'.[33]

O'Connell and D'Esterre had each brought a case containing two pistols and Bennett loaded O'Connell's. However Stanley had no experience of firearms and asked a friend, Frederick Piers, to load D'Esterre's pistol. Stanley placed D'Esterre on his spot, but McNamara objected, saying that the choice of ground should be determined by tossing a coin.[34] Stanley conceded the point and McNamara won the toss, allowing McNamara to choose O'Connell's position. Handing O'Connell his two pistols, he then attended to some other details. He cast an eye over him looking for any conspicuous items that might help D'Esterre's aim. Seeing some problems, he removed a large bunch of seals from O'Connell's watch-chain (which could injure him if the bullet hit there), and replaced his white cravat with a black stock. Then he proceeded to give O'Connell a series of instructions about how to fight the duel. O'Connell stopped him and said with much solemnity, 'I have one earnest request to make of you.' 'What is it, my dear fellow?' replied McNamara anxiously. 'Let me beg of you', said O'Connell, 'not to say another word to me—until the duel is over.'[35] McNamara stopped talking.

In most duels the combatants waited until a signal was given before firing. But in a previous duel D'Esterre had fired at his man before this signal, and so it was agreed that once the parties were placed on the ground they could fire at their own discretion.[36] Somewhat theatrically, D'Esterre crossed his two pistols on his chest before taking his position.[37] D'Esterre fired first and missed, the bullet entering the ground before O'Connell's feet. O'Connell aimed low and took his shot. The bullet hit D'Esterre. He bent a little on his right leg , turned round, and fell on his face. A loud triumphant cry from the crowd was said to have echoed across the ground. A young student, who later became a Protestant clergyman, was even said to have flung his hat in the air and shouted, 'Huzza for O'Connell.'[38] On the ground D'Esterre complained of a pain in his back. The surgeons rushed to attend to him but were unable to find the bullet; it seems it passed through the bladder to the lower part of his spine. O'Connell made his way back to Dublin. Rumours were rife. It was reported that O'Connell had been killed and a party of dragoons were dispatched to Bishop's Court to protect D'Esterre from any crowd violence. They met O'Connell's carriage leaving Kildare and the officer asked, 'Gentlemen, have you heard anything of a duel that was to take place in this neighbourhood?'[39] 'It is over,' replied McNamara. 'Mr D'Esterre has fallen.' The officer bowed his head, then turned to his men and said 'Right about face.'[40] The dragoons returned to Dublin. D'Esterre lingered for two days before dying at five p.m. on 3 February, apparently exculpating O'Connell from any blame with his last breath.

The duel answered, at least in the short term, the questions about O'Connell's bravery. Writing about the duel a few years later, a journalist noted that O'Connell had not lacked courage. He paraphrased Madame de Stael on Napoleon: 'Of death itself he had no fear; but death would have been a reverse, and to reverses of every kind he had a decided objection.'[41] There was much speculation about how D'Esterre, a noted marksman and fire-eater, could have lost. One interpretation blamed Frederick Piers, the man who had loaded his pistols. It was said that he had been too sparing of the gunpowder and the shot had therefore lacked distance. Others said that, in his haste to fire first, D'Esterre had fired too soon, before his pistol was at the right level.[42] Charles Dickens' magazine, *Household Words*, later had this to say: 'O'Connell and D'Esterre—a bad business with hints of not quite fair play on the part of the seconds.'[43] Nothing further was written in the magazine to explain this extraordinary claim. It was probably a reference to a popular belief that D'Esterre had been badly served by his inexperienced second, Stanley, who was said to have unknowingly placed him at a disadvantage, 'in a line with a tree, which afforded direction to his adversary's aim'.[44]

'The ground was white with snow and the oil lamps dimly burning when O'Connell and his brother returned in solemn silence to Dublin.'[45] Finally O'Connell spoke: 'I fear he is dead, he fell so suddenly.'[46] His companions wondered where D'Esterre had been hit and speculated that it had been a head wound. But O'Connell disagreed: 'That cannot be—I aimed low. The ball must have entered near the thigh.' His diagnosis was correct. O'Connell was a good shot, even under pressure. Indeed it was said that 'he could have hit his antagonist where he pleased'.[47] He told his brother to visit Daniel Murray, Archbishop Troy's coadjutor, and express his deep regret for what had happened. When told the news, Murray is alleged to have exclaimed, 'Heaven be praised! Ireland is safe!'[48] There remained a risk of arrest. Fearing being apprehended, O'Connell stayed away from his house at Merrion Square and went instead to the home of Denys Scully. He told his brother to visit the barrister Richard Pennefather, a Protestant, and retain him for his defence in case he was prosecuted. Writing to tell his wife everything, he apologised for the 'momentary absence' but reassured her that although the cause was to be regretted, it 'will purchase years of safety'.[49] Seven hundred men called to the house on Merrion Square to show their support; learning that O'Connell was absent they left their cards.[50] On 4 February O'Connell's mind was eased. Sir Edward Stanley wrote to reassure him that 'there is not the most distant intention of any prosecution whatever, on the part of the family or friends of the late Mr D'Esterre.'[51] Grateful for the communication, O'Connell replied that 'no person can feel for the loss society has sustained in the death of Mr D'Esterre with more deep and lasting sorrow than I do.'[52] Concerned for D'Esterre's widow, O'Connell contacted her and offered, in his own words, 'to share his income with her', meaning some form of annuity, apparently £150 per annum.[53] She refused, but he did persuade D'Esterre's daughter to accept an annuity and he paid this until his death. It was said that whenever O'Connell passed D'Esterre's house on Bachelor's Walk he raised his hat and said a prayer.[54] Watty Cox's *Irish Magazine* covered the duel in March 1815 and O'Connell was furious with the treatment, even though it reported that 'the ruffian was the victim of his own bloody speculations'.[55] He was upset by the engraving of the duel which showed a very short distance between the men and O'Connell standing over the body of D'Esterre with a smile on his face.[56] Few read anything into the illustration. Instead the duel enhanced O'Connell's standing in the country. He was the champion of the people, who had vanquished the Protestant assassin sent to kill him.

On the night of the duel, O'Connell's thoughts returned to the agitation for Catholic relief. He began planning the creation of a new Catholic organisation, which became the Catholic Association (distinct from the Catholic Association formed in 1823), with a loose organisation to avoid the provisions of the Convention Act. This Association met for the first time on 4 February 1815. An aggregate meeting of the Catholics had agreed to send a new petition to

Donoughmore and Grattan, but while the former agreed to present it in parliament, the latter gave an ambivalent response. O'Connell pressed that Sir Henry Parnell should be given the petition to present, and this was agreed by the Catholic Association's committee on 23 April 1815.[57] The legality of the new association was being challenged. Before the Westmeath grand jury in March 1815 Judge Day blamed the association for encouraging disturbances and said that in his opinion it was an illegal body.[58] Parnell presented the petition in favour of full emancipation in the House of Commons on 11 May and spoke on Catholic claims in 18 May. However his motion that the House would go into a committee on the Catholic claims was defeated by 228 to 147 on 30 May.[59] A section of the press blamed O'Connell and the hard-line leadership of the Catholics for the defeat.[60] Despite the setback, O'Connell remained confident that emancipation would soon be won.

Securities again became an issue. After all O'Connell had done to secure agreement on the issue, even to the extent of splitting the Catholic leadership, he was now willing to compromise. He was so anxious to secure emancipation, and so optimistic that it might be won soon, he suggested to Parnell that, if a relief bill was passed, a deal might be done on securities afterwards. He would not accept a relief bill accompanied by securities—such a bill 'we would one and all oppose'.[61] However 'if the bill be *first* carried' he promised there would be 'no popular opposition to the arrangement' of the securities. This was an extraordinary U-turn, but O'Connell claimed that the critical state of Ireland persuaded him to go further than 'my principles could justify at any other period'. In part this was spin, such as O'Connell's claim that agitators like himself did not 'direct the popular sentiment', they merely echoed it. But he also seems to have been prepared to compromise because he thought full emancipation was within reach. He was so confident of success that he even began discussing ways of reforming the Irish administration. For example he suggested promoting the lord chancellor to remove him from office, replacing him with McMahon, the Master of the Rolls. Saurin could then take McMahon's place, removing him from politics. However O'Connell was still insistent that if securities were part of a relief bill it would 'never, never be accepted'.[62] And he revealed that any Irish priest who was suspected of vetoism lost all respect.

Having already dispatched Fingall, O'Connell went after Grattan at an aggregate meeting on Thursday 16 June held at Clarendon Street Chapel. O'Connell was furious that Grattan had refused the request of his constituents: 'Thus, then, has Mr Grattan finally rejected you.'[63] O'Connell reflected on Grattan's career, 'his early and his glorious struggles for Ireland. I know he raised her from degradation and exalted her to her rank as a nation.'[64] And he praised him for his brave struggle to prevent Ireland being degraded to 'a pitiful province'. 'My gratitude and enthusiasm for those services will never be extinguished,' he insisted. But he suggested that since Grattan had moved to Westminster he had been diminished. Cruelly applying a quote Grattan had famously deployed against his great rival, Henry Flood, he said that 'he was an oak of the forest, too old to be transplanted.' O'Connell blamed 'the foul and corrupt atmosphere that fills some of the avenues to Westminster' for this decline. As a result, 'He has since the Union made no exertions worthy of his name and of his strength.'

O'Connell's problems with his finances were again causing problems. His wife was concerned that his spending was out of control and extracted promises that he would not lend money rashly. In March 1815 she was angered when she discovered he had decided to act as security for James O'Leary, even though he had given a specific promise that he wouldn't. James O'Connell unwittingly confirmed the story and O'Connell was furious with his brother for interfering. At the assizes in Limerick, O'Connell was distraught when he received a harsh letter from his wife; he was so upset that he destroyed it, as he did any letters from her that hurt his feelings. Admitting that he had cried for two hours after reading it, he swore that it was 'a loose and idle suspicion'. 'Darling,' he reassured her, 'you have no cause for your misery. Did I ever deceive you?'[65] But this was a lie. He had been persuaded by John Hickson, an unreliable friend, to support O'Leary and had entered into an arrangement with Pim's Merchants in William Street, Dublin.[66] It was not only his wife who had warned him against O'Leary. Hunting Cap believed that O'Leary's extravagant lifestyle would cause him to 'snap' and gave O'Connell strict instructions not to help him in any way.[67] Mary had a right to be worried as her finances were exhausted.[68] She was living in Dublin and struggled to meet the debts incurred running the household. On occasion she was obliged to borrow money from James O'Connell.[69] Believing her husband, she apologised for upsetting him over the O'Leary affair. O'Connell was also apologetic and told her that 'there never, *never, never* was a man so blessed in a wife. You are everything my most anxious heart could desire or even imagine'.[70] At the assizes O'Connell was having better results. He had been retained by the prosecution in Limerick, but then dismissed when the prosecutors decided they could do without him. However the prisoner then employed O'Connell and 'by my exertions *alone* I got him *easily* acquitted'.[71]

The escape of Napoleon from Elba was occupying O'Connell's thoughts. Despite his criticism of Napoleon in some public speeches the truth is that he was a great admirer. He was excited by the news and admitted he could 'scarce draw my breath'.[72] Updates were eagerly awaited: 'Good God, how I die with impatience for the next packet.' O'Connell's wife shared his enthusiasm, and grew worried in early April when it it was reported the allies were closing in on Napoleon. But O'Connell was not concerned. He believed that an attack would 'only tend to consolidate the great man's power'.[73] Full of praise, he noted that 'his popularity with the French people is the most glorious and extraordinary of his achievements.' Waterloo crushed O'Connell's hopes. Upon hearing the news he was 'horribly out of spirits' and he noted dejectedly that liberty had been for ever crushed in France.[74] In July 1823 O'Connell had dinner with Dr O'Meara, Napoleon's surgeon on St Helena, and he enjoyed hearing first-hand stories of 'the unfortunate great man'.[75] The defeat of Napoleon at Waterloo resulted in the suicide of Samuel Whitbread, one of the leading British opposition MPs and a great friend of emancipation. O'Connell mourned his death. 'Well, well, fate seems strangely perverse,' he said, unable to mask his despair. 'The scoundrels of society have now every triumph.' He used the same phrase in 1820 about the defeat of Napoleon when he attacked the way 'the scoundrels of society enjoyed the battle of Waterloo'.[76]

More popular than ever, O'Connell was hailed as the champion of the people. He spoke at a meeting in Cork on 9 August 1815 and afterwards the enthusiastic crowd wanted to carry him through the street. O'Connell escaped their attentions by using a ladder to climb to an adjoining yard.[77] The success of the duel had made him reckless and in a speech at the Catholic aggregate meeting of 29 August 1815 he delivered an intemperate attack on the chief secretary, Robert Peel. Peel had been highly critical of O'Connell in a recent speech and O'Connell decided to respond, but he did so in such a goading and aggressive manner that it is difficult to see it as anything other than a deliberate provocation. Aware that police informers were present, O'Connell called on them to report back these words, 'that Mr Peel would not DARE, in my presence, or in any place where he was liable to personal account, use a single expression derogatory to my interest, or my honour.'[78] Dismissing him as nothing more than 'the champion of Orangeism', he said, 'I have done with him, perhaps for ever.' In the language of the day this was tantamount to calling Peel a coward, and O'Connell left himself open to a response. Having recently killed a man in a duel it might have been expected that O'Connell would act cautiously, for a short time at least, but he seemed to be actively anticipating another challenge.

Peel was not O'Connell's only target. He went on to richly abuse Thomas Elrington, the provost of Trinity College Dublin, who he said had only been promoted because of a pamphlet he had written against the Catholics. 'But did anyone ever read the pamphlet through?'[79] O'Connell laughed that the 'most malignant sentence' he could pronounce on an enemy would be 'to condemn him to the reading, distinctly and without omission, the entire of that pamphlet. Human nature, I fear, could not bear it.'

Elrington was never likely to respond, but Peel was a different matter. He understood the nature of the insult that had been given and knew that it required action. Honour—as well as reputation—was at stake and he immediately employed his friend Sir Charles Saxton, under-secretary at Dublin Castle and MP for Cashel, to act as his second if an apology was not forthcoming. O'Connell enlisted his friend, George Lidwell, to act for him. A duel seemed inevitable. Saxton called on Lidwell twice on Friday 1 September, but he was not home. However the purpose of the meeting was clear and Lidwell urged O'Connell to have horses ready to take him to a field in Celbridge, Co. Kildare, which Lidwell would appoint as the site of the duel.[80] The duel was likely to take place that very day, although O'Connell would have preferred it the next morning. However he told Lidwell, 'Just do as you please.'[81]

But for some reason the arrangements for the duel were not made. Peel and Saxton blamed Lidwell and published a highly condemnatory account of the affair in the *Correspondent* the next evening, Saturday 2 September. This prompted Lidwell to proffer his own challenge to

Saxton, ruling both men out as seconds. The two men later met at Calais. Saxton fired and missed and Lidwell discharged his own pistol in the air.[82] O'Connell's reputation was at stake and he sent a letter to the editor of *Carrick's Post* on 3 September attacking Peel's 'paltry trick' in rushing to print to denounce his tardiness after just one day of discussion. O'Connell accused Saxton of inventing quotes for the newspaper and ended with a defiant statement: 'I have disavowed nothing; I have refused the gentleman nothing. I have only to regret that they have ultimately preferred a paper war.'[83]

The publication of this letter on the evening of Monday 4 September further enraged Peel. Furious at the mention of 'a paltry trick', he contacted O'Connell directly at six p.m. requesting that he would make arrangements with Colonel Samuel Brown, his new second, for an immediate duel.[84] O'Connell acted immediately and arranged for his cousin, Baldwin, to visit Brown at eight p.m. to confirm that the duel would take place. At nine p.m. O'Connell wrote to Richard Newton Bennett, who was near Castle Carbury, Co. Kildare, begging him to come to him '*instanter*'.[85] But O'Connell was aware that Bennett might not be able to arrive in time, and so thought of the knight of Kerry and Major McNamara as alternatives. The same night he wrote to the knight of Kerry asking him to take Lidwell's place as his second: 'I want a friend most sadly and venture to think of you.'[86] The knight of Kerry agreed.

As with the D'Esterre duel, O'Connell kept the entire matter secret from his wife. At this time his uncle, General O'Connell, was staying with him at Merrion Square. He was on a long visit home, accompanied by his step-daughter, Aimée de Bellevue. During this visit he resolved to leave his entire fortune to the younger sons of O'Connell and O'Connell's brother, John, and when he returned to France he rid himself of all unnecessary expenses so that they would have a decent inheritance.[87] General O'Connell opposed duelling, but he knew that his nephew had to fight and he knew that to refuse brought with it disgrace. O'Connell and his uncle discussed the arrangements for the duel in French, changing to Irish if someone who knew French came into the room.[88] This made O'Connell's wife suspicious and she guessed from the exchange in the newspapers that another duel was being arranged. Determined to prevent it, she sent word about the duel to the sheriff that night. On the morning of Tuesday 5 September two constables arrived at the house to take O'Connell temporarily into custody. General O'Connell was furious when he discovered Mary O'Connell's intervention. Rebuking her over breakfast, he said, 'Mary, this is the only time in my life I ever was angry with you, and you have made me very angry.' 'I am sorry to have annoyed you, uncle,' she replied, 'but I would much sooner vex you than let my husband be killed.'[89] This unexpected turn prevented the duel being arranged for that day. Hearing nothing, Colonel Brown grew impatient and at seven o'clock that evening wrote to O'Connell to criticise 'the impropriety of any delay in a case of so much delicacy'.[90] O'Connell replied within the hour explaining his wife's actions and how he would 'at the first possible moment' arrange the details with Brown.[91] The duel was delayed until O'Connell found a way to extricate himself from his wife's attentions.

A trip to the continent seemed the only way of avoiding the watchful eye of Mrs O'Connell and a second arrest. The duel was arranged to take place in Ostend. In the meantime O'Connell continued with the Catholic agitation and at a meeting of the Catholic Association on 8 September he moved to send a deputation to the pope to secure a pledge on the veto. A committee of seven was appointed to collect subscriptions in parishes to defray the deputation's expenses. O'Connell then set out with his wife to Killarney, ostensibly on legal business, but really so that he could leave her there, 'tranquil and unsuspicious', while he went with his brother, James, to Waterford to catch a boat to England.[92] He had arranged to meet Bennett there, but Bennett had not arrived by Wednesday 13 September, and O'Connell left him a message to get directions at the Spring Garden Coffee House. Bennett arrived before the boat left that evening and O'Connell and his friends debated whether they should travel under false names. However this was rejected for 'many reasons', and in particular because they did not believe any attempt would be made to intercept them.

Lord Norbury had once said that the first thing heard about a duel should be the sound of the pistols firing. But this duel had already raised far too much noise. This was not surprising. Peel was the chief secretary for Ireland, while O'Connell was the people's champion. O'Connell and Bennett arrived at Milford on Thursday 14 September, where their names were 'carefully inquired after and taken down'.[93] 'What was this done for?' he wondered, before deciding 'No matter.'

They travelled through Wales on the Friday and Saturday and planned
to reach London, to be joined by Lidwell, on Sunday 17 September.
From there they would travel to Dover to catch a boat to Calais, and
from there make their way to Ostend. O'Connell was full of high spirits:
'There never was such a battle. Waterloo was nothing to it.' He was
confident that victory was inevitable: 'I cannot bring myself even to
doubt success.' And he believed the real importance of the duel was not
the result, but the contest itself, the confrontation between government
and the people. There was something new and disturbing in
O'Connell's attitude, and he seemed to be enjoying the danger.

The duel did not get any further than England. As soon as he arrived
in London, Lidwell was arrested. A police spy had travelled on the
carriage with him. O'Connell escaped and hid until the morning of
Tuesday 19 September, when he boarded a carriage to Dover. But as
soon as he set foot on it he was arrested by a magistrate, Sir Nathaniel
Conant.[94] A warrant had been issued based on information provided
by Dublin Castle officials and it was made clear to O'Connell that he
would be prosecuted if he killed Peel, and vice versa, with 'a certain
execution in case of a conviction'.[95] This brought the affair to an end.
There was no way of proceeding. The government had gone to great
lengths to prevent the duel and it was claimed that a hundred
constables were on the Dover coast to arrest O'Connell if he made it
that far; some had apparently even gone to Calais, where they had
broken into a man's room in search of him. This seems more like
rumour than reality, but it was indicative of the interest the affair had
generated. Much can be read into O'Connell's belief that he had been
cheated: 'What a glorious opportunity have they deprived me of—
living or dying—but regret is vain.'[96] O'Connell was furious that so
much trouble had been taken to apprehend him, when Peel had been
allowed to travel unimpeded. But he realised that he could not now be
accused of cowardice: they had done 'all in their power to give the
gentlemen a meeting'.[97] He realised that he would have to tell his wife
the truth, and he decided reluctantly to write a long letter, asking his
brother, James, to prepare her for the news before she read it. In later
years, O'Connell came to regret his behaviour in this affair. 'The heat of
blood', he later accepted, and 'the vanity of a criminal obedience to a
more than criminal custom' had blinded his judgement.[98]

Despite her good intentions, Mary O'Connell had endangered her husband by stopping the duel in Dublin. Afterwards, when Lidwell advised O'Connell to tell her everything, he reflected on the danger. He realised that he had been very lucky that she had not suspected anything the second time, because if she had tried to stop the duel again she would only have succeeded in making him a target. All his enemies would have been encouraged to send him a challenge, knowing that they were safe to do so, and he would have been 'destroy(ed) for ever'.[99] Many men, then and now, would have been furious with their wife for interfering in such a public way and for leaving them open to ridicule. But O'Connell seems to have accepted his wife's actions and was more concerned with securing her forgiveness. Thus he attempted to win her sympathy by telling her about his journey home. On the crossing back to Dublin he was 'sick as a dog' on the cabin floor, 'with three gentlemen's legs on my breast and stomach, and the sea after dripping in on my knees and feet'.[100] This, he told her, made him feel 'completely punished'. During a visit to Hunting Cap the next month, O'Connell received a stern lecture, or as he called it 'a great rating from the old man', almost certainly about the business with Peel.[101] O'Connell 'promised to be a good boy in future'.

Chapter 9

DEBTS AND DESPAIR,
1816–1820

James O'Leary was declared bankrupt on 9 January 1816. This had been coming for some months and O'Connell was swept up in his failure. His foolish agreement to act as security now came back to haunt him. It is not clear how much O'Connell owed, but he admitted it was enough to ruin him and make 'a beggar' of his wife and children.[1] His brother, James, offered to help, and together they tried to raise the money. General O'Connell was persuaded to lend £3,600 to assist O'Connell with the O'Leary debt.[2] James was furious with O'Connell for having been taken advantage of so easily and told him that his 'too sanguine disposition' made him hope for 'some ideal *good* that may never occur'.[3] There was a further problem. O'Connell was terrified that Hunting Cap would hear that he had helped O'Leary. Hunting Cap had given O'Connell strict instructions on the subject and the exposure would have created another breach, perhaps irreparable, between the men. And if O'Connell was disinherited a second time there would be no hope of escaping his debts.

So how bad were O'Connell's finances? James O'Connell compiled a list of O'Connell's debts, or at least the ones he knew about, in 1817, and he concluded that £20,000 was probably 'a very low estimate'.[4] Given that O'Connell's income from legal fees was almost £4,000 in 1814, the scale of his indebtedness is clear.[5] O'Connell owed more than five times his annual professional income, and even though he owned land it was estimated that it would barely pay the enormous debt he owed if sold.[6] This land gave him an additional income of between £1,500 and £2,000 a year.[7] James calculated that his brother would have to use all this income just to pay the interest on his debts, and he was incredulous that O'Connell seemed to believe that within two years they would somehow all be discharged. The money was owed to a long list of creditors, £500 here, £200 there, with the largest amounts owed to General O'Connell (£3,600) and Denys Scully (£2,274). In addition he had borrowed £300 from his sister, Ellen, £100 from his mother, and £130 from Hunting Cap's clerk. The total came to £18,699 and James was also aware that O'Connell had borrowed £500 from a Limerick bank. Given that these were only the debts he had discovered, James despaired that the actual total was probably greater than £20,000.

So how on earth had he amassed such debts? In part it was because of serious financial misjudgements, such as acting as security for James O'Leary (a mistake that probably necessitated a number of the loans). For someone who was so shrewd in the courtroom and the political arena, he was remarkably naive when it came to the world of business. William Drennan, the former United Irishman, once told O'Connell that he possessed many of the characteristics of Charles James Fox, including his gullibility.[8] In his private life O'Connell was extravagant with money. He lived like an old tribal chieftain, offering hospitality to one and all, and in 1822 he reproached himself for 'that loose and profligate waste of money to many an ungrateful and undeserving object' which he blamed for his problems.[9] He knew that he would inherit land and a large sum of money when Hunting Cap died and this made him reckless. Knowing this money would come someday, he felt justified in paying for everything on credit. He later admitted that he went into debt 'on that speculation'.[10] Occasionally he wished for the death of his uncle, though he would regret bitterly these 'criminal' thoughts. Hiding his difficulties as best he could, he concealed his indebtedness from his wife, probably until 1822.

To maintain his status in society O'Connell spent widely and only too well. The house in Merrion Square and a carriage costing £500 were just part of the conspicuous consumption.[11] Other debts were a result of his political agitation. The Catholic cause was often close to bankruptcy in the 1810s. O'Connell kept it afloat, sometimes using his own money to pay for the meeting rooms and the other general costs. O'Connell personally paid for the rooms at Capel Street and when these proved too expensive moved to a smaller place at Crow Street.[12]

This was one of the most difficult periods in his life, he later told his children, as he faced an increasingly apathetic public and crippling financial debts.[13] On more than one occasion his wife had to plead with him, 'I *want* money, love.'[14]

In the middle of his financial crisis, O'Connell underwent a spiritual conversion. He had returned to the Catholic faith some years earlier, or at least for a short time, but this was something deeper and more sincere. Coming so soon after the killing of D'Esterre and the abortive duel with Peel it seems certain that there was a connection. O'Connell approached the Rev. F.J. L'Estrange, of the Order of Discalced Carmelites, at St Teresa's, Clarendon Street, Dublin, and began receiving religious instruction. L'Estrange would serve as his spiritual advisor for many years and would often accompany him on his travels. When a German nobleman visited O'Connell at Derrynane in 1828 he described L'Estrange as 'the ideal of a well-intentioned Jesuit'.[15] He was impressed by his 'philosophical mind and unalterable calmness' and said that his 'mildness cannot always conceal the sharp traces of great astuteness'. Mary was delighted with the news of the conversion and O'Connell himself admitted that he felt 'beyond any comparison happier in *this* change', hoping that it would 'prove complete'.[16] O'Connell's children were delighted by the news: Maurice 'thanked God with his hands clasped for your *conversion*'.[17] The outward manifestation of the conversion was a change in devotional practice. O'Connell became publicly devout, observing Lenten and Friday obligations and praying and attending mass regularly. Internal manifestations of the change are harder to gauge and while it did not affect his speeches (which were as aggressive as ever), he turned his back on duelling and from this time on began to express deep remorse over the killing of D'Esterre. He publicly avowed that he would never again consider 'what are called points of honour' and 'most heartily wish[ed] I never had'.[18] There was, he was convinced, 'a higher duty than any worldly notions which forbids that practice'. In later years, when O'Connell was accused of lacking courage by some newspapers, his public response was 'Would to heaven that in escaping with my own life I had not given a too sad but convincing proof that I did not want courage!'[19]

'What an absurd as well as criminal thing duelling is,' O'Connell exclaimed in 1824.[20] And yet he was almost drawn into another duel at the end of 1817. At a meeting of the Catholic Board on 4 December he insulted John Leslie Foster, a member of the British parliament, and Foster demanded an apology. None was forthcoming, so Foster issued a challenge. O'Connell backed down, issuing a statement that his comments were only directed at Foster's public character and this was accepted.[21] Care was taken that Hunting Cap did not hear of the conflict as he disapproved both of O'Connell's aggressive speeches and his duelling. Given O'Connell's finances this would have been disastrous; he stood to gain a large property and an estimated income of £4,000 a year when his uncle died.[22]

It took an incredible family effort to save O'Connell 'from [financial] *destruction*' in this period.[23] Despite great misgivings, James agreed to mortgage some of his land to save his brother. This, he admitted, made him 'exquisitely miserable' as he was no longer master of his time or his property. He also knew that Hunting Cap would disinherit him if the transaction was revealed. Full of bitterness for having been dragged into the affair, he told Daniel that he believed his 'prospects in life were for ever blasted'. He was disgusted with Daniel and rebuked him for involving him 'in the ruin you have been so long preparing for your amiable wife and interesting family'. His other brother, John, intervened to help and joined with James to give Daniel a loan of £1,700.[24] Great care was taken to ensure that Hunting Cap did not hear about O'Connell's dealings with O'Leary. The story of O'Leary's failure was first-class gossip in Kerry and its details were well known, with Daniel's involvement widely discussed. O'Connell's sister, Ellen, saved him. She positioned two men at Derrynane to intercept visitors and instruct them to refrain from mentioning the matter.[25]

When Lent began in 1816 O'Connell chose for the first time to engage in serious fasting. He avoided breakfast and refused to eat meat on abstinence days. Indeed he took to the matter with such zeal that his wife began to worry for his health, especially when he was ill on a number of nights. She ordered him to 'to give up fasting should you in the slightest degree find it disagrees with you'.[26] Years later O'Connell admitted, sheepishly, that he had drunk too much wine on these occasions, believing it was 'additional nourishment', and that this was responsible for making him ill.[27] As for him missing breakfast, his wife was uncomfortable with the idea of him spending all day in court (possibly from nine in the morning until ten at night) without eating anything. But O'Connell had the zeal of a convert and insisted that, although occasionally a little fatigued, fasting agreed with him perfectly. And he reassured her that on abstinence days he ate 'an enormous dinner of fish'.[28] When Lent came to an end he claimed that he 'hardly knew the taste of meat'.[29] Mary joked that he was now 'the better *Christian*' and that she would have to follow his example: 'The times are changed.'[30]

O'Connell's legal career was thriving. At the Ennis assizes in 1816 he boasted that his business was 'far beyond that of any other barrister'.[31] He was proud that he was 'without any rival at the head of this circuit'. Two hundred guineas were earned, even though it hadn't been a great circuit, and O'Connell promised his wife that this would 'work over the difficulties into which my most absurd credulity involved me'.[32] Judges were still being greeted with barely concealed contempt. O'Connell had little time for Judge Mayne, a justice of the common pleas, even though he was able to persuade him to 'agree perfectly' with him. As far as O'Connell was concerned, Mayne was '*an animal*, easily managed', and he enjoyed 'laughing at him by the hour'.[33]

In August 1816 O'Connell took part in the celebrated 'Nosegay' libel trial. John Philpot Curran, though retired, had also indicated that he would take part, but in the event did not attend. 'What a wavering inconsistent fellow!' exclaimed O'Connell.[34] Curran had probably declined because his health was failing and he died a few months later, in October. O'Connell was saddened and wrote: 'What a man has Ireland lost!'[35] He claimed that Curran's 'very soul was republican Irish' and he praised his courageous stands in 1778, 1782, 1798 and again during the Union, in other words, 'at all times, in all places'.

The 'Nosegay' case was taken by George Evans Bruce, a Limerick banker, against Thomas Grady, a barrister, over a scurrilous poem he had published called 'The Nosegay'. The men had once been friends but had fallen out over a loan. Bruce asked for £20,000 in damages, claiming that the poem had damaged his reputation.[36] Certainly the poem was scandalous, and included a suggestion that Bruce had incestuous relations with his sister, though in reality the relationship had been with his sister-in-law.[37] Thomas Goold was leading counsel for the plaintiff and spoke for three hours and three quarters, 'an excellent speech... but very tedious'.[38] O'Connell acted for the defence and spoke for an hour and a half, in what he thought was 'my best speech I think'. Never one to downplay the significance of anything he was involved in, O'Connell declared to the jury that it was 'a case of more importance in every result, whether social, moral, or constitutional, than any case that he ever remembered in this or the sister country'.[39] O'Connell mocked Goold for claiming the 'highest lineage' for George Evans Bruce and joked that 'I suppose he claims a descent from Robert Bruce'.[40] And he was defiant in his claims that he would prove the allegations in the poem, insisting that Bruce was 'a detected cheat in 1786', 'a defiler of his sister's bed in 1793' (she became pregnant and gave birth to a boy, Tommy Black), 'a tampering traitor in 1794', 'a pimp in 1804', and 'a usurer in 1807'. The *Limerick Evening Post* reporter was swept away by this attack and said that O'Connell's 'humour, wit and nervous eloquence were equal to anything we ever heard from the distinguished orator'.[41] The next day the jury awarded Bruce £500 with sixpence costs and O'Connell, pleased with the result, thought it was a 'shabby enough' sum.[42]

At the Galway assizes in March 1817 O'Connell claimed 'a complete triumph' after winning all of his cases.[43] On court days during Lent he continued to fast, going from morning until nine or ten at night without eating. His wife continued to worry about his health, but he reassured her that he was never 'in better health or spirits'.[44] In any case he claimed to have 'grown too fat' and said he would 'be quite a monster' if he ate at mid-day as his wife suggested.

Mary gave birth to a boy called Daniel on 22 August 1817.[45] O'Connell was delighted and said that, despite long hours in the courtroom, he 'never was better or in *half* such spirits'.[46] But anonymous letters began arriving again to threaten his domestic happiness. The letters were sent from Limerick and addressed to O'Connell. Although not extant, the letters were obviously malicious, and Mary believed the writer was 'insane'.[47] O'Connell claimed that the writer was Tom Codd, who had tormented him for years, but his explanation is not convincing.[48] Another letter arrived on 16 October and Mary became certain that the writer was the Bristol correspondent of 1812.[49] Despite the allegations in the letters, Mary was not too worried and she told O'Connell that he should not 'suffer the slightest uneasiness on *this* subject'.[50] She reassured him that 'the machinations of *our anonymous friend* have not lessened my confidence in you.' Ending her letter with a joke, she said that she would say no more until she saw him and then she would 'scold' him well. Feeling under pressure, O'Connell did not see the humour in the situation and reacted badly, writing an angry response which Mary said was 'the first *serious* letter I ever got from you' and which made her feel like a scolded child.[51]

Sometime during 1817 O'Connell fell ill with fever, after having been soaked after spending eight hours on a sailing vessel which was attempting to land at Caernarvon harbour. He was forced to rest at Capelcarrig, where he became very ill, and worried that if his life was threatened there was not a Catholic priest nearby.[52]

The seceders and the anti-seceders were still competing for the soul of the Catholic nation. On 13 February 1816 the seceders adopted a petition declaring that the Catholics of Ireland were willing to accept a qualified emancipation, in other words with securities.[53] This petition was circulated throughout the country for signatures and was then given to Henry Grattan to present in parliament. A rival petition was adopted by the Catholic Association calling for unqualified emancipation and was also in circulation. At a large meeting of the Limerick Catholics on 23 March 1816, O'Connell spoke in favour of resolutions condemning the veto and the seceders' petition. Similar resolutions were passed at a meeting of the Cork Catholics, which O'Connell attended, on 19 April 1816.[54] Having two separate Catholic petitions was hardly likely to strengthen the cause, or go down well in Britain where the split was barely understood. O'Connell himself admitted that the Catholic cause had been almost fatally undermined by the divisions in 1816.[55]

On 29 November a meeting of Catholic gentlemen was held at D'Arcy's Globe Tavern, on Essex Street in Dublin. At this O'Connell proposed preparing an address to the people of England, and this was accepted.[56] There was another meeting on 17 December, held at the Clarendon Street Chapel. It was agreed that the Catholic petition of 1812, which had been signed by Fingall and the seceders, should be readopted and presented to parliament. O'Connell wanted to pass a resolution calling for parliamentary reform, but there was not much support and he withdrew it for the sake of unanimity.[57] O'Connell was thinking a great deal about broadening his agitation. He was involved in the founding of the 'Friends of Reform in Parliament' on 13 January 1817, a body established to prepare petitions and spread information on parliamentary reform.[58] Membership was five shillings a year, but only about forty people (Catholics and Protestants) joined, and after a few meetings and dinners it came to an end.

In the spring of 1817 the seceders decided to petition the prince regent and a meeting was organised for No. 50 Eccles Street on 4 February to arrange the details. Admittance was limited by a resolution which declared that only those involved in sending the previous year's petition to Grattan could attend.[59] A loud knock at the hall door interrupted the meeting. The chairman looked embarrassed, but no one moved. 'The knock was both loud and long and terminated in a climax of sound. A general presentiment seemed to pervade the assembly, that there was but one person who would have the audacity to demand admittance in that manner.'[60] The secretary ran to the staircase to see who it was and then returned to his seat, whispering nervously to the chairman. The door opened and O'Connell and some friends walked in.

It was said that it would have required the pencil of a Hogarth to capture the scene.[61] Impatient, vexed men glared at O'Connell with barely concealed distaste. Lord Southwell asked the men to leave, reminding them of the notice in the hall that limited admittance. But O'Connell refused, saying that he would certainly not leave. In typical O'Connell style he then went on the attack. In a 'haughty tone' he interrogated them about why 'they dared to take upon themselves to act for the Catholics of Ireland' while at the same time excluding from the meetings those that were 'their superiors in every attribute'.[62] Sir Edward Bellew moved to adjourn the meeting, claiming that they were being treated with disrespect. But O'Connell opposed him and after a long debate the motion was withdrawn.[63] Bellew then proposed two motions, one of which called on Grattan to present their petition in parliament. This gave O'Connell an opportunity to deliver a lecture on the problems he had identified in the Catholic cause. The key problem, he believed, was the public divisions and dissentions, which had been responsible for 'the weakness and imbecility of the Catholic cause last year'. There was general agreement here. O'Connell suggested establishing a committee, composed of seceders and non-seceders (but not including himself), to meet and discuss a way of putting aside their differences and reuniting. But this was voted down by fourteen votes to four; only the seceders were allowed vote. Upon hearing the result, O'Connell rose and said that he had done his duty. He accused the seceders of seeking only 'dissention and distraction' and said he 'would no longer consent to remain among them'. Their support for a veto was dismissed as 'puny efforts' that were 'poor and impotent' and he said that it was ridiculous for them to expect success, 'from such miserable support, against the universal voice of Ireland'.[64] O'Connell and his friends then withdrew from the meeting. 'Dismayed and humiliated', the seceders were left defeated.[65]

In June O'Connell was forced to go to London to be discharged of his recognisances to keep the peace following the Peel duel.[66] Sir Nathaniel Conant, the magistrate who had arrested him, wanted the recognisances renewed as he feared that O'Connell would attempt to go to the continent again and fight the duel. At the hearing O'Connell's counsel was called to make the necessary motion, but the lawyer was nervous and began making mistakes. O'Connell stepped forward and, holding his hat, moved to have the recognisances discharged. The chief justice pretended not to notice that O'Connell was representing himself and nodded his assent. O'Connell bowed and left the court. His wife was unwell and went to Clifton, near Bristol, with her youngest children, to drink the waters and recuperate.

While in London O'Connell had friendly talks with Lord Fingall but held little hope that he would 'come back to the Catholics'.[67] Meeting with some leading figures in London only confirmed his high opinion of his own abilities. He believed the English bar was weaker than the Irish bar, and the British MPs 'so much my inferiors'. This appealed to his vanity but also reminded him 'how cruel the penal laws are which exclude me from a fair trial' with these men. One day, when walking through the lobby of the Commons, he was startled by a man in a hurry, wearing a blue coat, who brushed against him. O'Connell turned quickly and saw that the man was Robert Peel. It was the closest he had ever come to meeting him.[68] During this visit to London O'Connell enjoyed returning to the theatres he had frequented in his youth. A performance of the celebrated Edmund Kean at Drury Lane left him nonplussed; he thought Kean owed his success 'to a strange singularity of manner'. He also saw John Philip Kemble at Covent Garden, and went to the opera with a Colonel Smith and his wife. While there he ran into '*a flame* of mine, a Miss Finucane' and he teased his wife that she should be 'quite jealous'. O'Connell was proving quite a hit with the ladies and he flirted with a musician's wife who made him fancy himself 'young and well looking'. But he reassured his wife that her 'doating husband can be faithful even in temptation'.[69]

Mary O'Connell was having her own adventures in Bristol. A Captain John O'Connell (no relation) saw her every day. He was 'respectful' and 'very kind', and she asked her husband for permission to dine with him.[70] This aroused O'Connell's jealousy. He admitted that he tortured himself 'asking foolish questions' and was 'quite ashamed of my folly'. Mary sought to put his mind at ease and told him that, as they approached fifteen years of married life, she 'never had cause to regret it' thanks to her 'fond and indulgent husband'. And she reassured him that he was the 'continual subject' of conversation with their children. Whenever another man was praised, the daughters Ellen and Kate would exclaim, 'Mamma, sure he is not as good a husband or father as our father?'[71]

In Ireland, the Catholic Association was running out of energy. The general apathy was commented upon at a meeting on 28 June 1817 and it was decided to bring the organisation to an end. In its place a new, revised Catholic Board was formed in July 1817 and it was hoped that the seceders could be encouraged to return to form a unified body.[72] O'Connell, too, was beginning to wonder how his agitation could proceed given the 'want of animation' in the country.[73] Despite all his best efforts he could not rouse the Catholics to agitate, or even to adopt what his son later called 'a defensive position'. His son reported that

> O'Connell always spoke of this period as one of the most trying of his eventful life... a moral lethargy, a faint-hearted and hopeless apathy hung over the country, and, with the exception of himself, scarce anyone was in the field for Ireland.[74]

The seceders did not return to the new Catholic Board and the meetings dragged on as apathetic as before. Around £2,000 in debt, the Board decided to suspend its meetings at the end of 1817 and resolved on 29 April 1818 not to petition parliament that year.[75] Edward Hay, the secretary who had been instrumental in suspending the Board, then published an appeal for a subscription to pay for the debts he had incurred since 1811. O'Connell disapproved of these decisions, joking that '*Honest Ned* Hay has outlawed us all.'[76] Even though there was little support for further agitation O'Connell was determined to act: 'If I petition alone, I *will* petition.' He prepared a paper listing Catholic grievances, addressed to the Catholics of Ireland, which he published on 1 January 1819.[77] O'Connell was never as good in print as he was speaking; he was only an average writer. He unwisely made a reference to how much more he would earn as barrister (about a thousand guineas a year) if he was a king's counsel and some read his desire for emancipation as economic self-interest. The address was dismissed by the *Dublin Journal* as a 'strange jumble of egotism and mis-representation'.[78] But O'Connell ignored the criticism and decided to advance: 'We are thinking of agitating again.'[79] Seeing unity as the key to future success, O'Connell attempted to reconcile with his childhood hero, Henry Grattan. He approached him about the creation of a patriotic society, possibly named after Grattan himself, and celebrating the period of legislative independence from 1782 to 1800 ('the only period of Irish history', according to Grattan).[80]

In this period of despondency, it was only on the legal circuit that O'Connell was triumphant. In Ballinrobe, Co. Mayo, on 22 March 1819, he successfully represented a Captain Fitzgerald who had sued for criminal conversation when a Captain Kerr slept with his wife. Fitzgerald was awarded £1,500 damages, though not the £20,000 he had claimed. The trial lasted from nine in the morning until two a.m. the next day, and O'Connell fasted the entire time (he was still following his new Lenten practices).[81] At the Cork assizes on 9 April he enjoyed himself greatly 'bothering parsons'. He was representing Robert Morett, the rector of Castletownshend, who was being sued for defamation. The Rev. Horace Townsend, 'a celebrated wit and a kind of *star of the west*', was a hostile witness and attempted to mock O'Connell. But O'Connell was able to make him appear 'both ludicrous and dishonest' and 'got the laugh completely against him'.[82] The verdict was returned in Morett's favour.

Despite his legal successes he still struggled to pay his debts. An attempt to persuade General O'Connell to waive the interest on his £3,600 debt did not get far.[83] Instead his uncle advised him to live within his means and 'put less effort into emancipation'. The letter was written in French so that Mary would not be able to learn the extent of his problems. On the morning of 19 July O'Connell injured his leg when his horse fell on him in the Phoenix Park.[84] But he was well enough to attend a dinner that evening in Morrison's Hotel to honour

John Devereux, who was raising an Irish legion to assist Simon Bolívar in Venezuela and Columbia. O'Connell was a great admirer of Bolívar —the Liberator—and had helped organise the dinner. His son, Morgan, would later serve in this legion and O'Connell's own title of 'The Liberator' comes from his admiration of Bolívar, with whom he corresponded.[85]

Old quarrels were revisited at this time. Edward Hay gave an interview to the *Dublin Evening Post* in which he claimed that the infamous witchery resolutions of 1812, which had alienated the prince regent, had been devised by the Whig opposition in England and sent to Ireland by a relative of George Ponsonby. This claim was published, without attribution, on 29 June 1819.[86] O'Connell was furious and at the next Catholic meeting, on 1 July, he stated that he had drawn up the offending resolutions and that there was no connection to Ponsonby. A sheepish Hay was forced to admit his role in the story. 'Honest Ned' Hay's stock fell further with this revelation and Lord Donoughmore wrote to O'Connell to praise his conduct. O'Connell was delighted that Hay had been humiliated and hoped he would never 'again show his ugly nose and dirty person in Catholic affairs'.[87]

Henry Grattan died in the summer of 1820 and was buried at Westminster Abbey. O'Connell believed he should have been buried in Ireland and in later years blamed this publicly on 'the bad taste of his family'.[88] At a meeting at the Royal Exchange on 13 June 1820, called to discuss the Dublin by-election occasioned by the death, O'Connell paid tribute to 'the greatest man Ireland ever knew'.[89] He claimed he could 'exhaust the dictionary three times told' in finding words to enumerate his virtues. Grattan's son was running for the seat against Thomas Ellis, and O'Connell dismissed Ellis as a man who lacked 'knowledge', 'eloquence, talent, patriotism', and 'leisure'. And he mocked Ellis's campaign for misspelling 'candidate' as 'canditate' on its literature.[90] Ellis would become one of his favourite targets in the years ahead. On Wednesday 14 June a general meeting of the Catholic body (with Lord Fingall in the chair) was held at D'Arcy's Tavern to discuss how to proceed following Grattan's death. It was decided to give William Plunket the new relief petition and ask him to present it in parliament, but only if he agreed to campaign for emancipation without any securities.[91] If he refused, the petition would then be given to the knight of Kerry. Plunket, however, declined to give a commitment on securities, in a confidential letter, something that O'Connell leaked to the *Dublin Evening Post* a few days later. In fact Plunket had insisted that 'conditions and securities are just and necessary'.[92] O'Connell believed that Plunket's refusal settled the matter and the petition should automatically be given to the knight of Kerry, as agreed at the meeting. But at a committee meeting there was a split on the issue, with seven in favour of giving the petition to Plunket anyway, and seven wanting to give it to the knight of Kerry. Fingall cast the deciding vote in favour of Plunket. It was now O'Connell's turn to secede, and he and his friends withdrew from the meeting. O'Connell returned to the general meeting and secured an adjournment until 22 June. O'Connell made his opposition public in the *Dublin Evening Post*: 'Our first duty seems to be to procure emancipation *as Catholics*, if we can—and if we cannot, then, *as Catholics*, to remain unemancipated.'[93] At the adjourned Catholic meeting O'Connell secured agreement on opposing any relief which was accompanied by securities.

The death of George III, after a long period of mental instability, brought the prince regent to the throne as George IV. O'Connell was delighted that his estranged wife, Caroline, would be queen and he hoped she would 'flog the scoundrels, every one'.[94] The prince of Wales had been separated from his wife for a number of years, and she was rumoured to have amassed a enormous number of lovers during the 1800s and 1810s, a list which included some prominent politicians. The possibility that Caroline might become queen gave O'Connell an idea to cause trouble. He contacted his friends in Westminster to ask the MP, Henry Brougham, to use his influence to make him the queen's attorney general in Ireland.[95] There was no money attached to the position, but he wanted it to mortify the queen's (and O'Connell's) enemies in Ireland. It would give him a higher status in court: he could not then be 'flung into the back row'. The penal laws did not preclude him from the post and he enjoyed thinking about how it would 'annoy some of the greatest scoundrels in society'.[96] Not hearing an answer, O'Connell contacted Brougham directly, who was given permission by the queen to make a decision. In the event of the appointment being made, Brougham asked O'Connell to recommend an Irish Protestant to serve as the queen's solicitor general in Ireland and he nominated his old friend, Richard Newton Bennett.[97] O'Connell was confident of success—overconfident—but his hopes were eventually dashed.

Brougham hesitated for months before deciding against the appointments, as he was not certain that the queen's right was maintainable and he did not want to go against his own legal advice. O'Connell felt that Brougham had slighted him, and for almost three years held it against him.[98]

In the meantime Queen Caroline was put on trial for adultery. A public meeting of Co. Dublin freeholders took place at Kilmainham courthouse on 30 December where the high sheriff of Dublin and a pro-government party attempted to pass an address praising the new king and the recent actions taken against the queen. O'Connell attended the meeting and objected to the high sheriff's attempts to rig the matter by hand-picking a small committee to prepare the address. His presence at the meeting was challenged by the high sheriff, who wondered whether he was a freeholder of the county of Dublin. 'Speaking with great emphasis', O'Connell declared that he was a freeholder of the county and had an hereditary property 'which, probably, may stand comparison with the person who interrogates me'.[99] He then won loud applause for his defiant claim that he earned an annual income greater than any of the people there were able to raise from taxes. Lord Cloncurry was also present and objected to the high sheriff's attempts to select a committee, insisting that everyone at the meeting should be able to nominate. There followed a heated meeting and, seeing that he would not get his own way, the high sheriff dissolved it. But O'Connell refused to leave and moved that Lord Cloncurry should take the chair and continue the meeting until an address was written. This was passed and Cloncurry took the chair, but the high sheriff declared that such a move was illegal and threatened Cloncurry with arrest if he did not retire. O'Connell moved in for the kill, taunting him to 'Prepare your prison then!'[100] There was loud cheering for several minutes when he said he hoped it was big enough to hold him and all his supporters. Again the high sheriff called on Cloncurry to withdraw and the men to disperse or he would call in the army. But O'Connell jeered him, saying that the meeting was perfectly legal and if anyone was prosecuted, 'let me be that man; for I have, and shall everywhere avow, that I have advised and counselled you to continue the meeting'.[101] Faced with O'Connell's legal expertise and confidence, the high sheriff withdrew.

The meeting proceeded for a short time before the army stormed in to disperse it. Cloncurry refused to leave the chair and was removed by force. But O'Connell was not finished yet and he reassembled the gathering across the road with a chair for Cloncurry secured from a nearby house. They then passed an address attacking the recent proceedings against the queen as 'dangerous and unconstitutional' and asking that they would never be revived. The address also mentioned the 'distress and aggravated miseries' of the Irish since the passing of the Union. O'Connell then moved to establish a committee to report on the high sheriff's behaviour to the lord lieutenant. The Kilmainham incident was reported in detail in the British newspaper, the *Morning Chronicle*, and there was much interest in the case.

On 2 January 1821 at a meeting at D'Arcy's Tavern to discuss Kilmainham, O'Connell ended his speech by referring to the recent events in Portugal. A constitutional revolution had taken place in August 1820 and it had made an impression on O'Connell. He took inspiration from the fact that the changes had been achieved 'without bloodshed'.[102] This is what he wanted for Ireland: 'not one human life sacrificed, no plunder, no confiscation' and he imagined a day when Ireland was 'free and independent'. 'Now', he said, 'it is coming home to our own oppressors'. At the meeting at D'Arcy's Tavern O'Connell quoted Lord Byron, 'the poet of the age', who had claimed in 1818 that Portugal was full of 'base Lusian slaves—the lowest of the low'.[103] But O'Connell now declared that the country was 'a great nation', the 'freest of the free'. It remained to be seen whether O'Connell could achieve a similar transformation in Ireland.

Chapter 10

'AN UNPRINCIPLED LIBERTINE': THE PRIVATE LIFE OF DANIEL O'CONNELL

'It was said about O'Connell in his own day, that you could not throw a stick over a workhouse wall without hitting one of his children, but he believed in the indissolubility of marriage, and when he died his heart was very properly preserved in Rome.'

(SENATOR W.B. YEATS, 11 JUNE 1925).

'The charitable institutions of Dublin are favoured with many of O'Connell's illegitimate offspring.'

(ELLEN COURTENAY, *Narrative*, 1832).

Damaging allegations about O'Connell's private life were made public in 1832, but they have their origins in an event dating back to 1818. It was in that year that Ellen Courtenay, a young girl from Cork, gave birth to a son, who she later claimed was fathered by O'Connell. She alleged in 1832 that she had been raped by O'Connell during a visit to his house in Merrion Square and over the next four years she attempted to generate maximum publicity from the story. Courtenay's story has many problems, not least of all that in the 1830s it was seized upon and manipulated by O'Connell's political enemies in Britain. Her account is also unreliable—self-justificatory and selfish —and almost certainly edited and published to either blackmail O'Connell or damage him politically. It was published at the offices of the *Satirist*, a nasty magazine that often attempted to procure money from its targets in return for dropping stories.[1] But Courtenay possessed a lot of detailed information that appears genuine and this chapter will suggest that there was more to the story than has been accepted. Attempts to discredit Courtenay's account have been problematic. Denis Gwynn's short examination of the evidence in 1930 was heated and subjective.[2] More recent accounts have traced O'Connell's and his wife's movements in 1817, when Courtenay claimed to have first met O'Connell, but these are wide of the mark.[3] If anything did happen the key dates are the beginning of 1818 because the child was born on 4 November 1818.

Stories of O'Connell's philandering have been too readily dismissed by historians, often for quite preposterous reasons. Folklore experts have suggested that these stories were 'a product of the folk-mind', in other words that peasants wanted their Gaelic heroes to possess 'insatiable sexual' powers and so projected tales of philandering on to O'Connell.[4] That these stories were therefore 'a tribute' to his popularity does not convince. Others have insisted that any adultery was impossible given that the 'powerful evidence' which exists—the tender love letters between O'Connell and his wife which were exchanged throughout their marriage.[5] But if frequent expressions of love precluded adultery, affairs would be a novelty. It should also be remembered that O'Connell and his wife had received letters in 1812 and 1816 alleging various infidelities (and before the Courtenay incident), and these can hardly be seen as products of the folk-mind or (given their private nature) as politically motivated attacks. O'Connell himself told his wife in 1820 that his new religious beliefs (including a desire to attend mass every Sunday) meant that he 'would not, darling, now be unfaithful to you even by a look'.[6] Everything depends on the emphasis that is placed on the 'now'. If the Courtenay allegations are false then they are probably responsible for creating the legend about O'Connell's womanising from his own time all the way down to W.B. Yeats' famous speech in the Senate. The evidence is mixed, and is on both sides, but Courtenay's claims cannot be discarded lightly.

Ellen Courtenay moved from Cork to Dublin around April 1817 when she was, in her own words, 'scarcely fifteen years of age'.[7] She called to visit O'Connell at his home in Merrion Square, apparently to obtain his advice about a leasehold estate which her father had mortgaged. O'Connell saw her many times, but she grew uneasy about his attentions and resolved to communicate with him only by letter. For eight months she did not see him, and began teaching at a boarding school in Dublin. Then she received a letter asking her to visit him (this must have been in January 1818), and when she did she was subjected to 'the most remorseless and flagrant aggression which ever disgraced humanity'.[8] Afterwards to comfort her, O'Connell swore on a bible or prayer-book that he would provide for her. Even from her own account it seems unlikely that O'Connell raped Courtenay. It was almost certainly a seduction, and consensual, for she admits to being 'bewildered by the rank sophistry of an unprincipled libertine'.[9] Nor does it seem to have been limited to one occasion. When she visited O'Connell soon after she slept with him again, claiming that he had found 'fresh meshes in which to entrap my understanding and to lull the workings of my conscience'. Therefore her description of the event as a rape should be seen as part of her efforts in 1832 to exculpate herself from any responsibility for what had happened. Afterwards, 'fresh disgust' made her recoil and she resolved to leave the country. O'Connell paid her fare and she went to London only to discover she was pregnant. She claimed to have returned on a short visit to see O'Connell, but to have received little sympathy and no financial support. One of the most damaging of Courtenay's claims, given in a footnote to her *Narrative*, was that O'Connell had 'ten or twelve wretched females, whom he had seduced, hanging upon him for support'. These women were 'compelled' to visit him at his home to receive a 'wretched pittance, which he occasionally doled out to them, as a compensation for their ruined prospects, their estranged friends, their fall in society, their blasted happiness and their lost honour'.[10] This, no doubt, would have contributed to O'Connell's debts. It is possible that these entanglements were what his brother, James, was referring to in 1823 when he mentioned the 'heavy expenses that must attend your *former indiscretions* (which I thank God do not now exist)', and which he estimated to be £600 a year.[11]

Courtenay gives some idea of who these women were: 'They were chiefly the governesses of his children, and the companions of his wife.' A few, she claimed, became pregnant, but even then they received little additional support from O'Connell. The reference to the governesses is striking. For a long period, the governess of O'Connell's daughters was a Miss Gaughran. In 1823, when Mary O'Connell was out of the country with the younger children in a strange attempt to economise, O'Connell paid a number of visits to Gaughran. When Mary discovered this she was furious and administered a severe 'scolding'.[12] Suspecting an affair, Mary made him promise to never visit Gaughran again. O'Connell assured her that he 'never in my life showed the slightest tinge of preference to any being above you, and why *now*, when I would not look at any other woman for a moment'.[13] This was not the first time that Mary was jealous, and there are other instances from 1808 and 1812, for example when she complained of him being 'among all the pretty girls at Mrs Kenny's, a dangerous place... However I am not very *uneasy* about it.'[14] Later, when O'Connell was in London in 1825 and mentioned in a letter that he was going off to meet some women, Mary became jealous and he was forced to reassure her that 'the world's worth would not tempt me to give you cause.'[15]

Returning to England, Courtenay and O'Connell remained in touch by mail. Her son was born on 4 November 1818 and named Henry Simpson, apparently at O'Connell's request. Demands for money were refused with O'Connell pleading poverty, though he promised that when his rich uncle died she would receive a yearly provision.[16] O'Connell's financial state was not public knowledge, even in 1832, nor was his reliance on Hunting Cap to rescue him. During this period Courtenay seems to have resumed her career as a teacher. Hunting Cap died in 1825 and Courtenay returned to Ireland to receive her provision. She remembered this incorrectly as being four years later, or 1822, but this error does not necessarily discredit her tale. If the other details were invented she would surely have got her chronology correct and it is more likely that her memory was wrong.

In Dublin O'Connell refused for a month to see her. One night, she waited for him outside his house but when he arrived he told her to see Fr F.J. L'Estrange, his religious professor. Upon being told that her child was extremely ill, and that she needed support, he slammed the door shut on her 'with all the fury and gesticulation of an incensed drayman'.[17] Courtenay met with L'Estrange and was given a note for £20, payable in two months, and made swear on a bible that she would never again approach O'Connell for assistance. She claimed that L'Estrange blamed 'corrupt accessories' who had 'tempted him [O'Connell] into evil' and pleaded with her to destroy his letters.[18] The money barely paid for her debts and she considered suicide, but was talked out of it by a woman who supported her in this period.

Once back in England, Courtenay decided upon a career on the stage. She had been praised for having 'the power of creating sympathy in the bosoms of others' and secured money from friends to purchase a large wardrobe of clothes in March 1826 so that she could perform at the Royalty Theatre in London.[19] However disaster struck. There was a fire at the theatre in April and her wardrobe was destroyed. She claimed she never recovered from this calamity as she received no compensation and a wardrobe was 'absolutely necessary to every performer of respectability'. The fire at the Royalty Theatre did occur, on 12 April 1826, but whether the destruction of her wardrobe really would have blighted her prospects is implausible.[20] Again Courtenay was attempting to justify and explain every misfortune in her life. Afterwards Courtenay arranged for some benefits to be held at the English Opera House, but she claimed to have earned little from them. After eight years of raising her son, she decided to give him up. First she placed him in the care of a family at Holborn, whose children she had previously taught, and she paid for his upkeep. But his health was terrible and so Courtenay decided to give him to the care of Fr L'Estrange. Believing he was in a Dublin orphanage, she did not see him again until 1835. Fleeing her debts, Courtenay moved to Paris where she received some lucrative acting engagements, benefiting from the patronage of a rich nobleman, but this patronage ended abruptly following the 1830 revolution. She returned to London and was soon facing the debtors' prison. At this point she began trying to raise money from O'Connell's friends. She approached The O'Gorman Mahon (who had been at Clongowes with one of O'Connell's sons and who had played a leading role in the Clare election) in February and March 1831 to try and secure his assistance, but he refused to call at her house despite many pleas.[21] Following this, she wrote her account of what had happened. In November 1831 she contacted the radical MP, Henry Hunt, detailing O'Connell's 'catalogue of crimes and atrocities mingled with cruelty and meanness'.[22] Hunt believed her story. He later told O'Connell that he would never have done so had he 'not personally known your character'. Despite his dislike of O'Connell's 'cant and hypocrisy', he felt obliged to contact him and warn him of the impending publication so that it could be prevented. O'Connell reacted angrily, attacking Hunt's 'insane insolence'.[23] He denied the charge, suggesting that 'a calumny' against him 'would have been worth any money in Ireland at any time during the past twenty years, that is, if it had the least face of probability'. Arrested for her debts soon after, Courtenay was imprisoned at the Fleet Prison. There she published her account of O'Connell's mistreatment of her in January 1832. O'Connell declined to respond and advised his friends to avoid attacking her: 'What she wants most is to have a controversy raised.'[24] He was anxious to get a copy of the publication to see what she had written and wondered whether she specified 'the day on which she alleges the crime was committed'.

The aftermath of the story, entwined as it is in O'Connell's political career in Britain in the 1830s, will be left to a future work. Certainly the story was used against O'Connell by his enemies, exploited, for example, by *The Times* newspaper, which was having its own war with him. Released from prison, Courtenay contacted Christopher Fitzsimon, O'Connell's son-in-law, in 1834 to try and arrange a settlement but nothing came of it.[25] She was only reunited with her son in 1835. The serious illnesses which had afflicted him as a child had taken their toll and he was now lame and almost completely deaf.[26] A victim of neglect, both from his parents and his guardians, he was unable to read or write.[27] Courtenay began to teach him. She also attempted to cash in on her notoriety and took to the stage with him in July 1835, after an absence of five years, to perform the tragedy *Douglas* at the Victoria Theatre. This, ironically, had been one of O'Connell's favourite plays growing up and he had quoted lines from it on his sick-bed in 1798. *The Times* reported that Henry Simpson (now calling himself Henry O'Connell) did not 'bear a very close resemblance to the personage to whom the lady has attributed his existence'.[28] In the first months of 1836 Henry O'Connell began trying to meet O'Connell, following him to church every Sunday and then trying to talk him. He claimed to have talked 'kindly' with O'Connell on Sunday 6 March, with O'Connell advising him to return to Ireland.[29]

Unlikeable and unreliable, Courtenay was prone to lying to advance her own interests. In March 1836 she commissioned a friend, William Carmichael Smyth, to meet with Major McNamara (who she claimed had been appointed to act in the matter) to try and arrange a financial settlement from O'Connell. Smyth had been imprisoned himself in

November 1832 for refusing to support his wife, although he had claimed in his defence that she beat him.[30] Smyth met McNamara on Sunday 6 March and Courtenay claimed in print afterwards that McNamara had admitted everything: 'That Mr O'Connell does not attempt to deny the facts, and there was not a doubt but that the boy was his.'[31] But Smyth published a refutation of her claims in a letter to *The Times*, insisting that he had not spoken to Courtenay since the meeting.[32] He denied that McNamara had ever admitted to discussing the matter with O'Connell, but he did not discuss or deny O'Connell's alleged paternity and the letter is a strange piece of evidence. It certainly shows how quickly Courtenay alienated her friends from her cause. On Sunday 13 March Henry O'Connell set out again to intercept O'Connell on his way to mass. O'Connell was walking with his son, John, when Henry appeared with his mother. He said something to O'Connell, who, according to John, became 'a good deal excited'.[33] Seeing his father's state, John (who was on the other side of the street) crossed over and told Henry to go away, but he replied that he 'would follow my father in spite of you'. John grabbed Henry's cloak, knocked him down, and began hitting him with his umbrella. But O'Connell intervened and told him, 'Don't strike the boy, John.'[34] Both men then walked away. Henry O'Connell brought charges against John O'Connell and the case went to court on 16 March; Daniel O'Connell stayed away. Courtenay attempted to speak at the end of the hearing, but was refused permission, and she shouted that it was O'Connell's own fault if he was being harassed. Having denied any physical similarity the previous year, *The Times* now claimed that the resemblance between Henry and Daniel O'Connell was generally remarked upon in the court.

It is impossible to say with any certainty what really happened between Ellen Courtenay and Daniel O'Connell. We know that she pursued the matter, doggedly, between 1831 and 1836, with a determination that bordered on obsessional. Not all of her efforts to raise money were public, and the level of detail she possessed about O'Connell's household, family, friends, and associates suggests that there was some truth to her story. Certainly she was not as innocent as she claimed, and she showed little regret in abandoning her son in 1826 to pursue a career on the French stage. O'Connell's position was difficult, but he never denied the story publicly even though it should have been easy to contradict many of the details of her story (for example by calling on Fr L'Estrange to make a statement). The balance of evidence suggests that there was some brief liaison with Courtenay and that O'Connell avoided being dragged into a commitment he could not afford financially nor accept for personal and political reasons.

Further attempts by Courtney to raise money ended in farce. On Thursday 17 June 1836 Courtenay and her son arranged a new benefit concert at the Queen's Theatre. It was another performance of *Douglas* and Henry O'Connell attempted to give a speech before the performance but he was not audible.[35] The theatre manager had not been paid in advance and the fiddlers in the orchestra refused to play. An argument broke out between Henry and the manager and when the performance began the fiddlers decided to disrupt the performance from the orchestra pit. The audience began throwing orange peel, gooseberries, and coins at the fiddlers, and a fight broke out between the musicians and the audience. Eventually things calmed down, and the performance resumed, but occasionally a fiddler would raise his head and shout out a cheer for Daniel O'Connell.

Chapter 11

'A RESTLESS EXISTENCE': DECIDING ON NEW STRATEGIES, 1821–1824

'Master Ellis, what an orator! I once heard Master Ellis attempt a speech and I laughed a considerable time after.'
(DANIEL O'CONNELL AT THE AGGREGATE MEETING OF THE CATHOLICS OF IRELAND, 2 DECEMBER 1824.)[1]

On New Year's Day 1821 O'Connell wrote another address to the Catholics of Ireland, in what was becoming an annual event. It was answered in print a few days later, by Richard Sheil, who accused O'Connell of inconsistency and attacked him for having revived the veto controversy and insulted Plunket.[2] Sheil scored some hits, dismissing O'Connell as someone who followed rather than led, and who was torn between wanting 'public praise' and following 'his sense of public duty'; this, claimed Sheil, made him reflect the moods of 'popular excitation'. Sheil was now a barrister on the Leinster circuit, but despite his great reputation for oratory he was unable to make much of an impression. His knowledge of the law was limited, and he was not a versatile debater, being more suited to set-piece orations. While he could sometimes use his oratorical genius to sway a jury, he never became more than 'a passable general lawyer'.[3] O'Connell responded on 12 January and joked that 'like the rabid animal in the fable, Mr Shiel is not half so mad as he pretends to be.'[4] He praised Plunket's personal qualities and professional accomplishments ('I cheerfully acknowledge his professional superiority and excellence'), but attacked him over political differences.[5] The Peterloo massacre of 1819 was mentioned, when the army had opened fire on political protestors in Manchester, as Plunket had voted against an inquiry into it. O'Connell claimed this showed that Plunket had supported the dispersion. O'Connell called Peterloo 'the most portentous event of modern times' and suggested that it might very well be the first step to military despotism.

Plunket, meanwhile, was about to surprise everyone. On 7 March he introduced two bills in the House of Commons, the first in favour of Catholic emancipation, the second conceding to the government a veto over the appointment of Catholic bishops and deans. This was unexpected. O'Connell was on circuit in Limerick, and rushed into print with a further two letters addressed to the Catholics of Ireland. These letters were written in instalments between cases and were sent to the *Morning Herald* for publication as soon as a part was completed. In the first letter, dated 17 March, O'Connell gave qualified support to the first bill, but dismissed the second as 'a penal and restrictive law of the worst description'.[6] Insisting that no Irish Catholic bishop had ever been disloyal to the crown (except, he joked, for one who 'bore the inauspicious name of Plunket(t)', though 'he was certainly innocent'), O'Connell rejected the need for a board of control to monitor the Irish bishops.[7] He also put his professional reputation on the line ('I forego that reputation... unless what I say to you now be true'), and declared that sections of the bill were 'false in point of law and of fact'. A veto over the appointment of deans had never been mentioned before and O'Connell attacked Plunket for 'out-Heroding' Herod by offering to extend the veto. He ended the letter by calling the second bill 'an act to "decatholicise" Ireland' and insisted it was as bad as, or worse than, any of the penal laws. The second, unfinished letter was dated 20 March and O'Connell continued the attack. His tone was defiant: 'I would infinitely rather perish with disgrace on a scaffold than assent to such a law.'[8]

On 26 March Plunket's bills were merged into a single piece of legislation. This new bill passed through the House of Commons on 2 April, but was defeated on 17 April in the House of Lords by 159 votes to 120.[9] O'Connell was delighted: he had hoped that 'the present rascally Catholic bill' would be 'flung out' by the 'rascals' in parliament.[10] If the bill had passed O'Connell would have been finished in politics. His attempt to call an aggregate meeting of the Catholics in Dublin to discuss the bill had failed because he had not been able to raise enough signatures. People had decided to wait and see what would happen at Westminster. O'Connell had gambled everything on securing emancipation his way, with no conditions, and he would have paid the price if emancipation had been secured through Plunket. Afterwards it was said openly that if emancipation had been secured, O'Connell would have been denied office, even if it 'rained places'.[11] 'What is to be done now?' wondered O'Connell in the aftermath.[12] He hoped the rejection of Plunket's bill would make the vetoists realise that securities were a dead issue as a bill with them was 'kicked out' as unceremoniously as one without them.

George IV decided to visit Ireland in the summer of 1821, in the first royal visit since 1690 (and in far different circumstances). After years of abusing the prince regent, O'Connell decided on a new strategy: conciliation. George IV was promising a new direction and it was believed that a show of loyalty might persuade him that there was no danger in emancipation. O'Connell proposed calling a meeting of the Catholics to discuss how to honour the king as well as to discuss the state of Catholic affairs, but this attempt to link the two was opposed by Lord Fingall and a number of other Catholic aristocrats and O'Connell backed down. At the meeting on 10 July at D'Arcy's Tavern to prepare the congratulatory address to the king, an envoy arrived bearing an offer from the lord mayor, Abraham Bradley King[13]. This was an offer for a joint meeting to discuss the king's visit at the Royal Exchange on 19 July, with the Catholic body and Dublin corporation uniting to honour him. This was accepted, with O'Connell one of the most enthusiastic supporters of the new departure. As part of this deal it was agreed that there would be no triumphalist celebration on 12 July in Dublin and the statue of King William III in College Green would not be covered in orange ribbons, something that was seen as a deliberate insult to the Catholics. This agreement was broken on the day, apparently by a drunken mob which was determined to decorate the statue. But O'Connell urged restraint at the next Catholic meeting and was determined to maintain the truce.[14] Here he was in a minority. But in the weeks ahead he managed to persuade the Catholics to trust his strategy and join with the Protestants in honouring the king. At a subsequent meeting O'Connell again repeated his long-held belief that dissension was at the heart of Ireland's problems and that there was but one solution: 'unanimity'. Old insults had been forgiven, he said, when the Catholics had accepted the offer of conciliation from Dublin corporation, and this newer insult should also be forgotten for the sake of unity.[15] This was a very different O'Connell from the agitator of old.

At the meeting at the Royal Exchange on 19 July various suggestions were made for erecting a permanent monument to George IV in Ireland. The three main suggestions were for a column, a palace, or a bridge, and O'Connell spoke in favour of the second (though he did not propose it). This was agreed and O'Connell pledged to give an annual sum of twenty guineas from his own income for that purpose.[16] A conciliation dinner was also hosted by the lord mayor on 1 August to celebrate the coronation. O'Connell and Sheil attended along with about 330 others; he later described himself as 'Daniel in the lion's den'.[17] Royal fever seemed to sweep the country; Lord Cloncurry later said that 'a strange madness seemed at that conjuncture to seize people of all ranks in Ireland.'[18] The king arrived in Dunleary (renamed Kingstown in his honour) on 12 August and held his first levee in Dublin Castle on 20 August. O'Connell and his brother, John, were among nearly one hundred prominent Catholics who were presented to the king.[19] He was also chosen as one of the men to accompany the king on his journey to the Curragh for the races on 31 August; they left the king at Celbridge where he was met by the duke of Leinster.[20] On the day of the king's departure, Monday 3 September, O'Connell was in Wicklow, but he rode back to Dunleary to make a presentation. This presentation left O'Connell open to much ridicule in the months and years ahead, especially given his championing of the queen (who had died a month earlier on 7 August) and his years of abusing the king when he had been prince regent. O'Connell met the king in his tent, knelt on one knee, and presented him with a laurel crown. It became an integral part of the story that a 'tear of manly sentiment' glistened in the king's eye.[21] Years later, the *Courier* newspaper in London had great fun mocking O'Connell and alleged that the idea for the royal palace was his, that he had pledged to give a thousand pounds a year from his income to build it, and had followed the king into the sea to present him with the laurel crown, kneeling in the water to do so.[22] O'Connell was furious with the allegations of 'unbecoming servility' and denied them all. Indeed he boasted that when the king held out his hand for him to kiss it he had declined to do so. This seems true enough; it was noted in the newspapers at the time that the two men had merely shaken hands.[23]

Even in the short term, O'Connell's behaviour at Kingstown was much commented upon. He began wearing a fur cap with a gold band while travelling on circuit, and started boasting that it was a present from the king, who had worn it himself on his visit.[24] O'Connell denied in print having said this 'in earnest', and suggested that if it had been said it in jest it must have been 'a dull joke'. He was astonished that a serious newspaper could be 'so exquisitely silly' as to notice his cap. But the truth is that it was O'Connell who was drawing attention to his new-found friendship with George IV and the fur cap was an integral part of the story. At a county meeting of the Catholics in October O'Connell was teased about his fur cap by Nicholas Mahon. But he turned the joke to his advantage by suggesting that he 'would call my cap the cap of unanimity, but then the cap would not fit Mr Mahon'.[25] Laughing afterwards, O'Connell told his wife that she had never seen 'or heard of anything that took better than my hit at Mahon'.

In December 1821 the Marquess Wellesley, who was sympathetic to the Catholics, arrived as lord lieutenant for Ireland. The older brother of the duke of Wellington, Wellesley was small of stature but large in ego. He was described by Walter Scott as 'talking politics like a Roman emperor' and in Ireland he exclaimed boastfully, 'The Irish government! Sir, I am the Irish government'.[26] Saurin was removed as attorney general and Plunket took his place; O'Connell rejoiced that 'our mortal foe is, I trust, extinguished for ever'.[27] The arrival of Wellesley was feared by Protestant loyalists and made O'Connell optimistic that emancipation would follow soon. He reconciled with Plunket, and looked forward to the time when he would be a king's counsel and 'get *fair play* in my profession'.[28] In his address to the Catholics of Ireland in January 1822 he began by quoting Byron's 'hereditary bondsmen' lines to remind his 'fellow countrymen—you can never obtain your liberty without an exertion on your own part'.[29] In this letter he promised his readers that there was no possibility of a return to the penal laws. And he ended the letter by quoting Shakespeare to suggest that any such attempt would be to 'cry havoc and let slip the dogs of war'.[30]

A new Catholic petition was adopted at an aggregate meeting of the

Irish Catholics, held at Denmark Street Chapel, on Wednesday 13 February. This was then sent to Lord Donoughmore and William Plunket to be presented in parliament. O'Connell took a battering at the meeting. When he rose to speak his attempt to discuss the merits of the petition were opposed vigorously. He was also challenged as soon as he attacked Lord Castlereagh (now Lord Londonderry) and was asked if he was there to abuse members of parliament. His discussion of European politics was also criticised; Hugh O'Connor interrupted and wanted to know if he planned 'to occupy the time of this meeting with such ridiculous nonsense'.[31] The attack was applauded. But O'Connell was at his best when provoked and replied, 'Whether it be ridiculous or sensible, I am determined I will not be prevented from going on.' This broke the tension and there was much laughter. O'Connell followed up by moving successfully a resolution from 1813 declaring that the Catholics would not accept any concession inconsistent with their honour, a coded declaration against securities.

'How I *long* to be out of debt.'[32] Money was still the biggest problem bedevilling O'Connell. But after years of concealing the extent of the problem from his wife, 'to save you from mental suffering', he had finally confessed the extent of his problems.[33] In March 1822 he and his wife decided upon a quixotic strategy to ease their debts. They agreed that she and the younger children would move to France where, it was believed, the cheaper standard of living would allow for savings to be made. Away from Ireland, Mary could also avoid giving money to relatives and dependents who called to the door, and this seems to have been a major consideration. She later discussed 'the eternal *relay* of cousins' which made living in Kerry impossible, as 'your door could not be kept shut to your connections or to mine'.[34] But, even then, it seems to have been a crazy scheme and given that travel, accommodation, and food would have to be paid for it is difficult to see how any savings could be made. O'Connell was optimistic that he could clear his debts within two years and it was decided that the family would remain abroad until that time. To finance the move O'Connell was forced to borrow £600 from his brother, James, further adding to his debts.[35] The family departed on 2 May, heading first to Bordeaux. O'Connell was wracked by guilt, aware that his profligacy had brought about this separation from his family. He knew that his wife did not blame him, 'but my own heart does, and the misery I now endure is nothing but the punishment I deserve for not being more attentive'.[36] Worried about his children, he warned his wife to watch the 'rascally French' and not let them near his 'darling girls'.[37]

Hunting Cap fell ill in May and O'Connell was once more 'tempted to great sin' in hoping he would die and thus provide him with the inheritance to release him from his debts.[38] The feeling was short-lived and O'Connell realised that he did not want to inherit the property in this 'wrong' way. Hunting Cap's legs were swollen, but he soon recovered and O'Connell marvelled that he was 'a surprising old man'.[39] O'Connell's law practice was 'flourishing' and, his family away, he was able to devote all his time to his career. He rose at four a.m., breakfasted at a quarter past eight, had dinner after five, and then went to bed between nine and ten p.m.[40] There was also time to have his portrait taken. O'Connell was often disappointed with the portraits and engravings of himself. He had more hope for the work of B. O'Reilly which began in June (and which was completed in February 1823). O'Connell requested that he did not want anything written under it except his name and the two lines of 'hereditary bondsmen'.[41] 'I think *this time*', he told his wife, 'we shall not be disappointed'. The picture, which proudly displays the silver cup that O'Connell was awarded in 1814, provides the cover for this book.

In August O'Connell travelled to France to visit his wife and family, who were staying at Pau. On his travels he was abused by a French sea-captain who tried to wind him up by attacking England in general and Englishmen in particular.[42] O'Connell just smiled, provoking the captain into more vehement attacks. Still O'Connell refused to respond, until finally the captain asked 'Do you hear me, monsieur? Do you understand me?' 'Perfectly,' replied O'Connell quietly. The captain was astonished that O'Connell was so calm and asked him why he didn't resent this attack on his country and countrymen. But O'Connell replied simply: 'I have no cause to resent anything you have said. On the contrary I think much of it is richly deserved. Besides you have not attacked *my* country, nor *my* countrymen.' Confused, the captain asked O'Connell if he was English. O'Connell replied in French that he was Irish, and from that moment on the captain gave him every attention. On the final part of his journey, O'Connell took a wrong turn, taking the road to Bayonne instead of the road to Pau. Only discovering his mistake at night-time, but anxious to see his family, he decided to keep riding overnight. Exhausted after all this travelling, he finally arrived at Pau, and often told this 'disagreeable' story of getting lost afterwards.[43]

Home in Ireland following this visit, O'Connell continued to miss his wife and family. When Thomas Moore's poem 'Loves of the Angels' was published in December 1822 he was touched by the description of a separated husband and wife. He regretted that he was not able to read it to his children and praised it for being 'full of Moore's magic'.[44] Despite the criticism of Moore in literary magazines, O'Connell believed that he was 'the prince of poets', and that there was 'more melody and harmony in his versification than in any other poet I have read'.

The separation from his wife and children made O'Connell resentful. He vented his frustrations on the French people and throughout 1823 he made numerous criticisms of their character and politics. Agreeing with his youngest son, Danny, he claimed that 'the French are very inferior to the Irish.'[45] He also wrote that 'the French people are probably the only people in the world utterly unfit for liberty... They want moral temperament.'[46] These criticisms were new for O'Connell and he had not expressed himself so harshly before. But his new opinion was that 'they are indeed an odious people.' Even O'Connell's hero Napoleon was not exempt from the attacks: 'His colossal power was wielded to enslave the Church... to discountenance the mild and modest virtues of the Christian.' O'Connell insisted that these thoughts were the product of 'deep reflection' and that he had long been thinking of them. None the less it is clear he was also sublimating his frustration at missing his wife, for in a later letter he regretted the absence of his 'saucy' and 'cocknosed' wife and concluded: 'How sore my heart is at times, and I hate France with a mortal hatred.'[47] Mary and the children moved from Pau to Tours, and spent the summer in Paris, and from there arranged to go to England for the final part of their tour.

There was other evidence that O'Connell missed them deeply. In March he teased his wife by telling of the impression he had made on the coach journey from Killarney to Cork. A woman was travelling with her two daughters and she told O'Connell as they left the coach that he had 'quite won her daughters' hearts'. 'Only think of that, my old woman,' he told his wife, 'as a puff to my vanity.'[48] He joked that this showed there was more for her to worry about than just his fasting, 'about which you are so saucy'. He was also anxious about his children and worried about the effects of his long absence. His son, John, who had been 'a *great great* favourite', had been criticised by Mary for being idle, and O'Connell despaired because 'idleness is so miserable and mean a quality' and he thought he could 'entertain no great hope of him if he were idle'.[49] O'Connell had clearly forgotten his own youth: 'It is a sad thing for me to have my boys disappoint me thus.'

On 14 December 1822 the lord lieutenant, Wellesley, attended a performance of Oliver Goldsmith's *She stoops to conquer* at the New Theatre Royal in Dublin. During the playing of 'God save the king' there was a riot, started by Orangemen who were furious at the government's banning of the traditional dressing of the statue of William III earlier in the year, and a quart bottle and then a large piece of wood, part of a watchman's rattle, were thrown at Wellesley's head. Wellesley was terrified, believing it was part of a larger assassination conspiracy, and there were immediate repercussions. A 'grand public meeting' was called by the lord mayor for 20 December at the Royal Exchange to discuss the matter. At a Catholic meeting on 19 December O'Connell pressed that he and other Catholics should also attend this meeting and this was agreed 'by a great majority'.[50]

The meeting at the Royal Exchange was packed. It began at noon and a number of people spoke, including the duke of Leinster, the governor of the Bank of Ireland, Lord Cloncurry, and O'Connell. 'There never was such a meeting in Ireland,' O'Connell wrote afterwards.[51] He was also proud of his own contribution as he was the only person 'who made himself heard throughout'. The *Dublin Evening Post*, no friend to O'Connell since the Magee trials, eulogised O'Connell for his speech and said that 'no man can speak to the public with greater effect'.[52] Though it also noted that he did not always exert himself 'in the right way'.

The loyalist Trinity College Dublin students were becoming a source of irritation to O'Connell. One night in March, when it was reported that they were going to attack his house, a group of his supporters gathered round Merrion Square to defend him. O'Connell assured them that he was 'prepared to meet any assault'.[53] Around this time O'Connell began thinking of forming a new Catholic body to renew agitation. The recent ones had fallen away because of apathy, but even though little had changed, O'Connell was determined to act anyway. At a dinner party in Glencullen, in the Dublin mountains, on 8 February 1823, he first revealed his ambition.[54] Following this, a preliminary meeting of the Catholics took place on 25 April at Dempsey's City of Dublin Tavern in Sackville Street, but it was not well attended.[55] O'Connell spoke of his desire to form a new Catholic body, to represent the people, counsel them in times of distress, and give vent to their complaints.[56] At a meeting in the same venue five days later, arranged to prepare for a forthcoming aggregate meeting, O'Connell set out his core principle, his challenge to the Irish people: 'Will you, like torpid slaves, lie under the lash of the oppressor? If we are not free, let us, at least, prove ourselves worthy of being so.'[57] This drew several minutes' applause. O'Connell proposed a resolution to establish a new Catholic Association and this was carried unanimously.

The foundation meeting of the Catholic Association (formally called The Irish Catholic Association) was held at rooms rented in Dempsey's City of Dublin Tavern, on Monday 12 May. Fifty men attended and O'Connell proposed an annual subscription of one guinea. Hugh O'Connor objected and suggested doubling the subscription, but O'Connell opposed this vigorously and won the point. It was agreed that future meetings would be held at Coyne's, No. 4 Capel Street. The Catholic Association met again on Tuesday 13 May. At this meeting it was agreed to send a deputation to the king with the address agreed at the recent aggregate meeting. This deputation would consist of the earl of Fingall, a number of Catholic peers, and two gentlemen from each county. The first proper debate at the Catholic Association took place on 20 May but the matters discussed were not too serious and O'Connell's resolution about the Catholic chaplain at Newgate Prison was passed unanimously.

The first test for O'Connell at the Catholic Association came on Saturday 24 May. For O'Connell it was a busy working day. He stayed in bed until seven a.m., later than usual, because it was the second fast day in succession and he did not want to exhaust himself.[58] He was then in court from eleven a.m. until after three p.m., where he made three speeches to juries; he was 'very successful' with his first two and had no complaints about the third. Finished in court, he then attended the meeting of the Association. O'Connell wanted to give Protestants (and people of other religions) permission to attend all meetings of the

Association, although they would not be able to speak or vote unless they were subscribers. Catholics, however, could only attend if they were a member. Eneas MacDonnell objected to this and suggested that Catholics should have the same rights to attend as those from other religions.[59] But O'Connell was adamant there was a difference and that Catholics were 'unworthy' of attending if 'they did not take a guinea's worth of interest in the Catholic cause'. He won this vote 'by a triumphant majority'. MacDonnell and two others then objected to allowing Protestants to become members as emancipation was not in their interests, but O'Connell answered that since they must win emancipation from Protestants there was no one better equipped to discuss the matter with them or to advise them. And he joked that it was unlikely Orangemen would flock in with guineas to disrupt proceedings. O'Connell again won the vote by a large majority. He told his wife that 'we have in our little parliament set the Protestants a good example'.[60] To help matters in England, O'Connell decided to reconcile with Henry Brougham in May 1823. He apologised for the 'idle, private or personal pique' which had disrupted their working relationship, following his attempt to become the queen's attorney general for Ireland.[61] Brougham was entrusted with the Catholic petition, as well as a petition for the administration of justice in Ireland.

Detailed rules for the Catholic Association were drawn up by O'Connell. For example, no member could speak twice on a motion, unless he was the proposer, in which case he had the right of reply. Catholic priests were given automatic membership of the Association. Meetings began at three p.m., but according to the 'no house' rule, if fewer than ten members were present by three thirty p.m. then the meeting adjourned automatically. The 'no house' rule was first enforced at the meeting of Saturday 31 May and in the months ahead was a source of frustration for O'Connell as meetings were adjourned even though he had plenty of business he wanted to get through. It was a sign of how little interest there was in the new Catholic Association that so many meetings were attended by fewer than ten people. O'Connell's son, John, having returned to Ireland to be educated at Clongowes, attended a meeting of the Association in late October or early November. He was astonished that the two-room floor in Capel Street was but half-full, with 'scanty returns of money, few communications from the country, and informal haste' in the management of business.[62] The men who attended did not make a good impression: he felt they were 'captious, uncertain, half-timid', and he had little faith in the new body.

In June 1823 O'Connell received a hint that he would be awarded a patent of precedence. This was an honour rarely granted by the crown and it enabled a barrister to wear a silk gown ('take silk') and practice as a king's counsel. O'Connell was desperate for the honour; it would be worth over £1,000 a year to his professional income and 'help bring home my wife and children', and best of all he would not have to 'sacrifice one particle of my independence to get it'.[63] O'Connell was determined to reject any 'place, pension or office', but he was willing to accept this conciliatory gesture from the government. In the event, the patent of precedence was not forthcoming and O'Connell would wait years, until his legal career was effectively over, before it was finally awarded. This refusal to grant him a patent of precedence gnawed away at him for the rest of the decade. Every year he became more and more bitter at seeing younger and inferior lawyers advancing ahead of him and it only fuelled his anger and ambition.

Despite not being a king's counsel (and therefore unable to charge higher fees or take certain cases) O'Connell had never been more successful at the bar. He had become the celebrity lawyer of the day. Contributing to his fame was the *New Monthly Magazine* (which O'Connell called 'one of the best in London'), which published a detailed profile of him in July.[64] The article was unsigned, though it was later revealed that the author was William Henry Curran. The article described a typical working day for O'Connell. It began with O'Connell starting early and:

> If any one of you, my English readers, being a stranger in Dublin, should chance, as you return upon a winter's morning from one of the 'small and early' parties of that raking metropolis, that is to say, between the hours of five and six o'clock, to pass along the south side of Merrion Square, you will not fail to observe that among those splendid mansions, there is one evidently tenanted by a person whose habits differ materially from those of his fashionable neighbours. The half-opened parlour shutter, and the light within, announces that someone dwells there whose time is too precious to permit him to regulate his rising with the sun's.[65]

This was O'Connell preparing for his work in court, in a room with 'book-cases clogged with tomes in plain calf-skin binding' and 'blue-covered octavos' lying on the tables. But if the same visitor saw O'Connell later that day in the Four Courts they would not think it was the same man. They would find

> the object of your pity miraculously transformed from the severe recluse of the morning into one of the most bustling, important, and joyous personages in that busy scene. There you will be sure to see him his countenance braced up and glistening with health and spirits—with a huge, plethoric bag, which his robust arms can scarcely sustain... You perceive at once that you have lighted upon a great popular advocate.

The article revealed that by three o'clock in the afternoon O'Connell would have finished an enormous amount of legal business and 'you would naturally suppose that the remaining portion of the day must of necessity be devoted to recreation or repose'. However if you then went to one of the many public meetings, held in Dublin, you would find him there, 'before you, the presiding spirit of the scene, with a strength of lungs, and redundancy of animation, as if he had that moment started fresh for the labours of the day'. There he would remain, 'until, by dint of strength or dexterity, he had carried every point'. Afterwards he might attend a public dinner, before going home, and he 'is sure to be found before day-break next morning at his solitary post, recommencing the routine of his restless existence'. O'Connell was understandably delighted with the article: it gave a 'brilliant character of me', he wrote to his wife, though he joked that it had 'the extreme folly to describe me as a handsome man'. He said that she might agree with that, 'but others will laugh'.

O'Connell had promised his wife in January 1823 that he would 'never again conceal a thought of mine from you'.[66] It was not a promise he would keep. He had been referring specifically to his debts, and his confidence that after another year they would be all paid. But in the autumn of 1823 the folly of sending his family to the continent was exposed. O'Connell was forced in September to admit to his brother, James, that his finances were as bad, if not worse than ever.[67] He faced ruin. James was shocked by 'the state of embarrassment'.

Three times O'Connell begged his brother for money and three times he was refused. James was implacable and attacked his brother's 'very novel' scheme of sending his family to the continent. He wondered how they could even think they were saving money when they were travelling all the time, including a stay in 'the most expensive part of Paris', and were thinking of moving to 'England, the dearest country in Europe to live in'.[68] James blamed his brother for having 'squandered or dissipated' his enormous professional income and reminded him that he must put his own wife and family first. O'Connell promised to repay the loan in November, but James was incredulous: 'In the name of common sense, how?'[69] He also reminded O'Connell that neither he, nor John, had received a shilling of interest on the loan they had given him in 1816. He also owed them a further £1,000 for a mortgage they had signed over to him. James warned him that if Hunting Cap heard of the state of his affairs he would be finished, and he advised him to do something quickly as 'surely *ill-health* or *arrest for debt* would completely knock you up'.[70]

By November Mary and the children had settled in Southampton, unaware of the magnitude of O'Connell's debts. O'Connell planned to remove them to Derrynane the following summer, to live with Hunting Cap (who was 95). But Hunting Cap refused, saying that he did not want anyone to visit for more than two days at a time (his nephews excepted).[71] James was certain that the '*tour* to the continent' was to blame for the new crisis. But by now he had given up advising his brother and he noted archly that 'if what you have suffered heretofore by your waste of money has not cured you, anything I could say would make no impression'. The debts were estimated to be more than £20,000 (so little progress had been made since 1816) and James had proof of three-quarters of them.[72] James believed that his brother had always been 'of a most sanguine disposition' and blamed this for his carelessness. To make matters worse, O'Connell's creditors started to reclaim their money. Denys Scully was upset at never having had his loan repaid and eight years on demanded his money.[73] Despite his promise, O'Connell did not tell his wife about the failure of their economising. First, he thought she was pregnant, following his visit to Paris in the summer of 1823, though it turned out to be a false hope. O'Connell was disappointed: he had wanted 'another doat'.[74] Second, his instinct was always for concealment and avoiding embarrassment.

He assured her that if his legal practice continued to thrive he might soon be able to bring her and the children home, even though there was little evidence to support him. Once again, somehow, O'Connell avoided disaster and was able to raise enough money to placate his creditors in the short term. Even James praised him in February 1824 for having finally come to terms with his 'embarrassments'.[75]

'How monotonous my life is,' complained O'Connell in January 1824.[76] He told his wife that 'the history of one day is the story of all'. He was still rising early, around five a.m., and would work until eight fifteen. Then he breakfasted, two fresh eggs every day, which he feared were making him fat. He would work at home until ten forty-five, and then head to the courts. At home by five p.m., he would dine and then read until about nine thirty p.m., when he would go to bed. O'Connell was much concerned with his weight. Even though he was not drinking wine or punch, he was still growing 'daily more and more corpulent'.[77] He blamed his eating habits, as he rose early, spent much time on his feet, and walked 'very fast through the streets'. Even during Lent he continued to gain weight, though he enjoyed his 'beefsteak' when Lent was over, which he ate with 'a *ferocious* appetite'.[78] At the Four Courts O'Connell was having great success and his professional income for the year was £6,045.[79] The lord chancellor, Lord Manners, long an enemy, had even begun laughing at jokes he made in court: 'He has not smiled on me so for some time.' At a dinner given by the lord lieutenant, Manners spoke highly of O'Connell's talents and praised his argument in a case before him as 'one of the best' he had heard since he had arrived in Ireland.[80]

Lord Norbury was still an irritation. He was now 'cruelly deaf' and barristers were forced to shout to make themselves heard. There were also further run-ins with 'that snivelling Serjeant Lefroy'.[81] O'Connell was defending two men 'for their lives' when he was stopped during the cross-examination of 'the single identification witness'.[82] This enraged him and he launched into a vicious denunciation of Lefroy. The jury acquitted the prisoners, saving O'Connell from bringing the matter before parliament, and afterwards he wondered 'what a miserable creature he is... He is a strange instance of what puffing will do to exalt, even in a difficult profession, a being of little intellect and no heart.' In April, three prisoners O'Connell defended were sentenced to death though he was not convinced they were guilty. 'It is a wretched profession when one has the agony of playing for the human life,' he bemoaned, though he believed that if they were 'really guilty twenty hangings would be too good for them'.[83]

The great idea of the Catholic Association was now unveiled. O'Connell first suggested the idea of a national subscription—the Catholic rent, a small amount to be collected monthly, which would allow even the poorest supporters to feel involved—at a meeting on 24 January. This was not an original idea, Lord Kenmare had first suggested it back in the 1780s, as O'Connell himself acknowledged, and O'Connell had attempted something similar on a temporary basis in 1812. But this was a more radical scheme, and O'Connell was determined to extend the rent to every parish in the country.[84] He was confident it could raise £50,000 if collected.[85] As Oliver MacDonagh has noted, 'O'Connell saw the rent as the transformer of sentimental support into real commitment.'[86] Unfortunately, O'Connell's attempts to gain approval for the rent at subsequent meetings were stymied by the 'no house' rule. Nicholas Purcell O'Gorman, the secretary, was infatuated with rules and would always adjourn the meeting at three thirty if a quorum was not present. Despite O'Connell's best efforts to secure promises of attendance, he struggled to get enough men to attend, or attend on time. At three twenty O'Gorman would make a great show of taking out his watch and leaving it on the table, and at three thirty he would hold it up and say, 'Gentlemen, it is half past three o'clock and ten members not present we must adjourn!'[87]

On Wednesday 4 February there were only seven people present, and this included O'Connell and O'Gorman in the chair. It was three twenty-three, and the watch was already in O'Gorman's hand. Unable to remain seated as the time counted down, O'Connell ran downstairs to Coyne's shop, desperate to find some members. On the stairs he met an eighth member heading up, but he needed two more. In the shop he spotted two young Maynooth priests and, remembering that all Catholic clergymen were honorary members, he pleaded with them to attend the meeting. They refused, as they did not want to get involved in politics, but O'Connell ignored them. He talked over them and eventually started pushing them up the stairs. They arrived in the room just as O'Gorman was about to adjourn the meeting and so it was allowed to proceed.[88] William Coppinger took the chair, allowing the two priests to sneak away (there was no further counting of the house).

O'Connell rose to discuss his idea of a national subscription, and he gave clear reasons why it would not affect the legality of the Association. He gave his word that he would attend to every detail and act as secretary in the collection of the rent. Five distinct purposes of the rent were outlined. The first was to finance regular Catholic petitions to parliament, including hiring a parliamentary agent in London to represent them (£5,000 a year). The second was on public relations, supporting sympathetic newspapers and opposing 'the Orange press' (£15,000 a year). The third was offering legal protection to Irish Catholics (£15,000 a year), the fourth educating the Catholic poor (£5,000 a year). The fifth and final purpose was for the training of Irish priests, especially so priests could be sent to North America where there was a shortage (£5,000 a year). The surplus £5,000 would be allowed to accumulate and would be used for the building of chapels, accommodation for the clergy and so on.[89] In this way O'Connell cleverly ensnared the Catholic clergy in his plans, making it in their best interests to encourage and support the rent. However not everyone saw the value of the scheme and O'Connell was mocked for his ambition; some wondered how sending priests to North America would help emancipation and others doubted anything would come of it.[90] Even John O'Connell, in school at Clongowes, was teased about his father's 'penny-a-month plan for liberating Ireland'.[91]

A committee appointed to consider the plan approved it on 14 February.[92] But again there was some criticism with O'Gorman claiming that its report was the work of O'Connell and had never been shown to the committee.[93] Details of 'The monthly Catholic rent' were published in the *Dublin Evening Post* on 19 February. There were fourteen resolutions, with the eleventh stating that each subscriber must pay not less than a penny a month and not more than two shillings. The fourteenth resolution appointed O'Connell as secretary to collect the subscriptions. This was the making of the Catholic movement in the 1820s. As O'Connell anticipated, 'The Catholic rent will surely emancipate us.'[94] O'Connell also changed the 'no house' rule on 21 February; the meetings would no longer adjourn automatically at three thirty, but instead would wait until five p.m. for ten members, and if ten members were present at any point before this it could begin. His popularity among Catholics, and his profile in the country, was greater than ever. Full of confidence, O'Connell decided to become even more aggressive in his speeches. On 21 February he denounced the duke of York at a meeting of the Catholic Association in such strong terms that the *Courier* suggested Catholics would have to behave better if they wished to obtain emancipation. O'Connell also broke with Plunket once more, telling the Catholic Association that he could not be trusted as his political interests and views were opposed to theirs.[95]

The Catholic Association began taking the lead at the aggregate meetings of the Catholics of Ireland. At the aggregate meeting on Friday 27 February at the Old Townshend Street Chapel, a petition was presented which had been agreed at the Association meeting three days earlier. But an attempt was made to block it, with one speaker calling for it to be referred back to the Association for revision before it was presented to parliament. There was little support for this motion (it was not seconded) and O'Connell rose to speak 'amidst the most enthusiastic cheering'.[96] Unable to speak for several minutes, as 'deafening shouts' echoed throughout the chapel, he began by quoting his 'old and favourite motto' of 'Hereditary bondsmen'. Addressing the criticism that the Catholic leaders were merely agitators, he said that 'he thanked his God for being one'.[97] He insisted that whatever they had won they had won through agitation, and whatever they had lost they had lost by moderation. And as for 'moderation', he said the very word made him sick and he wondered why certain men who said it so often didn't just teach a parrot to repeat it.

On 15 May a meeting of the Catholic Association was disrupted by a young man who heckled Richard Sheil throughout his speech. The members wanted to evict him, but O'Connell intervened and invited the man to speak. He refused, but he came back on 24 May and gave an impassioned speech attacking the Catholics and denouncing O'Connell for being the worst of them. Several men interrupted him, as he wasn't a member and therefore had no speaking rights, but O'Connell insisted that he should be allowed to continue as it should never be said that a Protestant was denied a hearing. Disconcerted, the young man sat down soon after. O'Connell rose to respond. He speculated that the young man might be 'a bravo hired by the Orange club to assail my character and motives'. This made him think back to D'Esterre, though he insisted that he had 'passed that time of life when mere personal ribaldry can make me forgetful of the obedience I owe my Maker and of my duty to my family, and would to God, sir, I had ever been guided by the same feeling'.[98] After giving 'instruction' to 'this temperate youth', O'Connell sat down to great applause. The young man was then insulted in a speech by Kirwan. Afterwards he asked for Kirwan's card so he could challenge him, but this was refused as he declined to give his own name. Humiliated, the man left the meeting.

Those who attacked O'Connell in public received similar treatment. Colonel Frederick Trench mocked O'Connell in parliament and dismissed him as 'Lawyer O'Connell'. Responding, O'Connell recollected that when he had been called to the bar the 'gallant colonel' was also pacing the Four Courts trying to make a career as a barrister, 'and the only difference between them was, that the colonel paced the hall and failed, while he (O'Connell) walked it and succeeded'. As a result, he said, he had felt no need to transform himself from a lawyer to a colonel.[99] Attacks on the Catholics were also answered. Thomas Ellis, an MP and alderman, had published a pamphlet claiming that Catholics were mentally inferior to Protestants and O'Connell remembered that Ellis had also been on circuit with him and had received every encouragement from the judges, whereas he had had to insist upon being heard.[100] But while O'Connell secured so much business that he struggled to carry all his briefs into court, Ellis had so much free time he was able 'to put on his dancing shoes'. O'Connell enjoyed baiting Ellis and this animosity went back a number of years. On 2 April 1821 Ellis had given a speech in the House of Commons on the Catholic relief bill in which he wondered aloud why O'Connell was 'the acknowledged organ of the Catholic body'.[101] He insisted that it could not be because of his family which, 'though respectable, was of yesterday'. Nor could it be because of his talents, 'for his eloquence was but of mushroom celebrity and was far outshone by the talents opposed to him'. Responding, O'Connell's assessment of Ellis's career was even more brutal: he said it was one of total 'professional incapacity, an acknowledged total failure in every way'.

Death threats were becoming a regular occurrence. In June O'Connell claimed to have received twelve in recent weeks, some threatening to slit his throat.[102] The Catholic rent was slow coming in, but O'Connell created a comprehensive parish-by-parish system to organise and collect it. He was still supremely confident that it would succeed and he told the Catholic Association on 4 July that 'for the first time in his life the Catholic people would owe him a debt of gratitude' if it succeeded to the extent he expected.[103] The Association was gradually growing in strength and by the end of the year it was receiving weekly returns of £1,000 on average.[104] Hunting Cap also showed his support and sent £10 and a long letter full of praise on 10 December.[105]

The Trinity College Dublin students were still causing problems. Large numbers began attending the meetings of the Association to heckle and disrupt and O'Connell struggled to find a way of stopping them. For example, the meeting of 27 October, which Mary O'Connell and her daughters attended, was disrupted by the students and it took much time to restore order. Growing frustrated, O'Connell found premises at the Corn Exchange on Burgh Quay in November, and there found a solution by accident. The entrance was near the coal-porters' stand (with about one hundred and fifty men) and the men promised to keep guard and throw the students in the Liffey if they tried to cause trouble.[106] The rooms at the Corn Exchange were perfect, and there was a large meeting area which could accommodate up to a thousand people. In later years O'Connell would joke that it was the Dublin coal-porters who had saved the agitation and that therefore they deserved the credit for carrying emancipation.[107]

Meanwhile Plunket attempted to get his revenge on O'Connell. At a meeting of the Catholic Association on 16 December O'Connell announced that

> He hoped Ireland would be restored to her rights—but, if that day should arrive—if she were driven mad by persecution, he wished that a new Bolívar may be found—may arise—that the spirit of the Greeks and of the South Americans may animate the people of Ireland.[108]

As far as Plunket was concerned this was incitement to rebellion and he decided to prosecute. The home secretary was Peel, and he saw in O'Connell's words nothing more than a coded announcement that 'I hope the people will rise in arms against their lawful government.'[109] At five thirty p.m. on Monday 20 December, as O'Connell was returning from a meeting of the Catholic Association, he was visited at home by Alderman Darley and a police constable. Darley informed him that he was obliged to enter into a recognisance to appear at the next sessions.

O'Connell was astonished to learn that it was upon a charge of having spoken seditious words at the Catholic Association. The men shook hands and parted.[110] O'Connell's first concern was to ensure that Hunting Cap, who would disapprove, would not hear of it. So he begged a friend in Kerry to leave out anything to do with the prosecution when he was reading the *Dublin Evening Post* to him.[111] O'Connell had visited Hunting Cap in September and found him 'a great deal broken'.[112] Asked to help with the arrangements for when he died, O'Connell wrote his epitaph, which included the tribute, 'They loved him most who knew him best.'[113]

The charges over the 'Bolívar speech' were dropped on 1 January 1825 when the newspaper reporters refused to co-operate. For example, the reporter for *Saunder's News-Letter* claimed to have been asleep during the speech and to have taken his account from another person. O'Connell was in great spirits at the hearing, joking so much with one of the prosecution lawyers that *The Times* complained that it made the whole thing 'rather ludicrous'.[114] On leaving Green Street Courthouse O'Connell was greeted by a huge crowd of supporters and they followed him, cheering, all the way to Merrion Square, despite his best efforts to disperse them. The grand jury dismissed the bills of indictment that evening by fifteen to eight.[115]

At the next meeting of the Catholic Association, on Saturday 8 January 1825, O'Connell was acclaimed by the gathering. For 'nearly ten minutes' there was applause, waving of hats, and cheering and O'Connell delivered an emotional speech in response. He said that the real reason for his arrest had been to find an excuse to suppress the Catholic Association, but he told the gathering that he was up to the challenge and that 'if any man was to be sacrificed for that purpose, I was that man.'[116] This produced further cheering and O'Connell declared that he was the instrument which would bring about emancipation. He then asked the gathering to admit his claim as a right, so 'that I may be at all times the victim, when their liberty or their rights are to be sacrificed upon the altar of persecution'. This was O'Connell at his most defiant, revealing that if the Catholic Association was suppressed he would merely change its name and call it a board, or a committee, or even a directory. This was a time of rumours and uncertainty, with some entertaining stories circulating Dublin about how the Catholic question would be resolved. It was said that Sir

Harcourt Lees, a leading Orangeman, would race Daniel O'Connell from the Corn Exchange to Maynooth College with the winner getting to choose whether the government's policy should be emancipation or legitimate coercion. Lees was amused by the idea that so much would depend on 'the ultra perspiration of these two political and religious antagonists'. In a letter to *The Times* he joked that he would bet 'ten to one' that he would 'beat Dan'.[117] Meanwhile, after almost two years away, Mary O'Connell and her children were back in Ireland. They had arrived home in the summer of 1824, returning to their house at Merrion Square. Mary joked that it was about time as their youngest child, Danny, had taken to abusing the English on the streets of Southampton: 'such a little patriot as he is'.[118] He was clearly his father's son.

Chapter 12 ∾

BIG O AND SIR GLORY: A COMEDY IN THREE ACTS, 1825

'*Big O: A super-human Counsellor, intensely bent upon delivering (after the Orange fashion) the entire of the forty-shilling freeholders of their votes, even with the certainty of being compelled to endure a patent of precedency, as a reward for "all his sacrifices" in effecting the said deliverance*'.
(WILLIAM COBBETT, *Big O and Sir Glory, A Comedy in Three Acts*, SEPTEMBER 1825).

1825 was the worst year of O'Connell's political career. The Catholic Association was suppressed, a new Catholic relief bill was defeated, and, worse, his leadership of the Irish Catholics was undermined and his reputation assailed. Believing that 'the game was won',[1] he had decided to compromise, agreeing to a qualified emancipation with two conditions imposed by the government—disenfranchisement of the forty-shilling freeholders and a state provision for the Catholic clergy. They were not the same as a veto but they were securities none the less, and it was a high-risk gamble to take. However, even with these concessions, emancipation was still rejected and O'Connell was left exposed and vulnerable, with many suspecting that he had compromised for selfish reasons because of his desire to gain a patent of precedence and advance his own career. This was a time when O'Connell's judgement was doubted and his leadership questioned, as people began to wonder if he had lost his way and even if he could still be trusted.

O'Connell's frustration at not being advanced at the bar had been growing for some time. Every year he saw inferior lawyers being promoted ahead of him, receiving the silk gown and thus having precedence in the courtroom, and it rankled. He was in his fiftieth year, and had been a barrister for almost twenty-seven of those, and he struggled to contain his bitterness over what he saw as a terrible personal injustice. In January 1825 he compared himself to one of his contemporaries on the circuit, Edward Pennefather, someone he had once been able to 'compete with easily', but who now moved '*hours* before me' because he was a king's counsel.[2] The financial implications of not being promoted were also a factor, as he continued to struggle with his debts. O'Connell presided over a charity dinner at the end of the month but refused to drink the health of the lord lieutenant, Wellesley, because of his prosecution in December, insisting that it was safer to be his enemy than his friend. And it is significant that in his attack on Wellesley he emphasised the injustice of being denied a silk gown.[3] *The Times* was disgusted by what it called O'Connell's 'egregious folly' in insulting Wellesley. This was a difficult time for O'Connell and his leadership was being increasingly challenged. As a result, he was growing irritable about the 'miserable and unnecessary jealousy' which he faced daily at the Catholic Association. A new emancipation petition had been prepared for the British parliament and a deputation carried it to London. O'Connell was due to join them in February and this mission was weighing on his mind as he knew he would suffer financially from missing the assizes. The new Catholic petition was entrusted to Sir Francis Burdett (the 'Sir Glory' of Cobbett's satire) to present in the House of Commons (in a pointed snub to Plunket) and there was a belief that London would be the theatre where Irish hopes would be decided.

The government now decided to suppress the Catholic Association, something it had long wanted to do, and legislation was prepared to declare it illegal. In the king's address to parliament he spoke of how the Catholic Association was 'irreconcilable with the spirit of the constitution' and called for this 'evil' to be removed.[4] An unlawful societies in Ireland bill was presented to the House of Commons on 15

February by the chief secretary for Ireland, Henry Goulburn. In his speech he denounced the Association for squashing dissent and claimed that it had links with the traitors of old, Wolfe Tone, Thomas Russell and Robert Emmet.[5] O'Connell realised his presence in London was more important than ever so that he could present their case before the bar of the House of Commons. He set off with his son, Maurice, and Richard Sheil, following the death of Hunting Cap on 10 February 1825 at the age of ninety-seven.

William Cobbett, the crusading journalist and radical reformer, had been championing the cause of Catholic emancipation in Britain and was full of advice for O'Connell before he arrived. He urged him to be 'bold' and to make sure that his thoughts were not 'castrated'.[6] Cobbett's weekly paper, the *Political Register*, became part of the concerted effort to convince the British public that emancipation could be granted without any danger either to society or to the constitution. O'Connell had been looking forward to meeting Cobbett (they shared many similarities, including a physical resemblance) and was not disappointed when he met him, thinking him 'a bold clear-headed fellow' with 'distinct and well-intentioned' views.[7] According to Cobbett, his first words when he met O'Connell were the dramatic: 'Well, Mr O'Connell, let me beseech you to bear in mind that you are come into hell and that you have, of course, devils to deal with.'[8] In London various strategies were discussed to generate public interest in the Catholic cause and emancipation. One idea the delegation had brought from Dublin was to present the Catholic petition before the bar of the Commons and this was attempted on Friday 18 February. A motion to allow this was proposed in the Commons by Henry Brougham and seconded by Sir Francis Burdett, but it was voted down. During this debate Peel gave a violent speech against the Catholic Association and was so exultant at one point that he walked over to the bar of the Commons and shook O'Connell's hand, apparently not recognising him.[9] Prevented from presenting his case, instead O'Connell followed the debates on the unlawful societies in Ireland bill closely. The quality of oratory on display left him cold. The solicitor general he dismissed as 'a blockhead', the president of the board of control as 'just one of the worst speakers I ever heard'. He had no doubt that he would be their superior in debate, finding them a 'stupid set... altogether'. But he also worried that their English allies were not as zealous as he expected—'there is an English coldness'—and he wondered if they would really mind if the Irish Catholics were crushed.[10] Burdett presented the Catholic petition on 1 March and, pressed by O'Connell, also proposed a motion that the Commons should take into consideration the laws against the Catholics to see if they should be changed. Although opposed by Henry Goulburn the motion was carried by 247 to 234.[11] This thirteen-vote victory created the momentum for a new Catholic relief bill. O'Connell later boasted that he had forced Burdett to bring forward his motion and became convinced it would bring about emancipation.

The unlawful societies in Ireland bill passed inexorably through the Commons, with its third reading on 25 February. It received the royal assent on 9 March. O'Connell joked to his wife that everyone in parliament pronounced 'association' the way she did, as 'asso-she-ation', 'so you triumph over us all'.[12] He was clearly missing his wife, writing to her once or twice a day, calling her his 'darling, cocknosed, sweetest, saucy, best of women' and reminiscing about the first time they had held hands.[13] Maurice spoke at many of the public meetings in favour of emancipation, and O'Connell worried that he was copying too many of his own bad habits and was 'too personal' in his attacks. He believed this 'propensity to personality' was dangerous, especially as it had 'an hereditary source'.[14] In this period the deputation met with many of the leading English Catholics and their supporters, and O'Connell became optimistic that the cause of emancipation was being advanced by their mission: 'We are certainly working on the English mind.' The Commons committee to inquire into Irish affairs was set up on 17 February, and a week later Lord Donoughmore presented the Catholic petition in the House of Lords.[15] On 25 February O'Connell was examined by the committee for Irish affairs and he discussed the state of the peasantry, land issues, and legal proceedings. He was pleased with his performance, noting that Peel attended most of the examination.[16] A number of MPs even made a point of stopping him afterwards to tell him that his answers had removed their doubts about emancipation.[17] O'Connell believed that a 'great battle' would be fought in England and he was quite vain of his success.[18] 'We are to be emancipated,' he told his wife, confidently.[19]

A major public meeting of the English Catholics was held at Freemasons' Tavern on 26 February to discuss petitioning the House of

Lords to reject the bill suppressing the Catholic Association.[20] O'Connell was determined to make an impression and made sure he was well prepared. He visited the hall in advance and practised speaking from different positions to find the best place to position himself. The acoustics in the hall were terrible and it was difficult to make oneself heard. Thus, at the meeting on 26 February, most of the audience stood as they strained to hear the different speakers. O'Connell discovered that he could be heard most clearly from a position leaning against a pillar, and it was here that he delivered his speech.[21] The preparation paid off. His three-and-a-half-hour speech was a triumph, praised by Lord Stourton as superior to the oratory of Pitt and Fox, and by Charles Butler as being as good as that of the great Lord Chatham.[22] Sheil noted that the newspaper reporters had looked upon O'Connell with a great deal of 'supercilious distaste' at the start of his speech, but that by the end he had won most of them over. The reporter from *The Times*, however, refused to be be impressed and described his voice as 'powerful, but without modulation', and his gestures as 'violent and theatrical, without being impressive'.[23] O'Connell began the speech confidently. He assured his listeners that they could remain seated as 'I promise you it will not be difficult to hear me,' and he made jokes at the expense of previous speakers who had gone on for too long.[24] Referring to the 'considerable pecuniary sacrifice' he had made by coming to London, and his sadness as leaving his home, 'and a happy home it is', he expressed his disgust that the House of Commons had refused to hear the delegation. He had come to London to vindicate the Catholic Association, but he rejoiced that instead he had an opportunity to appeal to '*you*, the people of England'.

The old enemy was attacked. O'Connell claimed (and this was one of his regular allegations in this period) that a lodge of the Orange Order had as its password a quote from the 68th psalm: 'That thy foot may be dipped in the blood of thine enemies; and that the tongue of thy dogs may be red with the same.'[25] A man in the audience objected and cried, 'No!' But O'Connell stood over his claim and said that if he failed to prove his words he would give up on emancipation for ever.

In a theatrical moment O'Connell held up the act suppressing the Catholic Association and then flung it away. He dismissed it as 'this Algerine Act' (which soon became its popular designation), because it was not clear whether the legislation had 'been framed in England or

Algiers'.[26] 'What legislation, I will ask, is this?', he said, to loud cheers. 'I am sure it ought not to be English'. The speech was a mixture of the personal and the political. He talked about how a new alderman, a man called Hamilton—'there's nothing like naming names'—had celebrated his elevation by getting 'drunk into intoxication with champagne furnished from the taxation of poor Catholics'. He had then called round to O'Connell's house and demanded admission, suspecting that some illegal meeting was taking place there. 'Oh you may call me an agitator,' O'Connell told the crowd, 'but I must say that I do not think existence worth having, when it must be purchased by such degradation.' O'Connell sat down to 'long continued cheering which was accompanied by waving of hats and handkerchiefs'. It was his greatest success in London.

William Fagan later reflected that one of O'Connell's greatest skills was his ability to choose the best time to speak, neither too early nor too late. He arrived at meetings at 'the opportune moment', creating a 'sensation when he appeared', and reviving 'the flagging spirits of the crowd'.[27] Nowhere was this skill more in evidence than here, and 'in no part of Ireland could he have been more enthusiastically received'. Shiel was less astute and unwisely chose to speak after O'Connell, by which time the audience was exhausted and unwilling to listen to a speech heavy in statistical data. His effort, 'comparatively speaking, was a failure'. Sheil himself admitted that he felt like an actor surveying an empty house, and he 'became disheartened, and lost his command over his throat'.[28] Even he was bored by his speech and its 'laborious detail of uninteresting facts'.

Two days later, on 28 February, O'Connell sent a letter to William Plunket, requesting a meeting. O'Connell later admitted that he had gone to London irritated at Plunket and 'much and personally offended with him'.[29] But now that the Catholic question was about to be discussed once more, he realised it was necessary to reconcile, to put aside his dislike for Plunket, 'my personal enemy', for the sake of the Catholic cause. As he admitted later in the year, he recognised that the delegation needed Plunket's backing for the debates in parliament and so he 'flung to the winds my personal wrongs, I discarded my individual resentments' and 'I sought, I courted.'[30] They met later on the 28th, and the meeting marked the beginning of a new strategy of conciliation. Plunket was still supportive of a veto to ease British fears, and O'Connell spent much time trying unsuccessfully to argue him out of this position. On 2 March O'Connell called to Plunket's house and it was here that Plunket helped persuade him to accept some form of securities if it meant winning emancipation. Plunket also invited him to help draft a new relief bill and this appealed to him greatly. The disenfranchisement of the forty-shilling freeholders and the state provision for the clergy were mooted (what became known as the 'wings'), as, it seems, was the reward of a patent of precedence for O'Connell if emancipation passed. Another meeting was arranged for the following day and O'Connell was invited to bring along another representative from the Irish delegation.

On 3 March O'Connell and Lord Killeen, the eldest son of Lord Fingall, went to Plunket's house, where the 'wings' were presented formally. O'Connell gave his support, Killeen objected, and both men returned to the delegation to report on the offer.[31] As a former vetoist, Sheil supported the 'wings', but he noted afterwards that many resented O'Connell's 'dictatorial tone'.[32] At this meeting O'Connell used all his powers to defend the principle of the 'wings' and, although the delegation was split, he seems to have carried the argument. O'Connell was certain that 'we have won the game'.[33] Not only that, he was convinced that he deserved the credit for winning it. It was precisely because victory was so close that O'Connell was prepared to compromise to guarantee it. It was the first of many mistakes. There were a number of factors which persuaded him to accept the 'wings'. He had little faith in the forty-shilling freeholders and believed, wrongly as events would later demonstrate quite spectacularly, that they would always be the puppets of their landowners and vote as instructed. The provision for the clergy he viewed as harmless and he thought the payments would bring £250,000 of 'English money into Ireland' every year, without any state interference.[34] But what was really driving him was the prospect of success, and it seemed so close that any concessions could be tolerated if they would confirm victory. The difference emancipation would make to his own professional career was inevitably a factor and the patent of precedence dangling before his eyes distracted him. He had also succumbed to the attention and adulation in London. Everyone was telling him that it was he who would carry emancipation, and even though he recognised that he was being 'lost *by flattery*', he still could not think clearly. As he admitted to his wife, 'I wish to God I could make my motives so pure and disinterested as to care little for gratitude and applause'.[35]

A new emancipation bill was prepared to be presented in parliament, and O'Connell and Plunket joined forces with Burdett to draft it. John Cam Hobhouse was surprised to note that 'the greatest harmony reigns between the two'.[36] O'Connell was examined again by the committee for Irish affairs on 4 March and was questioned about the Catholics of Ireland, 'the people, the church, the friars, the priests, the Jesuits'.[37] The Orange Order was a particular target for O'Connell, and he insisted that its oaths were shadowy and suspicious, and that 'the peasantry speak of them as *Exterminators*'.[38] He also blamed the Orange lodges for the outbreak of the 1798 Rebellion, accusing them of having fomented the civil unrest in the country for their own purposes. When addressing the remaining restrictions on the Catholics, he made a point of discussing his own failure to be made a king's counsel. He called it 'an excessive grievance' and discussed at length the income it cost him.[39] The suggested disenfranchisement of the forty-shilling freeholders was defended as making no real difference if emancipation accompanied it, as he insisted they were too easily controlled by their landlords. O'Connell's ignorance of the province of Ulster was evident. Under questioning he admitted that he had never been to the counties of Antrim, Derry, Armagh, Fermanagh or Donegal, and had only been in Down and Tyrone when travelling to Monaghan. He was examined before the Lords on 9 March and was described by Lord Colchester, an aggressive opponent of emancipation, as 'a stout built man with a black wig, and light-coloured eyebrows, above the middle stature, pale countenance, square features, blue eyes... respectful and gentle, except in a few answers where he displayed a fierceness of tone and aspect'.[40] From the way the examination went O'Connell left with a confident but ultimately mistaken belief that the prime minister, Lord Liverpool, would support emancipation.

Cobbett met with O'Connell on 8 March and begged him to reject the 'wings', but O'Connell was evasive and refused to admit that he had conceded the point.[41] The next day Sheil told Cobbett that O'Connell had been promised a patent of precedence and immediately his faith was shattered. He now turned on O'Connell with a vengeance, determined to punish what he perceived as this betrayal of the Irish Catholics and, most importantly, of himself. Not part of the deputation, but in London none the less, Jack Lawless joined in the opposition to the 'wings'. He published an angry tirade against both the 'wings' and O'Connell on 15 March in the *Morning Herald*, which was reprinted in the *Freeman's Journal* on 18 March. Lawless believed that a state provision for the clergy would allow the government to corrupt them, and that agreeing to the disenfranchisement of the forty-shilling freeholders was a sell-out. Claiming to be a member of the delegation, he also accused O'Connell of making these concessions for selfish reasons, because emancipation would give him a silk gown.[42] By this time it had leaked that O'Connell would receive a patent of precedence from the government in the event of emancipation and so this charge stung.[43] Lawless's opposition to the 'wings', subsequently vindicated, earned him the nickname 'Honest Jack'. O'Connell, though, was furious with him, denouncing him as 'that miserable maniac Lawless'. But he was so convinced that the emancipation bill would pass through both houses of parliament that he was not too uneasy—'the game is won—it is only the manner of playing it that makes any difference'.[44] He looked forward to entering the House of Commons as an MP and had little doubt that he would make an impression. His vanity was commented upon by those in the delegation. 'The Irish tell me he is very vain', wrote John Cam Hobhouse in his diary, after meeting the full delegation at a dinner on 13 March. Hobhouse believed that O'Connell was someone who liked people to point him out in a crowd and say, 'This is he.' Nevertheless he found him 'very pleasant, natural and easy' but thought that he was 'not what is called a man of the world, or with the airs of a town-bred gentleman'.[45] He also noted that the same Irish who found him vain admitted that he was 'a most powerful speaker and a very learned lawyer' and he, himself, was impressed that 'he rises very early in the morning'.

On 17 March O'Connell attended the annual dinner of the benevolent society of St Patrick at the City of London Tavern, wearing a 'flaming shamrock'. However the dinner ended early when Lawless stormed in and began ranting about the 'wings'. A number of men attempted to restrain him but failed.[46] The next day the Catholic Association voted its own dissolution in Dublin, and arranged to give its funds to Lord Killeen for safekeeping. It also passed a resolution asserting that O'Connell still enjoyed 'the *undivided* and *undiminished* confidence of the Catholic Association', suggesting that the divisions in

London were making an impression, though O'Connell was still ascendant.[47] Deciding to return home to assist in the winding-up of the Catholic Association, O'Connell set out for Dublin on 21 March. He also made it clear that he would refuse to accept any money for his expenses while in London, insisting that no man should even speak of paying him.[48]

Sir Francis Burdett introduced the emancipation bill on Wednesday 23 March in the Commons, and Robert Peel, the home secretary, decided not to oppose it at the first reading, but wait for the debate on the second reading in April.[49] Deciding to return to England, O'Connell arrived in London on 18 April, afraid the Whigs, 'our hollow friends', would desert the cause.[50] He began attending the debates in the Commons and was shrewd in his analysis of the different speakers, reviewing not only what they said but how they said it. For example, he noted the contribution of John Henry North, who made a speech which 'reads well in the newspapers' but which made no impression on the House and thus was 'a total failure'.[51] The vote on the second reading of the emancipation bill passed in the Commons on 21 April by 268 to 241. O'Connell was impressed by the speech of George Canning, 'one of the best I ever heard anywhere', but was repulsed by the bigotry on display in so many of the other contributions. The bill in favour of disenfranchising the forty-shilling freeholders was introduced the next day and O'Connell recognised that it was 'a very hard card to play' as it risked alienating some friends even as it offered the possibility of winning over some enemies.[52] O'Connell was in high spirits, as indeed was his son, Maurice. In the Commons Maurice jumped over some banisters and down a flight of stairs showing off, and O'Connell was amused that they would 'have been all thrown out' if he had been caught.[53]

Emancipation appeared inevitable and O'Connell was prepared to make any sacrifice to guarantee it, even if it meant 'personal humiliation'. And so he decided to make an apology to Peel for the events which had almost led to them fighting a duel a decade earlier. There were a number of reasons why he decided to take this step. First, he had come to accept that he had been 'clearly in the wrong' in 1815 and had long decided to make a 'painful but just' admission of this fact. He had also come to respect Peel for the reforms he had introduced as home secretary, in particular the way he had changed the mode of electing juries in Britain and his reform of the criminal code. But the main reason was that he believed Peel was the type of man who would allow 'personal hostility to, and the sense of an injustice done by a person styled a leader of the opposite party' to cloud his judgement when it came to the Catholic question.[54] In other words, he feared that Peel's inveterate opposition to emancipation was personal, and he blamed himself for it. And so he asked Richard Newton Bennett to carry a message to Colonel Brown, Peel's second in 1815, in which he accepted that he had offered the first provocation.[55] Brown asked that this apology should be made in writing and Bennett did so, although he did not write as strongly as O'Connell would have wished. Peel accepted this apology and sent O'Connell a letter in response, 'just such as a kind and warm-hearted gentleman would write'.[56] The approach to Peel was, as he admitted later in the year, 'painful to my pride'. But he was prepared to do it if it helped assuage Peel's determination to block emancipation. News of the apology was soon made public, though it was said that Peel had made no response. It gave ammunition to O'Connell's enemies who believed that he had 'crouched to Mr Peel' out of selfish motives, namely his greed for a patent of precedence.

The duke of York, the younger brother of George IV, made a violent speech against emancipation in the House of Lords on 25 April. In it he discussed the coronation oath and made emotive use of 'the ten years of misery, which had clouded the existence of his illustrious and beloved father,' because of the emancipation question. His intervention was important, because he was in line to succeed George IV, and his declaration that he would never give the royal assent to a Catholic relief bill, 'whatever may be the situation of his life', influenced many.[57] O'Connell, however, mistakenly believed that the speech would work to their advantage as it was so extreme it might turn people in favour of emancipation. O'Connell attended the levee on 27 April and kissed the hand of the king, George IV. The next day he was in Birmingham for the annual general meeting of the Midland Catholic Association and he delivered a speech for an hour and three quarters which was cheered throughout. O'Connell boasted to his wife that he had been described as 'a first rate orator' and he joked that she would agree. On 30 April he attended an anti-slavery meeting in London and when he was spotted in the crowd he was ushered to the front and asked to speak. In his oration he talked of how 'the blacks, having become free, would in time become members of society, would fill offices of importance and finally work out their independence'.[58] He praised 'the glorious Bolívar' for freeing the slaves (making sure to note that it would have been 'dangerous' to say this in Ireland), and attacked the United States for allowing slavery while preaching freedom ('you boast of your love of liberty, but you are tyrants, not friends of liberty—you are hypocrites').[59] And he stoked controversy by bringing Irish politics into the meeting when he declared that 'he himself was a slave'.

The split within the Irish deputation, caused by the 'wings', widened. Nicholas Purcell O'Gorman refused to accept the disenfranchisement of the forty-shilling freeholders and O'Connell quarrelled with him after a dinner at Lord Fitzwilliam's on 1 May. O'Connell was feeling the pressure and fought with O'Gorman 'in a rare passion', so much so that afterwards he believed the breach was irreparable. On 3 May Thomas Denham, a Nottingham MP, spoke in the Commons in favour of emancipation and mentioned the injustice of withholding a silk gown for so long from O'Connell. O'Connell was flattered by the tribute, but it provided fuel for his enemies who believed that self-interest was clouding his judgement.[60] When a deputation was sent to consult with Burdett and Donoughmore, which included Fingall and O'Connell, O'Gorman insisted on going even though he had not been chosen, further alienating him from O'Connell. May was the critical month, as the bill had its third and final reading in the Commons and faced the 'proud and vile peers' in the Lords.[61] Some observers believed emancipation might be postponed until the following year but O'Connell was convinced that 'it is *now* or never'.

This was a tense time. O'Connell spoke at a bible meeting on 9 May about Ireland and was booed by some listeners, which made him reflect on the 'state of ignorance' in England when it came to Irish affairs.[62] On 9 May he attended the debate in the Commons on the forty-shilling disenfranchisement bill and was furious with Henry Grattan's son, James, for opposing it. Grattan had suggested that if the forty-shilling freeholders were unfit to vote then they were also unfit to be emancipated and claimed confusingly 'I do not think this bill will cure the remedy.'[63] O'Connell despised him for being so inarticulate and mocked him viciously afterwards. He told his wife, 'Only think, darling, of such blockheads being the persons who govern and make laws for us.' The vote on the third reading of the emancipation bill was won in the Commons on 10 May by 248 to 227. Everything depended on the Lords and the attitude of the king. The crucial vote was on 17 May and O'Connell stood for eight hours among a huge crowd of spectators in the gallery of the House of Lords. The debate went on until five thirty a.m. but the final vote was crushing, 130 consenting to the bill (which was made up of 84 peers present and 46 proxies), and 178 against (113 present and 65 proxies).[64] The planned celebrations turned into a wake. Despite the humiliating disappointment, O'Connell refused to give up. Returning home at six a.m., he wrote to his wife to say, 'We must begin again.'[65] In the middle of his greatest disappointment his old resilience and defiance had been restored. This was a time for reconciliation with his allies and war with his enemies. Now that the bill had been defeated, and the 'wings' abandoned, O'Connell tried to make his peace with Lawless and O'Gorman.[66] But he was determined to go after the prime minister, Lord Liverpool, who he believed had acted dishonestly over relief. In his mind Liverpool was now 'a public enemy and must be hunted down like a wild cat'. He was also frustrated with the English Catholics and he despised their timidity for making a new strategy more difficult. But most of all O'Connell was frustrated with himself, feeling he had been tricked into agreeing to the 'wings' and thus compromising his principles for nothing.

On Saturday 21 May O'Connell delivered a lengthy speech to the British Catholic Association at the Crown and Anchor Tavern, London, which was 'applauded to the skies'.[67] Fagan later said that it was 'full of fire, and of real classic eloquence'.[68] O'Connell's spirits were returning and he knew that the only strategy was to return to agitation in Ireland. His thoughts were also on repeal of the Union and he wished that someone would take up the cause.[69] The prospect of 'a better agitation than ever' cheered him and he began making plans for how to proceed. He decided that a New Catholic Association would have to be formed, and it should have its own uniform, 'a blue frock and white pantaloons in summer—blue pantaloons in winter—a blue velvet cape' and a coat. The frock-coat would have two gold buttons with the Irish crown and harp on them and he wanted supporters to wear the uniform in both Britain and Ireland as 'a pledge of hostility to Lord Liverpool'.[70] He even ordered Christopher Fitzsimon, who was marrying his daughter, Ellen, to get married in the uniform. The prospect of a new agitation energised him and he assured his wife that he 'never was *up* to agitation till now'.[71] He boasted that the government would 'not get one hour's respite'.

The defeat of the emancipation bill brought with it a backlash, and those who disagreed with O'Connell's leadership took this opportunity to strike. Some retained their faith in him, but others were disillusioned and believed he had lost his way. After all, O'Connell himself had been the one who had demanded unqualified emancipation and had crushed anyone who supported securities. He was even taunted by Robert Peel and Sir Charles Wetherall, the British attorney general, and accused of having 'betrayed popular rights in order to obtain the objects of my personal ambition'.[72] Thomas Wyse, who wrote an account of the Catholic Association a few years later, believed the failure cast 'a slur on the negotiators' and he referred to a 'host of errors and sins'.[73] Over the summer the first murmurings of discontent with O'Connell were heard back in Ireland. It was clear there were divisions, with his leadership under threat. But there were also public displays of support, arranged to show that he still had the confidence of a large number of people and would not be abandoned just yet. O'Connell was fortunate that he was able to draw upon deep reserves of goodwill, built up over decades, but in this period he came close to exhausting them. He arrived back in Ireland on 1 June and was met at Howth with a public procession which escorted him back to his house at Merrion Square. From the balcony he delivered an address to the crowd and to great cheering insisted that despite the recent setback emancipation would soon be achieved.[74] On 8 June he spoke at an aggregate meeting, held at St Michan's Church, North Anne Street, where it was estimated that between six and seven thousand people attended. He wanted to send a clear signal that a new campaign was about to begin and so wore the blue uniform of the New Catholic Association.[75] Lawless provided the main opposition, but he was received badly, with many hisses, even though O'Connell pleaded for him to be heard. In a vehement attack Lawless rounded on 'the unfortunate credulity of the last three or four months' but the crowd was against him and shouted 'Off! Off!' until he could no longer be heard. O'Connell then rose to speak and while he accepted that ''tis true we have been defeated', he insisted 'we are not dismayed'. 'We have been betrayed, but we are unconquered.'[76] He ended by promising that there would be a new campaign, with a New Catholic Association formed and a new rent collected. Afterwards O'Connell's carriage was escorted by a procession back to Merrion Square.

But there was also evidence that O'Connell's reputation had been damaged. Sir Edward Bellew insisted on a vote to elect the committee of twenty-one which would organise the foundation of the new Catholic body. O'Connell's declining popularity was shown by the fact that, although he was elected unlike Bellew, he only came sixth in the poll with 311 votes. Richard Sheil topped the poll with 317 votes, John Lawless was near the bottom with 6.[77] William Bellew, Sir Edward's brother, a lawyer, then published a legal opinion against the formation of a new association. But he was dismissed by O'Connell, in a public letter to the Catholics of Ireland on 28 June, as someone who received a pension from the Castle and therefore couldn't be trusted, a typical line of abuse for anyone who differed from him.[78]

The New Catholic Association met at the Corn Exchange on 16 July, with ninety-six members subscribing.[79] O'Connell had been careful to avoid any illegality and it deliberately curtailed its powers to evade the government's restrictions. It would not petition parliament, and would limit its activities to non-political matters like the state of education and the burial of the dead. The old aggressive O'Connell was clearly back. At a meeting in Limerick he delivered a scathing attack on Lord Colchester, for comments he had made about the Catholics, and dismissed him in a wonderful put-down as having 'spoke, and sipped some gin-toddy that he had by him, and spoke and sipped—and spoke *unutterable* nonsense'.[80] In another speech he blamed Britain for turning Ireland into 'a pitiful province'.[81] 'Ireland to themselves' was now his demand, an extension of his favourite toast, 'Ireland as she ought to be'.

Comments O'Connell at made at a meeting of the Dublin Catholics at St Audeon's parish in Bridge Street Chapel on 9 July generated controversy. O'Connell had defended his actions in London by insisting that it had the 'entire concurrence and sanction' of two leading Irish prelates, Bishop Doyle and Archbishop Murray.[82] This was widely reported, prompting Cobbett to publish a denunciation on 19 July in which he accused O'Connell of having acted from corrupt personal motives. This took the form of a letter to the Catholics of Ireland which was published first in the *Political Register* and then reprinted in the Dublin *Morning Register* on 26 July. Cobbett blamed O'Connell's acceptance of the 'wings' for the failure of emancipation. One of his main allegations, and he cited Sheil as his source, was that O'Connell would have been granted a patent of precedence after emancipation and this prompted him to speculate that personal ambition had meant that he had been willing to sacrifice the best interests of the cause.[83] The attack was personal, with O'Connell accused of 'inconsistency' and 'inordinate vanity'. In response, O'Connell published a letter in the Dublin *Morning Register*, dated 21 August, in which he called Cobbett 'a comical miscreant'.[84] Addressing the charges of inconsistency and vanity, he joked that if these were crimes he would make no other apology than to say, 'The bed is large enough for both of us—share the blanket, friend Cobbett.' O'Connell also insisted that Cobbett never had a friend that he did not betray. But O'Connell was embarrassed further when his claims were refuted publicly by the Rev. Professor William Kinsella, of Carlow, who denied that O'Connell had received any sanction from Doyle to support the 'wings'. O'Connell attempted to spin his way out of trouble, pretending that he had been misquoted and that he had only been referring to the clerical provision. But Doyle then made public that he would have resigned rather than accept a 'paltry bribe' from the government.[85] Great damage was done and for months a wounded O'Connell wondered what he had done to alienate Doyle.[86]

On Saturday 24 September Cobbett published his satire 'Big O and Sir Glory, or, Leisure to laugh: a comedy in three acts' in his *Political Register*, and within a week it was being sold as a pamphlet. It was a curious mixture of dialogue and documentation, reviewing what had taken place in London and who was to blame. Too rambling and disjointed to be actually funny, it was none the less effective, and provided a damaging critique of O'Connell's actions. As far as O'Connell was concerned Cobbett was now 'a vile vagabond'. The ferocity with which O'Connell abused his enemies shocked some of his friends, but he later defended it by saying that 'if he did not use the sledge hammer to smash his opponents, he could never have succeeded'.[87]

O'Connell refused to admit that he had been wrong as he worked to rebuild his reputation. In newspapers and at meetings he was criticised, but, unusually for him, he was keen not to react too strongly.[88] At a meeting of the Co. Louth Catholics in Dundalk on 17 October there was some opposition when a vote of thanks to O'Connell was proposed.[89]

Anthony Marmion, the secretary of the meeting, interrupted to propose an amendment censuring O'Connell for supporting the 'wings' and he accused O'Connell of acting from 'corrupt and personal motives'. After a heated debate the amendment was defeated and the vote of thanks passed. O'Connell felt obliged to address a letter to the Catholics of Co. Louth, which was published in the *Dublin Evening Post* on 3 November. In this letter he explained the reasons for his apology to Peel and defended himself from all of Marmion's charges. He also addressed, for the first time, the bribe which the government had offered him in 1811. He was making it public to show that if money had been motivating his actions in London then he would not have turned down an annual payment of £1,200, nor would he have sacrificed almost £10,000 in legal earnings lost because of the time he spent agitating. In an emotional plea to the people, he wrote of the time, money and pride he had sacrificed to the cause, and how he had even sacrificed 'the glowing years of my youth and manhood' which had passed over him 'like the troubled dream of restless sleep'.

The letter had the intended impact and O'Connell received a better reception at the Munster provincial meetings of the Irish Catholics, held at St Michael's Chapel in Limerick, on 24 October. He was greatly relieved by the response he received on the streets, with a large crowd escorting him to the chapel. His speech at the meeting was also applauded and he told his wife afterwards that he was 'in great *fresh* spirits'.[90] The prospect of a new agitation excited him, and he claimed that he 'never began a winter's campaign with better health or more animation'.[91] At this time, O'Connell was amused by a story he had heard about Saurin. Lord Wellesley was engaged to an American widow, Marianne Patterson, who was a Catholic. Saurin was unaware of her religion and at a dinner launched into an attack on the pope and the Catholic faith. Afterwards she made a point of telling Saurin that she was a Catholic and he was mortified, sending her a profuse apology which she ignored.

An aggressive speech towards the end of the year almost resulted in a fresh duel. During a speech to the New Catholic Association, O'Connell accused a Kerry barrister called Maurice Leyne of having converted to Protestantism purely to inflict pain on his father. Offended, Leyne sent O'Connell a challenge, accusing him of being a liar, a slanderer and a coward, but it was declined. O'Connell was determined never to fight another duel and reported the challenge to the authorities, resulting in Leyne being bound to the peace by large securities. Embarrassed by this, O'Connell's son, Maurice, decided to take his father's place and sent Leyne a message suggesting that he fight him instead. But this, in turn, was declined as Leyne had no quarrel with him. Furious, Maurice and his brother, Morgan, attempted to horse-whip Leyne (in an unintended *homage* to D'Esterre) as he left the Four Courts, but they fled when they were recognised. This caused O'Connell great embarrassment and he reported his sons (and his son-in-law Christopher Fitzsimon, who had also become involved) the next day at the head police office. Morgan was arrested at the theatre that evening, Fitzsimon at O'Connell's own house, and Maurice in Tralee; all were bound to keep the peace.[92]

The opposition to O'Connell for his support of the 'wings' came to a head in December. The backlash had been growing for some time, and his opponents, led by William F. Finn (who was married to O'Connell's sister) and Nicholas Purcell O'Gorman, arranged to attack him at the meeting of the Leinster provincial Catholics held in Carlow on 15 December. O'Connell was worried. He knew that 'a most violent party' had been raised against him and he feared that it might be impossible to resist. 'What a world we live in!' he exclaimed to his wife, fearing that 'the object probably is to drive me off the stage of Catholic politics'.[93] But he was determined to fight back, accepting that 'obloquy and reproach have been the certain salary of those who in every age or country have honestly struggled for the welfare of their native land'. This was a tense time and his wife was anxious about the 'trial' in Carlow. She was also furious about how cruelly and ungratefully the Catholics were behaving. 'Is it not enough to make you retire with disgust from their service?' she wondered.[94] She shared her husband's views that the Catholics acted like slaves and she was equally unsympathetic: 'They deserve to be slaves and such they ought to be left.' Mary seems to have been serious about O'Connell retiring from the campaign for Catholic emancipation. More than once she mentioned that she was surprised he was still determined to persevere and she admitted it was 'enough to drive one to distraction to think of all you have lost in the Catholic cause in a pecuniary and in every other possible way'. Thinking about all he had sacrificed in the Catholic cause, and the 'foul ingratitude and base duplicity' he faced, made her 'almost cry'.

The meeting in Carlow assumed a critical importance, with O'Connell himself fearing that he would be 'defeated and put down for ever'.[95] But, much to his relief, '*We were triumphant.*'[96] O'Gorman was 'heartily hissed and all but pelted to pieces' and O'Connell boasted that 'we beat the Wingers out of the field'. O'Connell's faith in the Irish people had been restored and he was relieved they had not listened to 'the Wingers and their fantasies'. The delegation from Wexford made a public show of presenting O'Connell with a salver, along with an address of support. Rather than being seen as a sign of his popularity, the tribute should rather be seen as a sign of how vulnerable he was perceived to be. O'Connell was grateful for the 'popular kindness' he had received and he blessed 'the good sense, the good feeling of *my* poor people'. Despite this victory, the attacks on O'Connell continued for some time. Jack Lawless denounced him at a meeting of the 'Catholic Association for 1826' (a fourteen-day association formed in January of each year, thus evading legal restrictions, organised in parallel with the New Catholic Association) and proposed a resolution to have the men who supported the 'wings' 'stamped with the reprobation of the country'.[97] However Lawless' rants were not heeded and O'Connell was given another chance. It was a close run thing but he had come through the trial.

In time O'Connell came to accept that his support of the 'wings' had been a mistake and that his opponents had a point. He believed that conciliation was taken as weakness, and as a result was abused. In December 1826 he told the knight of Kerry that 'we *never, never, never* got anything by conciliation' and he cited as evidence the deputation to London in 1825: 'Could it be possible to be more conciliatory than we were?'[98] But instead of being rewarded or treated with respect they had been 'flung back'. O'Connell believed that '*temperateness, moderation and conciliation*' were 'suited only to perpetuate our degradation' and that if they were serious about succeeding, 'we must call things by their proper names—speak out boldly, let it be called intemperately, and rouse in Ireland a spirit of *action*'. Some people continued to blame O'Connell for the failure to secure emancipation in 1825, and indeed for the fact that emancipation had not been won 'long since' despite his many years of campaigning. O'Connell was aware of these criticisms, but tried his best to ignore them. Whenever he did address them he always said in his defence that 'the fault-finders' had no idea of 'the species of *material* with which I have to deal'.[99] They were 'the kind of persons who eternally clog every movement', men who 'would prefer breaking my head to smashing the pates of 500 Orangemen'. In September 1828, following his victory in the Clare election, when O'Connell looked back to what he called 'the experiment of 1825', he admitted he had 'foolishly acceded to the securities called "the wings"'.[100] His view now was that the government had gone along with the emancipation bill because of its fear of violence in Ireland following the suppression of the Catholic Association. He believed the correct strategy would have been to have 'kept up that salutary apprehension'. But, instead, in 'an evil hour' he had listened to Plunket and agreed to the 'wings' to guarantee passing the measure. Looking back, O'Connell believed that his support had been decisive in keeping the country tranquil, as he was 'the only man who could succeed in causing a perfect silence to reign amongst the universal Catholic body. I procured for this purpose public tranquility.' Seeing that he had 'appeased the storm' the ministry had abandoned emancipation, knowing that the danger was past. O'Connell now knew he had been deceived, and he was determined it would not happen a second time: 'I should be more than insane, I should indeed be "a knave or a fool" if I were to be deceived in the same way again.'[101] O'Connell had learned his lesson. The 'rotten reed of "securities"' would never again be accepted.

Chapter 13

'THE WAND OF THE ENCHANTER': MOBILISING THE MASSES, 1826–1827

'The rod of oppression is the wand of this potent enchanter of the passions, and the book of his spells is the Penal Code.'
(RICHARD SHEIL ON DANIEL O'CONNELL, 5 JULY 1828)[1]

The general election of 1826 signalled an unexpected change of direction in the campaign for Catholic emancipation. As Fergus O'Ferrall has written, '1826 is the great turning point in Irish popular politics'.[2] And the driving force here was not O'Connell, but men who grasped the importance of the forty-shilling freeholders. This was the clearest demonstration yet that the 'wings' had been a trap, but fortunately for O'Connell he had weathered the storm and had been forgiven for his mistake. Having abandoned that compromise he was once again dominant. On 16 January 1826 the 'Catholic Association of 1826' met for fourteen days, the legal limit, to discuss the continuing campaign for emancipation. Here Thomas Wyse, a new leader from Waterford, presented the case for mobilising the rank-and-file Catholics for the approaching election to unite 'the whole nation in one cry'.[3] It was Wyse who became the architect of the Waterford campaign, a campaign to unseat the sitting MP, Lord George Thomas Beresford, whose family believed it had a right to control the representation for the county, and replace him with a young, liberal, Protestant landlord, Henry Villiers Stuart. Wyse had only recently returned from the continent, where he had been living for ten years, and where he had married a niece of Napoleon, Letitia Bonaparte. His energy and organisational ability provided a new model for the campaign for emancipation. To the dismay of many Catholics Richard Sheil accepted a retainer from Beresford to act as his counsel in the election, but O'Connell defended him in public and insisted that as a lawyer he was bound to act for whoever employed him, thus ending the debate.[4]

A dinner was arranged for 2 February to gauge support for emancipation. Various Irish MPs and dignitaries were invited, but many, like Alexander Robert Stewart, MP for Co. Londonderry and a nephew of Lord Castlereagh, refused because they saw it as a reorganisation of the Catholic Association in a different shape.[5] Others, like the duke of Buckingham, refused because they did not want 'to flatter the personal vanity of Mr O'Connell'.[6] O'Connell meanwhile was busy feuding with the Dublin newspapers, angry that his speeches were not being reported properly. He refused to allow the reporters to attend the dinner on 2 February without paying, and when this was opposed by the committee organising it, he declared that he would not attend unless they were excluded.[7] He won this point, but the reporters got their revenge by refusing to cover any of his speeches until a compromise was agreed.

On 12 March O'Connell and Lord Killeen attended a private party at Dublin Castle. It was a diverse gathering, also present were the novelist Lady Morgan (Sydney Owenson), the lawyer and politician John Henry North (who was O'Connell's neighbour on Merrion Square and who was described by Morgan as one of 'the doctrinaires of our country'), and Colonel Blacker, the grand master of the Orange lodge, who was popularly known as 'the roaring lion'.[8] O'Connell was a great admirer of Morgan's novels, but his admiration was not reciprocated. During the meal Morgan became nostalgic for the 1790s, when the Castle would rather have tortured men like O'Connell than dine with them. She believed that O'Connell wanted back to the days of Brian Boru,

> himself to be the king, with a crown of emerald shamrocks, a train of yellow velvet... a sceptre in one hand and a cross in the other, and the people crying, "Long live King O'Connell!" This is the object of his views and his ambition.

It was clear she despised O'Connell. She refused to accept that he was 'a man of genius' as some people had insisted. Rather, she claimed he had only 'a sort of conventional talent', useful in the courtroom, which had won him 'local popularity'.

The approaching contest in Waterford began to generate enormous interest. On 28 March the *Dublin Evening Post* explained the significance of the election: 'It will be a battle... which... will decide the Catholic question... The election of Mr Stuart must be considered as the harbinger of civil freedom in Ireland.'[9] Despite lacking any experience in election campaigns, Wyse and his committee created an incredible local machine to mobilise support. The framework which had been constructed to collect the Catholic rent was adapted for this new purpose, the priests were brought on board and, as Wyse later noted, there was 'almost an individual appeal to the forty-shilling constituency of the county'.[10] The role of the priests became contentious, with Beresford accusing them of abusing their powers to support Stuart. Even the *Dublin Evening Post* on 5 June referred to the priests' 'crusade' in Waterford. National attention focused on Waterford as the most significant constituency in the June election. In this period polling was an open process, often lasting a number of days until all the freeholders had an opportunity to cast their vote. It was generally believed that Beresford would win one of the two seats on offer, having an estimated 600 more registered votes than Stuart (there was little doubt that Richard Power, one of the sitting MPs, would take the first seat). Things looked desperate for Stuart. It was only on 9 June that he wrote to O'Connell inviting him to assist in the campaign. O'Connell accepted and his intervention proved decisive.

'This is the greatest contest ever known,' boasted O'Connell soon after arriving in Waterford. 'We *will* win.'[11] On 18 June 1826 O'Connell visited Kilmacthomas, a town controlled by the Beresfords, where he was greeted by a large crowd waving green boughs. O'Connell 'harangued them' from the window of his inn, and 'we had a great deal of laughing at the bloody Beresfords'.[12] There followed a 'tremendous' meeting at Dungarvan later the same day; O'Connell spoke from a platform erected by the walls of a new chapel and the success of the meeting made him realise that Wyse was right and that popular declamation could achieve great things. The priests in the town assisted their campaign and O'Connell was convinced they would secure all the votes in the town. From there he visited Dromona, Cappoquin, the residence of Villiers Stuart, and was much taken by the beauty of the area, making him appreciate why Lady Morgan used it so much in her 1818 novel *Florence McCarthy: an Irish tale*. From Dromona he went to Cappoquin town with Stuart, and their carriage was then drawn by enthusiastic voters all the way to Lismore.[13] 'I never had a notion of popular enthusiasm till I saw that scene,' O'Connell admitted afterwards. His name was shouted almost as much as Stuart's and he delivered a strong speech at the chapel at Lismore. His wife had been unwell, but hearing that she was recovering boosted his spirits and he was buoyant, looking forward to 'all the *racy* triumphs at the success of agitation'.[14] O'Connell was even proposed as a candidate, but this was just a device so that he could speak at the hustings, and he withdrew as pre-arranged afterwards. His speech was described by Wyse as 'one of the most truly eloquent harangues' and he believed that he might very well have won the election had he not withdrawn.[15]

By Sunday 25 June O'Connell was certain that Stuart would win the second seat, even though the Beresfords were 'determined to die hard' and planned on continuing the poll for a few more days. O'Connell was delighted that they were 'beating those bigoted and tyrannical wretches', and believed the Beresfords were merely resorting to 'practicing every species of delay and spinning out the time'.[16] He was also delighted that he had been able to keep the people tranquil, and away from any activity that could have led to violence. This was in contrast to the election campaign in Tralee, where a crowd had thrown stones at some magistrates, and were fired on by soldiers, killing five people and wounding twelve more.[17] Polling in Waterford continued on Wednesday 28 June and O'Connell predicted 'a most enormous majority'.[18] The election finally ended the next day and the result was announced, with victory for Stuart, who received 1,357 votes, to Beresford's 527; Power topped the poll and took the first seat with 1,424 votes. It was a humiliating defeat for Beresford. At a dinner in his honour in Cavan a few weeks later, Beresford complained that he had been defeated because the priests threatened to excommunicate anyone who voted for him, though this was swiftly denied.[19] There were also victories for new pro-emancipation candidates in a number of counties, and in Louth, Monaghan, Westmeath and Cavan there were similar revolts by forty-shilling freeholders against their landlords' wishes.[20] The *Dublin Evening Post* recognised immediately that what had been done in these counties could soon be done in every county where Catholic voters outnumbered Protestant voters and that 'a revolution' had been 'conceded to Ireland'.[21]

Retribution was swift in coming for those forty-shilling freeholders who had defied their landlords' wishes. Evictions were widespread throughout the country to punish and intimidate. The Waterford Protection Association was established to represent local freeholders, and similar organisations were formed in other counties. The victory at Waterford convinced O'Connell that the Catholic rent should be revived and in July he began a campaign to renew the collection.[22] To avoid any legal restrictions, O'Connell insisted that the money was given along with a pledge that it was for 'all useful purposes not prohibited by law', and in particular for national education.[23] But the real reason was to protect the forty-shilling freeholders threatened with eviction. O'Connell was determined not to draw upon the reserves from the old rent because it would create legal difficulties and also remove the impetus for the new rent. Rather than wanting large donations from individuals, he preferred every parish contributing, and as many people as possible sending a penny a month. O'Connell believed that the existing rent was 'a sacred fund' to be used only in emergencies, as he knew that once spent it could not be replaced without 'violating the Algerine Act and making the new rent illegal'.[24] Lawless opposed assisting the forty-shilling freeholders, believing that landlords would deliberately target their tenants if they knew they would be compensated. But O'Connell argued him down, insisting that unless the forty-shilling freeholders were aware they would be compensated they would never go against their landlord's wishes.[25] To celebrate the recent victory, a grand provincial meeting for Munster was organised for Waterford in late August and Lord Fitzwilliam, the lord lieutenant for Ireland who had been sacked in 1795 because of his support for emancipation, accepted an invitation to attend.

O'Connell decided to launch a new organisation in August, the 'Order of Liberators', copying the example of Simon Bolívar. Membership was exclusive, dependent on having performed an act of distinctive service to Ireland, and O'Connell decided upon a bright green uniform to distinguish members.[26] The order was unveiled to much mocking, but O'Connell boasted that 'they will make a noise yet'.[27] His brother, John, was one of the sceptics and suggested that he did not know what he was doing, but O'Connell scorned him and his other critics for 'their sapient advice'. The Order of Liberators proved a failure and had to be re-launched in 1828, though it helped give O'Connell his title of 'The Liberator' following emancipation. He certainly left himself open to ridicule in the enthusiastic way he took to the streets, 'in the full dress of a verdant liberator', as William Curran wrote to Lady Morgan, 'green in all that may and may not be expressed, even to a green cravat, green watch-ribbon, and a slashing shining green hat-band'.[28] *Blackwood's Edinburgh Magazine* was full of contempt for his decision to style himself 'one of the Order of Liberators' and said that he was traversing 'Ireland dressed in green, and decorated with green ribbons, after the fashion of a madman, to stimulate the atrocious conduct of the priesthood'.[29] 'It is sufficient to make a man sick to read the speeches of this fellow', it claimed, suggesting that he should instead be called 'the toadeater of superstition and bigotry' or the 'licker of the pope's great toe'.

On 5 August 1826 an English barrister, Henry Crabb Robinson, the same age as O'Connell, landed in Cork. He was curious to see the courts of justice and was given a tour two days later by some barristers he met in a coffee-room. In the *Nisi Prius* court a case was being argued and he was impressed with 'the prominent man at the bar', a 'thick-set, broad-faced, good humoured, middle-aged person, who spoke with the air of one conscious of superiority'.[30] The man was O'Connell. When the case was over O'Connell began talking to one of the barristers and was delighted to find that Robinson shared their profession. Taking him by the arm, he led him from court to court, 'as he had business in most cases', chatting with him at intervals all throughout the day. Robinson was greatly impressed by O'Connell as a lawyer. He noted that he was a 'sort of pet' with the judges, and that his good humour compensated for what they viewed as 'his political perversities'. They became unlikely companions. After all, Robinson was a Dissenter and believed that the Roman Catholic church was 'the greatest enemy to civil and religious liberty'.[31] But the sheer force of O'Connell's personality made it impossible to dislike him.

Deciding to visit Kerry, Robinson set out on the Killarney coach on 9 August. The coach was packed, with 'a crowded mass of passengers and luggage, heaped up in defiance of all regulations'. But, as it happened, O'Connell was on the same coach, and when he saw Robinson he insisted on him joining him at the front. Robinson kept a detailed diary and in his entry for that day he noted that it was 'as interesting a ride as can be imagined' with 'the glorious Counsellor' hailed along the road wherever they went. He found him 'a capital companion, with high animal spirits, infinite good temper, great earnestness in discussion, and replete with intelligence'. Wanting to be honest up front, Robinson told him that he was a Dissenter and that the Roman Catholic church was, 'from a religious point of view', the 'object of my abhorrence'. But he also told him that he thought emancipation was a right and that, politically, he could not have 'a warmer friend'. Upon hearing this O'Connell seized him by the hand and said, 'I would a thousand times rather talk with one of your way of thinking that with one of my own.'[32] It was known that O'Connell was travelling that day and whenever the coach stopped at a village to change horses a crowd of people gathered to cheer him. At one posting-house he was stopped by an old woman who said, 'with a piercing voice, "Oh, that I should live to see your noble honour again! Do give me something your honour."' 'Why, you are an old cheat!' exclaimed O'Connell. 'Did you not ask me for a sixpence last time, to buy a nail for your coffin?' The woman admitted that she had, upon which he threw her a shilling. 'Well, then, there's a shilling for you, but only on condition that you are dead before I come this way again.' The woman caught the money and gave a cry of joy, saying that she would buy a new cloak. 'You foolish old woman,' said O'Connell, 'nobody will give you a shilling if you have a new cloak on.' But the woman replied that she would not wear it when begging.

This was O'Connell country. The crowd shouted 'praises of "the glorious Counsellor"' as the coach set off, and Robinson noted that O'Connell was 'the object of warm attachment' wherever he went. The coach arrived in Killarney at about four o'clock in the afternoon. As they were about to get out, O'Connell invited Robinson to dinner. 'You are aware by this time that I am king of this part of Ireland,' he told him. 'Now, as I have the power, I tell you that I will not suffer you to alight until you give me your word of honour that on Monday next you will be at the house of my brother-in-law... and you must then accompany me to Derrynane, my residence. Now promise me instantly!' Robinson conceded that he was 'too well aware of your power to resist you', and gave his word. 'King Dan commands attendance' was the heading for the published diary entry. The men went to the Kenmare Arms and O'Connell introduced Robinson 'as a particular friend', which guaranteed him preferential treatment while he was there.

The dinner on Monday 14 August was in Cahir, Co. Tipperary, and was attended by numerous members of the O'Connell family. There Robinson met Mrs O'Connell, her health still not good as he described her as 'an invalid' as well as 'very lady-like and agreeable'. Because it was a strict fast day O'Connell had not eaten all day. When the dinner arrived he 'begged a blessing in the usual way' and then added 'something in an inaudible whisper'. Robinson was impressed that although O'Connell was 'rigid in the discharge of all formalities of his Church' he showed the 'utmost conceivable liberality towards others'; he also found 'great hilarity' in his table manners. A dinner-party took place the next day, beginning in the afternoon and continuing until late, with music and dancing. Here O'Connell was 'very lively—the soul of the party'. On Wednesday 16 August they all set out for Derrynane, with the women in a carriage, and the men on horseback. When they came to O'Connell's land they were greeted by large numbers of his tenants. Sometimes men would be waiting for them in lanes and would run alongside O'Connell's horse, 'vehement in their gesticulations and loud in their talk'. Trying to get away, O'Connell asked Robinson to 'trot a little faster'. O'Connell explained that a condition he imposed on his tenants was they 'should never go to law, but submit all their disputes to him'. Throughout the journey O'Connell adjudicated in a number of cases. Finally they reached Derrynane, which O'Connell described as 'the wreck' of the family fortune, having suffered from confiscations in every reign. The house was of plain marble, but new, larger rooms had been added by O'Connell 'to render the abode more suitable to his rank'. O'Connell's nurse, now old and toothless, lived there and when he saw her he jumped from his horse and kissed her. O'Connell took Robinson for a walk and showed him the cemetery of the O'Connell family, 'a sacred spot'. They discussed the events that had radicalised O'Connell and he reflected back to the 1790s when the government might have secured the Irish Catholics as '"their steadfast friends, at least," said he, significantly, "but for the Union"'.[33] The Union was much discussed, and Robinson expressed his approval of it. But O'Connell would not insult his guest and 'spoke gently' about it. Insurrections were also mentioned and O'Connell admitted that 'I could never allow myself to ask whether an insurrection would be right, if it could be successful, for I am sure it would fail'. They had 'an excellent dinner' that night, with the parish priest (who said mass there every morning) in attendance and a piper playing music. The next day it rained constantly and the group remained indoors. Robinson noted that everyone did as they liked: 'Some played backgammon, some sang to music, many read.'

Friday 18 August was a nicer day and O'Connell went for a walk with Robinson and the parish priest. Religion was discussed and O'Connell admitted that 'there can be no doubt that there was great corruption in the Church at the time what you call the Reformation took place, and a real reform did take place in our Church'. Upon hearing this, the priest bolted. O'Connell did not notice but when Robinson mentioned it he was apologetic. 'Oh,' he said, 'I forgot he was present, or I would not have given offence to the good man... He is an excellent parish priest... He is always with the poor.' Mass was said every morning at the house but no pressure was ever put on Robinson to attend. Robinson left that day, and travelled to Limerick and then Waterford.

Robinson arrived in Waterford in time for the grand provincial Catholic meeting for Munster. There was a public meeting at Waterford Cathedral on Monday 28 August with a dinner in honour of Lord Fitzwilliam planned for the next day. O'Connell, having learned that Robinson was in town, sent him a ticket to attend the dinner as his guest. Robinson also decided to attend the meeting in the cathedral, and was impressed to find 'some thousands' in attendance. It was evident that O'Connell was 'the idol of the people and he was loudly applauded when he entered'. Many people spoke, but Robinson noted that O'Connell 'was the orator of the day'. For about an hour and a half he addressed the gathering with 'power and effect', his 'language vehement, all but seditious'.[34] Robinson was impressed that O'Connell could adjust his oratory to suit the audience and the subject before him. Here 'his manner is colloquial, his voice very sweet'. O'Connell himself admitted afterwards that 'they say I made a *brilliant* speech' and although he was not convinced—'nobody is half as bad a judge of his speech as the speaker himself'—he was pleased that he 'never was more cheered, neither did I ever *move* an assembly so much'.[35] Twenty resolutions were passed at this meeting, and one was in support of the forty-shilling freeholders, declaring that the Catholics would never accept an attempt to limit that franchise and that any attempts to punish voters would be resisted by all legal means.[36] The next day there was a committee meeting in the sacristy of the cathedral, where a committee arranged what would be done at the public meeting that afternoon. Robinson noted that O'Connell always spoke last and 'his opinion invariably prevailed'. O'Connell later addressed the public meeting, 'with no less energy and point than yesterday'.

One reporter arrived too late to record one of the speeches. Terrified that he would be punished by his employers, he begged O'Connell to tell him what he remembered so he could have something to report. O'Connell went one better: he delivered an entire speech for him. 'As I had nothing better to do,' he later remembered, 'I consented, and delivered a much better speech, walking up and down the room, than the one I had pronounced at the meeting.'[37] O'Connell was greatly amused that the 'very best report' of his speech appeared in the newspaper that had not even a reporter present.

The dinner in honour of Lord Fitzwilliam took place at seven p.m. on Tuesday 29 August and was well attended. Fitzwilliam gave a short speech, 'scarcely audible, with his eyes fixed on the ground', in which he spoke of his wish to serve Ireland. The only remarkable speech, according to Robinson, was that of O'Connell, and it was short. O'Connell was delighted, telling his wife that he 'made a famous speech; everything was superb'.[38] After midnight, when most of the noblemen had left, various toasts were given. One was addressed to the English bar and Robinson was invited to speak. His speech was hilariously awful, as he completely misjudged the mood of the crowd and gave unintentional offence to almost everyone present. It is not clear what he was getting at when he suggested that, because he was a Protestant and an Englishman, he believed that if he was met by an Irish Catholic, 'I should expect him to hang down his head while I looked him boldly in the face.' There was 'an appalling silence—not a sound', as Robinson, himself, admitted sheepishly afterwards. But he recovered to rescue his speech, ending it by claiming that because of the liberal sentiments he had heard that day he was now 'of your Church, whether you will receive me or no'. Another dinner was held in honour of O'Connell in Waterford on Thursday 31 August and for this he wore the full regalia of the Order of Liberators. The dinner was a success, though O'Connell struck a somewhat incongruous figure as the only person present wearing the flamboyant green uniform.

O'Connell missed the Catholic meeting on 7 September when the treatment of the forty-shilling freeholders was discussed. It was agreed that the new Catholic rent would be used to support those being evicted for how they voted, with the old rent loaned to the fund if that was not sufficient. But afterwards O'Connell vetoed the idea. A loan would risk making the new rent illegal, though a gift of some money could be given without any danger. O'Connell had great hopes for the new rent, believing that if it succeeded they would be emancipated, even if a new Algerine Act was passed.

The death of the duke of York, the king's brother and heir to the throne, who had done so much to destroy the 1825 relief bill, on 5 January 1827 raised hopes further. At a Catholic meeting in Dublin on 10 January there was a series of sustained attacks on him, but O'Connell intervened, declaring, 'We war not with the dying or the grave. Our enmities are buried there. They expired with the individual.'[39] Afterwards, O'Connell reflected that 'we are a strange people, perhaps the most sensitive in the world to the kindly and affectionate motives of the heart, but we can be fierce too'.[40] He asked his friend, Richard Newton Bennett, in London seeking a judicial appointment in Ceylon, to try and discover what were the views of the duke of Clarence, the new heir to the throne, on the Catholic question. He wanted 'the map of the land', insisting that if he had 'the compass' he could 'steer by it'.[41] The 'Catholic Association for 1827' met for fourteen days, starting on 16 January. O'Connell launched an attack on the prime minister, Liverpool, and his old enemy, Peel, and called on England to become 'really powerful by conciliating Ireland'.[42] When it was announced that the duke of Wellington had replaced the duke of York as commander-in-chief of the army, he was denounced by O'Connell as deserving the 'execration' of the people of Ireland as he had won his title with Catholic blood and then had voted against 'the freedom of the Catholics of Ireland'. At the meeting on 22 January (day five) O'Connell delivered an attack on George Canning and declared that it was necessary to distinguish between their 'real friends' and 'disguised enemies'.[43] This was objected to by James Dwyer, who intervened to attack O'Connell as 'a person of warm temperament' who 'sometimes suffers his judgement to be held captive by his imagination'.[44] Two days later, on 24 January, O'Connell made an important public admission. He accepted that he had been wrong in 1825 to support the disenfranchisement of the forty-shilling freeholders and that he now had 'the zeal of a convert returning to his original principle', a public confession which ensured his rehabilitation was complete.[45] At a meeting of the Catholic Association on 3 February O'Connell, in the middle of another rant, attacked Scotsmen for being hypocrites. When challenged by Lawless, who listed a number of honourable Scotsmen, O'Connell merely shrugged that this 'only proved the generality of the rule'.[46]

The meeting a week later on 10 February proved highly controversial. O'Connell used the opportunity of the death of his friend, John Bric, to launch an attack on William Cobbett and press for the Catholic Association to discontinue taking the *Political Register*. When delivering his lengthy tribute to Bric he also decided to fire a warning to the British government. He suggested that the safety of the state depended on them not goading the people into resistance and he asked 'How long can the present state of things last?'[47] He warned the government that it was mistaken if it assumed that just because the Catholics seemed to be 'shrinking from any combat' it meant there was no danger to the state. At this point O'Connell was interrupted by a young member of the Association, who questioned the relevance of what O'Connell was saying. This lit the fuse on O'Connell's temper and the result was explosive. Shaking with anger, he asked repeatedly whether he was to be interrupted and demanded to know if it had 'come to this that the youths of Ireland will not allow a man who has laboured long in their cause to speak for his dead friend'. There was uproar at the meeting, worse than anything which had ever been seen before, with constant shouting and hats waved in anger. When O'Connell resumed his speech he continued to make reference to the interruption, provoking further shouting and unrest. He called upon the chairman to command the man 'to allow me to stand on the grave of my dead friend without presuming to interrupt me. Have I his permission to go on?' The note-taker for the Association recorded that this was greeted by 'violent tumult'. A number of people spoke in defence of Cobbett, with Lawless the most notable. Lawless suggested that on this occasion O'Connell was 'the last man whose advice ought to be followed. Why? Because his heart gets the better of his head.'[48] He also noted that O'Connell had disagreed with Bric on a number of issues when he was alive and had 'waged a petty war with him'. O'Connell interrupted to say that Bric had agreed with him on the 'wings', but Lawless just shrugged and said that 'in those wings he lost his feathers.' Lawless pleaded for the people 'not to be swept away by that torrent of eloquence which so copiously flows from the lips of my friend' and moved an amendment in favour of Cobbett. At the end of the debate there was complete chaos, with ten or twenty men trying to speak at once: 'The tumult was inconceivable.'[49] But O'Connell was triumphant. Lawless's amendment was defeated and O'Connell's motion removing Cobbett's newspaper was passed 'amidst acclamations'.

Liverpool suffered a stroke on 15 February, bringing his long premiership to an end. For a time it appeared that Wellington would succeed him as prime minister, much to the alarm of O'Connell who feared that 'all the horrors of actual massacre threaten us'.[50] Instead the sympathetic George Canning became prime minister, prompting six resignations from the cabinet, including those of Wellington and Peel. The new ministry prompted Sir Francis Burdett to introduce a fresh motion for Catholic relief in the House of Commons on 5 March. There was a two-day debate, but it was defeated by 276 votes to 272, the first time since 1819 that a Catholic relief bill failed to pass in the Commons.[51]

O'Connell was prepared to give Canning's ministry a chance. His instincts were always those of a fighter, but a fighter who believed that knowing when to duck and give ground was as important as knowing when to hit out. This was a time for ducking, and O'Connell spoke at a Catholic meeting on 18 April urging the postponement of an aggregate meeting on 1 May. He wanted to avoid any discussions that might make things difficult for the new administration and suggested a wait-and-see policy. His motion was carried, provoking the wrath of Eneas MacDonnell, the Catholic Association's agent in London, who feared another return to the failed policy of conciliation of 1825. He rebuked O'Connell for 'a most grievous error' in postponing the aggregate meeting and insisted that he was 'the maddest man on the earth' if he had any faith in William Plunket. It was a harsh comment not likely to endear him to O'Connell, especially the abrupt postscript: 'You are grossly misled, believe me. Remember 1825!'[52]

Richard Newton Bennett continued to act as O'Connell's emissary in London. A meeting was arranged with the new chief secretary for Ireland, William Lamb (the future Lord Melbourne), who gave him this message: 'Tell Mr O'Connell I must for a time be worse than Peel but, when we can, we will do all the good we can. Beg of him to have confidence, though we cannot do much, or worse men will come.'[53] O'Connell was 'greatly alarmed' at this news, and took it to mean that Lamb would side with the 'Orange faction' to show 'his *candour and liberality*'.[54] Lamb had little interest in Irish affairs, but at forty-seven years of age, was grateful to be finally in office. Dublin Castle officials disliked his open approach to government, and later recalled that 'when Mr Lamb was here the only orders were "Show him in"'.[55] O'Connell became disillusioned with the direction of Canning's government, especially because of its failure to replace 'the *old warriors*' in Ireland. True, the octogenarian chief justice of the common pleas, Lord Norbury, was 'bought off the bench', persuaded to retire in return for being advanced in the peerage as Viscount Glandine and earl of Norbury. But even though O'Connell hated Norbury, 'a sanguinary buffoon... irritable, impatient, bigoted', he thought it 'a most shameful traffic' to have secured his retirement in this way.[56] The result of all these transactions was that he was losing confidence in the new administration, he admitted it 'is worn out or rather trodden to rags'.[57] He still hoped for a patent of precedence, having received a promise by a back channel that it would be awarded by the new government once a new lord chancellor for Ireland was appointed, and perhaps before. A rumour of this award was attacked by the *Courier* newspaper as a 'revolting absurdity' as it claimed O'Connell was 'a loud-tongued brawler', guilty of treason and sedition, who had only escaped prosecution because 'the lawyer predominated over the rebel'.[58]

At a major Catholic meeting in Dublin on 16 June O'Connell outlined a dual strategy, urging every Irishman, whether in a palace or a lowly cottage, to give Canning's ministry their support but also calling for new meetings to be arranged all over the country to mark the new start of parliament, as 'we ought not to throw ourselves into the hands of any administration'.[59] At this meeting he also announced that in future the Catholics should petition parliament for 'freedom of conscience' rather than emancipation as it was now a campaign for 'universal liberty'. But the death of Canning on 8 August dashed these hopes, however qualified they may have been. 'Another blow to wretched Ireland', wrote O'Connell to his wife.[60] Any chance of a patent of precedence was once again lost and O'Connell was left further embittered. A new ministry was formed with a non-entity, Lord Goderich, as prime minister. But O'Connell refused to bargain with the new administration, 'who are to this hour piddling with me as a mere act of justice'.[61]

'My affairs are so deranged that I do not know what to do.'[62] Despite all his promises and predictions, O'Connell had still not cleared his debts and owed about £10,000. Following the death of Hunting Cap he had inherited Derrynane, and received about £14,000 for his third of the personal property. But this did not solve all of his financial problems.[63] He was able to pay off most of his debts but not all, and he continued to struggle with his finances. His creditors included a number of Iveragh neighbours (even the local priest), and his brother, James, was quick to demand the payment of the money he was owed, close to £3,000.[64] O'Connell moaned in November 1825 that he was 'quite sick of being in debt' and hoped that two years of 'strict economy' would clear all his problems. He was worn out from paying interest on all his debts and looked forward to the time when he would be free of them and able to pay the dowry of his daughter, Kate. He promised his wife that when he debts were all paid she could 'command every shilling I have in the world'.[65] General O'Connell was astonished that his inheritance from Hunting Cap, when combined with the money he had lent him (which together came to £20,000), had not been able to clear his debts.[66] He warned O'Connell that 'the very existence of your large family hangs on your life'. But O'Connell had no idea what 'strict economy' meant. Inheriting Derrynane had dragged him further into debt, especially as he had decided to renovate the house. In October 1827 he regretted that he had spent 'a foolish deal of money' improving Derrynane, which he admitted was a 'cruel extravagance and folly'.[67] Expensive sofas had been purchased from the auction of the property of the former lord chancellor, Lord Clare, and O'Connell liked to joke that they were 'once present at high Orange orgies'.[68] With economising like this it was no wonder that he remained in massive debt. In May 1827 his brother, James, regretted that his 'pecuniary embarrassments are so great' but insisted he was unable to help.

Guilty about the continued absence of his wife from Dublin, in October O'Connell lamented that his misjudgements had caused so much trouble.[69] However he still clung to the forlorn hope that strict economising would clear all his debts and enable him to start saving for Kate's dowry. But he kept finding that he owed more money than he thought.[70] He was earning over £7,000 a year at the bar and rather optimistically believed that if he could apply all of this income to his debts for eighteen months (and live off his property) he would be clear.[71]

Money aside, he was content. At his house in Merrion Square he had installed a shower-bath, and he was taking great pleasure from this new invention. He would rise at five a.m., work until eight-thirty or nine, and then take a shower-bath, with the cold splash of water from the barrel providing an initial 'shock' but leaving him feeling and looking 'as healthy after it as if I were young again'.[72] In at least three letters to his wife he boasted of the effects of the shower, and how he felt its benefit all day. He was also impressed that the system was so well 'contrived that it makes no kind of *splash* or wet'.[73] Refreshed, and feeling as if he had a sleep-in, he would eat 'a voracious breakfast' and then work until ten thirty. His professional career was going well, he admitted he was 'very, very busy', and he retired to bed every evening at nine thirty. He said he slept soundly, with his 'heart warm with the fondest love for my wife and children and filled however occasionally with *pecuniary* anxieties'.[74] He had also decided to stop drinking wine, and now found that he needed much less sleep, and felt 'cool and pleasant' when in bed.[75]

The failure to secure a patent of precedence continued to distress him. Towards the end of the year he changed his mind and decided to apply to the government for one, via Thomas Spring Rice, the under-secretary for the home department in charge of Irish affairs. In his application on 29 November he discussed the injustice which was being done to him and his clients by withholding one. He was also clear that he was tired of being mocked for his inferiority by lawyers junior to him by many years, such as John Henry North (who 'taunted me with his station') and Leslie Foster (who 'asserted his superior station most unpleasantly').[76] As part of his argument O'Connell claimed that this 'act of justice to me' would be seen as 'a kindness to the Irish people', although he admitted this might be down to his vanity. He predicted that his work would increase in quantity and quality if he had the patent and he requested to be placed after Wallace, the first man to receive a silk gown after the time O'Connell felt he should have received one. But Rice was unsuccessful in his attempt and O'Connell wrote him an angry letter, with much 'bitterness of feeling'.[77]

In December O'Connell represented a charismatic Catholic priest accused of having seduced a young Protestant woman, in a case that attracted an 'extraordinary degree of public interest'.[78] The Rev. Thomas Maguire, thirty-five years old, was the parish priest of Drumkerrin, Co. Leitrim, and it was alleged that he had slept with Anne McGarrahan, the daughter of the village innkeeper, that he had married her in secret, and that she had become pregnant with his child.[79] The innkeeper, Bartholemew McGarrahan, sued for £500 in damages and the case went to trial on 13 December. Maguire was an instantly recognisable figure, having engaged in a debate against a leading Protestant, the Rev. Richard Pope, on doctrinal differences earlier in the year (in a meeting that was co-chaired by O'Connell).[80] During this 'Discussion' (as it became known), Pope was defeated and 'Fr Tom' was hailed as the Catholic champion and became 'the object of popular adoration'.[81] The salacious details of the case, Maguire's high profile, and the possibility that it might be a conspiracy to do down a Catholic priest, all added to the public interest. O'Connell was assisted during the trial by Sheil and it became a part of Drumkerrin folklore that O'Connell visited the village in disguise before the trial to investigate what had really transpired.[82]

The case was heard in the court of exchequer before Baron Smith, after O'Connell had failed in his attempt to get it heard outside of Dublin. O'Connell's hated foe, John Henry North, was the leading counsel for McGarrahan providing an extra level of interest. Outlining the case for the plaintiff, George Bennett explained that Maguire had arrived in the parish in February 1825 and had stayed for six weeks at McGarrahan's inn. In September 1826 McGarrahan had been imprisoned for debt, and it was claimed that during this period Maguire seduced his daughter and even married her in a private ceremony. Anne became pregnant and went to England, where she gave birth to a still-born child in July 1827. From there she returned to Drumkerrin in August, when her family decided to sue Maguire.

Anne McGarrahan, twenty-three years old, was the first witness called. She was, according to contemporary accounts, a plain-looking woman, though dressed very stylishly. O'Connell was vicious in his cross-examination, questioning her about who had paid for her clothes (hinting that they were gifts she had been given in return for sexual favours) and challenging her to admit that she had once denied the allegations on oath. When asked whether she had once sworn the allegations were false, Anne became confused and replied, 'I never offered to swear, but I said I would.' The men and women in the packed courtroom burst out laughing. McGarahan's counsel called for order, but Baron Smith noted with a half-smile that while he hoped 'order will in future be preserved, at the same time persons cannot always refrain from laughing'.[83] O'Connell then produced a letter from Anne to Maguire, dated September 1827, in which she admitted that she was 'the innocent cause of your present persecution: the Protestants hate and fear you, therefore, they would sacrifice my honour and character to destroy yours'.[84] But Anne insisted that this letter had been dictated by Maguire, and that she had written it in the presence of him and the local bishop after having visited Maguire to ask for money. Becoming upset, she turned to Maguire and shouted, 'O you villain! You villain!'

Reviewing the case now it is difficult to separate fact from fiction. Some things, however, appear likely. It seems almost certain that Fr Tom Maguire had embarked on a sexual relationship with Anne McGarrahan. For one thing, numerous letters between them were presented in court (some but not all of them dismissed by O'Connell as forgeries), and the letters proved that the relationship was not as innocent as Maguire (or O'Connell) claimed. Second, O'Connell refused to call some of his own witnesses (notably a servant girl) for fear of incriminating his client. Less conclusive, but also suggestive, the Drumkerrin locals remembered seeing the two walking hand-in-hand on numerous occasions. That said, it also appears certain that Bartholemew McGarrahan was encouraged to take the case to ruin Maguire's reputation and damage the Catholic church. It was revealed during the trial that McGarrahan was almost bankrupt, and yet he had no trouble paying his legal fees or retaining some of the country's leading barristers. It is no longer difficult to accept that a charismatic Catholic priest might have an affair with a younger woman, but there is evidence to suggest that the case was prompted and supported financially by men with their own agenda. The jury eventually decided in Maguire's favour, but it is significant that this verdict was set aside in February 1828 by a tribunal, making a new trial possible, though this never happened. O'Connell's behaviour during the trial was extraordinary. It provides an important insight into his character as we see exactly what he was prepared to do, or say, to win the case.

O'Connell was determined to destroy Anne's character and he was brutal in his cross-examination. He attempted to show that she was a 'vile prostitute' (at one point he called her a 'practiced prostitute' who suffered from 'moral leprosy') who had slept with any number of men in return for favours. However he was sceptical that she had ever been pregnant, though he admitted 'she often got abundant provocation to be pregnant'.[85] He was determined to establish that 'a diabolical conspiracy' existed to destroy Maguire. Turning to Anne, he enquired whether her father was a Freemason and an Orangeman and, when this was confirmed, he asked, 'Do Orangemen love the priests much?' In a brilliant but virulent closing speech, O'Connell dismissed the evidence of Anne McGarrahan as that of a 'strumpet of fifty paramours' and insisted his client was the victim of 'a cold-blooded assassination' attempt. The oration lasted three hours and he ended it by claiming that Maguire would never have 'stooped from his heavenly feast to feed on such wretched carrion as Anne McGarrahan'. It was a nasty comment, made worse by his follow-up question, 'What beauty, what fascination is there about her?' When he finished, the packed courtroom burst into applause, but they remained silent when North concluded for the plaintiff. O'Connell was delighted with his speech, which was described by some at the bar as 'the best speech he ever made'.[86] According to the *Dublin Evening Post* no reporter could convey 'the energy, the critical acumen... and the burst of eloquence which electrified the audience'.[87] The next day, after further evidence, the jury returned with a verdict in favour of Maguire. That night there were extensive celebrations in Dublin, as Maguire's supporters went on the rampage, smashing windows that were not illuminated. The army was called out to restore order and quell the riots. The case soon became the subject of a satirical poem, 'The nymphs of Drumkerrin', which praised O'Connell as the 'triumphant chief/ In every cause where justice claims relief'. O'Connell was delighted was the result. 'My heart is light,' he admitted afterwards.[88] He ended the year in high spirits, unaware that the long campaign for emancipation was entering its final stage.

Chapter 14 ∿

| LIBERATION, 1828–1829

'Agitator, n. *person who agitates—D. O'Connell especially.*'
(FLÜGEL'S *German and English Dictionary*, 1830).

On Saturday 28 June 1828 O'Connell set out for Ennis, Co. Clare, on a mission to stand for election to the British parliament and challenge the very foundation of the Protestant Ascendancy. He had spent the day working in the Four Courts until a green carriage pulled up to the yard, which was his signal to leave. News of his departure raced around the Four Courts, and courtrooms were emptied as barristers, jurors, and curious onlookers rushed outside to see O'Connell off; a large crowd of well-wishers had already gathered to cheer him on his way. The coach was certainly difficult to ignore; it was covered in green decorations and the coachmen were also wearing 'pure, unmitigated green' uniforms. At about three fifteen p.m. O'Connell left the courts, in the elaborate green uniform of the Order of Liberators. He called out, 'O'Gorman' and Nicholas Purcell O'Gorman (wearing a green coat with a white lining) and Richard Newton Bennett came out to join him in the carriage. Once they were inside, O'Connell mounted the box and gave the signal, 'All right.' Three cheers were given as the carriage drove off, which O'Connell acknowledged by raising his hat. But some opponents had also gathered and hissed at the carriage as it departed.[1] The countryside was expecting O'Connell and bonfires were lighted along the road to greet his arrival.[2] The journey became a pageant, with men attempting to take the place of the horses to draw the carriage into towns, forcing

O'Connell to remonstrate with them. It was perhaps no wonder that the journalist for the *Freeman's Journal* was obliged to insist that this was 'no visionary story'.

The series of events which had brought O'Connell to that point were equally dramatic. Lord Goderich had resigned as prime minister on 8 January 1828 and was succeeded by the duke of Wellington, with Robert Peel returning as home secretary. The Catholic Association passed a resolution to oppose all future election candidates in Ireland unless they gave a pledge against Wellington's government. The irony is that this resolution was almost revoked by O'Connell himself, following the repeal of the Test and Corporation Acts which affected Dissenters. Lord John Russell wrote to O'Connell acknowledging the support he had received from Wellington and suggesting that, in recognition of this, the anti-Wellington resolution should be withdrawn. O'Connell was anxious to maintain Russell's friendship and presented a motion withdrawing the resolution at the very next meeting of the Catholic Association. Hatred of Wellington ran deep, however, and he was roundly opposed. Unable to get his own way, O'Connell conceded the point.[3]

The very first election to fall under the terms of this resolution came in Co. Clare. William Vesey Fitzgerald, the son of James Fitzgerald who had been sacked as prime serjeant in 1799 because of his opposition to the Union, received a new office in Wellington's government and thus had to seek re-election. Fitzgerald was widely respected, he was a supporter of emancipation (although he had voted for the suppression of the Catholic Association), and was a benign landlord. But the resolution did not recognise such distinctions and after a heated debate in the Catholic Association it was decided he would be opposed. The choice of the Association was William Nugent McNamara, O'Connell's second in the fatal duel of 1815. McNamara was a wealthy Protestant, with extensive holdings in Co. Clare, and was seen as the only man who could run Fitzgerald close in a contest. Victory, even for him, seemed out of the question. An invitation to stand was quickly sent to him in Clare and O'Connell was convinced he would accept the nomination. However he was preoccupied with work and decided not to go to Clare to assist in the campaign; Vesey Fitzgerald boasted privately that it was because he 'was afraid of personal risk and danger'.[4] On Monday 23 June, O'Connell gave a speech at the Corn Exchange where he

announced that a victory in Clare would destroy the ministry of Peel
and Wellington and, at the very least, show that the Catholics were
determined to be free. He was so certain that McNamara had, by now,
accepted the nomination that he told the gathering that if 'his friend
had not offered himself, he [himself] would certainly have stood'. 'Clare
would not be without a candidate,' he announced to cheers, and he
promised that he would stand for the very next vacancy, in any county,
as long as it did not interfere with a liberal and independent candidate.[5]
This heralded a radical new departure in Irish politics.

The next day, Tuesday 24 June, O'Connell organised a meeting at the
Corn Exchange to revive the Order of the Liberators. As president of
the order he took the chair, and outlined its ten ideals and objectives.[6]
Later in the day news arrived from Clare that McNamara had refused
the invitation. Now O'Connell's bluff (if it was a bluff) had been called.
David Roose, a Dublin stockbroker and admirer of O'Connell, met
O'Connell's friend P.V. Fitzpatrick in a bookshop around this time and
suggested that O'Connell should run. Fitzpatrick remembered back to
the days of John Keogh, when Keogh had argued that emancipation
would never come until a Catholic was returned to parliament
(although he had assumed this would be for a borough and not an
open seat).[7] Fitzpatrick rushed to convince O'Connell to stand.
Afterwards, Roose and Fitzpatrick would receive the credit for giving
O'Connell the idea to stand for election. But the speech to the Catholic
Association on 23 January shows that O'Connell was also thinking
along those lines and had already made the decision to stand for
parliament, if not then, then at the very next opportunity. The road to
Clare was paved with O'Connell's intentions.

There was an unstoppable momentum to push O'Connell into
declaring his candidacy. A large meeting of the Catholics was held at
the Corn Exchange that same day to discuss who should stand instead
of McNamara. Various names were suggested, but they were all
drowned out by 'deafening cries of "Mr O'Connell, Mr O'Connell"'.
O'Connell was finally called upon to speak and he announced that
despite his 'humble pretensions' he was ready 'to obey the voice of the
nation'.[8] 'The days of compromise and of half measure are gone,' he
declared to much cheering. An article on the 'Great Agitator' in the *New
Monthly Magazine* in 1829 claimed that his decision to stand in Clare
was 'the most daring, and the boldest which this man ever took, or ever

will take. Were he to live a century he could do nothing which would show so much of daring and intrepid talent.'[9] And the journalist paraphrased Voltaire to suggest that it was one of those decisions 'that vulgar men would call rash, but great men would call bold'. There were daily meetings of the Catholic Association. O'Connell announced on Wednesday 25 July that he was standing, not because of any personal ambition, but rather to 'advocate a principle, which may in my person be vindicated'. Because of his professional commitments, O'Connell was not able to leave Dublin for some days. So the Catholic Association decided to send Jack Lawless and Thomas Steele, all extraordinary firebrands, ahead to Clare to kick-start the campaign. A new member, Charles James Patrick O'Gorman Mahon, a twenty-eight year old who styled himself The O'Gorman Mahon, was also despatched and he would play a key role in Clare. In O'Connell's words, they were being sent 'to ride on the whirlwind and direct the storm'.[10]

For the first couple of days of the campaign O'Connell believed that if he was elected he would be fined £500 for every day he did not take his seat in the British parliament. But he quickly discovered his mistake and made sure to publicise that he had been in error. On Thursday 26 June, at a Catholic meeting, he stated that this was an experiment which would open the eyes of Europe to the state of the Catholics and he declared himself ready to take part in that experiment.[11] 'Ours is a moral not a physical force,' he insisted, as he called on the people of Clare to keep the peace and abstain from any violence, or any kind of illegal activity. This had become O'Connell's core belief, that 'moral strength' would defeat the 'physical force of any nation' and the 'union of physical force with moral sentiment' would give Peel no option but to concede emancipation.[12] The next day O'Connell gave a defiant speech to the Catholic Association about the validity of his candidacy. Any attempt to disqualify him, he insisted, would be a violation of the Act of Union, and he announced that he would love the opportunity to fight Peel and 'the bigots' face-to-face. To great cheers and laughter he insisted that he looked forward to giving them all 'a piece of my mind'.[13] This was also the message of his address to the electors of Clare, drafted on 24 June, in which he gave a solemn pledge that he would take his seat at Westminster without having to swear the 'obnoxious, horrible oaths' against the Catholic faith, namely the oath that 'the sacrifice of the mass and the invocation of the blessed Virgin, Mary and other saints, as now preached by the Church of Rome, are impious and idolatrous'. The appeal was to 'Old Ireland for ever' and he called on the people to choose between a 'friend of Ireland' and 'the friend of an anti-Irish intolerant administration'.

The journey to Ennis became a procession and a race; a procession because O'Connell's carriage was greeted along the way by hundreds of thousands of supporters and a race because nominations were closing on Monday morning and he would be prevented from standing if he did not arrive in time. All along the way he was hailed as the 'Man of the people'. At Toomavara, near Nenagh, O'Connell was met by a crowd so large that his carriage was unable to move and he gave a short speech in which he proclaimed that he had 'dared your foes and bearded your enemies'. Urging conciliation, he begged the local gangs to forget their feuds and work together for 'Old Ireland'.[14] He arrived at the outskirts of Nenagh, Co. Tipperary, at midday on Sunday 29 June, where he was met by 2,000 people on foot and horseback, with a further 50,000 (100,000 according to other reports) cheering him as he made his way into the town.[15] He stopped at an inn for refreshments, while a band played 'Garryowen' and men, women and children gathered to sing for his entertainment. Following his meal he addressed the crowd while standing on the high seat of his carriage. The reporter for the *Morning Register* said that he had never in his life witnessed 'so grand or magnificent a scene. In whatever direction the eye was turned it fell on a dense and solid mass of people, while the ear was assaulted by a shout which you could hear reverberated for miles around'.[16] The final stage of the journey was to Ennis. Even though it was late at night, everyone wanted to see O'Connell. One reporter was amazed how 'men in their shirts and women in their (what shall I call them) *inexpressibles*, rushed to their doors' to catch a glimpse as he passed.

It was two a.m. on Monday morning when O'Connell finally arrived in Ennis. Despite the lateness of the hour there was still a massive procession to greet him, an outpouring of support and adulation. The reporter for *The Times* said that it would be impossible to describe this procession, or 'the shouts, the tumultuous and deafening cheers with which they were received as they came into the town'.[17] 'For good or evil', the reporter noted, Irish politics had been changed dramatically, and the contest was recognised as being much more intense than the 1826 campaign in Waterford. O'Connell's son, Maurice, had already arrived in the town and was acting as O'Connell's agent. More importantly, the work of O'Gorman Mahon, Steele, and Lawless was already bringing results. They had transformed the county and Sheil later admitted that much of O'Connell's success was down to their campaigning and the machine they had put in place.[18] Steele had even threatened to fight any landlord who tried to intimidate his tenants. Fr Tom Maguire, who O'Connell had famously defended in the McGarrahan trial, decided to repay the favour and arrived in the county to rally support; his rabble-rousing skills proved invaluable. Sheil also arrived to act as O'Connell's counsel and his oratorical skills were another addition to the arsenal. One man who did not remain in Clare to assist with the campaign was Major McNamara. Having turned down the opportunity to stand himself, he now fell into a terrible sulk, and flounced off to the Aran Islands.[19] But he still managed to cause O'Connell problems, even in his absence, for O'Connell felt obliged to make him a written promise that he would vacate the seat in his favour at some future point (if he won it), a promise that McNamara later insisted he honour.

Nomination of candidates was at eleven a.m. at the courthouse on Monday and it proved to be the most dramatic day of the campaign. Fitzgerald had brought a large entourage with him, and they arrived early, taking all the best seats at the front. When O'Connell arrived at eleven he accused the sheriff of a breach of faith, having been told that no-one would be admitted before that time. However, to loud cheering, he declared that he did not care as he was happy to remain standing with the people.[20] The first candidate to be nominated was Vesey Fitzgerald, but the process was interrupted when the high sheriff noticed O'Gorman Mahon ('a handsome young man with enormous whiskers'[21]) in the gallery, wearing the distinctive uniform of the Order of Liberators. Waving his wand of office, he demanded to know, 'Who, sir, are you?' 'My name is O'Gorman Mahon,' came the reply. Disapproving of the overtly political symbol of the green medal of the Order of Liberators, the high sheriff demanded that it was removed. O'Gorman Mahon was enraged and announced, 'This gentleman *(laying his hand on his breast)* tells that gentleman *(pointing with the other to the sheriff)*, that if that gentleman presumes to touch this gentleman, this gentleman will defend himself against that gentleman or any other gentleman, while he has got the arm of a gentleman to protect him.'[22] It was, as Sheil rightly noted, an 'extraordinary sentence' and won a large burst of applause from the gathering. O'Connell looked at O'Gorman Mahon with 'gratitude and admiration'. He joined the discussion, suggesting that 'green is no party colour' and that while it might be hateful to some of their enemies it was a 'darling colour' and would never be put down by Wellington or his cabinet. O'Gorman Mahon then declared, 'I shall not lower the green badge for any man. I owe the sheriff no courtesy and he shall receive none from me.'[23] The sheriff sat down, dejected and defeated. The first blow had been struck.

Fitzgerald was proposed by Sir Edward O'Brien and seconded by Sir Augustine Fitzgerald. After a dramatic pause, O'Gorman Mahon then rose to nominate O'Connell. He made a long speech proposing him, and the nomination was seconded by Richard Steele, who called O'Connell 'the man of the people'.[24] Before the candidates were invited to speak, Francis Gore, an unsuccessful barrister and Clare proprietor who was supporting Fitzgerald, rose to attack O'Connell, the involvement of the priests in the election and the Catholic Association. He delivered his speech in a tone so low that it was difficult to hear him, but he succeeded in angering O'Connell by raising his willingness to abandon the forty-shilling freeholders in 1825 when his own personal ambitions had been at stake. O'Connell was at his best when under fire and responded in his own speech the only way he knew how, with brutal, crushing, unrelenting abuse. He told the gathering that the law had not prevented Gore from advancing in his career: 'want of talent did'. And he followed it by asking the crowd if he was to be 'subjected to the taunts of a briefless barrister—a bigot without business?'

Before this, though, it was Fitzgerald's turn. As soon as he rose to speak it became obvious that he was a well-liked candidate, with his speech regularly cheered and applauded. He insisted that he was a friend of the Catholics and defended his vote for the suppression of the Catholic Association by saying that he had followed the lead of George Canning, and had been acting in the best interests of the Catholic cause. The cheers became louder as he went on, with the crowd urging him to continue speaking when he apologised for having detained them for too long. Towards the end of his speech he made reference to his father, who despite being caught up in a sex and money scandal in the 1800s (which involved the duke of York and his mistress), was a much respected and loved figure, especially because of his opposition to the Union. Fitzgerald spoke movingly about how his father was right now 'stretched out on a bed of sickness', unaware that his son's seat was under threat. Here he broke down in tears, moving many in the audience to join him, and it was a few minutes before he was able to resume his speech. His voice shaking, he concluded by praising the electors for all the support they had shown him in the past, and he sat down to 'a burst of acclamation'. Sheil called it 'one of the most effective and dexterous speeches' he had ever heard.[25]

What could O'Connell do? He knew he was in a tricky position, especially as he admired Fitzgerald on a personal and political level (his support for suppressing the Catholic Association in 1825 and for Wellington excepted). But he also knew from years of addressing public gatherings that a moderate line would not work, and that the only chance he had was to eviscerate Fitzgerald and make him a figure to be hated and despised. As he rose to speak it was obvious to those who knew him well that he was 'collecting all his might'.[26] His speech was nasty, brutish, and brilliant, without doubt one of the greatest of his life. It was also one of the most personal, and he deployed humour, insult and smear tactics to devastating effect. Sheil afterwards noted that in such a warfare 'a man must not pause in the selection of his weapons, and Mr O'Connell is not the man to hesitate in the use of the rhetorical sabre'. O'Connell claimed to have been insulted by Fitzgerald's talk of his support for the Catholic cause, and insisted that it was not enough for Catholics to be hated by the cabinet of which Fitzgerald was a member, they must also be treated with contempt. Allegations of improper use of official funds had been circulated by O'Connell's agents for some days, and O'Connell addressed that point. Reviewing Fitzgerald's years of public service, he suggested that he talked of public principles, while at the same time 'the public money is going into his pocket'. It was a cruel and dishonest smear, and prompted Fitzgerald to interrupt and plead, 'Do I deserve these observations?' But O'Connell was relentless and said that while it might have been unfair to accuse him of pocketing £100,000, as some of his campaign team had, it was probably true that he taken £20,000. Gore's charge of having abandoned the forty-shilling freeholders in 1825 was addressed. O'Connell admitted that at the time he had believed they were the slaves of their landlords, but that now he knew different: 'It was a fault in me to have consented to their disenfranchisement; but I have made full and ample reparation; and sooner now would I shed the last drop of my blood than consent to their disenfranchisement.' Gore was roundly abused, and O'Connell compared their respective careers at the bar (they were almost exact contemporaries), and how one was a failure, the other a complete success. 'But what use is my success to me?' he asked, reflecting on the 'cruel fate' which meant that he could not rise at the bar because he was a Catholic, and all that this had cost him. Addressing Gore, but aiming at Fitzgerald, he destroyed them both with his pointed remark: 'I have wept over my lot in private, for I never shed my tears in public.' It was a direct hit. Fitzgerald's tears were neutralised, his support evaporating, as O'Connell attacked every aspect of his character and politics.

The suppression of the Catholic Association was raised, and O'Connell discussed the double standard in Ireland where Catholics could be murdered by Protestants without fear of prosecution, but any attempt to mobilise the Catholics was prevented by the law. 'Is our blood like ditch-water,' he asked, 'thus to be let run into waste, and no man be called to account for shedding it?' Fitzgerald's conduct in this period was dismissed in the strongest language as 'barefaced and miserable hypocrisy'. O'Connell showed him no sympathy for siding with Canning and Plunket and he quoted the saying, 'there is good company in hell.' 'Well,' said O'Connell, 'I shall not so apply the word in the present instance, but there is certainly good company in the political purgatory which the gentleman is at present enduring.' 'Will you vote for Fitzgerald who suppressed the Catholic Association?' he asked, to shouts of 'No, no.' He followed this by urging them to use their votes to give a hearty 'licking to V. Fitzgerald'. Now in full flow, he denounced Fitzgerald for being the friend of Peel, and for smiling while he had defended him. Choosing the first half of a famous Shakespearian quote, O'Connell suggested that 'A man may smile and…', leaving the rest hanging, and added that 'I will not use the word [villain]', before calling Fitzgerald 'the smiling gay deceiver'.

O'Connell even discussed his own early life, 'when the blood was bubbling in my veins' and 'my passions led me astray', and when he had been 'inattentive to the function of my religion'. But he rejoiced that even then he had never abandoned or denied it. The speech ended with a volley of execration for the combined enemies of the Catholic cause. Lord Lyndhurst, an anti-Catholic peer in the House of Lords, had claimed that he could not 'see his way through this question'. O'Connell suggested that if he was elected to parliament he would 'supply him with a pair of political spectacles in less than a week'. Those who hailed the duke of Wellington for defeating Napoleon were also denigrated. Was Wellington, he wondered, like Jack the Giant Killer, who had vanquished the enemy all on his own 'with his sword of sharpness?' Gore had praised the statesmanlike qualities of Wellington and had even compared him to the great Lord Chatham. This astonished O'Connell and he asked his audience to laugh at this for him, because he was too tired, and they duly obliged. The crowd was now cheering and laughing at everything he said, completely under his spell. He continued his attack on Wellington, claiming that 'a more stuttering, confused, unintelligible speaker' had never opened his mouth. And he called on the people to reject Fitzgerald, 'the sworn friend and kissing companion of Peel and Wellington'. The peroration was perfectly judged. '"Romans, countrymen and lovers", I came not here on my own account, but yours—I am not fighting my own but the Catholic cause.' And with that he sat down urging the people to reject Peel, Wellington, and Fitzgerald and instead make their cry 'O'Connell, the Catholic cause and Old Ireland'.

There remained the formality of the sheriff calling for a show of hands in favour of the candidates. Twenty-one men raised their hands for Fitzgerald. Everyone else in the packed courtroom raised their hands for O'Connell, and there was 'loud shouts and cheering for several minutes'. The sheriff attempted to claim that not all of these men were freeholders, but O'Connell argued that since he had no proof either way there was nothing he could do about it. It was decided that the formal polling would begin the next day and the meeting adjourned. Fitzgerald was furious with O'Connell for the way he had been treated. Contacting Peel he reported how 'nothing can equal the violence here', and he noted ruefully that 'the country is mad', and that 'madmen' had 'been allowed to proceed in the career of revolution'.[27]

For the next week the town of Ennis came to a standstill. Shops closed, and even the races were 'completely deserted' as everyone followed the election campaign. O'Connell was hailed as the Irish Washington and Bolívar, and instead of saying 'God be with you' people began saying 'O'Connell be with you'.[28] Everywhere you looked there were signs of the campaign. Even the children in the streets were active, singing songs like 'Green is my livery' and 'The liberty tree'.[29] There was also money to be made in merchandising. One wily merchant produced a supply of green silk handkerchiefs, with the 'Hereditary bondsmen' lines wrapped around O'Connell's portrait in the centre.[30] During the campaign, O'Connell demonstrated that he was a master of the political gesture. When he encountered the local bishop on the street he made a show of kneeling down to receive his blessing.[31] O'Connell had taken a room in a hotel opposite the courthouse, and his supporters erected a platform outside his window, large enough that twenty people could stand on it at any one time. It was from here that O'Connell and the other campaigners addressed the people every day. The results of each day's polling were announced in the Grand Jury Room after six p.m. At the end of the first day, Tuesday 1 July, the numbers were very close with 200 for O'Connell and 194 for Fitzgerald, though O'Connell complained that nearly fifty of his voters had been prevented from casting their votes that day.

It was claimed by the government that 150 priests had travelled to Ennis from all over the country to campaign for O'Connell. Whatever the number they were incredibly active, mobilising support, encouraging, cajoling, intimidating, persuading. Their influence was enormous. As a result, allegations of undue influence were made to the high sheriff and a Fr Murphy of Corofin was brought before him to answer charges of having terrified the voters into doing what he wanted. A lawyer for Fitzgerald accused Fr Murphy of having intimidated his voters by looking at them a certain way, but he was no match for Sheil, who defended the priest. Sheil enquired sharply whether a priest was to be prosecuted for his physiognomy. And he raised his hands in bafflement and asked, 'Do we live in a free country?'[32] There were other examples of the clergy's influence. A Fr Geoghegan gave a speech in Irish to the people from the platform outside O'Connell's window in which he told the story of a man who had pledged his vote to O'Connell, but who had then been persuaded to vote for Fitzgerald. This man, the priest revealed, had died that very night. He called on them to pray for the soul of the man, and as they went down on their knees he warned them to make sure the same fate did not befall them.[33] But the priests were not followed unconditionally. A Fr Coffey attempted to lead seventy-five freeholders to vote for Fitzgerald, but they were met by O'Gorman Mahon, who commanded a halt and marched them away with him instead.[34]

3,000 troops had been sent to Ennis to maintain order, but reporters were astonished that there was no drunkenness on the streets, and no violence; everything was perfectly tranquil.[35] An order had been given by O'Connell to endure everything and never retaliate. One night a supporter of Fitzgerald lashed out at a boy who was abusing him. Two men were about to intervene on the boy's behalf when they heard a voice, 'Remember the order—have you forgotten the order?'[36] Calm was immediately restored. One of the proudest things for O'Connell was the fact that 60,000 men could gather in Ennis every day, 'sinking under the heat', and not a single one would touch a drop of whiskey. 'No man was intoxicated,' he boasted, 'nor partook of that which was called the Elysium of savages, or degraded himself like a brute.'[37] In fact the people took it upon themselves to inflict a punishment for drunkenness. The guilty party was thrown into a certain part of the river and held there for two hours, during which time he was dunked repeatedly.[38] That is not to say that no alcohol was served. Wine, porter, and especially cider were provided by O'Connell's campaign.[39] But the amounts were small, and were only served as light refreshments. The absence of disorder and violence disturbed the government more than anything else. As a government agent reported to the lord lieutenant, 'The absolute quietness of the place is quite frightening.'[40] The polling book was closed at six p.m. on the second day with 850 votes for O'Connell to 538 for Fitzgerald, and it was rumoured that Fitzgerald had already brought out the men who were usually kept in reserve until the last day. Fitzgerald became increasingly withdrawn and depressed as the campaign went on, and kept shrinking from those who asked the question 'Where is this all to end?'[41] Meanwhile Lawless was going hoarse campaigning for O'Connell. He was amused, however, to learn that the beautiful girls in Clare had formed a 'general confederacy' to refuse to marry any man who voted for Fitzgerald.[42] O'Connell, himself, was attracting many favourable glances. Lawless later recounted to the Catholic Association how 'some of the most beautiful women he had ever beheld in Ireland' would come forward to get a glimpse of O'Connell and he joked that he had never, until then, 'pitied Mrs O'Connell half so much'.

At nine o'clock every evening the O'Connell campaign team would retire to a private room upstairs in Mrs Carmody's tavern for dinner.

'Crammed and piled upon one another', they would work their way through 'enormous masses of beef, pork, mutton, turkeys, tongues and fowl', saying very little until their appetite was satisfied. O'Connell abstained from alcohol, only ever drinking water, while the rest of the men drank tumblers of punch. Toasts were then given and the usual 'hip, hip, hurrah,' and only then would the events of the day be discussed. O'Connell was exhausted every evening, but seemed 'sustained by the vitality which success produces'.[43] Most evenings 'a solemn and spectral figure'—Fr Murphy of Corofin—would glide into the room, like 'the figure of Death which the Egyptians employed at their banquets'. He would then start crying, 'The wolf, the wolf is on the walk,' which was his way of urging the gathering to forget about their own pleasures and return to work. Lawless, having usually by this time settled down to enjoy his second tumbler, was particularly offended by this 'nocturnal molestation' and grew to hate this 'unrelenting foe to conviviality'. But Murphy usually succeeded in dragging the men downstairs, where they would find a crowd of priests directing the distribution of food throughout the locality for supporters who had not eaten that day.

There were various scuffles between O'Connell's campaign team and the high sheriff. O'Gorman Mahon became so frustrated with his actions that he told him directly that he would make him do his duty. Upon hearing this the assessor recommended that O'Gorman Mahon be taken into custody, but O'Gorman Mahon just gave him a contemptuous look. No challenges were issued, but only because O'Connell was insistent that there would be no fighting until the election was over. Edward Hickman, a wealthy landlord and notorious duellist, threatened to shoot O'Connell if he canvassed his tenants. But O'Connell deflected this threat with humour, suggesting to Hickman's tenants that 'sure boys, he's the greatest play actor in the world... Now that is what Mr Ned Hickman is about. He's well aware that every one of you is determined to vote for me, but he wants to keep square with Mr Vesey Fitzgerald, and that's what makes him play off the farce.'[44] O'Connell understood the theatrics needed to secure victory. When one landlord's tenants, numbering about 100, arrived to vote for Fitzgerald, O'Connell rushed on to the platform and slowly raised his arm in triumph. They all deserted the landlord and voted for him. The margin of victory grew each day; by the close of polling on Thursday 3

July there were 1820 votes for O'Connell to 842 for Fitzgerald.[45] It was no longer a contest. O'Connell gave a speech to the people who had gathered to hear the latest news, once again attacking Wellington for achieving his victories with Irish blood and then abandoning the Catholics afterwards. A voter in the audience said that he was one of those men, having fought nineteen times under Wellington and having been wounded three times. O'Connell then attacked those Catholics who had voted for Fitzgerald, men who had disgraced their religion and who were determined to act as slaves. There was also a threat for the British government. He declared that if he was prevented from taking his seat he would regard it as a breach of the Union, and in fact as having repealed the Union. In that case he promised to restore the Irish parliament in Dublin and 'all the privileges of the glorious year of 1782'. The totals at the end of polling on Friday were 2027 for O'Connell and 936 for Fitzgerald. In Fitzgerald's own famous description he had polled 'the gentry to a man' but it had not been enough. 'The desertion has been universal,' he conceded.[46]

The next day, Saturday 5 July, polling came to an end and O'Connell was returned as the new MP for Co. Clare with 2,057 votes to Fitzgerald's 982. The assessor ruled that the election was valid, leaving the matter of what oaths must be taken by O'Connell to the House of Commons. In his acceptance speech O'Connell began by apologising for anything he might have said, 'produced by the strong excitement of the moment', against Fitzgerald. Fitzgerald was now praised as 'a gentleman of whose honour and integrity I feel as convinced as I do of my own existence'. O'Connell also praised the people of Clare for their 'extraordinary tranquillity' during the campaign and said they had performed 'a great national and religious duty'. He promised the gathering that he would be able to take his seat at Westminster and that he would continue to act as a 'radical reformer' in parliament. Repeal of the Union was clearly on his mind. Some people had claimed recently that this would be impossible, but O'Connell declared that a similar victory had been obtained in 1782 and 'I hope I shall show that it may be done again'. Fitzgerald made a dignified concession speech, to much applause, although he was much more bitter and scathing in private. Following his speech, Sheil also made conciliatory remarks about Fitzgerald and hailed O'Connell as 'the mighty agitator of Ireland'. It was in this speech that Sheil discussed 'the wand of this potent enchanter of the passions', and insisted that the only way forward was to remove his 'volume of magic' and 'break his wand', then 'he will evoke the spirits which are now under his control no longer'.

MPs were entitled to free postage so O'Connell sent a number of letters that afternoon, all franked, to send news of his victory. According to the *Limerick Chronicle* his first four letters were sent to the duke of Wellington, Lord Eldon, Peel, and Goulburn.[47] Peel was horrified by the news of O'Connell's victory and admitted privately that the 'instrument of political power' in Ireland had been 'shivered to atoms'.[48] Peel and Wellington had been moving to a recognition that emancipation was inevitable; the Clare election was the catalyst that speeded up the process.

On Sunday 6 July crowds of well-wishers arrived in Ennis to cheer the newly elected member of parliament. Every window in the town was decorated with flowers, every door with green branches of laurel. A large chair was placed in the centre on the platform, inscribed with the 'Hereditary bondsmen' lines. At one thirty p.m. O'Connell arrived at the platform and was raised on the chair and then carried throughout the town, where he was cheered and saluted. The green silk O'Connell handkerchiefs had obviously sold well, for they were waved enthusiastically wherever he went. Following this O'Connell was carried on the chair all the way to Limerick, despite his protestations that travelling by carriage would be easier, and he was 'met, at every step, by hundreds'. The army kept a close watch on his movements but it was clear that even here he had his support. Once, when passing a marching detachment, he was stopped by the young sergeant, a man called Ryan, who walked away from his men to shake hands with him. Ryan told O'Connell that he might very well be flogged or demoted for this breach of military discipline, but that he did not care because he had 'had the satisfaction of shaking the hand of the father of my country'.[49] O'Connell came to believe that it was moments like this which convinced Wellington that he could not rely on his own army.

O'Connell arrived in Limerick at dusk and was greeted by a triumphant procession which escorted him to Moriarty's Hotel. There, from the balcony, he gave a speech to 'the immense multitude', which was 'received with the most deafening cheers'. For perhaps the only time in his life O'Connell was not heard clearly. Ever single sentence was cheered so loudly that it was impossible for the reporters to make out what he was saying. There followed a public dinner in his honour. At two p.m. the next day, O'Connell and his entourage began the journey to Dublin, bringing with him, according to one reporter, 'the blessings of a liberated people'.

On Thursday 10 July O'Connell arrived in Dublin, in time to make a triumphant late entrance to a packed meeting of the Catholic Association at the Corn Exchange. When he arrived there was 'general exultation' and he had to make his way 'through the dense assembly, amid the most rapturous and enthusiastic demonstrations of applause. Every man in a room rose to offer his heartfelt congratulations and the ladies in the gallery waved their handkerchiefs.'[50] O'Connell was in great form, telling the gathering that that he was so happy he would rather laugh than do anything else. He then told them to sit back and enjoy something they had never heard before, a speech from a Roman Catholic member of parliament. A sign of his confidence was his willingness to address the events of 1825, when he said he had attempted to forge 'a golden link' between the Catholic church and the state and had been prepared to sacrifice the forty-shilling freeholders. To great applause he declared that he would 'rather die on the scaffold than give them up'. He had but one demand: 'unconditional, unqualified, free and unshackled' emancipation. There was also a clear threat to the British government: they must either conciliate or crush the Irish Catholics. O'Connell mentioned the 300 soldiers who had cheered him as he left Ennis, and the support he had received on the way home. This was a time to either secure the loyalty of the Irish Catholics, or lose it for ever. For the British government the way O'Connell had been able to maintain control over the people in Clare was as worrying as his election victory. It was a clear signal that the people were in his power to do with as he liked.

On 27 July O'Connell had a private meeting with the lord lieutenant, Lord Anglesey, to discuss the state of Ireland. O'Connell had requested the meeting, ostensibly to discuss an incident in Longford when a Catholic had been killed during an Orange march, but really to discover what might happen in the months ahead. Anglesey was surprised to find O'Connell speaking with 'peculiar calmness and mildness of manner', blaming the 'unhappy state of the country' on the 'frequent and unnecessary interference of the police and by the Protestants being generally armed'.[51] Worried that the details of the conversation might become public, Anglesey sought assurances that everything would remain confidential. O'Connell put his hand on his heart and bowed ('obsequiously' according to Anglesey), promising that nothing would be leaked by him. He also took great pains to emphasise 'his abhorrence of insurrection and his conviction that none was to be expected'. The loyalty of the priests and bishops was discussed, and O'Connell emphasised that they could be controlled quite easily, and he 'seemed to hold quite cheap any doubt as to the management of the priests'.

Anglesey took the opportunity to lecture O'Connell about the behaviour of the Catholic Association, and especially its treatment of the duke of Wellington. During this lecture Anglesey let slip that Wellington had converted to the cause of Catholic emancipation and would acquiesce in the measure, but not immediately, and only if the country remained tranquil. The shape of this 'adjustment' was then discussed. When the question of the forty-shilling freeholders was raised O'Connell conceded that the freeholders 'would never stand in the way of an adjustment'.[52] This was an incredible concession, especially given all of the public declarations of the subject, and showed that some of the old spirit of 1825 remained. O'Connell left the meeting in great form and 'appeared much pleased with his reception'. Lord Forbes, who had also been in attendance, escorted O'Connell out and they continued to discuss what would happen in the months ahead. In an outer room O'Connell remarked that he saw 'but one difficulty. It is the forty-shilling freeholders. We cannot *all at once* give them up. We must have time!' Anglesey was delighted when this was reported back and thought that the declaration was 'the most remarkable and satisfactory of all that took place'. He was full of glee and mocked O'Connell as 'the vainest of men', believing that he 'is easily taken by a good bait'.

But it seems clear that O'Connell was also trying to hook Anglesey. During the discussion O'Connell made a great show of how he was not motivated by any self-interest and was even prepared to sacrifice himself for the sake of a deal. When Anglesey assured him that he would, 'of course, be in parliament', O'Connell shook his head and said that 'this he did not wish'. This shocked Anglesey and he spent much time urging him to reconsider, praising his talents and discussing the high situations he was suited for. Comparing O'Connell to George

Washington, Anglesey insisted that he would be called by the people to serve. Following the meeting, Anglesey was convinced that O'Connell was 'perfectly sincere', though he admitted that he 'should be laughed at for my gullibility' if he was wrong. He believed that O'Connell had a 'good heart and means well and means indeed always what he says' but 'he is volatile and unsteady and so vain that he cannot resist momentary applause'.

Prince Hermann Louis Henri Pückler-Muskau, a minor Prussian nobleman, visited O'Connell in Derrynane in late September. Pückler-Muskau was a keen traveller, on a tour of Britain and Ireland, and he definitely left an impression on O'Connell, who was so amused by him that he used three exclamation marks ('I have had Prince Pückler-Muskau!!!') when discussing his visit afterwards.[53] Even Pückler-Muskau's arrival at Derrynane was entertaining. He paid a messenger to carry news of his coming to O'Connell, but the man immediately spent the money on whiskey, and then had an accident while riding while drunk, falling off his horse.[54] However another message was sent and O'Connell invited Pückler-Muskau to join him at his home. Delayed because of terrible weather, Pückler-Muskau arrived at eleven p.m. on the evening of 28 September, just as the extended O'Connell family were finishing their wine and dessert.[55] 'A tall handsome man, of cheerful and agreeable aspect' rose to greet Pückler-Muskau, introduced him to his family, and then showed him to his bedroom: 'This was the great O'Connell.' Leaving his bags in his room, Pückler-Muskau returned to the dining room and was entertained by all the family, and O'Connell's 'old and capital wine' made an even better impression. After the women retired, O'Connell drew his seat closer and they began discussing Ireland. O'Connell asked if he had seen the Giant's Causeway, but Pückler-Muskau laughed and said that he had a greater interest in seeing 'Ireland's Giants'. It was flattery that bordered on the fulsome, but it went down very well all the same.

Pückler-Muskau's account of O'Connell, though subjective, is revealing. He was hugely impressed with O'Connell, a man who had it in his power to 'raise the standard of rebellion from one end of the island to the other', but who was 'too sure of attaining his end by safer means to wish to bring on any such violent crisis'. As far as he was concerned, O'Connell had as much power in the country as King George IV, perhaps more, because without any 'arms or armies' he was master of the people and had persuaded tens of thousands of Irishmen to abstain from drinking whiskey in Clare during the recent election campaign. O'Connell exceeded all his expectations, though he could still be extremely critical. 'One frequently perceives too much design and manner in his words,' he admitted, and he also thought there was too much of the actor about him. O'Connell's manners, he regretted, were at times 'tinged' by 'vulgarity'. He was also amused by O'Connell's vanity. The next day O'Connell told him of his distinguished uncle, General O'Connell, but added 'not without a certain *pretension*' that *he* was the head of the family. He noted that O'Connell made no attempt to 'conceal his very high opinion of himself'. But while he thought that 'his desire for celebrity seemed boundless', he was in no doubt that once emancipation was won, O'Connell's career, 'far from being closed, will I think only then properly begin'.[56]

Estimating that O'Connell was 'about fifty years old, and in excellent preservation', it seems Pückler-Muskau had heard some stories about O'Connell's early life because he added, 'though his youth was rather wild and riotous'.[57] Impressed with his military bearing, he thought O'Connell looked more like a general of Napoleon's than an Irish lawyer. He had also heard all about the duel with D'Esterre, though he was not clear on the details, and believed that 'O'Connell lodged a bullet in D'Esterre's heart; D'Esterre's shot went through his hat.' The greatest gift he believed O'Connell possessed was his 'magnificent voice' which was 'invaluable for a party-leader'. Returning from a walk on the afternoon of 29 September, he found O'Connell on his terrace, surrounded like a chieftain by all his tenants and the neighbouring peasantry. There O'Connell gave his instructions and laid down the law and Pückler-Muskau learned that here in Kerry 'O'Connell and the pope are equally infallible'. There were no lawsuits 'within his empire', and this rule applied not just to his tenants, but extended throughout the whole region.

O'Connell had never been more popular in the country. But even at the zenith of his popularity he was still being challenged at meetings of the Catholic Association, especially by a more radical wing, unwilling to compromise. It is perhaps always thus. In politics the greatest adversaries, the most serious threats, are often to be found on one's own side, rather than amongst one's opponents. Thomas Hyde Villiers, a British MP, visited Ireland in this period and his observations on the

Catholic Association are instructive. He noted that 'O'Connell and Sheil detest each other, though Sheil does not oppose him', and that Lawless 'detests him too, and does everything he can to thwart and provoke him'.[58] But although challenged 'by a numerous party in the Association', O'Connell was still 'all powerful in the country' and there was not 'one individual who has a chance of supplanting him in the affections of the great mass of the Catholics'. It was clear to Hyde Villiers that O'Connell had made enemies. He noted that Dr Doyle, bishop of Kildare and Leighlin, hated O'Connell, but was obliged to work with him. When addressing the Catholic Association at one of these meetings, O'Connell revealed his confidence that he could keep the country tranquil for another year, and although this was challenged by the more radical wing, he managed to convince the majority that a cautious approach was best. O'Connell was not by temperament a gambler. He had risen at the bar by protecting his clients and the very same instincts were at work here.

After departing from Derrynane on 30 September, Pückler-Muskau saw his hero twice more, at meetings of the Catholic Association in Dublin. On 18 November he visited the Corn Exchange and was spotted by O'Connell, who made room for him beside him. The room was packed, the heat suffocating, and the debate lasted five hours. But Pückler-Muskau barely noticed as he watched the 'good and bad orators' on display. In his rankings, the three greatest speakers were O'Connell, Sheil, and Lawless. Sheil was too theatrical for his liking, 'too affected, too artificial', and lacked feeling in his delivery.[59] He also noted that although he was as vain as O'Connell, the vanity of O'Connell was 'more frank, more confiding, and sooner satisfied', while that of Sheil was 'irritable, sore and gloomy'. Sheil, he detected, was jealous of O'Connell, who 'he vainly thinks to surpass'. Pückler-Muskau was greatly entertained by Lawless, who he hailed as the Don Quixote of the Association, with a 'fine head and white hair' and a 'magnificent voice'. But he noted that his speeches, which began brilliantly, gave way to 'extravagancies and sometimes [fell] into total absurdity'. Friends and enemies were abused with equal fury, and as a result he was little heeded. Lawless was 'laughed at when he rages like King Lear', oblivious to the impression he was making. At the next meeting Pückler-Muskau attended, Lawless again 'spoke like a madman' and delivered a vehement attack on O'Connell. He noted that O'Connell almost lost his temper but instead defeated Lawless by making fun of him in a cruel but entertaining manner.

The tensions in the Catholic Association were partly a result of the uncertainty about what would happen next. The king refused to give any indication to Wellington about whether he would agree to emancipation and the government was paralysed on the issue. Some compromise to placate the ultras on the Protestant side became inevitable, as emancipation became impossible to resist. It seemed increasingly clear that this would involve the disenfranchisement of the forty-shilling freeholders. On 2 December O'Connell declared to the Catholic Association that he would never accept emancipation if it meant disenfranchising the forty-shilling freeholders. But he had already conceded the point in private and, no matter what he said in public, the game was over for the forty-shilling freeholders.

At this time rumours of financial misdeeds began to circulate. Towards the end of the year O'Connell was accused in print of misappropriating some of the Catholic rent for his own purposes. The allegations were made in a hand-bill called A rent-payer, and suggested serious financial abuse. Given the precarious state of his personal finances, O'Connell was vulnerable to allegations of this sort. However he was cleared by an investigation conducted by the finance committee of the Association on 1 January 1829.[60] It is impossible to investigate these charges now, but it is unlikely there was any real substance to them. While he may have taken money he felt was due to him for campaign expenses in Clare, or other expenses involved in running the Catholic Association, he certainly was not stealing from the fund.

On 6 February 1829 O'Connell set out for London to see if he could take his seat in parliament, which had met the day before. In his absence Sheil moved a motion on 10 February to dissolve the Catholic Association, and this was approved, despite the opposition of O'Connell's son, Maurice, and letters from O'Connell himself warning that they had always been betrayed in the past when they had been too trusting. However Sheil, and even Lawless, believed that emancipation was inevitable and that there was no need to continue agitating. In any case a new Algerine Act, suppressing the Association, was being prepared for parliament. But O'Connell remembered the failure of 1825 and knew that the pressure must be kept on the government, that the threat of civil war in Ireland must continue to terrify it, and that there should be no concessions until emancipation had been secured.

In London O'Connell waited to see what would happen. The king tried one last attempt to sabotage emancipation, even to the extent of attempting to change the government, but this proved impossible and he was forced to give in. Finally accepting that emancipation could not be stopped, he gave his consent to an emancipation bill in early March.[61] Bitter at his defeat, George IV lamented that O'Connell was now 'King of Ireland', and he was reduced to 'Dean of Windsor'.[62] O'Connell was jubilant.[63] The emancipation bill was announced on 6 March, with no veto or ecclesiastical arrangements as part of it. There was an attempt to include a clause preventing the expansion of the Jesuits and the monastic orders, but O'Connell correctly realised that he could 'drive a coach and six through it'. 'I tread on air' he wrote ecstatically to his wife.[64] Overall, O'Connell was impressed with the emancipation bill: it was 'frank, direct, complete'.[65] But there was one blot. As expected, the freehold qualification was raised to ten pounds, thus eliminating the forty-shilling freeholders. They had won the election for him, and he felt guilty about having to abandon them and so made a last-ditch attempt to save them. However he received almost no support from the British MPs, even the radical ones, and it proved impossible. The forty-shilling freeholders were disenfranchised as the price to be paid for emancipation.

The emancipation bill received the royal assent on 13 April. The next day, when writing a letter, O'Connell dated it 'The first day of freedom!'[66] It marked the culmination of almost a quarter of a century of hard work, agitation, and sacrifice. He had never been happier, having won what he called 'one of the greatest triumphs recorded in history—a bloodless revolution more extensive in its operation that any political change that could take place'. However he was still not able to take his seat for Co. Clare, after the government decided that the emancipation legislation would not be back-dated to cover his election. But, in the event, he was re-elected unopposed in the summer. O'Connell was finally, at long last, able to enter the House of Commons. That year he was praised in print as a new Brian Boru and hailed as 'The Liberator' who had won his country's freedom.[67]

In later years O'Connell admitted that there was no way he could have returned to being 'a poor barrister' after 'the character and publicity I gained by emancipation'. With great honesty (and refreshing self-awareness) he conceded that 'human vanity would not permit it'.[68] O'Connell was already looking to the future. On the night that emancipation passed he was slapped on the shoulder by a friend who joked that his career was now over as he no longer had any reason to agitate, thus 'Othello's occupation's gone!'[69] 'Gone!' exclaimed O'Connell with a smile. 'Isn't there a Repeal of the Union?'

ABBREVIATIONS

DDA   Dublin Diocesan Archives
NLI   National Library of Ireland
RIA   Royal Irish Academy
UC   University of Chicago Library Archives
UCD   University College Dublin Archives
PRONI   Public Record Office of Northern Ireland

DAUNT, *Personal recollections*
William J. O'Neill Daunt, *Personal recollections of the late Daniel O'Connell* (2 volumes, London, 1848).
FAGAN, *Life*
William Fagan, *The life and times of Daniel O'Connell* (2 volumes, Cork, 1847–8).
FITZPATRICK, *Correspondence*
W.J. Fitzpatrick (ed.), *Correspondence of Daniel O'Connell, the Liberator* (2 volumes, New York, 1888).
HOUSTON, *Journal*
Arthur Houston, *Daniel O'Connell: his early life and journal, 1795 to 1802* (London, 1906).
O'CONNELL, *Speeches*
John O'Connell (ed.), *The life and speeches of Daniel O'Connell* M.P. (2 volumes, Dublin, 1846).
O'CONNELL *Corr.*
M.R. O'Connell (ed.), *The correspondence of Daniel O'Connell* (8 volumes, Shannon and Dublin, 1972–80).
PÜCKLER-MUSKAU, *Tour in England, Ireland and France*
[Prince Hermann Pückler-Muskau], *Tour in England, Ireland and France in the years 1829 and 1830. By a German prince* (2 volumes, London, 1832).
SHEIL, *Sketches*
M.W. Savage (ed.), *Sketches, legal and political, by the late right honourable Richard Lalor Sheil* (2 volumes, London, 1855).

REFERENCES

Introduction (pp vii–ix)

1. Speech 10 February 1827 (DDA 59/1/XVI f.21).
2. Seán O'Faoláin, *King of the beggars: a life of Daniel O'Connell* (Dublin, 1986, first published in 1938), pp 181–2. He suggested that 'O'Connell did a great deal to kill gentle manners in Ireland, to vulgarise and cheapen us'.
3. W.E.H. Lecky, *Leaders of public opinion in Ireland* (2 vols., London, 1903), ii, conclusion.

Prologue: The Doneraile Conspiracy, 1829 (pp 1–12)

1. *Freeman's Journal*, 29 October 1829.
2. D.O. Madden, *Ireland and its rulers since 1829* (2 vols., London, 1843–4), i, 83.
3. Pückler-Muskau, *Tour In England, Ireland and France*, i, 320–21.
4. See Daniel O'Connell to Edward Littleton, 9 October 1833 (*O'Connell Corr.*, v, 79).
5. Judgement of Mr Justice Hardiman, 30 March 2007 (*O'Callaghan & ors–v– Judge Alan Mahon & ors*).
6. Thomas Sheahan, *'Articles' of Irish manufacture, or, Portions of Cork history* (Cork, 1833), p. 129.
7. J. R. O'Flanagan, *The Munster Circuit* (London, 1880), p. 325.
8. Madden, *Rulers*, i, 83.
9. Sheahan, *'Articles' of Irish manufacture*, p. 134.
10. See Francis L. Wellman, *The art of cross-examination* (New York, 1923), for one account of the trial.
11. Sheahan, *'Articles' of Irish manufacture*, p. 134.
12. Madden, *Rulers*, i, 84.
13. Sheahan, *'Articles' of Irish manufacture*, p. 137.
14. *Freeman's Journal*, 29 October 1829.
15. See John Adolphus, *The royal exile* (2 vols., London, 1821), ii, 56–7.
16. *The Times*, 31 October 1829.
17. O'Flanagan, *The Munster circuit*, p. 329.
18. Sheahan, *'Articles' of Irish manufacture*, p. 136.
19. This was normal practice was jury trials in the nineteenth century. See Niamh Howlin, 'The nineteenth-century Irish jury: a study in depth', unpublished Ph.D. thesis, University College Dublin (2007).
20. *Freeman's Journal*, 30 October 1829.
21. *Freeman's Journal*, 2 November 1829.
22. Ibid.

23. Speech of O'Connell in Waterford, 8 November 1829 (*The Times*, 9 November 1829).
24. *O'Callaghan & ors -v- Judge Alan Mahon & ors* [2007] IESC 17 (30 March 2007) (*www.bailii.org/ie/cases/IESC/2007/S17.html*).
25. Seán O'Faoláin, *King of the beggars: a life of Daniel O'Connell* (Dublin, 1986, first published in 1938), p. 239.
26. Sheahan, *'Articles' of Irish manufacture*, p. 153.
27. *Freeman's Journal*, 3 November 1829.
28. *Freeman's Journal*, 2 November 1829.
29. Charles Phillips, *Curran and his contemporaries* (New York, 1862), p. 240.
30. Lord Colchester (ed.), *The diary and correspondence of Charles Abbot, Lord Colchester* (3 vols., London, 1861), iii, 612.

Chapter 1 'The Fortunate Youth' (pp 13–23)

1. Daniel O'Connell to Mary O'Connell, 25 December 1800 (*O'Connell Corr.*, i, 37).
2. Daunt, *Personal recollections*, ii, 119.
3. Houston, *Journal*, p. 1.
4. *The Times*, 24 May 1847.
5. Lady Gregory (ed.), *Mr Gregory's letter-box, 1823–1830* (London, 1898), p. 17.
6. See letter of one of Daniel O'Connell's sons to W.J. Fitzpatrick, 28 May 1888 (NLI MS 15476 item 2).
7. Houston, *Journal*, p. 5.
8. Fitzpatrick, *Correspondence*, i, 9.
9 Houston, *Journal*, p. 7. The poem was translated by Fr Charles O'Connor for Houston.
10. Daunt, *Personal recollections*, i, 308.
11. See O'Connell, *Speeches*, i, 4.
12. Daniel O'Connell to Walter Savage Landor, 4 October 1838 (Fitzpatrick, *Correspondence*, ii, 151).
13. Ibid.
14. NLI MS 1503, f. 29.
15. Daunt, *Personal recollections*, i, 116.
16. Ibid.
17. NLI MS 1503, f. 31.
18. Daunt, *Personal recollections*, ii, 77–8.
19. Daunt, *Personal recollections*, i, 116.
20. Ibid.
21. Houston, *Journal*, p. 15.
22. Daunt, *Personal recollections*, i, 101.
23. Ibid.
24. Daunt, *Personal recollections*, i, 101. His portrait also appeared in the *Dublin Magazine* in March 1813.

25. Daunt, *Personal recollections*, i, 49.
26. Daunt, *Personal recollections*, i, 111.
27. The story was told years later by a female relative of O'Connell's who was present at the evening (Fagan, *Life*, i, 81–2).
28. Fagan, *Life*, i, 82. Fagan said that this story was known by many of his relatives and could be 'abundantly confirmed'.
29. Daunt, *Personal recollections*, i, 51.
30. Daunt, *Personal recollections*, i, 62.
31. Daunt, *Personal recollections*, i, 178.
32. Daunt, *Personal recollections*, ii, 120.
33. Daunt, *Personal recollections*, ii, 205.
34. Daunt, *Personal recollections*, i, 135.
35. Daunt, *Personal recollections*, i, 135.
36. Entry for 31 December 1796 (Houston, *Journal*, p. 157).
37. *The Times*, 24 May 1847.
38. The bank went bankrupt in 1809 (see James O'Connell to Daniel O'Connell, 17 June 1809 (*O'Connell Corr.*, i, 203)).
39. Daunt, *Personal recollections*, ii, 40.
40. Daunt, *Personal recollections*, i, 116.
41. James Roche, *Critical and miscellaneous essays. By an octogenarian* (2 vols., Cork, 1850–51), ii, 99.
42. Houston, *Journal*, p. 31; see also O'Connell, *Speeches*, i, 6.
43. See, for example, [W.H. Curran], 'Sketches of the Irish bar, no. vi', *New Monthly Magazine*, vi (1823).
44. Fitzpatrick, *Correspondence*, i, 222.
45. Daniel O'Connell to Hunting Cap, 26 December 1793 (*O'Connell Corr.*, i, 13).
46. Daniel O'Connell to Hunting Cap, 3 February 1792 (*O'Connell Corr.*, i, 1).
47. Maurice O'Connell to Hunting Cap, undated (UCD MS P12/2/21).
48. Mary O'Connell to Daniel O'Connell, 23 January 1824 (*O'Connell Corr.*, iii, 7).
49. Daniel O'Connell to A.V. Kirwan, 8 November 1837 (Fitzpatrick, *Correspondence*, ii, 118).
50. Daniel O'Connell to Hunting Cap, 3 February 1792 (*O'Connell Corr.*, i, 1).
51. Daniel O'Connell to Hunting Cap, 16 April 1792 (*O'Connell Corr.*, i, 2).
52. A.V. Kirwan to Daniel O'Connell, 10 December 1837 (Fitzpatrick, *Correspondence*, ii, 122).
53. Daniel O'Connell to A.V. Kirwan, 8 November 1837 (Fitzpatrick, *Correspondence*, ii, 118).
54. M. F. Cusack, *The Liberator, his life and times, political, social and religious* (London, 1872), p. 51.
55. Fitzpatrick, *Correspondence*, i, 4.
56. Daniel O'Connell to Hunting Cap, 14 September 1792 (*O'Connell Corr.*, i, 3).
57. Daunt, *Personal recollections*, i, 103.

58. Daniel O'Connell to Hunting Cap, 17 January 1793 (*O'Connell Corr.*, i, 5).
59. See UCD P12/2/23; Daniel O'Connell to Hunting Cap, 21 March 1793 (*O'Connell Corr.*, i, 5).
60. Houston, *Journal*, p. 44.
61. Ibid., p. 45.
62. Daunt, *Personal recollections*, ii, 94.
63. Daunt, *Personal recollections*, ii, 95.
64. NLI MS 1503, f. 43.
65. Speech of 10 February 1827 (DDA 59/1/XVI f. 28).
66. Journal entry for 29 December 1796 (Houston, *Journal*, p. 155).

Chapter 2 Young Dan (pp 24–39)

1. Entry for 31 December 1796 (Houston, *Journal*, p. 158). Mahony was in one of the English (Irish) brigades.
2. Daniel O'Connell to Hunting Cap, 3 June 1793 (UCD P12/2/24).
3. Ibid.
4. Daniel O'Connell to Hunting Cap, 21 October 1793 (UCD P12/2A/26).
5. Mrs M.J. O'Connell, *The last colonel of the Irish brigade* (2 vols., London, 1892), ii, 121.
6. Daniel O'Connell to Hunting Cap, 24 November 1793 (*O'Connell Corr.*, i, 8-9).
7. Ibid., 9.
8. Daniel O'Connell to Hunting Cap, 26 December 1793 (*O'Connell Corr.*, i, 11).
9. Ibid., 12.
10. *The records of the honourable society of Lincoln's Inn: Admissions, 1420–1799* (London, 1896), i, 549.
11. Daniel O'Connell to Hunting Cap, 11 March 1794 (*O'Connell Corr.*, i, 14).
12. Houston, *Journal*, p. 49.
13. Maurice Morgan O'Connell to Daniel O'Connell, 21 November 1796 (*O'Connell Corr.*, i, 26).
14. Daniel O'Connell to Hunting Cap, 11 March 1794 (*O'Connell Corr.*, i, 14).
15. Ibid., 13.
16. Daunt, *Personal recollections*, i, 277.
17. Ibid.
18. Ibid., 277–8.
19. Fagan, *Life*, i, 10. O'Connell said that he was at Gray's Inn, but he only moved there in 1796 and only as a means to allow him to complete his training in Dublin.
20. Fagan, *Life*, i, 10.
21. He discusses the watch in a journal entry for 5 January 1796 (Houston, *Journal*, p. 104).
22. Daniel O'Connell to Hunting Cap, 22 April 1794 (*O'Connell Corr.*, i, 16).
23. Daniel J. Boorstein, *The mysterious science of the law: an essay on Blackstone's Commentaries* (Chicago, 1996), p. 2.

24. See Brian Dirck, *Lincoln the lawyer* (Chicago, 2007), p. 17.
25. Quoted in Oliver MacDonagh, *The hereditary bondsman: Daniel O'Connell, 1775–1829* (London, 1988), p. 28.
26. Houston, *Journal*, p. 50; O'Connell, *Speeches*, i, 11.
27. *The speeches of John Horne Tooke during the Westminster election, 1796* (London, n.d. [1796]), p. 16.
28. Speech of 10 February 1827 (DDA 59/1/XVI f. 41).
29. Daniel O'Connell to Hunting Cap, 22 April 1794 (*O'Connell Corr.*, i, 16).
30. Daniel O'Connell to Hunting Cap, 22 August 1794 (*O'Connell Corr.*, i, 18).
31. *Parliamentary history* (vol. xxxi, 1795), col. 1345.
32. Daunt, *Personal recollections*, i, 145.
33. Lady Gregory (ed.), *Mr Gregory's letter-box*, p. 37.
34. Daunt, *Personal recollections*, i, 145,
35. Daunt, *Personal recollections*, i, 138.
36. Entry for 18 February 1796 (Houston, *Journal*, p. 121) in which O'Connell detailed the events of the previous year.
37. Entry for 18 February 1796 (Houston, *Journal*, p. 122)
38. Entry for 30 December 1795 (Houston, *Journal*, p. 92).
39. Entry for 31 December 1796 (Houston, *Journal*, p. 158).
40. Daniel O'Connell to Hunting Cap, 10 December 1795 (*O'Connell Corr.*, i, 21).
41. Daunt, *Personal recollections*, i, 262.
42. Daniel O'Connell to Hunting Cap, 26 October 1795 (*O'Connell Corr.*, i, 19).
43. Houston, *Journal*, pp 63–4.
44. Daniel O'Connell to Hunting Cap, 10 December 1795 (*O'Connell Corr.*, i, 21).
45. Daniel O'Connell to Hunting Cap, 17 January 1796 (*O'Connell Corr.*, i, 22).
46. Ibid., 23.
47. Peter Rayleigh, *History of Ye Antient Society of Cogers, 1755–1903* (London, 1904), p. 10.
48. Houston, *Journal*, p. 66.
49. Rayleigh, *History of Ye Antient Society of Cogers*, p. 11 and p. 298.
50. Houston, *Journal*, p. 64.
51. Daunt, *Personal recollections*, i, 259.
52. Ibid., 260.
53. Journal entry for 11 December 1795 (Houston, *Journal*, p. 68).
54. Houston, *Journal*, p. 71.
55. Ibid., pp 71–2.
56. Entry for 16 December 1795 (Houston, *Journal*, p. 87).
57. Entry for 13 December 1795 (Houston, *Journal*, p. 77).
58. Ibid., p. 78.
59. Entry for 16 December 1795 (Houston, *Journal*, p. 85).
60. Ibid., p. 84.
61. Ibid., p. 85.
62. Daniel O'Connell to Mary O'Connell, 25 December 1800 (*O'Connell Corr.*, i, 37).

63. Mary O'Connell to Daniel O'Connell, 16 October 1816 (*O'Connell Corr.*, ii, 122). Emphasis as in original.
64. Mary O'Connell to Daniel O'Connell, 16 October 1816 (*O'Connell Corr.*, ii, 122).
65. Entry for 29 December 1795 (Houston, *Journal*, p. 90).
66. Douglas Thompson to Daniel O'Connell, 18 December 1795 (*O'Connell Corr.*, i, 22).
67. Entry for 29 December 1795 (Houston, *Journal*, p. 91).
68. Entry for 30 December 1795 (Houston, *Journal*, p. 93).
69. Houston, *Journal*, p. 92.
70. Entry for 30 December 1795 (Houston, *Journal*, p. 93).
71. Ibid., p. 92.
72. Entry for 3 January 1795 (Houston, *Journal*, p. 102).
73. Entry for 30 December 1795 (Houston, *Journal*, p. 92).
74. Mrs Hunter asked O'Connell to put her daughter's comment in his journal, see entry for 30 December 1795 (Houston, *Journal*, p. 95).
75. For a complete transcript of the trial see *www.oldbaileyonline.org*.
76. Entry for 6 January 1796 (Houston, *Journal*, p. 108).
77. Entry for 18 January 1796 (Houston, *Journal*, p. 114).
78. Daniel O'Connell to Mary O'Connell, 14 March 1807 (*O'Connell Corr.*, i, 160). Although he joked after he was married that he had less sympathy for convicted men who were bachelors (Daniel O'Connell to Mary O'Connell, 17 January 1809 (*O'Connell Corr.*, i, 190)).
79. Entry for 13 January 1796 (Houston, *Journal*, p. 110).
80. Entry for 30 January 1796 (Houston, *Journal*, p. 119).
81. Entry for 3 January 1795 (Houston, *Journal*, p. 102).
82. Entry for 31 January 1796 (Houston, *Journal*, p. 120–21).
83. Entry for 14 January 1796 (Houston, *Journal*, p. 113).
84. Entry for 20 January 1796 (Houston, *Journal*, p. 119).
85. Entry for 6 January 1797 (Houston, *Journal*, p. 171).
86. RIA MSS 12 P13.
87. Entry for 1 January 1796 (Houston, *Journal*, p. 98).
88. Ibid., p. 97.
89. Entry for 2 January 1796 (Houston, *Journal*, p. 98).
90. Entry for 18 January 1796 (Houston, *Journal*, p. 115).
91. Entry for 2 January 1796 (Houston, *Journal*, p. 100).
92. Entry for 5 January 1796 (Houston, *Journal*, p. 106).
93. Ibid.
94. Entry for 6 January 1796 (Houston, *Journal*, p. 108).
95. Entry for 19 January 1796 (Houston, *Journal*, p. 117).
96. Daunt, *Personal recollections*, i, 35.
97. Entry for 31 January 1796 (Houston, *Journal*, p. 120).
98. Entry for 18 February 1796 (Houston, *Journal*, p. 123).

99. Daniel O'Connell to Hunting Cap, 26 February 1796 (*O'Connell Corr.*, i, 23).
100. *The records of the honourable society of Lincoln's Inn: The black books* (London, 1902), iv, 68.
101. *The register of admissions to Gray's Inn, 1521–1889* (London, 1889), p. 400.
102. Daniel O'Connell to Hunting Cap, 5 April 1796 (*O'Connell Corr.*, i, 24).
103. Daniel O'Connell to Hunting Cap, 17 May 1796 (*O'Connell Corr.*, i, 25).
104. Houston, *Journal*, pp 52–3.
105. Daniel O'Connell to Hunting Cap, 17 May 1796 (*O'Connell Corr.*, i, 25).
106. O'Connell, *Last colonel*, ii, 272.
107. Entry for 31 December 1796 (Houston, *Journal*, p. 156).

Chapter 3 O'Connell in Dublin (pp 40–55)

1.   Houston, *Journal*, p. 154.
2.   Entry for 24 December 1796 (Houston, *Journal*, p. 148).
3.   W.E.H. Lecky, *Leaders of public opinion in Ireland* (2 vols., London, 1903), i, 90.
4.   Entry for 3 December 1796 (Houston, *Journal*, p. 126).
5.   Entry for 13 January 1798 (Houston, *Journal*, p. 230).
6.   Entry for 7 December 1796 (Houston, *Journal*, p. 129).
7.   Entry for 17 December 1796 (Houston, *Journal*, p. 146).
8.   Entry for 7 December 1796 (Houston, *Journal*, p. 134).
9.   Entry for 10 December 1796 (Houston, *Journal*, p. 137).
10. Entry for 29 December 1796 (Houston, *Journal*, p. 154).
11. Daunt, *Personal recollections*, ii, 14.
12. Entry for 13 December 1796 (Houston, *Journal*, p. 138).
13. Entry for 22 January 1797 (Houston, *Journal*, p. 184).
14. See entries for 13 December 1796 and for 9 February 1797 (Houston, *Journal*, p. 138 and p. 196).
15. See Daniel O'Connell to Mary O'Connell, 1 February 1803 (*O'Connell Corr.*, i, 89).
16. Entry for 10 December 1796 (Houston, *Journal*, p. 137).
17. Ibid., p. 138.
18. Entry for 23 December 1796 (Houston, *Journal*, p. 147). The Historical Society in Trinity College Dublin debated a different motion that evening (see the records of the Historical Society in the Trinity College Dublin Muniments).
19. Entry for 29 December 1796 (Houston, *Journal*, p. 156).
20. O'Connell, *Last colonel*, ii, 197.
21. Entry for 29 December 1796 (Houston, *Journal*, p. 155).
22. Entry for 31 December 1796 (Houston, *Journal*, p. 159).
23. Entry for 5 January 1797 (Houston, *Journal*, p. 168).
24. Entry for 5 January 1797 (Houston, *Journal*, p. 169). The emphasis is mine.
25. Entry for 2 January 1797 (Houston, *Journal*, p. 166).
26. Daniel O'Connell to Hunting Cap, 3 January 1797 (*O'Connell Corr.*, i, 28).
27. Entry for 23 February 1797 (Houston, *Journal*, p. 204).

28. Daniel O'Connell to Hunting Cap, 3 January 1797 (*O'Connell Corr.*, i, 27).
29. Entry for 14 January 1797 (Houston, *Journal*, p. 175).
30. Entry for 19 January 1797 (Houston, *Journal*, p. 178).
31. Entry for 28 January 1797 (Houston, *Journal*, p. 193).
32. Entry for 12 February 1797 (Houston, *Journal*, p. 198). The woman mentioned in the diary is named as 'Miss Upton', but from internal evidence it seems this was the same 'Sweet Eliza'.
33. Entry for 18 January 1797 (Houston, *Journal*, p. 177).
34. Ibid., p. 176.
35. Daniel O'Connell to Hunting Cap, 23 and 24 January 1797 (*O'Connell Corr.*, i, 29–30).
36. Entry for 6 February 1797 (Houston, *Journal*, p. 195); Daniel O'Connell to Hunting Cap, 3 January 1797 (*O'Connell Corr.*, i, 28).
37. Houston, *Journal*, p. 204.
38. Entry for 25 January 1797 (Houston, *Journal*, p. 182).
39. Entry for 25 January 1797 (Houston, *Journal*, p. 190).
40. Entry for 28 January 1797 (Houston, *Journal*, p. 193). The emphasis is O'Connell's.
41. Entry for 20 February 1797 (Houston, *Journal*, p. 202).
42. Entry for 20 February 1797 (Houston, *Journal*, p. 202).
43. Entry for 4 March 1797 (Houston, *Journal*, p. 206).
44. Entry for 4 March 1797 (Houston, *Journal*, p. 205).
45. Daunt, *Personal recollections*, ii, 98.
46. Ibid.
47. Daunt, *Personal recollections*, ii, 131.
48. Daniel O'Connell admitted this in Daunt, *Personal recollections*, ii, p. 99; see also Slieve Gullion, 'Leinster and Munster in the summer of 1844', in *Irish Monthly*, xl (Oct. 1912), p. 589.
49. Daunt, *Personal recollections*, ii, 99.
50. Daunt, *Personal recollections*, i, 205.
51. Ibid.
52. T. Sadleir (ed.), *Diary, reminiscences, and correspondence of Henry Crabb Robinson* (3 vols., London, 1869), ii, 350.
53. Daunt, *Personal recollections*, i, 6–7.
54. Ibid., 7.
55. Ibid., 7–8.
56. Ibid., 9.
57. John P. Prendergast's introduction to Charles Haliday, *The Scandinavian kingdom of Dublin* (Dublin, 1881), p. xviii.
58. O'Connell, *Speeches*, i, 68.
59. O'Connell, *Speeches*, i, 393.
60. Daniel O'Connell to John Primrose, 9 January 1819 (*O'Connell Corr.*, ii, 188).
61. *The Freemason's Quarterly Review* (London, 1847), p. 295. While there is no

doubt that O'Connell was a Freemason, the question of whether the other men listed were is unproven.

62. W.R. Denslow, *Ten thousand famous freemasons* (2 vols., Missouri, 2004), ii, 280–81.

63. *Freemason's Quarterly Review*, p. 295.

64. Petra Mirala, *Freemasonry in Ulster 1733–1813* (Dublin, 2007), p. 274.

65. Daniel O'Connell to Richard Barrett, 19 April 1837 (Fitzpatrick, *Correspondence*, ii, 86).

66. Mirali, *Freemasonry in Ulster*, p. 20.

67. Entry for 24 March 1797 (Houston, *Journal*, p. 211).

68. Entry for 25 March 1797 (Houston, *Journal*, p. 213).

69. Entry for 31 March 1797 (Houston, *Journal*, p. 215).

70. Ibid.

71. Entry for 1 May 1797 (Houston, *Journal*, p. 215).

72. See C.J. Woods, 'Was O'Connell a United Irishman?', in *Irish Historical Studies*, xxxv, 138 (2006), p. 177.

73. Examination of Robert Hobart, quoted in C.J. Woods, 'Was O'Connell a United Irishman?', in *Irish Historical Studies*, xxxv, 138 (2006), p. 176.

74. Houston, *Journal*, p. 216.

75. Entry for 13 January 1798 (Houston, *Journal*, p. 229).

76. Ibid., p. 216.

77. Hunting Cap to Daniel O'Connell, 15 February 1797 (*O'Connell Corr.*, i, 31).

78. Ibid., 32.

79. I would like to thank my research student Lisa-Marie Griffith for tracking down Regan's details.

80. Daniel O'Connell to Hunting Cap, 1 March 1798 (*O'Connell Corr.*, i, 32–3).

81. W.J. Fitzpatrick, '*The sham squire' and the informers of 1798* (Dublin, 1895), pp 307–8.

82. Houston, *Journal*, p. 217.

83. Houston, *Journal*, p. 130; see also Thomas Bartlett (ed.), *Revolutionary Dublin, 1795–1801 : the letters of Francis Higgins to Dublin Castle* (Dublin, 2004), pp 227–8.

84. Houston, *Journal*, p. 204.

85. Ibid., pp 204–5.

86. O'Connell, *Speeches*, i, 95–6.

87. Entry for 25 March 1797 (Houston, *Journal*, p. 213).

88. Daunt, *Personal recollections*, i, 86.

89. Entry for 31 December 1798 (Houston, *Journal*, p. 232).

90. Houston, *Journal*, p. 219.

91. Daunt, *Personal recollections*, i, 117.

92. Daunt, *Personal recollections*, ii, 9.

93. See letter of one of Daniel O'Connell's sons to W.J. Fitzpatrick, 28 May 1888 (NLI MS. 15476 item 2).

94. Daunt, *Personal recollections*, i, 48.
95. Ibid.
96. Ibid., 49.
97. Ibid.
98. Ibid.
99. Entry for 31 December 1798 (Houston, *Journal*, p. 231).
100. In later years he told O'Neill Daunt that as a youth he could not drink more than three glasses of wine without being sick (Daunt, *Personal recollections*, i, 156), but O'Connell was not always completely honest in his reminiscences.
101. Entry for 31 December 1798 (Houston, *Journal*, p. 233).
102. Entry for 2 January 1799 (Houston, *Journal*, p. 236).

Chapter 4 Daniel O'Connell and the Law (pp 56–84)

1. J.R. O'Flanagan, *Bar life of O'Connell* (London, 1875), p. 55. I am grateful to Mr Justice Adrian Hardiman for his comments on all the chapters and in particular for his guidance on legal points in this chapter.
2. D.O. Madden, *Revelations of Ireland in the past generation* (Dublin, 1877), p. 2.
3. W.H. Curran, *Sketches of the Irish bar* (2 vols., London, 1855), i, 167.
4. Madden, *Revelations of Ireland*, p. 3.
5. Ibid.
6. Ibid., p. 59.
7. D.O. Madden, *Ireland and its rulers*, i, 23.
8. Fagan, *Life*, i, 90.
9. Madden, *Ireland and its rulers*, i, 24.
10. Curran, *Sketches of the Irish bar*, i, 157.
11. Daunt, *Personal recollections*, i, 118.
12. Ibid., 119.
13. [Anon.], *Anecdotes of O'Connell, John Philpot Curran, Grattan, Father O'Leary, and Swift* (Dublin, n.d.), p. 10.
14. [Anon.], *Anecdotes of O'Connell*, p. 10.
15. Daunt, *Personal recollections*, i, 119.
16. Daunt, *Personal recollections*, ii, 55.
17. Daunt, *Personal recollections*, i, 230.
18. Daunt, *Personal recollections*, ii, 56.
19. O'Flanagan, *Bar life of O'Connell*, p. 59.
20. Daunt, *Personal recollections*, i, 230–31.
21. Ibid., 231.
22. Entry for 4 January 1799 (Houston, *Journal*, p. 241).
23. Entry for 2 June 1802 (Houston, *Journal*, p. 249).
24. Entry for 3 June 1802 (Houston, *Journal* p. 250).
25. Ibid.
26. See Daniel O'Connell's Legal Fee Book, 1798–1814 (UCD P12/5/152).
27. For the legal papers of Daniel O'Connell c. 1809–1823 see NLI MS. 8004.

28. Daunt, *Personal recollections*, i, 85.
29. Daniel O'Connell to A.V. Kirwan, 8 November 1837 (Fitzpatrick, *Correspondence*, ii, 118). McMahon's rise was helped by the fact that his brother was secretary to the prince regent.
30. A.V. Kirwan to Daniel O'Connell, 10 December 1837 (Fitzpatrick, *Correspondence*, ii, 122).
31. Daniel O'Connell to Mary O'Connell, 15 April 1806 (*O'Connell Corr.*, i, 153).
32. Curran, *Sketches of the Irish bar*, p. 169.
33. Ibid.
34. Daniel O'Connell to Mary O'Connell, 6 September 1805 (*O'Connell Corr.*, i, 146).
35. O'Flanagan, *Bar life of O'Connell*, p. 75.
36. [Anon.], *Anecdotes of O'Connell*, p. 8.
37. Fagan, *Life*, i, 89.
38. O'Flanagan, *Bar life of O'Connell*, p. 76.
39. Fagan, *Life*, i, 57.
40. Daniel O'Connell to Mary O'Connell, 2 March 1811 (*O'Connell Corr.*, i, 283).
41. Daunt, *Personal recollections*, i, 43.
42. Daunt, *Personal recollections*, i, 207.
43. Daunt, *Personal recollections*, i, 43.
44. Daunt, *Personal recollections*, i, 207.
45. Ibid.
46. Daniel O'Connell to Mary O'Connell, 6 March 1803 (*O'Connell Corr.*, i, 94).
47. O'Connell came to enjoy the Ennis assizes because 'there is a laudable spirit of litigation' (Daniel O'Connell to Mary O'Connell, 14 March 1810 (*O'Connell Corr.*, i, 217)).
48. NLI MS 130, f. 2.
49. Ibid., f. 3.
50. Fagan, *Life*, i, 88; see also J.A. Lovett Fraser, 'Daniel O'Connell as an advocate' in *Law Mag. And Rev. Quart. Rev. Juris.* 5th series, vol. 38 (1912–13), p. 64.
51. Fagan, *Life*, i, 89. Fagan claimed that 'there are lawyers living who witnessed this ebullition'.
52. Houston, *Journal* pp 140–41, and p. 222.
53. Daunt, *Personal recollections*, ii, 113.
54. Ibid., 113–14.
55. O'Flanagan, *Bar life of O'Connell*, p. 48.
56. Lovett Fraser, 'Daniel O'Connell as an advocate' in *Law Mag. And Rev. Quart. Rev. Juris.* 5th series, vol. 38 (1912–13), p. 63.
57. Daunt, *Personal recollections*, i, 279.
58. Ibid., 278.
59. Ibid., 232.
60. Ibid., 232–3.
61. Flanagan, *Munster circuit*, p. 287.

62. Ibid.
63. Ibid., p. 288.
64. Cusack, *Liberator*, p. 489.
65. 'Lame Galen and Counsellor O'Connell' in *Irish Magazine and Monthly Asylum for Neglected Biography*, (February 1810), p. 61.
66. Flanagan, *Munster circuit*, p. 288.
67. O'Flanagan, *Bar life of O'Connell*, p. 59.
68. Daunt, *Personal recollections*, i, 105.
69. Ibid.
70. Daniel O'Connell to Mary O'Connell, 15 March 1820 (*O'Connell Corr.*, ii, 243).
71. Flanagan, *Munster circuit*, p. 298.
72. Daunt, *Personal recollections*, i, 164.
73. Flanagan, *The Irish Bar*, p. 32.
74. Daunt, *Personal recollections*, i, 96.
75. Ibid., 97.
76. Daunt, *Personal recollections*, ii, 34.
77. Daunt, *Personal recollections*, i, 121.
78. Ibid., 124.
79. Ibid.
80. Fagan, *Life*, i, 133.
81. In Fagan this is the John Boyle trial told further on, but internal evidence suggests it was a different trial.
82. O'Flanagan, *Bar life of O'Connell*, p. 66.
83. Ibid., p. 57.
84. Madden, *Revelations of Ireland*, p. 61.
85. Ibid., p. 63.
86. Fagan, *Life*, i, 236–7.
87. O'Flanagan, *Bar life of O'Connell*, p. 42.
88. Ibid., pp 64–5.
89. Madden, *Revelations of Ireland*, p. 68.
90. Ibid.
91. Fagan, *Life*, i, 134.
92. O'Flanagan, *Bar life of O'Connell*, p. 55.
93. [Anon.], *Anecdotes of O'Connell*, p. 3.
94. Daniel O'Connell to Mary O'Connell, 30 March 1808 (*O'Connell Corr.*, i, 171).
95. Ibid.
96. O'Flanagan, *Bar life of O'Connell*, p. 62.
97. Daunt, *Personal recollections*, ii, 57.
98. O'Flanagan, *Bar life of O'Connell*, p. 56.
99. Ibid., p. 57.
100. Daniel O'Connell to Mary O'Connell, 3 April 1813 (*O'Connell Corr.*, i, 326).
101. O'Flanagan, *Bar life of O'Connell*, p. 58.
102 Flanagan, *Munster circuit*, p. 289.

103. Ibid., p. 290.

104. [Anon], *Memoirs of John Howard Payne, the American Rosicus... compiled from authentic documents* (London, 1815), p. 123.

105. Ibid., p. 124.

106. Ibid., p. 123.

107. O'Flanagan, *Bar life of O'Connell*, pp 60–61.

108. [Anon.], *Anecdotes of O'Connell*, p. 4.

109. Ibid.

110. Daniel O'Connell to William Plunket, 4 April 1822 (*O'Connell Corr.*, ii, 368).

111. O'Connell, *Speeches*, ii, 175.

112. Ibid., 176.

113. Ibid., 176–7.

114. See, for example, *Taaffe v. the Queen's Bench*, November 1812 (O'Connell, *Speeches*, i, 121–32).

115. O'Flanagan, *Bar life of O'Connell*, p. 61.

116. Ibid.

117. Fagan, *Life*, i, 444.

118. John P. Prendergast introduction to Charles Haliday, *The Scandinavian kingdom of Dublin*, p. xlii.

119. Ríonach Uí Ógáin, *Immortal Dan: Daniel O'Connell in Irish folk tradition* (Dublin, n.d.), p. 126.

120. Madden, *Revelations of Ireland*, p. 65.

121. [Anon.], *Anecdotes of O'Connell*, p. 14.

122. O'Flanagan, *Bar life of O'Connell*, p. 165.

123. Ibid., p. 166.

124. Fitzpatrick, *Correspondence*, ii, 285.

125. Ibid.

126. Daunt, *Personal recollections*, i, 170.

127. Lovett Fraser, 'Daniel O'Connell as an advocate' in *Law Mag. And Rev. Quart. Rev. Juris.* 5th series, vol. 38 (1912–13), p. 60.

128. Daunt, *Personal recollections*, i, 56.

Chapter 5 Opposing the Act of Union (pp 85–93)

1. Daunt, *Personal recollections*, i, 202.

2. Speech of 2 July 1812 (O'Connell, *Speeches*, i, 82).

3. Hunting Cap to Daniel O'Connell, 30 January 1800 (*O'Connell Corr.*, viii, 167).

4. See P.M. Geoghegan, *The Irish Act of Union* (Dublin, 1999) for a complete account of the passing of the Union.

5. Daunt, *Personal recollections*, ii, 111.

6. Daunt, *Personal recollections*, i, 203.

7. Daunt, *Personal recollections*, ii, 111.

8. Daniel O'Connell to Hunting Cap, 17 January 1796 (*O'Connell Corr.*, i, 23).

9. O'Connell, *Speeches*, i, 8.

10. Daunt, *Personal recollections*, ii, 111.

11. Tom Taylor (ed.), *The autobiography and journals of Benjamin Robert Haydon* (3 vols., London, 1853), ii, 389.

12. Daunt, *Personal recollections*, i, 204.

13. O'Connell, *Speeches*, i, 8.

14. Ibid., 9.

15. T.M. Ray to W.J. Fitzpatrick, 5 September 1865 (Fitzpatrick, *Correspondence*, ii, 312, fn. 1); W.E.H. Lecky also heard this from one of his relatives (W.E.H. Lecky, *Leaders of public opinion in Ireland* (2 vols., New York, 1903) ii, 198).

16. Fagan, *Life*, i, 338.

17. Ibid.

18. [W.H. Curran], 'Sketches of the Irish bar, no. vi', *New Monthly Magazine*, vi (1823), p. 8.

19. William Tait, *Ireland and O'Connell* (London, 1835), final part, p. 16.

20. Robert Moore to Daniel O'Connell, 27 September [1813], (*O'Connell Corr.*, i, 342).

21. Author of *An address to the people of Ireland on the projected Union* (Dublin, 1799), written from Kinsale on 1 January 1799.

22. Daunt, *Personal recollections*, i, 112.

23. Ibid., 61.

24. Ibid., 138.

25. Entry for 1 March 1834 (Taylor (ed.), *The autobiography and journals of Benjamin Robert Haydon*, ii, 389).

26. Daunt, *Personal recollections*, i, 225.

27. O'Connell, *Speeches*, i, 17.

28. Ibid., 18.

29. Ibid., 19.

30. Ibid.

31. Ibid., 20 and 23.

32. Ibid., 21. Andrew Strahan was MP for Carlow, James Stephen was MP for Tralee, Henry Martin was MP for Kinsale; none was Irish. There were no MPs called Crile or Cackin, but this was more probably inaccurate reporting of the speech. O'Connell may have been talking about MPs such as William Congreve Alcock or William Wigram.

33. O'Connell, *Speeches*, i, 24.

34. Daunt, *Personal recollections*, i, 202.

35. Daniel O'Connell to his brother, 15 January 1835 (Fitzpatrick, *Correspondence*, i, 516).

36. Daunt, *Personal recollections*, i, 203.

37. Ibid.

Chapter 6 Confronting a Culture of Defeat (pp 94–112)

1. Daunt, *Personal recollections*, ii, 148.
2. Ibid.
3. This contradicts another O'Connell story where he claimed that as a youth he could not 'drink more than three glasses of wine without being sick' (Daunt, *Personal recollections*, i, 155).
4. See Mary O'Connell to Daniel O'Connell, 7 November 1804 (*O'Connell Corr.*, i, 118), when she discussed the first time he '*spoke*' to her.
5. See Mary O'Connell to Daniel O'Connell, 24 September 1818 (*O'Connell Corr.*, ii, 183), when she revealed that she was born 25 September 1778.
6. Daunt, *Personal recollections*, i, 133.
7. Daniel O'Connell to Mary O'Connell, 29 November [1802] (*O'Connell Corr.*, viii, 169–70).
8. Daniel O'Connell to Mary O'Connell, postmarked 11 March 1827 (*O'Connell Corr.*, iii, 299).
9. Fitzpatrick, *Correspondence*, i, 12; Daunt, *Personal recollections*, i, 194.
10. Daunt, *Personal recollections*, i, 133.
11. Daniel O'Connell to Mary O'Connell, 28 November 1800 (*O'Connell Corr.*, i, 34).
12. Daunt, *Personal recollections*, i, 134.
13. Ibid.
14. Daniel O'Connell to Mary O'Connell, 25 December 1800 (*O'Connell Corr.*, i, 37).
15. Daniel O'Connell to Mary O'Connell, 30 December 1800 (*O'Connell Corr.*, i, 38).
16. Daniel O'Connell to Mary O'Connell, 24 January 1800 (*O'Connell Corr.*, i, 41).
17. Mary O'Connell to Daniel O'Connell, c. 24 April 1801 (*O'Connell Corr.*, i, 46).
18. Mary O'Connell to Daniel O'Connell, 8 May 1801 (*O'Connell Corr.*, i, 50).
19. Mary O'Connell to Daniel O'Connell, 25 May 1801 (*O'Connell Corr.*, i, 54).
20. Daniel O'Connell to Mary O'Connell, 7 July 1801 (*O'Connell Corr.*, i, 58).
21. Daniel O'Connell to Mary O'Connell, 9 February 1802 (*O'Connell Corr.*, i, 70).
22. See *O'Connell Corr.*, i, 73.
23. Daniel O'Connell to Mary O'Connell, 5 and 8 August 1802 (*O'Connell Corr.*, i, 75).
24. Daniel O'Connell to Mary O'Connell, 25 November 1802 (*O'Connell Corr.*, i, 82).
25. Ibid.
26. Daniel O'Connell to Mary O'Connell, 30 November 1802 (*O'Connell Corr.*, i, 83).
27. Daniel O'Connell to Mary O'Connell, 4 December 1802 (*O'Connell Corr.*, i, 84).
28. Daniel O'Connell to Mary O'Connell, 1 February 1803 (*O'Connell Corr.*, i, 89).
29. Daniel O'Connell to Mary O'Connell, 4 December 1802 (*O'Connell Corr.*, i, 85).
30. Daniel O'Connell to Mary O'Connell, 27 January 1803 (*O'Connell Corr.*, i, 86).

31. Daniel O'Connell to Mary O'Connell, 29 January 1803 (*O'Connell Corr.*, i, 87).
32. John O'Connell to Daniel O'Connell, [January 1803], (*O'Connell Corr.*, i, 87).
33. John O'Connell to Daniel O'Connell, [January 1803], (*O'Connell Corr.*, i, 87–8).
34. O'Connell, *Last colonel*, ii, 243.
35. Daniel O'Connell to Mary O'Connell, 3 February 1803 (*O'Connell Corr.*, i, 90).
36. Daniel O'Connell to Mary O'Connell, 5 February 1803 (*O'Connell Corr.*, i, 91).
37. *O'Connell Corr.*, i, 87.
38. Daniel O'Connell to Mary O'Connell, 7 August 1803 (*O'Connell Corr.*, i, 98).
39. Mary O'Connell to Daniel O'Connell, [12 August 1803] (*O'Connell Corr.*, i, 98).
40. Daniel O'Connell, 28 August 1803 (*O'Connell Corr.*, i, 99).
41. Cusack, *Liberator*, pp 266–7.
42. These letters are discussed in Mary O'Connell to Daniel O'Connell, 16 October 1816 (*O'Connell Corr.*, ii, 122).
43. Daniel O'Connell to Mary O'Connell, 29 September 1816 (*O'Connell Corr.*, ii, 121).
44. Daunt, *Personal recollections*, ii, 99.
45. Ibid., 100.
46. Ibid.
47. Ibid., 9.
48. Daniel O'Connell to Mary O'Connell, 28 August 1803 (*O'Connell Corr.*, i, 99).
49. Daunt, *Personal recollections*, ii, 8.
50. Ibid., 8–9.
51. Daniel O'Connell to W.J. O'Neill Daunt, 1844 (Fitzpatrick, *Correspondence*, ii, 345).
52. This statement was recorded by his relative, Rickard O'Connell (quoted in Fitzpatrick, *Correspondence*, ii, 430).
53. Daniel O'Connell to Mary O'Connell, 17 November 1803 (*O'Connell Corr.*, i, 101).
54. Mary O'Connell to Daniel O'Connell, [18 November 1803] (*O'Connell Corr.*, i, 102).
55. Daniel O'Connell to Mary O'Connell, 17 November 1803 (*O'Connell Corr.*, i, 101–2).
56. Daniel O'Connell to Mary O'Connell, 26 November 1803 (*O'Connell Corr.*, i, 105).
57. Mary O'Connell to Daniel O'Connell, [18 November 1803] (*O'Connell Corr.*, i, 102).
58. Daniel O'Connell to Mary O'Connell, 3 December 1803 (*O'Connell Corr.*, i, 108).
59. Mary O'Connell to Daniel O'Connell, [13 December 1803] (*O'Connell Corr.*, i, 112).
60. Quoted in Dirck, *Lincoln the lawyer*, pp 146–7.

61. Quoted in Fitzpatrick, *Correspondence*, ii, 430.

62. Fitzpatrick, *Correspondence*, ii, 430.

63. Ibid.

64. [W.H. Curran], 'Sketches of the Irish bar, no. vi', *New Monthly Magazine*, vi (1823), p. 5.

65. The speech is from 24 July 1812 (O'Connell, *Speeches*, i, 102), but there are other examples.

66. Daniel O'Connell to P.V. Fitzpatrick, 14 May 1839 (Fitzpatrick, *Correspondence*, i, 62).

67. Fagan, *Life*, i, 25.

68. Daniel O'Connell to Mary O'Connell, 13 November 1804 (*O'Connell Corr.*, i, 120).

69. Daniel O'Connell to Mary O'Connell, 17 November 1804 (*O'Connell Corr.*, i, 122).

70. Fagan, *Life*, i, 28; for a detailed account see Brian MacDermot (ed.), *The Irish Catholic petition of 1805: the diary of Denys Scully* (Dublin, 1992), pp 24–5.

71. Daniel O'Connell to Mary O'Connell, 17 November 1804 (*O'Connell Corr.*, i, 122).

72. Daniel O'Connell to Mary O'Connell, 4 December 1804 (*O'Connell Corr.*, i, 127).

73. Daniel O'Connell to Mary O'Connell, 6 December 1804 (*O'Connell Corr.*, i, 128).

74. Daniel O'Connell to Mary O'Connell, 15 December 1804 (*O'Connell Corr.*, i, 130).

75. Ibid.

76. Daniel O'Connell to Denys Scully, [19 December 1804], (*O'Connell Corr.*, i, 131) and Daniel O'Connell to Denys Scully, 23 December 1804, (*O'Connell Corr.*, i, 132).

77. *O'Connell Corr.*, i, 134.

78. Fagan, *Life*, i, 28.

79. Daunt, *Personal recollections*, ii, 149.

80. Fitzpatrick, *Correspondence*, ii, 285.

81. Ibid., 284.

82. *O'Connell Corr.*, i, 135.

83. Daniel O'Connell to Hunting Cap, 21 March 1805 (*O'Connell Corr.*, i, 135).

84. Mary O'Connell to Daniel O'Connell, 12 August 1805 (*O'Connell Corr.*, i, 142).

85. Daniel O'Connell to Mary O'Connell, 23 August 1805 (*O'Connell Corr.*, i, 144).

86. Daniel O'Connell to Mary O'Connell, 31 March 1806 (*O'Connell Corr.*, i, 149).

87. Daniel O'Connell to Hunting Cap, 8 April 1806 (*O'Connell Corr.*, i, 151).

88. Mary O'Connell to Daniel O'Connell, 2 April 1806 (*O'Connell Corr.*, i, 150).

89. Mary O'Connell to Daniel O'Connell, 18 April 1808 (*O'Connell Corr.*, i, 176).

90. Mary O'Connell to Daniel O'Connell, 16 April 1805 (*O'Connell Corr.*, i, 137).

91. Mary O'Connell to Daniel O'Connell, 16 August 1805 (*O'Connell Corr.*, i, 143).

92. Mary O'Connell to Daniel O'Connell, 27 March 1810 (*O'Connell Corr.*, i, 219).

93. Fagan, *Life*, i, 65.

94. Ibid., 39.

95. Ibid., 40.

96. Ibid., 41.

97. Ibid., 42.

98. Ibid., 43.

99. Ibid.

100. Ibid.

101. Ibid., 51.

102. Ibid., 44.

103. Ibid., 60.

104. Daunt, *Personal recollections*, i, 7.

105. Ibid., 25.

106. See *Cornwallis corr.*, iii, 108–9; MacDermot, *Petition of 1805*, p. 155.

107. Fagan, *Life*, i, 65.

108. Geoghegan, *The Irish Act of Union*, p. 66.

109. Fagan, *Life*, i, 72.

110. Ibid., 74.

111. Daniel O'Connell to Mary O'Connell, 28 March 1809 (*O'Connell Corr.*, i, 197).

112. Daniel O'Connell to Mary O'Connell, 6 April 1809 (*O'Connell Corr.*, i, 200).

113. Daunt, *Personal recollections*, i, 171.

114. Mary O'Connell to Daniel O'Connell, 15 March 1809 (*O'Connell Corr.*, i, 193).

115. James O'Connell to Daniel O'Connell, 8 September 1823 (*O'Connell Corr.*, ii, 506).

116. *O'Connell Corr.*, i, 205. This is now number 58.

117. Mary O'Connell to Daniel O'Connell, [September 1809] (*O'Connell Corr.*, i, 205).

118. Mary O'Connell to Daniel O'Connell, 21 March 1809 (*O'Connell Corr.*, i, 194).

119. Daniel O'Connell to Mary O'Connell, 24 March 1809 (*O'Connell Corr.*, i, 195).

120. Daunt, *Personal recollections*, i, 271.

121. Ibid., 272.

122. Ibid., 273.

123. Ibid.

124. *Freeman's Journal*, 14 July 1810; see also *Freeman's Journal*, 17 July 1810.

125. Daunt, *Personal recollections*, i, 273.

126. Ibid.

127. Ibid.

128. Report of T. Mulock (W.J. Fitzpatrick, *Secret service under Pitt* (Dublin, 1892), p. 198).

129. Daniel O'Connell to Mary O'Connell, 17 August 1810 (*O'Connell Corr.*, i, 231).

130. *Freeman's Journal*, 7 August 1810.

131. Daniel O'Connell to Mary O'Connell, 27 September 1810 (*O'Connell Corr.*, i,

234).

132. Mary O'Connell to Daniel O'Connell, 29 September 1810 (*O'Connell Corr.*, i, 234).

133. *O'Connell Corr.*, i, 241; *Freeman's Journal*, 18 December 1810.

134. Daunt, *Personal recollections*, i, 138–9.

135. Ibid., 139.

136. Ibid., 51.

Chapter 7 The Agitator (pp 113–46)

1.   O'Connell, *Speeches*, i, 376.

2.   *O'Connell Corr.*, i, 243.

3.   James O'Connell to Daniel O'Connell, 17 January 1811 (*O'Connell Corr.*, i, 245).

4.   O'Connell, *Speeches*, i, 50.

5.   Hunting Cap to Daniel O'Connell, 16 May 1811 (*O'Connell Corr.*, i, 257).

6.   Daniel O'Connell to Mary O'Connell, 15 March 1811 (*O'Connell Corr.*, i, 248).

7.   Daniel O'Connell to Mary O'Connell, 1 April 1811 (*O'Connell Corr.*, i, 253).

8.   Daniel O'Connell to William O'Brien, 13 February 1817 (*O'Connell Corr.*, ii, 133); Myles McSwiney to Daniel O'Connell, 25 December 1816 (*O'Connell Corr.*, ii, 129).

9.   See Pole to Ryder, 12 February 1811 (PRONI T3228/5/28).

10. Spy's report on the Catholic Committee, endorsed 17 February 1811 (PRONI T3228/5/31).

11. Ryder to Pole, 13 July 1811 (PRONI T3228/5/59).

12. *O'Connell Corr.*, i, 265.

13. James Roche, *Critical and miscellaneous essays. By an octogenarian* (2 vols., Cork, 1850–51), ii, 103.

14. Pole to Ryder, 20 July 1811 (PRONI T3228/5/65).

15. Public letter of Daniel O'Connell, 31 October 1825 (*Dublin Evening Post*, 3 November 1825).

16. *O'Connell Corr.*, i, 270.

17. O'Faoláin, *King of the beggars*, p. 129.

18. Fitzpatrick, *Secret service under Pitt*, p. 200.

19. *O'Connell Corr.*, i, 273; Fagan, *Life*, i, 75.

20. *O'Connell Corr.*, i, 273.

21. O'Connell, *Speeches*, i, 249.

22. *O'Connell Corr.*, i, 282; *Dublin Evening Post*, 31 December 1811.

23. See Fitzpatrick, *Correspondence*, ii, 420.

24. *O'Connell Corr.*, i, 290.

25. Ibid., 300–301.

26. O'Connell, *Speeches*, i, 72–3.

27. Ibid., 73–4.

28. Ibid., 79.

29. Henry Grattan Jnr, *Memoirs of the life and times of the Rt. Hon. Henry Grattan*

(5 vols., London, 1846), v, 483.

30. Daunt, *Personal Recollections*, i, 285.

31. O'Connell, *Speeches*, i, 356–7.

32. See speech of 4 February 1824 (O'Connell, *Speeches*, ii, 277).

33. See O'Connell's report of 15 June 1813 (O'Connell, *Speeches*, i, 206).

34. Speech of 25 June 1824 (O'Connell, *Speeches*, ii, 352).

35. O'Connell, *Speeches*, i, 114; see also Brian MacDermot (ed.), *The Catholic question in Ireland and England: the papers of Denys Scully* (Dublin, 1988), p. 383.

36. O'Connell, *Speeches*, i, 114.

37. Ibid., 108.

38. Ibid., 109.

39. Ibid., 120.

40. Daunt, *Personal Recollections*, i, 26.

41. Ibid., 27.

42. *O'Connell Corr.*, i, 330.

43. See Samuel Stephens to Daniel O'Connell, 10 May 1813 (*O'Connell Corr.*, i, 329).

44. O'Connell, *Speeches*, i, 160.

45. Ibid., 161.

46. Ibid., 163.

47. Ibid., 162.

48. S.J. Connolly, 'Union government, 1812–23', in W.E. Vaughan (ed.), *A new history of Ireland* (Oxford, 1989), v, 53.

49. O'Connell, *Speeches*, i, 179.

50. Ibid., 166.

51. Ibid., 170.

52. Ibid., 176.

53. Ibid., 190.

54. Ibid., 193.

55. Ibid., 194.

56. Ibid., 211.

57. Ibid., 214.

58. Ibid., 216.

59. Ibid., 215.

60. Ibid., 221.

61. DDA 54/1/VIII numbers 6 and 7; see also Mary O'Connell to Daniel O'Connell, 10 April 1811 (*O'Connell Corr.*, i, 255); and O'Connell, *Speeches*, i, 221.

62. O'Connell, *Speeches*, i, 226.

63. Ibid., 227.

64. Ibid., 245.

65. E.B. to Daniel O'Connell, 28 July 1813 (*O'Connell Corr.*, i, 336).

66. O'Connell, *Speeches*, i, 245.

67. Ibid., 247.
68. Ibid., 248.
69. Ibid., 262.
70. Ibid., 267.
71. Ibid., 269.
72. Ibid., 270.
73. Fagan, *Life*, i, 97.
74. O'Connell, *Speeches*, i, 287.
75. Ibid., 296.
76. Ibid., 281.
77. Charles Phillips, *Curran and his contemporaries* (New York, 1862), p. 242.
78. O'Faoláin, *King of the beggars*, p. 156.
79. O'Connell, *Speeches*, i, 303.
80. *O'Connell Corr.*, i, 353.
81. Fagan, *Life*, i, 527.
82. Ibid.
83. Daniel O'Connell to Mary O'Connell, 19 November 1804 (*O'Connell Corr.*, i, 123).
84. Nicholas Purcell O'Gorman to Daniel O'Connell, 19 August 1813 (*O'Connell Corr.*, i, 338).
85. O'Connell, *Speeches*, i, 309.
86. Ibid., 313.
87. Ibid., 319.
88. Daniel O'Connell to Pierce Mahony, 30 March 1829 (*O'Connell Corr.*, iv, 37).
89. O'Connell, *Speeches*, i, 332.
90. Ibid., 331.
91. Ibid., 334.
92. Ibid., 341.
93. Ibid., 342.
94. Ibid., 343.
95. *O'Connell Corr.*, i, 368.
96. Speech of 4 July 1824 (O'Connell, *Speeches*, ii, 365); although see also *Freeman's Journal*, 10 May 1815.
97. See speech of John Finlay, 11 December 1813 (O'Connell, *Speeches*, i, 364).
98. Hunting Cap to Daniel O'Connell, 14 December 1813 (*O'Connell Corr.*, i, 347).
99. Daniel O'Connell to Hunting Cap, 28 December 1813 (*O'Connell Corr.*, i, 349).
100. Daniel O'Connell to Hunting Cap, 28 December 1813 (*O'Connell Corr.*, i, 350).
101. Daniel O'Connell to Hunting Cap, 6 January 1814 (*O'Connell Corr.*, i, 351).
102. Ibid.
103. O'Connell, *Speeches*, i, 347.
104. DDA 54/1/IX number 45.
105. O'Connell, *Speeches*, i, 362.
106. Ibid., 366.

107. Ibid., 369.
108. Ibid., 391–2.
109. R.S. Mackenzie (ed.), *Sketches of the Irish bar by the Rt. Hon. Richard Lalor Sheil* (2 vols., New York, 1854), p. 9.
110. O'Connell, *Speeches*, i, 348.
111. Charles Gavan Duffy, *Young Ireland: a fragment of Irish history* (2 vols., final revision, London, 1896), i, 23.
112. Fagan, *Life*, i, 337.
113. O'Connell, *Speeches*, i, 349.
114. Ibid., 353.
115. Ibid., 359.
116. *Monthly Museum, or, Dublin Literary Reportory of Arts, Science, Literature and Miscellaneous Information* (November 1813), p. 126; *O'Connell Corr.*, i, 361.
117. O'Connell, *Speeches*, i, 424.
118. *O'Connell Corr.*, i, 361.
119. O'Connell, *Speeches*, i, 411.
120. Ibid., 414.
121. 'The Ribbon-men and Counsellor O'Connell', in *Irish Magazine and Monthly Asylum for Neglected Biography* (January 1814), p. 12.
122. *O'Connell Corr.*, i, 353.
123. Daniel O'Connell to George Bryan, 11 February 1814 (*O'Connell Corr.*, i, 354).
124. *O'Connell Corr.*, i, 355.
125. Daniel O'Connell to Owen O'Conor, 21 December 1818 (*O'Connell Corr.*, ii, 184).
126. O'Connell, *Speeches*, i, 415.
127. Ibid., 424–5.
128. Quoted in O'Faoláin, *King of the beggars*, p. 192.
129. General O'Connell to Daniel O'Connell, 16 June 1814 (*O'Connell Corr.*, i, 370–71).
130. MacDermot (ed.), *The Catholic question in Ireland and England, the papers of Denys Scully*, p. 525.
131. *O'Connell Corr.*, i, 372.
132. Myles McSwiney to Daniel O'Connell, 30 June 1814 (*O'Connell Corr.*, i, 372).
133. Daniel O'Connell to Mary O'Connell, 13 September 1814 (*O'Connell Corr.*, i, 379).
134. Daniel O'Connell to Mary O'Connell, 23 September 1814 (*O'Connell Corr.*, i, 381).
135. Fitzpatrick, *Correspondence*, ii, 422.
136. *O'Connell Corr.*, i, 388.
137. Phillips, *Curran and his contemporaries* (London, 1850), p. 259.
138. Ibid., p. 241.
139. Ibid.

140. O'Connell, *Speeches*, i, 438.

141. Fagan, *Life*, i, 135.

142. O'Connell, *Speeches*, i, 438.

143. Ibid., 439.

144. Ibid., 441.

145. Ibid., 442.

146. Ibid., 444.

147. Ibid., 445.

148. Ibid., 449.

149. Fagan, *Life*, i, 136.

150. See Fagan, *Life*, i, 111–12.

151. O'Connell, *Speeches*, ii, 12. The speech is incorrectly dated as 1814.

152. Ibid., 15

Chapter 8 Affairs of Honour (147–63)

1. 'The duel of D'Esterre and Daniel O'Connell' in *Bentley's Magazine*, xxxiii (London, 1853), p. 543; also printed in *The Eclectic Magazine* (New York, 1853).

2. Rickard O'Connell to Daniel O'Connell, 4 February 1815 (*O'Connell Corr.*, ii, 7).

3. Fitzpatrick, *Correspondence*, i, 27.

4. 'The duel of D'Esterre and Daniel O'Connell' in *Bentley's Magazine*, p. 542.

5. Denys Scully to Daniel O'Connell, 31 January 1815 (UCD P12/B/15).

6. *Irish Magazine and Monthly Asylum for Neglected Biography*, viii (March 1815), p. 101; see also the letter of a ninety-two-year-old descendant, R.C. D'Esterre Spottiswoode, to *The Times*, 11 May 1934.

7. *The Times*, 24 May 1847.

8. J.N. D'Esterre to Daniel O'Connell, 26 January 1815 (Fitzpatrick, *Correspondence*, i, 28).

9. Daniel O'Connell to J.N. D'Esterre, 27 January 1815 (Fitzpatrick, *Correspondence*, i, 28).

10. James O'Connell to J.N. D'Esterre, 27 January 1815 (Fitzpatrick, *Correspondence*, i, 29).

11. George Lidwell to Daniel O'Connell, 30 January 1815 (*O'Connell Corr.*, ii, 5).

12. Daniel O'Connell to Nicholas Purcell O'Gorman, 28 January 1815 (Fitzpatrick, *Correspondence*, i, 29).

13. 'The duel of D'Esterre and Daniel O'Connell' in *Bentley's Magazine*, p. 538.

14. Sheil, *Sketches*, ii, 103.

15. George Lidwell to Daniel O'Connell, 30 January 1815 (*O'Connell Corr.*, ii, 5).

16. James P. Gilchrist, *A brief history of the origin and history of ordeals... Also, a chronological register of the principal duels* (London, 1821), p. 245.

17. *Irish Magazine and Monthly Asylum for Neglected Biography*, viii (March 1815), p. 102.

18. Daniel O'Connell to Richard Newton Bennett, 31 January 1815 (Fitzpatrick, *Correspondence*, i, 30).

19. Fitzpatrick, *Correspondence*, i, 30.
20. Daniel O'Connell to Richard Newton Bennett, 31 January 1815 (Fitzpatrick, *Correspondence*, ii, 30).
21. Denys Scully to Daniel O'Connell, 31 January 1815 (UCD P12/B/15).
22. 'The duel of D'Esterre and Daniel O'Connell' in *Bentley's Magazine*, p. 540.
23. Ibid.
24. *Irish Magazine and Monthly Asylum for Neglected Biography*, viii (March 1815), p. 99.
25. Ibid., p. 100.
26. NLI MS 1504, f. 46.
27. Daniel O'Connell to George Lidwell, n.d. (quoted in 'The duel of D'Esterre and Daniel O'Connell' in *Bentley's Magazine*, p. 539).
28. Fitzpatrick, *Correspondence*, i, 34.
29. Ibid., 31.
30. Ibid.
31. *Freeman's Journal*, 2 February 1815.
32. Charles Phillips, *Curran and his contemporaries* (New York, 1862), p. 244.
33. Ibid., p. 244–5.
34. *Irish Magazine, and Monthly Asylum for Neglected Biography*, viii (March 1815), p. 100.
35. Fitzpatrick, *Correspondence*, i, 32.
36. 'The duel of D'Esterre and Daniel O'Connell' in *Bentley's Magazine*, p. 544.
37. Lorenzo Sabine, *Notes on duels and duelling* (Boston, 1855), p. 256; Charles Phillips, *Curran and his contemporaries* (New York, 1862), p. 244.
38. Fagan, *Life*, i, 152.
39. John P. Prendergast introduction to Charles Haliday, *The Scandinavian kingdom of Dublin*, p. vii.
40. Ibid.
41. 'The duel of D'Esterre and Daniel O'Connell' in *Bentley's Magazine*, p. 543.
42. Ibid., p. 544.
43. 'Duelling in England', in *Household Words*, xv (New York, 1857), p. 599.
44. J.G. Millingen, *The history of duelling* (2 vols., London, 1841), ii, 217.
45. Fitzpatrick, *Correspondence*, i, 33.
46. Fagan, *Life*, i, 152.
47. Ibid.
48. MacDonagh, *Hereditary bondsman*, p. 137.
49. Daniel O'Connell to Mary O'Connell, 3 February 1815 (*O'Connell Corr.*, ii, 7).
50. Fagan, *Life*, i, 152.
51. Sir Edward Stanley to Daniel O'Connell, 4 February 1815 (Fitzpatrick, *Correspondence*, i, 33).
52. Daniel O'Connell to Sir Edward Stanley, 5 February 1815 (Fitzpatrick, *Correspondence*, i, 33–4).
53. Fitzpatrick, *Correspondence*, i, 34; James Grant, *Random recollections of the*

House of Commons (Philadelphia, 1836), p. 169.

54. Fitzpatrick, *Correspondence*, i, 84.
55. *Irish Magazine and Monthly Asylum for Neglected Biography*, viii (March 1815), p. 101.
56. Daniel O'Connell to Mary O'Connell, 6 March 1815 (*O'Connell Corr.*, ii, 11).
57. *Freeman's Journal*, 26 April 1815.
58. *Dublin Evening Post*, 25 March 1815.
59. *O'Connell Corr.*, ii, 39.
60. *Dublin Evening Post*, 6 June 1815.
61. Daniel O'Connell to Sir Henry Parnell, 13 June 1815 (*O'Connell Corr.*, ii, 50).
62. Ibid., 47.
63. O'Connell, *Speeches*, i, 453.
64. Ibid., 455.
65. Daniel O'Connell to Mary O'Connell, 13 March 1815 (*O'Connell Corr.*, ii, 14).
66. Daniel O'Connell to Pim's Merchants, 23 December 1815 (*O'Connell Corr.*, ii, 76).
67. James O'Connell to Daniel O'Connell, 17 February 1816 (*O'Connell Corr.*, ii, 83).
68. Mary O'Connell to Daniel O'Connell, 13 March 1815 (*O'Connell Corr.*, ii, 15).
69. Mary O'Connell to Daniel O'Connell, 16 March 1815 (*O'Connell Corr.*, ii, 18).
70. Daniel O'Connell to Mary O'Connell, 17 March 1815 (*O'Connell Corr.*, ii, 19).
71. Ibid.
72. Ibid.
73. Daniel O'Connell to Mary O'Connell, 2 April 1815 (*O'Connell Corr.*, ii, 26).
74. Daniel O'Connell to Mary O'Connell, 12 July 1815 (*O'Connell Corr.*, ii, 53).
75. Daniel O'Connell to Mary O'Connell, 4 July 1823 (*O'Connell Corr.*, ii, 498).
76. Daniel O'Connell to Mary O'Connell, 19 March 1820 (*O'Connell Corr.*, ii, 246).
77. *O'Connell Corr.*, ii, 57.
78. O'Connell, *Speeches*, ii, 20.
79. Ibid., 23.
80. George Lidwell to Daniel O'Connell, 1 September 1815 (*O'Connell Corr.*, ii, 61).
81. Daniel O'Connell to Lidwell, 1 September 1815 (*O'Connell Corr.*, ii, 62).
82. Fitzpatrick, *Correspondence*, i, 42.
83. Daniel O'Connell to editor, 3 September 1815 (Fitzpatrick, *Correspondence*, i, 41).
84. Robert Peel to Daniel O'Connell, 4 September 1815 (Fitzpatrick, *Correspondence*, i, 41).
85. Daniel O'Connell to Richard Newton Bennett, 4 September 1815 (*O'Connell Corr.*, ii, 63).
86. Daniel O'Connell to knight of Kerry, 4 September 1815 (Fitzpatrick, *Correspondence*, i, 42).
87. General O'Connell to Daniel O'Connell, 30 July 1819 (*O'Connell Corr.*, ii, 204).
88. O'Connell, *Last colonel*, ii, 253.

89. Ibid., 254.

90. Colonel Brown to Daniel O'Connell, 5 September 1815 (*O'Connell Corr.*, ii, 65).

91. Daniel O'Connell to Colonel Brown, 5 September 1815 (*O'Connell Corr.*, ii, 65).

92. Daniel O'Connell to Denys Scully, 13 September 1815 (*O'Connell Corr.*, ii, 66).

93. Daniel O'Connell to Denys Scully, 16 September 1815 (*O'Connell Corr.*, ii, 67).

94. Daniel O'Connell to James O'Connell, 19 September 1815 (*O'Connell Corr.*, ii, 68). The recipient is incorrectly given as James Connor, but see Fitzpatrick, *Correspondence*, i, 44, for contradictory evidence, for example the salutation 'your affectionate brother'.

95. Daniel O'Connell to Denys Scully, 20 September 1815 (*O'Connell Corr.*, ii, 69).

96. Ibid., 68. My emphasis.

97. Daniel O'Connell to James Connor, 19 September 1815 (*O'Connell Corr.*, ii, 68).

98. *Dublin Evening Post*, 3 November 1825.

99. George Lidwell to Daniel O'Connell, 25 September 1815 (*O'Connell Corr.*, ii, 70).

100. Daniel O'Connell to Mary O'Connell, 30 September 1815 (*O'Connell Corr.*, ii, 70).

101. Daniel O'Connell to Mary O'Connell, 26 October 1815 (*O'Connell Corr.*, ii, 72).

Chapter 9 Debts and Despair (pp 164–78)

1. Daniel O'Connell to Mary O'Connell, 23 July 1817 (*O'Connell Corr.*, ii, 158); James O'Connell to Daniel O'Connell, 1 March 1817 (*O'Connell Corr.*, ii, 135).

2. James O'Connell to Daniel O'Connell, 12 July 1819 (*O'Connell Corr.*, ii, 202).

3. James O'Connell to Daniel O'Connell, 4 January 1816 (*O'Connell Corr.*, ii, 77).

4. James O'Connell to Daniel O'Connell, 1 March 1817 (*O'Connell Corr.*, ii, 136).

5. NLI MS 130.

6. James O'Connell to Daniel O'Connell, 1 March 1817 (*O'Connell Corr.*, ii, 135).

7. General O'Connell to Daniel O'Connell, 30 July 1819 (*O'Connell Corr.*, ii, 205).

8. William Drennan to Daniel O'Connell, 30 January 1819 (*O'Connell Corr.*, ii, 195).

9. Daniel O'Connell to Mary O'Connell, 4 May 1822 (*O'Connell Corr.*, ii, 382).

10. Daniel O'Connell to Mary O'Connell, 24 January 1823 (*O'Connell Corr.*, ii, 429).

11. Daniel O'Connell to Mary O'Connell, 9 April 1814 (*O'Connell Corr.*, i, 365).

12. O'Connell, *Speeches*, ii. 38.

13. Ibid., 38.

14. Mary O'Connell to Daniel O'Connell, 29 and 30 March 1816 (*O'Connell Corr.*, ii, 91).

15. [Puckler-Muskau], *Tour In England, Ireland and France*, ii, 337.

16. Daniel O'Connell to Mary O'Connell, 13 January 1816 (*O'Connell Corr.*, ii, 79).

17. Mary O'Connell to Daniel O'Connell, 1 April 1816 (*O'Connell Corr.*, ii, 93). Emphasis as original. The editor suggests that this 'conversion' was financial (a promise not to lend money or act as a security) rather than religious, but the religious content in the letters between O'Connell and his wife disproves this clearly. In addition the use of the word 'conversion' makes little sense if the change was something to do with O'Connell's future financial dealings.

18. Daniel O'Connell to Edward John Fitzsimon, 5 November 1824 (*O'Connell Corr.*, iii, 87).

19. Speech of 2 December 1823 (O'Connell, *Speeches*, ii, 263).

20. Daniel O'Connell to Mary O'Connell, 11 February 1824 (*O'Connell Corr.*, iii, 26).

21. *O'Connell Corr.*, ii, 169.

22. Daniel O'Connell to Mary O'Connell, 26 March 1818 (*O'Connell Corr.*, ii, 175).

23. James O'Connell to Daniel O'Connell, 22 January 1816 (*O'Connell Corr.*, ii, 80).

24. James O'Connell to Daniel O'Connell, 16 September 1823 (*O'Connell Corr.*, ii, 509).

25. James O'Connell to Daniel O'Connell, 17 February 1816 (*O'Connell Corr.*, ii, 83).

26. Mary O'Connell to Daniel O'Connell, 11 March 1816 (*O'Connell Corr.*, ii, 85).

27. Daniel O'Connell to Mary O'Connell, 25 March 1823 (*O'Connell Corr.*, ii, 453).

28. Daniel O'Connell to Mary O'Connell, 20 March 1816 (*O'Connell Corr.*, ii, 88).

29. Daniel O'Connell to Mary O'Connell, 14 April 1816 (*O'Connell Corr.*, ii, 101).

30. Mary O'Connell to Daniel O'Connell, 26 March 1816 (*O'Connell Corr.*, ii, 90).

31. Daniel O'Connell to Mary O'Connell, 13 March 1816 (*O'Connell Corr.*, ii, 86).

32. Daniel O'Connell to Mary O'Connell, 21 March 1816 (*O'Connell Corr.*, ii, 88).

33. Daniel O'Connell to Mary O'Connell, 13 March 1816 (*O'Connell Corr.*, ii, 86).

34. Daniel O'Connell to Mary O'Connell, 4 August 1816 (*O'Connell Corr.*, ii, 104).

35. Daniel O'Connell to Charles Phillips, 16 October 1817 (*O'Connell Corr.*, ii, 165).

36. *O'Connell Corr.*, ii, 105.

37. *O'Connell Corr.*, ii, 108.

38. Daniel O'Connell to Mary O'Connell, 8 August 1816 (*O'Connell Corr.*, ii, 107).

39. *An authentic report of the interesting trial for a libel, contained in the celebrated poem called 'The Nosegay'* (Limerick, 1816), p. 23.

40. Ibid., p. 34.

41. *O'Connell Corr.*, ii, 109.

42. Daniel O'Connell to Mary O'Connell, 9 August 1816 (*O'Connell Corr.*, ii, 107).

43. Daniel O'Connell to Mary O'Connell, 29 March 1817 (*O'Connell Corr.*, ii, 140).

44. Mary O'Connell to Daniel O'Connell, 11 April 1817 (*O'Connell Corr.*, ii, 142); Daniel O'Connell to Mary O'Connell, 15 April 1817 (*O'Connell Corr.*, ii, 143).

45. *O'Connell Corr.*, ii, 114.
46. Daniel O'Connell to Mary O'Connell, 31 August 1816 (*O'Connell Corr.*, ii, 116).
47. Mary O'Connell to Daniel O'Connell, 28 September 1816 (*O'Connell Corr.*, ii, 120).
48. Daniel O'Connell to Mary O'Connell, 29 September 1816 (*O'Connell Corr.*, ii, 121).
49. Mary O'Connell to Daniel O'Connell, 16 October 1816 (*O'Connell Corr.*, ii, 122).
50. Ibid.
51. Mary O'Connell to Daniel O'Connell, 17 October 1816 (*O'Connell Corr.*, ii, 123).
52. Daunt, *Personal recollections*, i, 137.
53. *O'Connell Corr.*, ii, 94.
54. Ibid., 99.
55. O'Connell, *Speeches*, ii, 39.
56. *O'Connell Corr.*, ii, 126.
57. Ibid., 127.
58. Ibid., 132.
59. O'Connell, *Speeches*, ii, 39.
60. Fagan, *Life*, i, 124.
61. Ibid., 125.
62. Ibid.
63. O'Connell, *Speeches*, ii, 39.
64. Ibid.
65. Fagan, *Life*, i, 125.
66. *O'Connell Corr.*, ii, 145.
67. Daniel O'Connell to Mary O'Connell, 10 June 1817 (*O'Connell Corr.*, ii, 147).
68. Fagan, *Life*, i, 210.
69. Daniel O'Connell to Mary O'Connell, 10 June 1817 (*O'Connell Corr.*, ii, 148).
70. Mary O'Connell to Daniel O'Connell, 12 June 1817 (*O'Connell Corr.*, ii, 149); Daniel O'Connell to Mary O'Connell, 24 June 1817 (*O'Connell Corr.*, ii, 152).
71. Mary O'Connell to Daniel O'Connell, 14 July 1817 (*O'Connell Corr.*, ii, 155).
72. *O'Connell Corr.*, ii, 157.
73. Daniel O'Connell to Charles Phillips, 26 September 1817 (*O'Connell Corr.*, ii, 165).
74. O'Connell, *Speeches*, ii, 38.
75. *O'Connell Corr.*, ii, 184–5.
76. Daniel O'Connell to Owen O'Conor, 21 December 1818 (*O'Connell Corr.*, ii, 184).
77. *O'Connell Corr.*, ii, 185.
78. Ibid., 187.
79. Daniel O'Connell to Owen O'Conor, 6 January 1819 (*O'Connell Corr.*, ii, 186).
80. Henry Grattan to Daniel O'Connell, 3 January 1819 (*O'Connell Corr.*, ii, 186).
81. Daniel O'Connell to Mary O'Connell, 23 March 1819 (*O'Connell Corr.*, ii, 199).
82. Daniel O'Connell to Mary O'Connell, 13 April 1819 (*O'Connell Corr.*, ii, 199).

83. General O'Connell to Daniel O'Connell, 30 July 1819 (*O'Connell Corr.*, ii, 205).
84. *O'Connell Corr.*, ii, 208.
85. Daniel O'Connell to General Bolívar, 17 April 1820 (*O'Connell Corr.*, ii, 257).
86. *O'Connell Corr.*, ii, 209.
87. Daniel O'Connell to Mary O'Connell, 18 August 1819 (*O'Connell Corr.*, ii, 214).
88. Speech of 10 February 1827 (DDA 59/1/xvi f. 22).
89. O'Connell, *Speeches*, ii, 72.
90. Ibid., 75.
91. O'Connell to the editor of the *Dublin Evening Post*, 17 June 1820 (O'Connell, *Speeches*, ii, 76).
92. O'Connell, *Speeches*, ii, 79.
93. O'Connell to the editor of the *Dublin Evening Post*, 17 June 1820 (O'Connell, *Speeches*, ii, 78).
94. Daniel O'Connell to Mary O'Connell, 11 October 1820 (*O'Connell Corr.*, ii, 285).
95. Daniel O'Connell to Thomas Spring Rice, 16 November 1820 (*O'Connell Corr.*, ii, 287).
96. Daniel O'Connell to Lord Cloncurry, 16 November 1820 (*O'Connell Corr.*, ii, 288).
97. Henry Brougham to Daniel O'Connell, 25 November 1820 (*O'Connell Corr.*, ii, 293); Daniel O'Connell to Henry Brougham, 15 December 1820 (*O'Connell Corr.*, ii, 298).
98. Daniel O'Connell to Henry Brougham, 26 May 1823 (*O'Connell Corr.*, ii, 479).
99. O'Connell, *Speeches*, ii, 84.
100. Ibid., 85.
101. Ibid., 86.
102. Daniel O'Connell to Mary O'Connell, 20 September 1820 (*O'Connell Corr.*, ii, 281).
103. O'Connell, *Speeches*, ii, 90.

Chapter 10 The Private Life of Daniel O'Connell (pp 179–86)

1. *The Times*, 1 March 1832.
2. Denis Gwynn, *O'Connell and Ellen Courtenay* (Oxford, 1930).
3. See Erin I. Bishop, 'Was O'Connell faithful? Ellen Courtenay revisited', in *Éire-Ireland*, 31: 3–4 (1996), pp 58–75. Bishop does conclude, however, that the case is an open one.
4. See Diarmaid O'Muirithe, 'O'Connell in the Irish folk tradition' and J.J. Lee, 'Daniel O'Connell', both in M.R. O'Connell (ed.), *Daniel O'Connell: political pioneer* (Dublin, 1991), p. 78 and pp 2–3.
5. This was Helen Mulvey's interpretation in her introduction to the first volume of the O'Connell correspondence.
6. Daniel O'Connell to Mary O'Connell, 3 August 1820 (*O'Connell Corr.*, ii, 266).
7. Ellen Courtenay, *A narrative by Miss Ellen Courtenay, of most extraordinary cruelty, perfidy and depravity, perpetrated against her by Daniel O'Connell,*

Esq., MP for Kerry (London, 1832), p. 7. Her reference from the local bishop shows that she was in Cork until the end of March 1817. It should also be noted that she gets O'Connell's constituency wrong in the title.

8. Courtenay, *Narrative*, p. 9.
9. Ibid., p. 10.
10. Ibid., p. 32.
11. James O'Connell to Daniel O'Connell, 19 November 1823 (*O'Connell Corr.*, ii, 517). Emphasis as in original.
12. Daniel O'Connell to Mary O'Connell, 7 December 1823 (*O'Connell Corr.*, ii, 524).
13. Daniel O'Connell to Mary O'Connell, 3 December 1823 (*O'Connell Corr.*, ii, 522).
14. Mary O'Connell to Daniel O'Connell, 1808 (*O'Connell Corr.*, i, 174); Mary O'Connell to Daniel O'Connell, 19 March 1812 (*O'Connell Corr.*, i, 287).
15. Daniel O'Connell to Mary O'Connell, 28 April 1825 (*O'Connell Corr.*, iii, 156).
16. Courtenay, *Narrative*, p. 13.
17. Ibid., p. 17.
18. Ibid., p. 34.
19. Ibid., p. 20.
20. *The Times*, 13 April 1826.
21. Ellen Courtenay to The O'Gorman Mahon, 19 February 1831 (UC The O'Gorman Mahon papers, Box 1, Folder 13); Ellen Courtenay to The O'Gorman Mahon, March 1831 (UC The O'Gorman Mahon papers, Box 1, Folder 13).
22. Henry Hunt to Daniel O'Connell, 25 November 1831 (*O'Connell Corr.*, iv, 363).
23. Daniel O'Connell to Henry Hunt, 30 November 1831 (*O'Connell Corr.*, iv, 369).
24. Daniel O'Connell to Walter J. Baldwin, 29 April 1832 (*O'Connell Corr.*, iv, 415).
25. Ellen Courtenay to Christopher Fitzsimon, 25 March 1836 (*The Times*, 26 March 1836).
26. See Henry O'Connell's letter to *The Times*, 30 June 1836.
27. Ibid.
28. *The Times*, 23 July 1835 (reprinted in *The Times*, 23 July 1935).
29. *The Times*, 17 March 1836.
30. *The Times*, 9 November 1832.
31. Ellen Courtenay to Christopher Fitzsimon, 25 March 1836 (*The Times*, 26 March 1836).
32. *The Times*, 2 April 1836.
33. *The Times*, 17 March 1836.
34. Ibid.
35. *The Times*, 17 June 1836 (reprinted in *The Times*, 17 June 1936).

Chapter 11 Deciding on New Strategies (pp 187–208)

1. O'Connell, *Speeches*, ii, 432.

2. Response of Richard Sheil (O'Connell, *Speeches*, ii, 102–3).

3. R.S. Mackenzie (ed.), *Sketches of the Irish bar by the Rt. Hon. Richard Lalor Sheil* (2 vols., New York, 1854), i, 7.

4. O'Connell, *Speeches*, ii, 104.

5. Ibid., 107.

6. Ibid., 113.

7. Ibid., 114.

8. Ibid., 127.

9. *O'Connell Corr.*, ii, 312.

10. Daniel O'Connell to Mary O'Connell, 14 April 1821 (*O'Connell Corr.*, ii, 315).

11. O'Connell, *Speeches*, ii, 130; *O'Connell Corr.*, ii, 314–15.

12. Daniel O'Connell to O'Conor Don, 23 April 1821 (*O'Connell Corr.*, ii, 319).

13. *O'Connell Corr.*, ii, 330.

14. O'Connell, *Speeches*, ii, 135.

15. Ibid., 136–7.

16. Fagan, *Life*, i, 271.

17. Speech of 30 April 1823 (O'Connell, *Speeches*, ii, 197).

18. Quoted in Fergus O'Ferrall, *Catholic emancipation: Daniel O'Connell and the birth of Irish democracy, 1820–30* (Dublin, 1985), p. 1.

19. *The Times*, 24 August 1821.

20. *The Times*, 4 September 1821.

21. *The Times*, 28 February 1825.

22. Fagan, *Life*, i, 272.

23. *The Times*, 8 September 1821.

24. Fitzpatrick, *Correspondence*, i, 75.

25. Daniel O'Connell to Mary O'Connell, 12 October 1821 (Fitzpatrick, *Correspondence*, i, 77).

26. O'Ferrall, *Catholic emancipation*, p. 10.

27. Daniel O'Connell to Hunting Cap, 5 January 1822 (*O'Connell Corr.*, ii, 346).

28. Ibid., 347.

29. O'Connell, *Speeches*, ii, 142.

30. Ibid., 152.

31. Ibid., 160.

32. Daniel O'Connell to Mary O'Connell, 31 May 1822 (*O'Connell Corr.*, ii, 396).

33. Daniel O'Connell to Mary O'Connell, 24 January 1823 (*O'Connell Corr.*, ii, 429).

34. Mary O'Connell to Daniel O'Connell, 4 February 1824 (*O'Connell Corr.*, iii, 18).

35. James O'Connell to Daniel O'Connell, 11 September 1823 (*O'Connell Corr.*, ii, 508).

36. Daniel O'Connell to Mary O'Connell, 4 May 1822 (*O'Connell Corr.*, ii, 382).

37. Daniel O'Connell to Mary O'Connell, 22 January 1823 (*O'Connell Corr.*, ii, 427).

38. Daniel O'Connell to Mary O'Connell, 14 May 1822 (*O'Connell Corr.*, ii, 388).

39. Daniel O'Connell to Mary O'Connell, 23 May 1822 (*O'Connell Corr.*, ii, 391).

40. Daniel O'Connell to Mary O'Connell, 14 May 1822 (*O'Connell Corr.*, ii, 388).

41. Daniel O'Connell to Mary O'Connell, 5 June 1822 (*O'Connell Corr.*, ii, 398).

42. O'Connell, *Speeches*, ii, 185.

43. Ibid., 186.

44. Daniel O'Connell to Mary O'Connell, 27 December 1822 (*O'Connell Corr.*, ii, 417).

45. Daniel O'Connell to Mary O'Connell, 19 February 1823 (*O'Connell Corr.*, ii, 441).

46. Daniel O'Connell to Mary O'Connell, 12 March 1823 (*O'Connell Corr.*, ii, 447).

47. Daniel O'Connell to Mary O'Connell, 20 March 1823 (*O'Connell Corr.*, ii, 452).

48. Daniel O'Connell to Mary O'Connell, 26 March 1823 (*O'Connell Corr.*, ii, 455).

49. Daniel O'Connell to Mary O'Connell, 14 June 1823 (*O'Connell Corr.*, ii, 486).

50. Daniel O'Connell to Mary O'Connell, 19 December 1822 (*O'Connell Corr.*, ii, 412).

51. Daniel O'Connell to Mary O'Connell, 20 December 1822 (*O'Connell Corr.*, ii, 412).

52. *O'Connell Corr.*, ii, 415.

53. Daniel O'Connell to Mary O'Connell, 25 March 1823 (*O'Connell Corr.*, ii, 454).

54. *O'Connell Corr.*, ii, 466.

55. O'Connell, *Speeches*, ii, 190.

56. Ibid., 191.

57. Ibid., 202.

58. Daniel O'Connell to Mary O'Connell, 24 May 1823 (*O'Connell Corr.*, ii, 476).

59. O'Connell, *Speeches*, ii, 208.

60. Daniel O'Connell to Mary O'Connell, 24 May 1823 (*O'Connell Corr.*, ii, 477).

61. Daniel O'Connell to Henry Brougham, 26 May 1823 (*O'Connell Corr.*, ii, 479).

62. O'Connell, *Speeches*, ii, 231.

63. Daniel O'Connell to Mary O'Connell, 19 and 20 June 1823 (*O'Connell Corr.*, ii, 489 and 490).

64. Daniel O'Connell to Mary O'Connell, 8 July 1823 (*O'Connell Corr.*, ii, 498).

65. [W.H. Curran], 'Sketches of the Irish bar, no. vi', *New Monthly Magazine*, vi (1823), p. 1.

66. Daniel O'Connell to Mary O'Connell, 24 January 1823 (*O'Connell Corr.*, ii, 429).

67. James O'Connell to Daniel O'Connell, 4 September 1823 (*O'Connell Corr.*, ii, 505).

68. James O'Connell to Daniel O'Connell, 8 September 1823 (*O'Connell Corr.*, ii, 506).

69. James O'Connell to Daniel O'Connell, 11 September 1823 (*O'Connell Corr.*, ii, 507).

70. James O'Connell to Daniel O'Connell, 16 September 1823 (*O'Connell Corr.*, ii, 509).

71. James O'Connell to Daniel O'Connell, 3 November 1823 (*O'Connell Corr.*, ii, 514).

72. James O'Connell to Daniel O'Connell, 19 November 1823 (*O'Connell Corr.*, ii, 518).

73. Denys Scully to Daniel O'Connell, 23 November 1823 (*O'Connell Corr.*, ii, 519).

74. Daniel O'Connell to Mary O'Connell, 30 November 1823 (*O'Connell Corr.*, ii, 521).

75. James O'Connell to Daniel O'Connell, 5 February 1824 (*O'Connell Corr.*, iii, 22).

76. Daniel O'Connell to Mary O'Connell, 27 January 1824 (*O'Connell Corr.*, iii, 10).

77. Daniel O'Connell to Mary O'Connell, 13 February 1824 (*O'Connell Corr.*, iii, 31).

78. Daniel O'Connell to Mary O'Connell, 10 and 19 April 1824 (*O'Connell Corr.*, iii, 64 and 65).

79. *O'Connell Corr.*, iii, 36.

80. Daniel O'Connell to Mary O'Connell, 18 February 1824 (*O'Connell Corr.*, iii, 36).

81. Daniel O'Connell to Mary O'Connell, 18 and 19 March 1824 (*O'Connell Corr.*, iii, 55).

82. Daniel O'Connell to Richard Newton Bennett, 21 March 1824 (*O'Connell Corr.*, iii, 56); *Morning Chronicle*, 30 March 1824.

83. Daniel O'Connell to Mary O'Connell, 10 April 1824 (*O'Connell Corr.*, iii, 64).

84. O'Connell, *Speeches*, ii, 276.

85. Daniel O'Connell to Mary O'Connell, 14 February 1824 (*O'Connell Corr.*, iii, 32).

86. MacDonagh, *Hereditary bondsman*, p. 210.

87. O'Connell, *Speeches*, ii, 274.

88. Ibid.

89. Ibid., 279–81.

90. O'Ferrall, *Catholic emancipation*, p. 55.

91. O'Connell, *Speeches*, ii, 286.

92. *O'Connell Corr.*, iii, 51.

93. *Dublin Evening Post*, 19 February 1824.

94. Daniel O'Connell to John Primrose, 18 December 1824 (*O'Connell Corr.*, iii, 89).

95. *O'Connell Corr.*, iii, 70.

96. O'Connell, *Speeches*, ii, 295.

97. Ibid., 299.

98. Ibid., 323.

99. Speech of 5 June 1824 (O'Connell, *Speeches*, ii, 334).

100. O'Connell, *Speeches*, ii, 439.

101. *Parliamentary Debates*, iv, col. 1534.

102. O'Connell, *Speeches*, ii, 345.

103. Ibid., 364.

104. Ibid., 438. By the end of 1824 approximately £8,000 from the rent had been invested in government securities (DDA 60/2).

105. O'Connell, *Speeches*, ii, 444.

106. Daunt, *Personal recollections*, ii, 136.

107. O'Connell, *Speeches*, ii, 380.

108. *O'Connell Corr.*, iii, 90.

109. Quoted in O'Ferrall, *Catholic emancipation*, p. 83.

110. O'Connell, *Speeches*, ii, 461.

111. Daniel O'Connell to John Primrose, 21 December 1824 (*O'Connell Corr.*, iii, 90.

112. Daniel O'Connell to Mary O'Connell, 26 September 1824 (*O'Connell Corr.*, iii, 79).

113. *O'Connell Corr.*, iii, 80.

114. *The Times*, 5 January 1825.

115. *O'Connell Corr.*, iii, 90–91.

116. O'Connell, *Speeches*, ii, 468.

117. *The Times*, 5 January 1825.

118. Mary O'Connell to Daniel O'Connell, 2 March 1824 (*O'Connell Corr.*, iii, 47).

Chapter 12 A Comedy in Three Acts (pp 209–28)

1. Daniel O'Connell to Mary O'Connell, 17 March 1825 (*O'Connell Corr.*, iii, 141).

2. Daniel O'Connell to Eneas MacDonnell, 11 January 1825 (*O'Connell Corr.*, iii, 96).

3. *The Times*, 25 January 1825.

4. 3 February 1825, *Parliamentary Debates*, xii (1825), col. 2.

5. 15 February 1825, *Parliamentary Debates*, xii (1825), col. 172.

6. William Cobbett to Daniel O'Connell, 12 February 1825 (*O'Connell Corr.*, iii, 111).

7. Daniel O'Connell to Mary O'Connell, 21 February 1825 (*O'Connell Corr.*, iii, 116).

8. O'Ferrall, *Catholic emancipation*, p. 91.

9. Sheil, *Sketches*, ii, 41.

10. Daniel O'Connell to Mary O'Connell, 21 February 1825 (*O'Connell Corr.*, iii, 116).

11. *O'Connell Corr.*, iii, 117.

12. Daniel O'Connell to Mary O'Connell, 22 February 1825 (*O'Connell Corr.*, iii, 118).

13. Ibid., 118 and 119.

14. Daniel O'Connell to Mary O'Connell, 22 February 1825 (*O'Connell Corr.*, iii, 118) and Daniel O'Connell to Mary O'Connell, 28 February 1825 (*O'Connell Corr.*, iii, 126–7).

15. *O'Connell Corr.*, iii, 121.

16. Daniel O'Connell to Mary O'Connell, 25 February 1825 (*O'Connell Corr.*, iii, 122)

17. Fagan, *Life*, i, 406.

18. Daniel O'Connell to James Sugrue, 25 February 1825 (*O'Connell Corr.*, iii, 124).

19. Daniel O'Connell to Mary O'Connell, 2 March 1825 (*O'Connell Corr.*, iii, 127).

20. *O'Connell Corr.*, iii, 127.

21. Entry of John Cam Hobhouse, 22 February 1827 (Lord Broughton, *Recollections of a long life* (ed. Lady Dorchester, 6 vols., London, 1909–11), iii, 170).

22. Daniel O'Connell to Mary O'Connell, 28 February 1825 (*O'Connell Corr.*, iii, 125)

23. *The Times*, 28 February 1825.

24. *The speech of Daniel O'Connell, Esq., at the Catholic aggregate meeting, at the Freemasons' Hall, on 26 February 1825, with a report of the proceedings thereat* (London, 1825), p. 4.

25. Ibid., p. 13.

26. Ibid., pp 19–20.

27. Fagan, *Life*, i, 407.

28. Sheil, *Sketches*, ii, 49.

29. Public letter of Daniel O'Connell, 31 October 1825 (*Dublin Evening Post*, 3 November 1825).

30. Ibid.

31. *Cobbett's Weekly Register*, 24 September 1825, p. 777.

32. Sheil, *Sketches*, ii, 34.

33. Daniel O'Connell to Mary O'Connell, 4 March 1825 (*O'Connell Corr.*, iii, 129).

34. Daniel O'Connell to Mary O'Connell, 14 March 1825 (*O'Connell Corr.*, iii, 136).

35. Daniel O'Connell to Mary O'Connell, 16 February 1825 (Fitzpatrick, *Correspondence*, i, 95).

36. Lord Broughton, *Recollections of a long life*, iii, p. 93.

37. Daniel O'Connell to Mary O'Connell, 4 March 1825 (*O'Connell Corr.*, iii, 129); *First report from the select committee on the state of Ireland* (London, 1825); see also George White, *A digest of the evidence of the first report from the select committee on the state of Ireland* (London, 1825).

38. White, *A digest of the evidence of the first report*, p. 40.

39. Ibid., pp 87–8.

40. Lord Colchester (ed.), *The diary and correspondence of Charles Abbot, Lord Colchester* (3 vols., London, 1861), iii, 372.

41. *Cobbett's Weekly Register*, 24 September 1825, p. 781.

42. Daniel O'Connell to Edward Dwyer, 15 March 1825 (*O'Connell Corr.*, iii, 140).

43. Richard Sheil to Daniel O'Connell, 11 August 1825 (*O'Connell Corr.*, iii, 188).

44. Daniel O'Connell to Mary O'Connell, 17 Mach 1825 (*O'Connell Corr.*, iii, 141).

45. Lord Broughton, *Recollections of a long life*, iii, 94.

46. Daniel O'Connell to Mary O'Connell, 18 March 1825 (*O'Connell Corr.*, iii, 142).

47. *O'Connell Corr.*, iii, 144.

48. Daniel O'Connell to Edward Dwyer, 14 March 1825 (*O'Connell Corr.*, iii, 137).
49. *Parliamentary Debates*, xii (1825), col. 114.
50. Daniel O'Connell to Mary O'Connell, 18 April 1825 (*O'Connell Corr.*, iii, 148); Daniel O'Connell to Mary O'Connell, 21 April 1825 (*O'Connell Corr.*, iii, 152).
51. Daniel O'Connell to Mary O'Connell, 20 April 1825 (*O'Connell Corr.*, iii, 151).
52. Daniel O'Connell to Mary O'Connell, 22 April 1825 (*O'Connell Corr.*, iii, 153).
53. Ibid.
54. *Dublin Evening Post*, 3 November 1825.
55. Fagan, *Life*, i, 380.
56. *Dublin Evening Post*, 3 November 1825.
57. *Parliamentary Debates*, xii (1825), col. 142.
58. Daniel O'Connell to Mary O'Connell, 30 April 1825 (*O'Connell Corr.*, iii, 157–8).
59. *The Times*, 2 May 1825.
60. Daniel O'Connell to Mary O'Connell, 4 May 1825 (*O'Connell Corr.*, iii, 161).
61. Daniel O'Connell to Mary O'Connell, 7 May 1825 (*O'Connell Corr.*, iii, 165).
62. Daniel O'Connell to Mary O'Connell, 9 May 1825 (*O'Connell Corr.*, iii, 167).
63. Daniel O'Connell to Mary O'Connell, 10 May 1825 (*O'Connell Corr.*, iii, 168).
64. *Parliamentary Debates*, xii (1825), col. 766.
65. Daniel O'Connell to Mary O'Connell, 18 May 1825 (*O'Connell Corr.*, iii, 176).
66. Daniel O'Connell to Mary O'Connell, 20 May 1825 (*O'Connell Corr.*, iii, 177).
67. Daniel O'Connell to Mary O'Connell, 21 May 1825 (*O'Connell Corr.*, iii, 178).
68. Fagan, *Life*, i, 438.
69. Daniel O'Connell to Mary O'Connell, 25 May 1825 (*O'Connell Corr.*, iii, 181).
70. Daniel O'Connell to Mary O'Connell, 28 May 1825 (*O'Connell Corr.*, iii, 183).
71. Daniel O'Connell to Mary O'Connell, 27 May 1825 (*O'Connell Corr.*, iii, 182).
72. Daniel O'Connell to Pierce Mahony, 17 September 1828 (*O'Connell Corr.*, iii, 408).
73. Thomas Wyse, *Historical sketch of the late Catholic Association of Ireland* (2 vols., London, 1829), i, 220.
74. *Dublin Evening Post*, 2 June 1825.
75. O'Ferrall, *Catholic emancipation*, p. 104.
76. *Dublin Evening Post*, 9 June 1825.
77. *Dublin Evening Post*, 25 and 28 June 1825.
78. O'Ferrall, *Catholic emancipation*, p. 108.
79. *The Times*, 20 July 1825.
80. *The Times*, 1 November 1825.
81. *The Times*, 26 November 1825.
82. *O'Connell Corr.*, iii, 215.
83. Ibid., 189.
84. Quoted in *Cobbett's Weekly Register*, 24 September 1825, p. 784.
85. O'Ferrall, *Catholic emancipation*, p. 112.
86. Daniel O'Connell to Rev. Dr Jeremiah Donovan, 18 December 1825 (*O'Connell Corr.*, iii, 215).

87. Fagan, *Life*, i, 472.
88. Daniel O'Connell to Mary O'Connell, 1 November 1825 (*O'Connell Corr.*, iii, 197).
89. *O'Connell Corr.*, iii, 198; *Dublin Evening Post*, 20 October 1825.
90. Daniel O'Connell to Mary O'Connell, 25 October 1825 (*O'Connell Corr.*, iii, 192).
91. Daniel O'Connell to Mary O'Connell, 29 October 1825 (*O'Connell Corr.*, iii, 194).
92. Fagan, *Life*, i, 473.
93. Daniel O'Connell to Mary O'Connell, 13 December 1825 (*O'Connell Corr.*, iii, 212).
94. Mary O'Connell to Daniel O'Connell, 16 December 1825 (*O'Connell Corr.*, iii, 212).
95. Daniel O'Connell to Mary O'Connell, 17 December 1825 (*O'Connell Corr.*, iii, 213).
96. Ibid.
97. *O'Connell Corr.*, iii, 227; *Dublin Evening Post*, 17 January 1826.
98. Daniel O'Connell to knight of Kerry, 31 December 1826 (*O'Connell Corr.*, iii, 283).
99. Daniel O'Connell to Edward Dwyer, 21 March 1827 (*O'Connell Corr.*, iii, 301).
100. Daniel O'Connell to Pierce Mahony, 17 September 1828 (*O'Connell Corr.*, iii, 407).
101. Ibid., 408.

Chapter 13 Mobilising the Masses (pp 229–47)

1. *Dublin Evening Post*, 5 July 1828.
2. O'Ferrall, *Catholic emancipation*, p. 143.
3. Ibid., p. 114.
4. R.S. Mackenzie (ed.), *Sketches of the Irish bar by the Rt. Hon. Richard Lalor Sheil* (2 vols., New York, 1854), i, 8.
5. Alexander Robert Stewart, 29 January 1816 (*O'Connell Corr.*, iii, 231).
6. Duke of Buckingham to William Plunket, 29 January 1826 (NLI MS PC 920).
7. Discussed in *The Times*, 19 July 1828.
8. Hepworth Dixon (ed.), *Lady Morgan's memoirs: autobiography, diaries and correspondence* (2 vols., London, 1863), ii, 225.
9. O'Ferrall, *Catholic emancipation*, p. 125.
10. Thomas Wyse quoted in O'Ferrall, *Catholic emancipation*, p. 127.
11. Daniel O'Connell to John Primrose, 19 June 1826 (*O'Connell Corr.*, iii, 250).
12. Daniel O'Connell to Mary O'Connell, 19 June 1826 (*O'Connell Corr.*, iii, 248).
13. Daniel O'Connell to Mary O'Connell, 21 June 1826 (*O'Connell Corr.*, iii, 250).
14. Daniel O'Connell to Mary O'Connell, 25 June 1826 (*O'Connell Corr.*, iii, 253).
15. Wyse, *Historical sketch*, i, 276–7.
16. Daniel O'Connell to Mary O'Connell, 26 June 1826 (*O'Connell Corr.*, iii, 253).

17. *O'Connell Corr.*, iii, 254.

18. Daniel O'Connell to Mary O'Connell, 28 June 1826 (*O'Connell Corr.*, iii, 255).

19. *O'Connell Corr.*, iii, 270.

20. O'Ferrall, *Catholic emancipation*, p. 133.

21. *Dublin Evening Post*, 5 July 1826.

22. Daniel O'Connell to Edward Dwyer, 13 July 1826 (*O'Connell Corr.*, iii, 259).

23. Daniel O'Connell to Edward Dwyer, 14 July 1826 (*O'Connell Corr.*, iii, 260).

24. Daniel O'Connell to Edward Dwyer, 31 August 1826 (*O'Connell Corr.*, iii, 268).

25. *The Times*, 13 July 1826.

26. *O'Connell Corr.*, iii, 259.

27. Daniel O'Connell to Mary O'Connell, 2 September 1826 (*O'Connell Corr.*, iii, 269).

28. Hepworth Dixon (ed.), *Lady Morgan's memoirs: autobiography, diaries and correspondence*, ii, 226.

29. *Blackwood's Edinburgh Magazine*, xx (1826), p. 311.

30. T. Sadleir (ed.), *Diary, reminiscences, and correspondence of Henry Crabb Robinson* (3 vols., London, 1869), ii, 334.

31. Ibid., 335 and 338.

32. Ibid., 338.

33. Ibid., 348.

34. Ibid., 353.

35. Daniel O'Connell to Mary O'Connell, 28 August 1826 (*O'Connell Corr.*, iii, 266).

36. *O'Connell Corr.*, iii, 266–7; *Dublin Evening Post*, 7 September 1826.

37. Daunt, *Personal recollections*, ii, 189.

38. Daniel O'Connell to Mary O'Connell, 2 September 1826 (*O'Connell Corr.*, iii, 268).

39. *Dublin Evening Post*, 11 January 1827; see also his speech of 22 January 1827 when he declared that 'We buried our passions and animosities in the tomb' (DDA 59/1/IV f. 35).

40. Daniel O'Connell to knight of Kerry, 15 January 1827 (*O'Connell Corr.*, iii, 287).

41. Daniel O'Connell to Richard Newton Bennett, 15 January 1827 (*O'Connell Corr.*, iii, 288).

42. *O'Connell Corr.*, iii, 290.

43. DDA 59/1/VII f. 60.

44. DDA 59/1/VIII f. 83.

45. DDA CP 59/1 VII f. 19.

46. DDA 59/1/xvi f. 33.

47. DDA 59/1/xvi f. 27.

48. Ibid., f. 63.

49. Ibid., f. 123.

50. Daniel O'Connell to knight of Kerry, 22 February 1827 (*O'Connell Corr.*, iii, 291).

51. *O'Connell Corr.*, iii, 301.

52. Eneas MacDonnell, 23 April 1827 (*O'Connell Corr.*, iii, 308).

53. Richard Newton Bennett to Daniel O'Connell, 9 June 1827 (*O'Connell Corr.*, iii, 322).

54. Daniel O'Connell to Richard Newton Bennett, 11 June 1827 (*O'Connell Corr.*, iii, 325).

55. O'Ferrall, *Catholic emancipation*, p. 162.

56. Daniel O'Connell to knight of Kerry, 9 June 1827 (*O'Connell Corr.*, iii, 323).

57. Daniel O'Connell to Richard Newton Bennett, 11 June 1827 (*O'Connell Corr.*, iii, 325).

58. *O'Connell Corr.*, iii, 327.

59. *O'Connell Corr.*, iii, 331.

60. Daniel O'Connell to Mary O'Connell, 9 August 1827 (*O'Connell Corr.*, iii, 340).

61. Daniel O'Connell to Richard Newton Bennett, 26 September 1827 (*O'Connell Corr.*, iii, 346).

62. Daniel O'Connell to Mary O'Connell, 4 December 1827 (*O'Connell Corr.*, iii, 360).

63. James O'Connell to Daniel O'Connell, 9 April 1825 (*O'Connell Corr.*, iii, 147).

64. James O'Connell to Daniel O'Connell, 27 January 1825 (*O'Connell Corr.*, iii, 103); Daniel O'Connell to Mary O'Connell, 18 March 1826 (*O'Connell Corr.*, iii, 240).

65. Daniel O'Connell to Mary O'Connell, 1 November 1825 (*O'Connell Corr.*, iii, 197).

66. General O'Connell to Daniel O'Connell, 10 February 1826 (*O'Connell Corr.*, iii, 234).

67. Daniel O'Connell to Mary O'Connell, 30 October 1827 (*O'Connell Corr.*, iii, 353).

68. Quoted in Fagan, *Life*, i, 448.

69. Daniel O'Connell to Mary O'Connell, 27 October 1827 (*O'Connell Corr.*, iii, 352).

70. Daniel O'Connell to Mary O'Connell, 20 November 1827 (*O'Connell Corr.*, iii, 356).

71. Daniel O'Connell to Mary O'Connell, 4 December 1827 (*O'Connell Corr.*, iii, 360).

72. Daniel O'Connell to Mary O'Connell, 8 November 1827 (*O'Connell Corr.*, iii, 354).

73. Daniel O'Connell to Mary O'Connell, 1 December 1827 (*O'Connell Corr.*, iii, 360).

74. Daniel O'Connell to Mary O'Connell, 8 December 1827 (*O'Connell Corr.*, iii, 362).

75. Daniel O'Connell to Mary O'Connell, 29 November 1827 (*O'Connell Corr.*, iii, 357).

76. Daniel O'Connell to Thomas Spring Rice, 29 November 1827 (*O'Connell Corr.*, iii, 358).
77. Thomas Spring Rice to Daniel O'Connell, 14 December 1827 (*O'Connell Corr.*, iii, 364).
78. *Report of the trial in the case of Bartholemew McGarahan versus the Rev. T. Maguire before Baron Smith and a special jury* (Dublin, 1862), introduction.
79. See Proinnsíos Ó Duigneáin, *The priest and the Protestant woman* (Dublin, 1997).
80. Ibid., p. 16.
81. Ibid., p. 17.
82. Ibid., p. 47.
83. *Report of the trial in the case of Bartholemew McGarahan versus the Rev. T. Maguire before Baron Smith and a special jury* (Dublin, 1862), p. 8.
84. Ibid., p. 30.
85. Ibid., p. 26.
86. Daniel O'Connell to Mary O'Connell, 15 December 1827 (*O'Connell O'Connell Corr.*, iii, 365).
87. *O'Connell Corr.*, iii, 366.
88. Daniel O'Connell to Mary O'Connell, 15 December 1827 (*O'Connell Corr.*, iii, 365).

Chapter 14 Liberation (pp 248–70)

1. *The Times*, 2 July 1828.
2. *The Times*, 3 July 1828.
3. Sheil, *Sketches*, ii, 102.
4. Vesey Fitzgerald to Robert Peel, 17 June 1828 (Lord Mahon (ed.), *Memoirs of the Right Honourable Sir Robert Peel* (2 vols., London, 1857), i, 107).
5. *The Times*, 27 June 1828.
6. *The Times*, 28 June 1828.
7. Sheil, *Sketches*, ii, 147.
8. *Dublin Evening Post*, 26 July 1828.
9. Anon., 'The Great Agitator', in *New Monthly Magazine*, xxv (1829), p. 254.
10. *O'Connell Corr.*, iv, 78.
11. Report of meeting of 26 June 1828 (*Dublin Evening Post*, 28 June 1828).
12. Speech of 16 January 1827 (DD 59/1/1 f. 32); Daniel O'Connell to knight of Kerry, 31 December 1826 (Fitzpatrick, *Correspondence*, i, 135).
13. *The Times*, 1 July 1828.
14. *Dublin Evening Post*, 1 July 1828.
15. *The Times*, 4 July 1828.
16. *Morning Register*, 3 July 1828.
17. *The Times*, 4 July 1828.
18. Sheil, *Sketches*, ii, 108-9.

19. Thomas Steele to Daniel O'Connell, 9 May 1846 (*O'Connell Corr.*, viii, 23).
20. *The Times*, 5 July 1828.
21. Pückler-Muskau, *Tour In England, Ireland and France*, ii, 131.
22. Sheil, *Sketches*, ii, 124.
23. *Morning Register*, 3 July 1828.
24. *Dublin Evening Post*, 3 July 1828.
25. Sheil, *Sketches*, ii, 127.
26. Ibid., 129.
27. Lord Mahon (ed.), *Memoirs of the Right Honourable Sir Robert Peel* (2 vols., London, 1857), i, 109.
28. O'Ferrall, *Catholic emancipation*, p. 193.
29. For a selection of election posters and addresses see DDA 60/1/11.
30. O'Ferrall, *Catholic emancipation*, p. 191.
31. Ibid., p. 197.
32. Sheil, *Sketches*, ii, 135.
33. *Morning Register*, 5 July 1828.
34. *Dublin Evening Post*, 10 July 1828.
35. *Dublin Evening Post*, 3 July 1828.
36. *The Times*, 12 July 1828.
37. *Dublin Evening Post*, 10 July 1828.
38. Pückler-Muskau, *Tour In England, Ireland and France*, i, 333–4.
39. Patrick Molony to Daniel O'Connell, 30 July 1828 (*O'Connell Corr.*, iii, 396).
40. Baron Tuyll to Anglesey, 4 July 1828 (PRONI D619/32A/82).
41. Sheil, *Sketches*, ii, 141.
42. *Dublin Evening Post*, 10 July 1828.
43. Sheil, *Sketches*, ii, 139.
44. MacDonagh, *Hereditary bondsman*, p. 252.
45. *Dublin Evening Post*, 5 July 1828.
46. Lord Mahon (ed.), *Memoirs of the Right Honourable Sir Robert Peel* (2 vols., London, 1857), i, 114–15.
47. *O'Connell Corr.*, iii, 387.
48. Lord Mahon (ed.), *Memoirs of the Right Honourable Sir Robert Peel* (2 vols., London, 1857), i, 116.
49. Daunt, *Personal recollections*, i, 28.
50. *Dublin Evening Post*, 10 July 1828.
51. Anglesey's signed memorandum of a conversation with O'Connell, 29 July 1828 (PRONI D.619/32B/2).
52. Emphasis as in original.
53. Daniel O'Connell to Edward Dwyer, 1 October 1828 (*O'Connell Corr.*, iii, 417).
54. Pückler-Muskau, *Tour In England, Ireland and France*, i, 321.
55. Ibid., 332.
56. Ibid., 335–6.
57. Ibid., 335.

58. Henry Reeve (ed.), *The Greville memoirs: a journal of the reigns of King George IV, King William IV and Queen Victoria. By the late Charles C.F. Greville* (8 vols., London, 1897–9), i, 148.

59. Pückler-Muskau, *Tour In England, Ireland and France*, ii, 118.

60. *O'Connell Corr.*, iv, 5.

61. Henry Reeve (ed.), *The Greville memoirs*, i, 206.

62. Lord Colchester (ed.), *The diary and correspondence of Charles Abbot, Lord Colchester* (3 vols., London, 1861), iii, 612.

63. Daniel O'Connell to Mary O'Connell, 5 March 1829 (*O'Connell Corr.*, iv, 19).

64. Daniel O'Connell to Mary O'Connell, 6 March 1829 (*O'Connell Corr.*, iv, 20).

65. Daniel O'Connell to Edward Dwyer, 6 March 1829 (*O'Connell Corr.*, iv, 1829).

66. Daniel O'Connell to Edward Dwyer, 14 April 1829 (*O'Connell Corr.*, iv, 45).

67. See the 'Clare Encore' (DDA 60/1/11/5).

68. Tom Taylor (ed.), *Life of Benjamin Robert Haydon, historical painter* (3 vols., London, 1853), ii, 390.

69. Fitzpatrick, *Correspondence*, ii, 229.

BIBLIOGRAPHY

PRIMARY SOURCES

Manuscript Sources

Dublin Diocesan Archives
DDA 54/1 to 60/2   Proceedings of the Catholic Association (and the earlier Catholic Committee)

National Library of Ireland
MS. 130   Daniel O'Connell's fee-book, 1798–1805
MSS 1503–1504   Reminiscences of Daniel O'Connell by his daughter, Ellen Fitzsimon, 1843 and 1876
MS. 8004   Legal papers of O'Connell, 1809–21
MSS 13,621–13,651   O'Connell correspondence
MS. 15,426   Papers relating to the Magee trial, 1813
MS 15,476   Papers of W.J. Fitzpatrick relating to his work on O'Connell
PC 920   Uncatalogued William Plunket papers

Public Record Office of Northern Ireland
T3228   Harrowby papers
D619   Anglesey papers

Royal Irish Academy
MSS 12 P 13   Daniel O'Connell's journal, 1795–1802

University College Dublin Archives
P12   Large collection of O'Connell papers including his second fee-book, 1798–1814 (P12/5/152)

University of Chicago Library
The O'Gorman Mahon papers

Printed Sources
I   PARLIAMENTARY AND LEGAL RECORDS
The register of admissions to Gray's Inn, 1521–1889. London, 1889
The records of the honourable society of Lincoln's Inn: Admissions, 1420–1799. London, 1896

The records of the honourable society of Lincoln's Inn: The black books. London, 1902
Parliamentary History
Parliamentary Debates

II PAMPHLETS

The speeches of John Horne Tooke during the Westminster election, 1796. London, n.d. [1796]

Collis, John. *An address to the people of Ireland on the projected Union.* Dublin, 1799

An authentic report of the interesting trial for a libel, contained in the celebrated poem called 'The Nosegay'. Limerick, 1816

The trial of John Magee. Dublin, 1815

First report from the select committee on the state of Ireland. London, 1825

The speech of Daniel O'Connell, Esq. at the Catholic aggregate meeting, at the Freemasons' Hall, on 26 February 1825, with a report of the proceedings thereat. London, 1825

Report of the trial in the case of Bartholemew McGarahan versus the Rev. T. Maguire before Baron Smith and a special jury. Dublin, 1862

White, George. *A digest of the evidence of the first report from the select committee on the state of Ireland.* London, 1825

III NEWSPAPERS AND MAGAZINES

Bentley's Magazine
Blackwood's Edinburgh Magazine
Cobbett's Weekly Political Register
Dublin Evening Post
Dublin Magazine
The Eclectic Magazine
Freeman's Journal
Freemasons' Quarterly Review
Household Words
Irish Magazine and Monthly Asylum for Neglected Biography
Monthly Museum, or, Dublin Literary Repertory of Arts, Science, Literature and Miscellaneous Information
Morning Chronicle
Morning Register
New Monthly Magazine
The Times

IV DIARIES, MEMOIRS, SPEECHES AND CORRESPONDENCE

[Anon]. *Memoirs of John Howard Payne, the American Rosicus... compiled from authentic documents.* London, 1815

Bartlett, Thomas (ed.). *Revolutionary Dublin, 1795–1801: the letters of Francis Higgins to Dublin Castle*. Dublin, 2004

Colchester, Lord (ed.). *The diary and correspondence of Charles Abbot, Lord Colchester*. 3 vols. London, 1861

Courtenay, Ellen. *A narrative by Miss Ellen Courtenay, of most extraordinary cruelty, perfidy and depravity, perpetrated against her by Daniel O'Connell, Esq., MP for Kerry*. London, 1832

Daunt, William J. O'Neill. *Personal recollections of the late Daniel O'Connell*. 2 vols. London, 1848

Dixon, Hepworth (ed.). *Lady Morgan's memoirs: autobiography, diaries and correspondence*. 2 vols. London, 1863

Dorchester, Lady (ed.). *Recollections of a long life [of Lord Broughton]*. 6 vols. London, 1909–11

Fitzpatrick, W.J. (ed.). *Correspondence of Daniel O'Connell, the Liberator*. 2 vols. New York, 1888

Grant, James. *Random recollections of the House of Commons*. Philadelphia, 1836

Grattan Jnr, Henry. *Memoirs of the life and times of the Rt. Hon. Henry Grattan*. 5 vols. London, 1846

Gregory, Lady (ed.). *Mr Gregory's letter-box, 1813–1830*. London, 1898

Houston, Arthur. *Daniel O'Connell: his early life and journal, 1795 to 1802*. London, 1906

Mackenzie, R.S. (ed.). *Sketches of the Irish bar by the Rt. Hon. Richard Lalor Sheil*. 2 vols. New York, 1854

Mahon, Lord (ed.). *Memoirs of the Right Honourable Sir Robert Peel*. 2 vols. London, 1857

MacDermot, Brian (ed.). *The Catholic question in Ireland and England: the papers of Denys Scully*. Dublin, 1988
— *The Irish Catholic petition of 1805: the diary of Denys Scully*. Dublin, 1992

O'Connell, John (ed.). *The life and speeches of Daniel O'Connell M.P.* 2 vols. Dublin, 1846

O'Connell, M.R. (ed.). *The correspondence of Daniel O'Connell*. 8 vols. Shannon and Dublin, 1972–80

[Pückler-Muskau, Prince Hermann]. *Tour in England, Ireland and France in the years 1829 and 1830. By a German prince*. 2 vols. London, 1832

Reeve, Henry (ed.). *The Greville memoirs: a journal of the reigns of King George IV, King William IV and Queen Victoria. By the late Charles C.F. Greville*. 8 vols. London, 1897–99

Ross, Charles (ed.). *The correspondence of Charles, 1st Marquess Cornwallis*. 3 vols. London, 1859

Sadleir, T. (ed.). *Diary, reminiscences, and correspondence of Henry Crabb Robinson*. 3 vols. London, 1869

Savage, M.W. (ed.). *Sketches, legal and political, by the late right honourable Richard Lalor Sheil*. 2 vols. London, 1855

Taylor, Tom (ed.). *The autobiography and journals of Benjamin Robert Haydon*. 3 vols. London, 1853

V CONTEMPORARY AND NEAR-CONTEMPORARY WORKS

Adolphus, John. *The royal exile*. 2 vols. London, 1821

[Anon.]. *Anecdotes of O'Connell, John Philpot Curran, Grattan, Father O'Leary, and Swift*. Dublin, n.d.

Cobbett, William. *Big O and Sir Glory: a comedy in three acts*. London, 1825

[Curran, W.H.]. 'Sketches of the Irish bar, no. vi'. In *New Monthly Magazine*, vi, 1823

Curran, W.H. *Sketches of the Irish bar*. 2 vols. London, 1855

Cusack, M.F. *The Liberator, his life and times, political, social and religious*. London, 1872

Duffy, Charles Gavan. *Young Ireland: a fragment of Irish history*. 2 vols. Final Revision. London, 1896

Fagan, William. *The life and times of Daniel O'Connell*. 2 vols. Cork, 1847–8

Fitzpatrick, W.J. *Secret service under Pitt*. Dublin, 1892

—'*The sham squire' and the informers of 1798*. Dublin, 1895

Gilchrist, J.P. *A brief history of the origin and history of ordeals... Also, a chronological register of the principal duels*. London, 1821

Gladstone, W.E. 'Daniel O'Connell'. In *The Nineteenth Century*, vol. xxv (1889)

Gullion, Slieve. 'Leinster and Munster in the summer of 1844'. In *Irish Monthly*, xl (Oct. 1912)

Huish, Robert. *The memoirs private and political of Daniel O'Connell*. London, 1836

Lecky, W.E.H. *Leaders of public opinion in Ireland*. 2 vols. London, 1903

Luby, T.C. *The life and times of Daniel O'Connell*. Glasgow, n.d.

Madden, D.O. *Ireland and its rulers since 1829*. 2 vols. London, 1843–4

—*Revelations of Ireland in the past generation*. Dublin, 1877

Maume, Patrick (ed.). *Reminiscences of Daniel O'Connell*. Dublin, 2005

Millingen, J.G. *The history of duelling*. 2 vols. London, 1841

O'Connell, Mrs M. J. *The last colonel of the Irish brigade*. 2 vols. London, 1892

O'Flanagan, J.R. *Bar life of O'Connell*. London, 1875

—*The Irish bar*. London, 1879

—*The Munster circuit*. London, 1880

O'Keeffe, C.M. *Life and times of Daniel O'Connell*. Dublin, 1864

Phillips, Charles. *Curran and his contemporaries*. Various editions, London, 1850 and New York, 1862

Prendergast, J.P. Introduction to Haliday, Charles, *The Scandinavian kingdom of Dublin*. Dublin, 1881

Rayleigh, Peter. *History of Ye Antient Society of Cogers, 1755–1903*. London, 1904

Roche, James. *Critical and miscellaneous essays. By an octogenarian*. 2 vols. Cork, 1850–51

Sabine, Lorenzo. *Notes on Duels and Duelling.* Boston, 1855

Sheahan, Thomas. *'Articles' of Irish manufacture, or, Portions of Cork history.* Cork, 1833

Tait, William. *Ireland and O'Connell.* London, 1835

[Taylor, W.F.]. *Reminiscences of Daniel O'Connell. By a Munster farmer.* London, 1847

Wyse, Thomas. *Historical sketch of the late Catholic Association of Ireland.* 2 vols. London, 1829

SECONDARY SOURCES

Aspinwall, Bernard. 'Was O'Connell necessary? Sir Joseph Dillon, Scotland, and the movement for Catholic emancipation'. In Loades, D.M. (ed.), *The end of strife.* Edinburgh, 1984

Bartlett, Thomas. *The fall and rise of the Irish nation: the Catholic question, 1690–1830.* Dublin, 1992

Bew, Paul. *Ireland: the politics of enmity 1789–2006.* Oxford, 2007

Bishop, Erin I. 'Was O'Connell faithful? Ellen Courtenay revisited'. In *Éire-Ireland,* 31: 3–4 (1996)

—*The world of Mary O'Connell [1778–1836].* Dublin, 1999

Boorstein, Daniel J. *The mysterious science of the law: an essay on Blackstone's Commentaries.* Chicago, 1996

Crimmins, J.E. 'Jeremy Bentham and Daniel O'Connell: their correspondence and radical alliance, 1828–1831'. In *Historical Journal,* 40 (1997)

Denslow, W.R. *Ten thousand famous freemasons.* 2 vols. Missouri, 2004

Dirck, Brian. *Lincoln the lawyer.* Chicago, 2007

Gash, Norman. *Mr Secretary Peel.* London, 1961

Geoghegan, P.M. *The Irish Act of Union.* Dublin, 1999

—*Lord Castlereagh.* Dundalk, 2002

—*Robert Emmet: a life.* Dublin, 2002

Gwynn, Denis. *O'Connell and Ellen Courtenay.* Oxford, 1930

Hilton, Boyd. 'The ripening of Robert Peel'. In Bentley, Michael (ed.), *Public and private doctrine: essays in British history presented to Maurice Cowling.* Cambridge, 1993

Howlin, Niamh. 'The nineteenth-century Irish jury: a study in depth'. Unpublished Ph.D. thesis, University College Dublin, 2007

Kelly, James. *'That damned thing called honour': duelling in Ireland.* Cork, 1996

Lovett Fraser, J.A. 'Daniel O'Connell as an advocate' in *Law Mag. And Rev. Quart. Rev. Juris.* 5th series, vol. 38 (1912–13)

MacCartney, Donal (ed.). *The world of Daniel O'Connell.* Dublin, 1980

MacDonagh, Michael. *The life of Daniel O'Connell.* London, 1903

MacDonagh, Oliver. *The hereditary bondsman: Daniel O'Connell, 1775–1829.* London, 1988

—*The emancipist: Daniel O'Connell, 1830–1847.* London, 1988

McElroy, Martin. 'The local Protestant landed elite and the impact of O'Connellism, 1826–35'. In *Irish history: A research yearbook*, 1. Dublin, 2002

McGrath, Thomas. *Politics, Interdenominational relations and education in the public ministry of Bishop James Doyle of Kildare and Leighlin, 1786–1834*. Dublin, 1999

Mirala, Petri. *Freemasonry in Ulster, 1733–1813*. Dublin, 2007

Moley, Raymond. *Daniel O'Connell: nationalism without violence*. New York, 1974

Nowlan, Kevin and O'Connell, M.R. (eds). *Daniel O'Connell: portrait of a radical*. Belfast, 1984

O'Connell, M.R. 'Daniel O'Connell: income, expenditure and despair'. In *Irish Historical Studies*, xvii (1970)

O'Connell, M.R. (ed.). *Daniel O'Connell: political pioneer*. Dublin, 1991

O'Dowd, Mary. 'O'Connell and the lady patriots: women and O'Connellite politics, 1824–1845'. In Blackstock, Allan and Magennis, Eoin (eds), *Politics and political culture in Britain and Ireland, 1750–1850: essays in tribute to Peter Jupp*. Belfast, 2007

Ó Duigneáin, Proinnsíos. *The priest and the Protestant woman*. Dublin, 1997

O'Faoláin, Seán. *King of the beggars: a life of Daniel O'Connell*. Dublin, 1986, first published in 1938

O'Ferrall, Fergus. *Catholic emancipation: Daniel O'Connell and the birth of Irish democracy, 1820–30*. Dublin, 1985

—'Daniel O'Connell, "the Liberator", 1775–1847 : changing images'. In *Ireland: A journal of history and society* (1994)

O'Flaherty, Hugh. 'Daniel O'Connell, the Counsellor, and our present constitutional disposition'. In *Journal of the Kerry Archaeological & Historical Society*, 27 (1994)

Ó hÓgartaigh, Margaret. 'Edward Hay: historian of 1798'. In *Eighteenth-century Ireland: Iris an dá chultúr*, 13 (1998)

Owens, Gary. '"A moral insurrection": faction fighters, public demonstrations and the O'Connellite campaign, 1828'. In *Irish Historical Studies*, 30 (1997)

—'Visualizing the Liberator: self-fashioning, dramaturgy, and the construction of Daniel O'Connell'. In *Éire-Ireland*, 33:3/4–34:1 (1998)

Tierney, Michael (ed.). *Daniel O'Connell: nine centenary essays*. Dublin, 1949

Trench, C.C. *The Great Dan: a biography of Daniel O'Connell*. London, 1984

Uí Ógáin, Ríonach. *Immortal Dan: Daniel O'Connell in Irish folk tradition*. Dublin, n.d.

Vaughan, W.E. (ed.). *A new history of Ireland: Ireland under the Union*. Volume V. Oxford, 1989

Wellman, Francis L. *The art of cross-examination*. New York, 1923

Woods, C.J. 'Was O'Connell a United Irishman?' In *Irish Historical Studies*, xxxv, 138 (2006)

WEBSITES

www.bailii.org/ie/cases/IESC/2007. Irish Supreme Court cases

www.oldbaileyonline.org. Complete transcripts of Old Bailey trials

www.oxforddnb.com. Matthew, H.C.G. and Harrison, Brian (eds). *Oxford Dictionary of National Biography.* 60 vols. Oxford, 2004

INDEX